aksa, 30 Oct 2016

Lovely lady, may God bless you!

Have You Considered
My Servant David?

Have You Considered My Servant David?

Denessa Luckett

Josiah Elisha Publishing, LLC
Indianapolis, Indiana

Cover illustrator: Dimitri Karetnikov

Published 2009

ISBN-13: 978-0-9821441-5-2; ISBN-10: 0-9821441-5-6

Publisher's Cataloging-in-Publication
(Provided by Quality Books, Inc.)

Luckett, Denessa.
Have you considered my servant David? / Denessa Luckett.
p. cm.
Includes bibliographical references and index.
LCCN 2008938859
Hardback edition ISBN-13: 978-0-9821441-5-2; ISBN-10: 0-9821441-5-6

1. David, King of Israel. 2. Leadership—Biblical teaching.
3. Jews—History—To 953 B.C. 4. Bible. O.T.
—Criticism, interpretation, etc. I. Title.

BS580.D3L83 2009 221.9'2
QBI08-600312

Printed in the United States of America

Contents

To God who has a sense of humor. You took a woman who could not write and asked her to write a book. Thank you for the journey. When life's experiences changed my voice, you nudged me to persist. Thank you for encouraging me to persevere. Thank you for allowing me to serve you in this way.

Monica and Herman D, I am a woman of my word. Selina O, God sent you at the right time to encourage me; thanks for the push.

To friends who poured healing oil and refused to give up, the Campbell family. May God bless you.

My dearest VKMS, may God be glorified in your life.

A special thanks to my reviewers:
Selina O
Bishop G. L. Mosley
Elder K. Jones

Editors:
Thank you for your expertise and unique perspectives. You enhanced me with your patience, teaching, and explanations.
L. Anderson
G. Anderson (in conjunction with L. Radke)
S. McCarthy and S. Nelson, you have been invaluable to me, and I could not have reached this point were it not for you. You are a godsend. I am deeply grateful that we have been able to work together.

To all of you who had a hand in producing this book, thank you for using your skills to make this project a reality.

To the reader, I thank you for the opportunity to serve you. May you be blessed by reading this book and may your relationship to Him soar.

Introduction

My first sermon in bible college was entitled "God Is Looking for David's Heart." It was directed toward future ministry leaders and pastors. Many people who receive the call to ministry have checkered pasts. God has a way of using people with checkered pasts to spread His gospel because they are living proof of God's power and can reach the unreachable through their testimonies.

Our class was as dysfunctional as you could ever imagine. One student made the news when he robbed a local bank at gunpoint, and others were caught while making midnight excursions to the dorm rooms of members of the opposite sex. Bible college gave a whole new meaning to the term *Christian*.

I began my studies at bible college shattered by my own set of troubles. The first guy who befriended me at school was a hard-core gangbanger named John. He admitted to having shot at people, and he referred to females in unflattering terms. Only weeks had transpired from the time he became a Christian to the time he was seated next to me in chapel. According to John, God had taken him from the world of gangs and brought him to bible college to save his life by getting him off the street.

Often during chapel, God would make his presence palpable, and whenever God overtook John, it was a most beautiful sight. John was a man who was used to being in control and controlling others. He was powerful in his own eyes, and when God's irresistible presence would attempt to overtake John, he would use his feeble human power to try to wrestle with and overpower God. It was like watching a young child trying to wrestle with and subdue his father. But God patiently tolerated John's resistance, and after a while God's love, sweetness, tenderness, and patience melted away all of John's hard-hearted resistance and need for control. Witnessing John's surrender was indeed a beautiful sight.

At bible college, there was also a sense of presumed holiness. Students had received and answered the call of God in their lives, and that call was viewed as a stamp of approval. Even though issues that needed to be addressed were still lurking under the surface, those issues were swept under the rug, ignored, or covered up.

Our instructors and those who preached in our chapel were emblems of righteousness who never admitted to any form of dysfunction. Everybody was a superhero at bible college, and no one ever admitted any flaws. To be fair, some of our instructors were indeed pure and had not erred in their lives. Unfortunately, that made them incapable of dealing with the imperfections they encountered in the student body. They believed that bible college was not the place to address such issues. They were insensitive to the need for deliverance because they had never felt such a need themselves. In such an atmosphere, unhealthy behavior was ignored because nobody wanted to address it. Students who could not manage to hide their flaws simply disappeared.

My sermon was written to address the cover-up problem at school. I admonished students not to get caught in the trap of ignoring the issues that needed to be addressed in their lives. I told them not to assume that they had arrived just because they had answered God's call.

King David was an example of a man who not only sought forgiveness for his sins but also pleaded with God to clean him of his unrighteousness. For King David, forgiveness was not enough. He understood that sin is an addictive, controlling beast and that committing a sin for the first time gave him a greater propensity to repeat it. Although God called people into the ministry, that call was not a rubber stamp of righteousness. God wanted to use each student's time in bible college for purification purposes. God had chosen bible college as the place of confrontation. He wanted to confront those He had called with their past behaviors, attitudes, thoughts, and unresolved issues so they could be addressed, thereby washing each student's slate clean. Those students who were unaware of what God was doing accused Satan of bringing up the past when all their ugliness resurfaced. Ironically, the very place that God had chosen for confrontation and purification was the place least tolerant of any display of dysfunction.

John eventually disappeared, but before he did, I witnessed a transformation in him. He found a woman at school who interested him, and what attracted him to her was not only her beauty but also her strength. She displayed a natural self-confidence that takes a woman years to develop. However, she did not appreciate his interest in her and told Dean B. that John was harassing her.

Dean B. had a private conversation with John that apparently made him snap, and after that John gradually stopped attending classes. Before he disappeared entirely, he picked me up one day in front of my dorm and we went for a ride. The look in John's eyes was bone-chilling; his eyes were glassy, wild, piercing, ravenous, and demonic, but I did not mention it. Instead, I tried to encourage him to return to school and to use his street toughness to endure the rigors of spiritual boot camp.

We ordered some food at a Wendy's drive-thru and then drove to a nearby park. As we sat in John's car, he brought up the subject that begged discussion.

He said, "I don't look the same, do I?"

"No, you don't," I said. "You don't look like the person I met at the beginning of the semester. In fact, you don't look like the person I know at all. What's the matter?"

"Denessa," he said, "all I want to do right now is see blood." Then he took a bite of his half-pound cheeseburger and added, "I want to see blood so bad, I can taste it."

A chill ran up my spine as the pinkish burger juice ran down his chin, because I could tell that he meant every word. He explained what had happened between the woman and him, and told me that he thought he'd been given an unfair shake.

"Do you understand that when a woman is referred to as 'my b--ch,' it's a compliment?" he asked.

"No, I do *not*," I said.

He gave me a quizzical look, and while he continued to tell me what Dean B. had said (and as far as I was concerned, Dean B. had come to the rescue of a damsel in distress), I silently prayed, "God, if you'll just get me out of this one, I promise . . . "

Later, John dropped me off at my dorm. As he drove away, I wished him well and whispered a prayer, "Dear God, please help him."

A couple years after graduating from bible college, I was sitting in a multivariable calculus class at Ohio State University when God spoke to me, saying, "This is not where I want you to be."

I responded silently, "Speak quickly and specifically, because I've already paid for my classes and books."

God answered, "I want you to study and write about the life of King David."

With apprehension, I dropped my classes and returned my books, wondering what I could possibly learn about King David.

Part One: Wayward

I.

Freedom at Last!

Though it is possible to study King David without an understanding of Israel's history, such a study would underestimate his impact on Israel. It would be difficult to see that King David was the greatest leader Israel ever had. As this book unfolds, you will begin to appreciate the significance of such a bold statement.

Saving Egypt from Starvation

The story starts in the land of Canaan when some of Jacob's sons sold their brother Joseph to a traveling Egyptian merchant. Joseph had been an obscure slave in Egypt for thirteen years when the pharaoh had two disturbing dreams that his wise men could not interpret. Because Joseph could interpret dreams, the pharaoh sent for him. Upon hearing the dreams, Joseph told the pharaoh that his dreams were a warning from God that a famine would plague his land for seven years. Since the dreams also revealed that seven years of prosperity would precede the famine, Joseph advised the pharaoh to collect and store 20 percent of the grain harvested during the next seven years.

The pharaoh used Joseph's interpretation and advice to prepare for the famine. He charged Joseph with the task of collecting and storing the grain. When the famine indeed struck, the pharaoh was able to sustain the Egyptians and keep them from dying of starvation. People from surrounding countries like Canaan turned to Egypt to buy grain because they, too, were affected by the famine.

Before the famine, Egyptians owned 100 percent of everything they possessed. They were free men and women who owned land, flocks, and herds, and they had disposable income. Before the famine, living hand to mouth was unheard of in Egypt. To live such a lifestyle was called poverty. However, the famine radically changed the wealth structure of Egypt and impoverished its people. To avoid starvation, they were forced to spend all their money on grain. When their money ran out, they sold their livestock, then their land, and finally they sold themselves to the pharaoh, becoming his servants. Although the pharaoh saved their lives, the famine reduced them to utter poverty. The pharaoh may have been seen as a hero because he saved his people from starvation, but by the end of the famine he had become incredibly rich, owning the entire land of Egypt, with the exception of the land belonging to the priests.

In modern times, the United States is regarded as the wealthiest nation in the world. While it is true that we have been blessed, we really are not the wealthiest nation, not in the least. We believe we are wealthy and cannot see how impoverished we are because of the wide availability and use of credit. If consumer lending were eliminated in America, it would level the playing field with other countries. Then we would realize that people in Third World countries are actually better off than the typical middle-class American. While they have little, everything they possess belongs to them. Some may live in a one-room shanty with dirt floors, cinder block walls, and a metal roof, but they own it free and clear. They may work hard all day to put food on the table with little change to spare, but at the end of the day, they are not in the red.

Today in America, the concept of full ownership is virtually unheard of. We lease our cars, we mortgage our houses, and we borrow money to buy the necessities of life. All that we earn and much of what we "own" is owed to lenders. For some, after all the bills are paid, there is not enough left over to buy food. We have nothing in storage and we have nothing to spare. At the end of a long, hard day of work, we find ourselves deeper in the red than the day before. We live in a world of sustainable poverty, yet we call it wealth.

Our society has nurtured a debt mentality and a consumer mind-set that has redefined the concept of wealth. American economists promote *comparative advantage* to encourage trade between countries. According to them, the country that can produce a product most cheaply should produce that item for other countries. Comparative advantage is good in theory, but in reality when individuals or nations consume more than they produce, they eventually become slaves to producers, just as the Egyptians became slaves to the pharaoh. In time, all consumers are reduced to utter poverty if they do not produce. They become slaves to producers.

There is a way out, but it requires redefining the concept of wealth, combined with extreme discipline. Wealth should be defined as the amount of time your assets can support you. In order to become wealthy in its truest definition, a person must operate profitably, obtain full ownership of all possessions, and become a producer by investing in or starting profitable businesses.

First, you must become a producer and operate profitably. Your revenue is your salary, and after you pay your expenses, what is left over is your *net income*. You only earn what you keep. In order to increase your net income you must either reduce your expenses or increase your revenues. In order to reduce expenses, you have to change the way you think. You do not have to have everything; focus on meeting your *needs*. Become a disciplined consumer.

Second, you must learn to live off less than you earn. Nearing the end of the famine, when Joseph gave seed to the Egyptians, he told them that they could not consume 100 percent of it. Twenty percent of the seed was to be used to pay the pharaoh (as taxes). The remaining 80 percent could not be completely consumed, either, since they had to set seed aside for the next year's crop. They had to live off less than they earned.

Finally, you must eliminate debt. Debt equals principal plus interest, and once it is eliminated, you not only achieve full ownership but also increase your cash flow. You can then use your increased cash flow for investing to increase wealth-generating assets instead of using it as disposable income.

Preserving the Seed

God intended to bless Jacob because he was Abraham's grandson. God told Abraham that he would bless his descendants through his son, Isaac. Between Isaac's sons, Esau and Jacob, Jacob was the son with the birthright, so God put Jacob's son Joseph into a position to bless his family.

The pharaoh would not withhold anything from Joseph, the man who had saved Egypt from starvation and increased the pharaoh's wealth beyond anything he could have imagined. When the pharaoh made Joseph ruler of Egypt, he also relinquished a tremendous amount of authority to Joseph. He appointed him coordinator of "Operation Feed Egypt." No one lifted a finger without Joseph's direction, and people bowed to him as he passed by. Joseph was a hero, second in command to the pharaoh.

Joseph had been second in command to the pharaoh for nine years when Jacob sent the majority of his sons from Canaan to Egypt to buy grain. It was only the second year of the famine; there were still five long years to follow. Joseph was trying to save his family from the utter poverty that Egypt was suffering as a result of the famine. When the pharaoh discovered that Joseph had family, he rolled out the red carpet for them, extending an invitation for them to live in Egypt and facilitating their move to Goshen, which contained the best pastureland.

Jacob had misgivings about moving to Egypt. His apprehension was not unfounded, because God had told Abraham that his descendants would be oppressed as slaves in a foreign land for four hundred years. Jacob's descendants were already living in the land that God promised Abraham, even though they did not possess it. Egypt was a foreign land, so what better place for the fulfillment of God's words? God assuaged Jacob's fears at Beersheba and promised to create a great nation, beginning with Jacob's seventy descendants. God also promised to be with them and to help them return to the land of Canaan. What could possibly go wrong when you have God's presence, His promises, and His provisions?

Over time, the pharaoh died, Joseph and his brothers died, and all the Egyptians of that era died, along with all memories of Joseph's contributions. The new pharaoh and the new generation of Egyptians no longer remembered their hero. However, it did not matter if the memory of Joseph's contributions was still at the forefront of public opinion, because the small, innocuous cluster of Israelites who had settled with Joseph in Egypt eventually grew to threatening proportions. The new pharaoh was concerned about the alarming growth rate of the Israelite population. Something had to be done to stem the tide and control the number of Israelites, because Egypt feared Israel would threaten its sovereignty.

The Israelite population explosion created a powerful political and military force. Jacob's descendants numbered seventy when they entered Egypt, but when they left Egypt, the number had grown to 600,000 men twenty years and older, not counting Levites, women, and children. The Israelite presence in Egypt also significantly benefited the country. Egypt could not afford to lose the Israelites, but neither could it afford the unwieldy power their growth represented. Egypt had to find a way to harness the power of the Israelites, so the Egyptians came up with two solutions: enslavement and genocide.

Under the Egyptians, the Israelites worked long hours and were driven mercilessly, suffering cruel and ruthless treatment. Egypt's oppression did not have the intended effect, however, because the harder things became, the more the Israelites grew in strength and numbers. Finally, the pharaoh implemented the last phase of his assault on the Israelites. Children are the future; kill them and society goes extinct. The strength of any society lies in its children—male children in particular, because men hold the power to resist domination. If the pharaoh destroyed that power center, he could maintain control.

The pharaoh decided to kill all newborn Israelite boys. He enlisted Egyptian midwives to kill Israelite boys at birth. Because the midwives often subverted his orders, he also enlisted Egyptian citizens to kill Israelite baby boys.

Egyptian citizens not only had the right to kill these boys with impunity, they also were mandated to do so. An Egyptian citizen could kill an Israelite male child without having to answer to the crime in a court of law, in order to preserve their way of life. If the crime ever did make it to court, a jury composed of their peers would acquit them.

The male children of any oppressed group are always an endangered species. In America, you will find them dead at a tender age, systematically barred from participating economically in society, enslaved to drugs and alcohol, or imprisoned.

Slave Mentality

Four hundred years of oppression and brutality at the hands of the Egyptians caused the Israelites to cry out to God. They cried to the God of all creation, who alone was powerful enough to bring them out of their condition.

> Years passed, and the king of Egypt died. But the Israelites still groaned beneath their burden of slavery. They cried out for help, and their pleas for deliverance rose up to God. God heard their cries and remembered his covenant promise to Abraham, Isaac, and Jacob. He looked down on the Israelites and felt deep concern for their welfare. *Exodus 2:23–25*

When God told Abraham that foreigners would enslave his descendants for four hundred years, He also promised to deliver and return them to Canaan. Everything happened according to God's word. Israel did become a great nation in Egypt, and the Israelites were slaves in Egypt for more than four hundred years. The Israelites built Egypt's wealth, working without compensation during their slavery. They built Egypt with the blood of their sons, the sweat of hard labor, and the tears of injustice. Egypt could not function without the labor Israel provided, and if it had not been for Joseph's contributions, the famine would have wiped Egypt out. So when the Israelites left Egypt, God made sure they received compensation. His promise that Israel would take the wealth of Egypt with her was fulfilled, and it was fair. God fulfilled all of His promises concerning the nation of Israel and her stay in Egypt.

> But I will punish the nation that enslaves them, and in the end they will come away with great wealth. After four generations your descendants will return here to this land, when the sin of the Amorites has run its course. *Genesis 15:14, 16*

Most people who read the story of Israelite slavery in Egypt feel indignation, taking the position that the Israelites deserved God's deliverance. They are sympathetic to the fact that all human beings have the right to be masters of their own lives. Slavery is an affront to humanity, no matter how "humanely" a slave is treated. No human has the right to enslave another. No human has the right to choose who will live and who will die. God commanded humans to be fruitful, multiply, and to subdue the Earth, giving them authority over aquatic and terrestrial animals. God gave humans dominion over the Earth and its contents, but He did not instruct humans to dominate each other. Most people feel that it is God's responsibility to defend the sanctity of human life when it is degraded and to see that justice is served. Although people feel that way, there is scriptural evidence that God does *not* condemn slavery.

God did not deliver the Israelites from Egypt on the basis of justice alone, but because of a promise. God promised Abraham that He would deliver his descendants from bondage, and He proved Himself a god of His word when He delivered an idolatrous people out of slavery. God had made a covenant with a righteous man (Abraham, blessed to be a blessing) and He had to honor that covenant on behalf of an unrighteous people. He accomplished what no other god had ever accomplished when He delivered an enslaved people from the hands of their oppressors. He was not halfhearted concerning His promise. He delivered the Israelites with His mighty power.

God responded to the cry of His people, even though He was aware of their idolatrous hearts. He looked beyond their shortcomings and faults and met their needs. It is far, far better to stand before God with a promise than with a false sense of self-righteousness. It also pays to have righteous ancestors. God blesses one thousand generations of descendants from righteous ancestors who love and serve Him. God is not slack concerning His promises. For the sake of an oath and love, God delivered His people.

> It was simply because the LORD loves you, and because he was keeping the oath he had sworn to your ancestors. That is why the LORD rescued you with such amazing power from your slavery under Pharaoh in Egypt. *Deuteronomy 7:8*

While it is true that God delivered the Israelites on the basis of a promise He made to their ancestors, He also responded to their cries of distress. God is sensitive and tenderhearted, and He can be touched by human infirmities. The Israelites were distraught as a result of the unrelenting cruelty of their oppressors. The Egyptians mistreated, humiliated, decimated, and degraded them. They were mere chattel, property, and were treated like objects, without concern for their emotional well-being, their intellect, or their desires. Any regard for their physical bodies only concerned a potential loss of labor.

Their irascible and insatiable oppressors drove them beyond the point of exhaustion, required superhuman feats, and assigned tasks and quotas without giving the Israelites the resources to accomplish them. The Israelites were discouraged, disheartened, and depressed because their lives were cheap. No one escapes the grave, but they were constantly faced with added threat because they could be killed at the whim of their oppressors. Their hope had long ago disappeared and they felt helpless because they had no power to create justice. They did not even have the luxury of being able to experience a mental breakdown. Finally they cried out in anguish, "God of our Fathers, we just can't take it anymore."

Slavery robbed Israel of her human dignity, and God wanted to restore it. God wanted to roll away the shame of slavery from His people. In some Christian circles, having self-esteem and a sense of self-worth is viewed as detrimental. Lacking self-esteem and a sense of self-worth, however, can cause people to treat themselves and others as if they are worthless. When people do not feel good about themselves, they lash out and destroy others, especially those who seem to have a high opinion of themselves. On the other hand, when God showers love on people, people begin to understand self-worth, and when people understand their worth, they love themselves and develop an appreciation for all of God's creation. When people love themselves, they are able to receive blessings instead of repelling them.

> I, the Lord, am your God, who brought you from the land of Egypt so you would no longer be slaves. I have lifted the yoke of slavery from your neck so you can walk free with your heads held high.
> *Leviticus 26:13*

People who have been abused continue to suffer from self-loathing long after the abuse has ended. They see no worth in themselves because they have been treated as if they were nothing. They reflect and internalize the hatred and low esteem of their abusers. They cannot meet the gaze of others, nor can they look into their own eyes lest they see their feelings of emptiness, shame, and worthlessness. It says a lot about the value God places on people that He would want to rebuild their self-esteem.

No, I created you in my image, I breathed the breath of life into you; you have divinity coursing through your veins. You will never achieve greatness or reach your potential as long as you are convinced that you are nothing. As long as you are convinced that you are nothing, you cannot receive my goodness because you won't believe you are worth it.

Often the oppressed look at themselves and wonder, "What is wrong with me? Why am I hated?" They think if they can answer those questions and devise solutions to "fix" themselves, they will gain respect from their oppressors and be treated well. However, the real question that needs to get asked (but never is) is, "What is wrong with my oppressor?"

Oppressed people suffer as a result of their oppressor's own low self-esteem. How people treat others is indicative of how they feel about themselves. If oppressors view other human beings as subhuman and use that view to justify ill treatment, it means that the oppressors also see themselves as subhuman. That means that fixing the oppressed so that they will become acceptable to their oppressors will never stop the oppression and abuse. The real issue that must be addressed is how to correct and heal the oppressor's low self-esteem and self-worth so that everyone can be healed.

Unfaithful

Israelites rubbed elbows with Egyptians for more than four hundred years, and idolatry became ingrained in them because it was an Egyptian way of life. Egypt practiced polytheism, worshiping a different god for every aspect of life. In addition, God called Abraham out of the land of the Chaldeans, another culture that was enveloped in idolatry.

It is easy for humans to fall into the trap of idolatry, because human beings are created to worship. We are worshipful beings, and worship is as important to the spiritual and soul fabric of humanity as air is to the physical body. It is not a matter of *whether* you worship; it is only a matter of *whom* or *what* you worship. A study of the Israelites represents a study of humanity. All the flaws and mistakes found in the Israelites can be found in people of any era. The Israelite condition represents the human condition. Because we are worshipful beings, no one is immune to the trap of idolatry, and even today, we are all guilty of idolatry to one degree or another.

Israel was in spiritual as well as physical bondage to her Egyptian oppressors. Although God removed Israel from slavery, she was still spiritually and mentally enslaved to the gods of Egypt because idolatry was still woven into the fabric of her soul. It is no wonder that Israel "reverted" to her idolatrous ways in the wilderness. It was easy for her to fall prey to idol worship, because it was already in her heart. Idolatry was her way of life. Worshiping the golden calf was not a fluke; it was the Egyptian way. Balaam's plot, which enticed the Israelites to marry foreigners who practiced idolatry, was effective because the Israelites had acquired an appetite for idolatry.

It is good to address a spiritual problem by first isolating it from its nurturing environment. What is even more crucial, but often overlooked, is to address the spiritual problem. Assuming that it will address itself is similar to sweeping dirt under a rug and assuming that since it cannot be seen, it is no longer there. Lack of expression of a spiritual problem is often assumed to be a signal of its absence, when it is really only dormant. If the spiritual condition of humanity's heart is not addressed, all efforts at changing location will be in vain. It is easy to change a person's circumstances but difficult to change a person's heart. Focus on changing the heart and everything else will change. Even if the circumstances do not change, they automatically lose their power when the heart changes.

God has a personality and characteristics that any human can relate to. However, it is difficult for many people to consider that God thinks, feels, desires a relationship with His creation, and wants to be loved and appreciated. When they consider God in this way, God ceases to be God in their eyes. If we are striving to know God, however, we must keep a balanced perspective. The reality of God's personality can be clearly seen through His interactions with the children of Israel. God loves and acts in love toward His creation, but God is also holy and hates sin and unfaithfulness.

God was incensed over Israel's response to His miracles and flabbergasted by her flippant treatment. He was baffled as to how the people He had just delivered could so quickly reject and betray Him. How could Israel attribute His miracles and handiwork to demons and credit other gods for her deliverance? God's gut reaction was to wash His hands of Israel. It would have been easier to cut the cord from the stiff-necked, incorrigible, unfaithful Israelites and to count His losses, but too much was at stake. His reputation was on the line. His involvement in Israel's plight caused the people of the world to focus their attention on Israel and her phenomenal God.

How could God defend a people and deliver them from bondage and then turn around and wipe them off the face of the planet? The world would think that God could not care for His people and that He had bitten off more than He could chew. "He had enough power to deliver them," they would say, "but He could not sustain them because His power was limited."

It would have been better for God not to have involved Himself with Israel in the first place than to back out midstream. Once God got involved, He was forever stuck with a people who would rather credit demons for their deliverance than glorify Him. God told Moses, "I'm so boiling mad that if I walk with these people, I'll wipe them out. It's better for your sake that I distance myself from you."

What it all came down to was loyalty, because the one who gives life deserves loyalty. A natural bond exists between the giver and the receiver of life. Loyalty to the giver of life develops naturally, but it is not obligatory. A cord that is not easily broken is created when life is given. In marriage, a man and a woman create a bond when they exchange life. In parent-child relationships, parents give life to a child, and the child's life is then intricately bound to the lives of his or her parents. Life that God gives supersedes all these relationships, and that is why He was stumped to find disloyalty in Israel.

God forever linked Himself to humanity when He gave life by creating Adam, and He strengthened the link when He gave His Son's life to restore a spiritually dead humanity. All life is inextricably linked to God. God is so intricately bound to humanity that He loses life when humanity loses life. Any parent who has lost a child can identify with the anguish God feels when countless people enter hell's portal. It grieves God to lose His creation, to lose life. *I have no pleasure in your death; why should you die?*

Whenever a person is in spiritual or physical bondage, their life belongs to what controls them, and they do not truly have a life. It stands to reason that if God delivers a person from bondage, restoring their life, their loyalty should belong to Him, and Him alone. He gave His life to give you life; therefore, your life belongs to Him.

God's problem with Israel was not only her refusal to give her life to Him, but also her refusal to accept the life He offered her. She deliberately rejected Him by crediting demons as her source of life and salvation.

> They offered sacrifices to demons, non-gods, to gods they had not known before, to gods only recently arrived, to gods their ancestors had never feared. You neglected the Rock who had fathered you; you forgot the God who had given you birth. *Deuteronomy 32:17–18*

Israel took advantage of God. She wanted to detach the giver of the gift of life from the gift. She did not want to be His by giving her life to God. Her devotion to God should have been unshakable, but Israel betrayed God. God invested heavily in Israel when He delivered her, but He brought heartache upon Himself because Israel did not appreciate His efforts. God came to the table in good faith, honoring His commitment to rescue Israel. He earned the right to be her God, but once He had delivered her and wanted to make their relationship permanent, Israel wanted nothing to do with God, preferring other gods to Him. Israel did not want a relationship with God; she just used Him to obtain her freedom. Once she got what she wanted, she tossed Him aside like a wadded-up gum wrapper. (Does that sound like anything *you* can relate to?)

We're in This Together

God walked into His marriage with Israel with His eyes wide open. He was dealing with a recalcitrant people in the same way a man (we'll call him Mr. Goodman) deals with a wife of ill repute. Before him, she had had many lovers; she had an appetite for variety. Monogamy was staid and stifling, but she decided to humor her husband. She was grateful to him because he brought her out of the dumps and nursed her back to health when no one else would have anything to do with her. He saved her from abuse, mistreatment, and untold atrocities and offered her a home with love and warmth and gave her a chance at life. He even told her, "I just want to be good to you."

For a time, she let him play the Good Samaritan. Life was good but predictable and boring with Mr. Goodman, so she eventually went back to her lovers. It did not take long for her to reach rock bottom, again becoming the object of many men's fantasies. To them, she was just an object, not a person of value. She finally found her way back to Mr. Goodman, shivering in her ragged clothes, her hair matted, her body emitting a foul stench, and her eyes glossy.

He took pity on her and took her back. It was a rocky road, but they managed to live peacefully for a while. Then, out of the blue, she left again, taking an even larger chunk of his heart with her. He wondered where he had gone wrong. What was it that he had not done for her? Why had she insisted upon blowing all his hard work on other men? Why was she so determined to allow others to tear down what he had built? Even with all those feelings going around in his head, when she called again, asking him to take her back, he did, knowing full well that she would one day break his heart all over again.

In the wilderness, God's response to Israel's unfaithfulness was to teach Israel the concept of spiritual monogamy. God's attitude about His relationship with Israel was one of permanence.

We're permanently bound, so let's make the best of it. If we're going to make this marriage work, there are some things you need to know; there are some things we need to get straight. Let me make it perfectly clear about who delivered you. You called upon all the gods who you now credit for your deliverance, but nothing happened. When you called on me for deliverance, I made it happen. These other gods you swoon over have never done anything except harm you. They don't love you like I do. You provoke me to jealousy when you shower your affections on those gods. Yes, I am jealous. I love you, and I refuse to share your affections with anyone else. You shouldn't have any other gods before me. There's only one God; every other god is a devil.

God reasoned that since it was not natural for Israel to love the one who had saved her and chosen her to be His very own, He would have to be patient and teach her how to please Him. He made His expectations very clear.

I can't tolerate unfaithfulness. Don't worship the things I made for your enjoyment as if they're greater than me. Don't give your affections to others; they belong to me. I'm jealous of your affection and appreciation; I don't share. If you're faithful to me, I'll shower my goodness upon you and yours, but if you despise and reject me by spurning my goodness, you will feel the consequences for generations. Don't treat me like I'm nothing, belittle me, disrespect me, blow me off, take me lightly, or disregard me. I created precedence when I created the world in six days. I've reserved the seventh day as a day of rest. Celebrate me and my accomplishments by resting with me.

Not only is it important how you treat me; I also care about how you treat others, because they belong to me too. Honor and obey your parents, for when you honor and obey them, you honor and obey me. I'll reward you with longevity if you do. Don't kill, don't destroy my creation, my work. Don't commit adultery; you know how I hate that. Don't lie to others. Don't take what doesn't belong to you. Don't covet (actively pursue) what belongs to another.

As in any new marriage, after the honeymoon comes the adjustment period. It is during the adjustment period that couples learn each other's likes and dislikes. That time is sensitive, because habits and customs once viewed as normal may start to seem offensive and unacceptable. The beginning stages of a marriage require tons of unfailing love and forgiveness if the marriage is to survive. It is a tumultuous time of change and struggle.

You know, she did that when you were dating, but you just swallowed hard and said nothing because you loved her and did not want to risk losing her. Besides, anything can be tolerated for a few hours. However, after you married her, you had to say, "Honey, I love you, but I don't like it when you flirt!"

In the wilderness, God was trying to get Israel ready to live successfully and harmoniously in the Promised Land, where He planned to dwell with her, but that meant eradicating personality quirks. There was a time when God involved Himself in the life of Israel and overlooked certain actions, but after they were married, God had to tell her that some of her behavior was offensive and could no longer be tolerated.

God made it a capital crime for Israelites to offer private sacrifices to evil spirits out in the fields, because they were using it as an opportunity to be unfaithful to God. If anyone wanted to offer a sacrifice, they had to bring it to the priest so the priest could present the sacrifice to the Lord as a peace offering. God was determined to eradicate idolatry. God forbade the Israelites or anyone else dwelling with them to eat animal fat or drink blood because the life of the flesh is in the blood. God would cut off from the community of Israel anyone who violated these rules.

It is a challenge to live in a society without adopting its customs, otherwise known as its culture. What the populace considers right is usually contrary to God's way. But God instructed Israel to shun Canaanite culture upon entering the land of Canaan. God called Abraham, their ancestor, away from his homeland to remove him from idolatry, and He expected his descendants to follow the same tradition. God instructed Israel not to adopt the practices of the current inhabitants or to continue the ways of the Egyptians where they came from.

Today I'm giving you a choice, and you need to make a decision right now. Will you live like your ancestors did? Will you live like the Egyptians where you came from? Will you adopt the culture of the people you'll be living around, or will you do things my way?

The Land Is Yours Because the Amorites Forfeited It by Their Sins

God did not give the land of Canaan to Israel as a reward for her righteousness He gave it to her because of the unrighteousness of its occupants. God told Abraham that He would return Israel to Canaan when the sins of the Amorites had run their full course. The occupants had been so vile that even the land of Canaan was repulsed, was revolted at their presence, and was ready to spew them out. God charged the occupants of Canaan with spiritual adultery and sexual immorality. Spiritual adultery and sexual immorality have contributed to the fall of every great civilization; none is immune. The way you handle your sexuality is indicative of the way you handle your spirituality, because both are influenced by the soul. To clear up any confusion, God explained exactly what the Canaanites had done to disgust Him so Israel would know what *not* to do.

The first charge of spiritual adultery was unfaithfulness to God by worshiping demons, consulting them for information, and using them to control others. Any activity that employed demons, God's enemies, was an affront to God. Employing demons is not interesting or intriguing and does not require scientific inquiry; it is deadly. God would not share Israel's affections, adoration, worship, and love with another. God had already taught Israel that a covenant relationship with Him required exclusivity via His commandments. To further emphasize the point, He explained the disgusting things the people of Canaan had done.

> When you arrive in the land the Lord your God is giving you, be very careful not to imitate the detestable customs of the nations living there. For example, never sacrifice your son or daughter as a burnt offering. And do not let your people practice fortune-telling or sorcery, or allow them to interpret omens, or engage in witchcraft, or cast spells, or function as mediums or psychics, or call forth the spirits of

> the dead. Anyone who does these things is an object of horror and disgust to the LORD. It is because the other nations have done these things that the LORD your God will drive them out ahead of you. You must be blameless before the LORD your God. The people you are about to displace consult with sorcerers and fortune-tellers, but the LORD your God forbids you to do such things. *Deuteronomy 18:9–14*

God gave prophets to satisfy Israel's need for information, direction, and instruction. The problem with witchcraft is that it subverts God's will. One of the biggest deceptions of demons is to make you think that you have mastery over them, that you are in control, and that they serve you. They let you think that they are your humble servants until they have you hooked; then they show you who is really boss. Their objective is to control, possess, and destroy you and to subvert the will of God in your life. Horoscopes, zodiac signs, fortune cookies, fortune tellers, psychics, cartoons, and movies and books about witches, warlocks, and the like are not acceptable entertainment for believers.

Furthermore, God warned that if the Israelites brought objects employed to worship other deities into their houses, it would harm them. Do not be attracted by the artistic beauty or the value of the idols, because they are deadly. Do not reason that just because the idols, objects, and images used to worship other gods do not hold the same meaning to you, they are harmless. The idols, objects, and images people employ to worship their deities have demons attached to them. There is no immunity for you if you possess accursed things, participate in detestable activities, or associate with idolatrous people.

> You must burn their idols in fire, and do not desire the silver or gold with which they are made. Do not take it or it will become a snare to you, for it is detestable to the LORD your God. Do not bring any detestable objects into your home, for then you will be set apart for destruction just like them. You must utterly detest such things, for they are set apart for destruction. *Deuteronomy 7:25–26*

Upon entering the land of Canaan with the Israelites, God planned to purify the land, using Israel to remove seven nations that were more powerful than she was. God gave Israel a mandate to purify the land, exterminating idolatry by breaking demonic strongholds. He called for reformation on a grand scale. God expected Israel to respond with such vehemence toward idolatry that she would tear down pagan altars, shatter sacred pillars, cut down Asherah poles, and burn idols. God determined that the occupants of Canaan were incorrigible, and His solution was to annihilate them completely.

Do not get mixed up with that bunch, because they will corrupt you. Do not make treaties or covenants with the inhabitants of the land because the unholy alliance will lead to your demise; your fate will be the same as theirs. God was disgusted with the immorality of the people of the land of Canaan, not their ethnicity. Be careful about your own associations, because your future depends upon it. Let your prayer to God be that He keep you from committing evil and keep you away from evil people.

> Be very careful never to make treaties with the people in the land where you are going. If you do, you soon will be following their evil ways. Instead, you must break down their pagan altars, smash the sacred pillars they worship, and cut down their carved images. You must worship no other gods, but only the Lord, for he is a God who is passionate about his relationship with you. Do not make treaties of any kind with the people living in the land. They are spiritual prostitutes, committing adultery against me by sacrificing to their gods. If you make peace with them, they will invite you to go with them to worship their gods, and you are likely to do it. And you will accept their daughters, who worship other gods, as wives for your sons. Then they will cause your sons to commit adultery against me by worshiping other gods. You must make no gods for yourselves at all. *Exodus 34:12–17*

God advocated a kind of intolerance of sin that compels believers to eradicate it. That admonition causes the Christian psyche to recoil. It seems ugly, judgmental, intolerant, and hypocritical, and goes against the concept of Christian passivity. Besides, the New Testament advocates mercy. In a democracy, you cannot go around destroying the lives of those who live contrary to your beliefs, because everyone has the right to life, liberty, and the pursuit of happiness. So how can you follow God's instructions without violating the rights of others?

You can please God without violating democratic tenets by taking a stand against sin but loving the sinner. Everybody has a right to free speech, so voice *your* convictions. When people demand the right to have government-sanctioned gay marriage, you can object by refusing to let your tax dollars support it. When people try to legalize abortion, you can protest. When people want to use tax dollars to do research on viable fetuses from fertility clinics, object. Who *is* the government, after all? The government is not an inanimate organization. The government is made of people. Remember, evil thrives when good men do and say nothing, and you will be held accountable for what you do or say. Silence is condoning, and passivity is not acceptable to God; it does not absolve you of guilt. It is your responsibility to speak out and to warn people about the evils they engage in; otherwise, their blood will be on your hands.

God charged the Canaanites not only with spiritual adultery, but also with sexual immorality. Just as God required Israel to have an exclusive relationship with Him, He also required sexual exclusivity in human relationships. God specifically forbade improper sexual relationships and conduct. The people living in Canaan were guilty of the lewd conduct that God warned the Israelites to avoid. Sexual intercourse with close relatives such as mothers, stepmothers, sisters, half sisters, granddaughters, aunts, daughters-in-law, and brothers' wives was unacceptable.

God forbade molestation, for a man to have sex with his wife's daughters and granddaughters, and for a man to have sex with his wife's sisters. Having sex with neighbors' wives was also outlawed. God prohibited homosexuality, bestiality, and for a man to have sex with his wife during her menstruation because it violated her. God also forbade the practice of burning children in a fire as a sacrifice to Molech. The way children are aborted today is essentially the same as sacrificing them to Molech.

This Earth desires righteousness; therefore, it groans under the weight of sinful humanity. Earth is a living organism, possessing its own intellect, feelings, and personality; it has a soul. We have labeled people with that understanding as primitive and superstitious, but they are correct. (God confirms this, but He warns us against worshiping the things He created.) The Earth is adversely affected by and convulses under the sins of humanity. The earth is repulsed by sin.

The challenge God gave the Israelites to conduct themselves as holy people still applies to every believer today. Before you received God as Lord and Savior, you lived according to customs established by your parents, their parents, and society. Some of those customs were contrary to God's expectations. When you receive God as your Lord, He teaches you how to live according to His instructions. He places you on a new plane (the kingdom of God) without removing you from a society that lives contrary to His will. God admonishes you not to live your life according to past habits and ideas that were contrary to Him, and He also tells you not to live your life according to the dictates of society that oppose His will. In the kingdom of God, there is no immunity from the consequences of living contrary to the will of God. Sin causes the place of blessing to become a place of cursing.

Take-home message: Humility is not having a low opinion of one's self—that is low self-esteem. God loves you very much and you are so valuable to Him that He wants to restore your self-esteem.

2.

Failure on the Border of Blessings

God instructed Moses to send twelve scouts, a representative from each tribe, into the wilderness to attest to the veracity of His claims. They were instructed to explore the land and see what it was like. Were the cities walled? How was the soil? Were there trees? They were also told to bring back samples of crops and to find out whether the people living there were strong or weak.

The men explored the land for forty days and returned with a mixed report. On one hand, the land was indeed all that God had said it was, fertile and productive (flowing with milk and honey), and they brought samples of fruit that grew there. The land was everything Israel had left behind in Egypt and more. However, the land was populated by Amalekites, Perrizites, Hittites, Jebusites, Amorites, and Anakites, just like God said, but their cities were advanced, developed, and well fortified, and the majority of the scouts doubted the Israelites' ability to defeat the Canaanites. They felt like grasshoppers in comparison to the giant Anakites, and they were sure they would be overpowered if they attempted to conquer the land. In fact, ten of the twelve scouts thought it would be a futile venture.

The report was a confounding blow, so discouraging that it inspired fear and caused Israel to weep. The Israelites actually began making plans to return to their former lives, preferring slavery to moving toward an uncertain future. They thought it would be better to go back to what they were used to, even if that meant losing their freedom and their lives and enduring intense hardship. Fear of the unknown makes present discomforts palatable. Israel had left certainty and embraced the unknown in the hope that things would be better, only to find herself in a worse position than when she started. She felt that God had betrayed her with empty promises. Israel had taken a risk, but she had nothing to show for her efforts. She felt as if God had not told her the whole story. If He had done so, it would have put things in a completely different perspective.

> Then all the people began weeping aloud, and they cried all night. Their voices rose in a great chorus of complaint against Moses and Aaron. "We wish we had died in Egypt, or even here in the wilderness!" they wailed. "Why is the LORD taking us to this country only to have us die in battle? Our wives and little ones will be carried off as slaves! Let's get out of here and return to Egypt." Then they plotted among themselves, "Let's choose a leader and go back to Egypt!"
> *Numbers 14:1–4*

Be careful what you say during setbacks. Better still, be careful what you say, period, because words are powerful. Israel said, "We wish we had died in Egypt or here in the wilderness. If we go forward with God, we will die in battle. Our families will be carried off as slaves." A study of her history shows that Israel got everything she spoke of.

Minority Report

Caleb and Joshua tried to counter the majority opinion by giving a faith report, but the Israelites would have none of it and wanted to stone them.

Faith does not ignore the facts nor deny the existence of obstacles; it simply looks at things from God's perspective. Faith sees giants but denies their power to conquer. Faith knows God made giants, and since He made giants, He has dominion over them. There are the facts of reality, but then there is faith. Rational thinking takes into account only the limited information that can be gathered via human physical senses. Then, based on the limited information our physical senses provide, we make faulty decisions. The ability to see the big picture means seeing what cannot be seen through conventional means. It means being connected to the One who sees all and relying on His perspective.

Israel did a self-evaluation and found herself lacking. "Our ability is no match for them. One of the giant descendants of Anak could wipe out twenty of us." There is no hope when you evaluate overpowering circumstances based solely on human ability. Indeed, if human ability is all you are working with, you are indeed hopeless. However, a faith mind-set incorporates reality and sees things as they are, but it also factors God into the equation and sees things as they *could be*. When God is involved in the equation, the possibilities are limitless and the outcomes are miraculous.

God gave Israel information. It was His intention to lead her from utter poverty where she was chattel to riches. He wanted to remove the shame of slavery and to restore her dignity, and He backed up His words by demonstrating that He had nothing but the best of intentions regarding her. He brought her out of Egypt, protected her from her Egyptian pursuers, and provided for her in the wilderness. He led Israel and was personally present to guide her, day and night. He took care of her needs for water, food, shelter, protection, discipline, and forgiveness.

I'm not asking you to blindly trust or even believe in empty promises. I am a god of my word; I am a god of substance. My word is more important to me than my name.

God holds His word higher than His name. By His word, He made the Earth. By His word, He created man and made him a living soul. By His word, He raised Jesus from the dead. Everything that He has accomplished has been done by His word. (Since human beings are made in His likeness and image, we also live by His principles and by the words we speak.) God's word goes forward and it will accomplish what He intends it to accomplish. Israel was dealing with a God of integrity. Who or what could resist His mighty power, His word? God gave His word to Abraham, who died without seeing God's word fulfilled. He promised to give Abraham's descendants Canaan, and God was ready to make good on His promise. Israel needed to rehearse God's promises; she needed to repeat what God had said.

> The Lord merely spoke, and the heavens were created. He breathed the word, and all the stars were born. He gave the sea its boundaries and locked the oceans in vast reservoirs. Let everyone in the world fear the Lord, and let everyone stand in awe of him. For when he spoke, the world began! It appeared at his command. But the Lord's plans stand firm forever; his intentions can never be shaken.
> *Psalm 33:6–9, 11*

Fighting Against the Miraculous

Despite all the failures, drama, and struggles in the wilderness, God was ready to fulfill His word. But even as He was trying to lead Israel into the blessing, she resisted Him. She followed Him every day while wandering about and getting nowhere, but when it was time to be blessed and to go where she had never been, she refused. In spite of God's efforts to prove Himself to Israel, she still refused to trust Him. Israel's relationship with God was always clouded by unbelief, doubt, and suspicion.

I cannot get you to trust me, no matter what I do. I am the one good thing that has ever happened in your entire life and all you do is fight against me. I am the one who has come alongside you to give you a happy ending, and yet you resist me. What else can I do to convince you that I am on your side and have your best interest in mind?

It takes trust to receive a miracle from God. God was trying to position Israel for a blessing. He was ready to fulfill the promise He had made to her ancestors, but she was not ready to cooperate with Him. It is impossible to please God without trust, because lack of trust blocks God from fulfilling His promise. God did not need Israel's assistance in fulfilling His promise. He just needed her to get into a position to receive it, but Israel resisted. If He moved forward, she stood still. If He gave her riches, she squandered them on demons. If He gave her talent, ability, and wisdom, she wasted them on useless things. She unraveled everything He was trying to do in her life. She sabotaged His efforts. No one could be a greater enemy than she was to herself!

Have you ever found yourself kicking and screaming, resisting God, when all He was trying to do was bless you? Have you ever found yourself fighting against the one thing that was meant to bless you? If so, you were your own worst enemy, the biggest hindrance to your blessing. How can you ever be blessed when you resist the One who is trying to do the miraculous in your life? He needs your obedient cooperation.

What is a miracle, anyway? A miracle occurs when God changes the unnatural order of things. What we view as normal and the natural progression of things is not the way God intended things to be. This planet and everything on it suffer from the curse of sin. Because of sin, we have sickness, disease, decay, death, disorder, and chaos. Ours is an accursed world. What is common and natural in our eyes is unnatural in the eyes of God. Thus, a miracle restores the natural order according to God's perspective and His intent; it is a reversal of the curse. A miracle, at its most basic root, is a change from the unnatural back to its original natural state according to God's perspective.

Miraculous change requires a change in perspective. Any agent of change, be it God, a physician, a leader, or a counselor, knows that in order for permanent change to take root in a person's life, that person has to take ownership of the change process; they must embrace change. God can do anything, absolutely anything. All He has to do is speak the word and He can transform any situation in the blink of an eye. God's action in miracles depends on the person receiving the miracle. God functions in a certain way and requires the person receiving the miracle to do certain things. Whatever God requires a recipient to do *involves* them in the miracle and causes them to take ownership to effect permanent change. If you do not appreciate what it takes to bring change, how do you know what to do to maintain it?

Put Up Your Dukes and Fight for It, Baby

What is it that causes us to fail on the border of a blessing? What is it that causes us to abort a blessing? Why do we fail to walk into blessings? Why do we repel blessings? The truth about most blessings is that you have to fight to get them. Whether you fight against your own mind-set cluttered with doubts and indecisions or whether you fight against a tangible enemy, you have to fight.

You do not just walk into a blessing; you have to *fight* your way into it, because the greater the blessing, the greater the resistance to receiving it. If you have not been taught that principle, a blessing loses its appeal; when in the pursuit of a blessing the obstacles start wearing you out, the first instinct is to back away. You do not want to embrace a thing that was meant as a blessing when it rejects, attacks, and destroys you. In fact, from a human viewpoint, something that wreaks havoc in your life is a curse. But the truth is that God often has a way of wrapping a blessing in what appears to be a curse.

God always tells you the end result without telling you about the process you will have to go through to get there. If He told you about the process, you would reject His offer. God showed Joseph his future in dreams, and oh what a glorious future it was! His parents and siblings would bow to him.

> "Listen to this dream," he said. "The sun, moon, and eleven stars bowed low before me!" *Genesis 37:9*

God did not tell him that he would be sold into slavery, falsely accused, and imprisoned, nor that thirteen years would pass before the dream became a reality. If God had told him that, the dream would have lost its appeal.

It seems to go against the meaning of a promise when you have to fight for it. After all, the maker of the promise is responsible for its fulfillment, right? In God's kingdom, however, this is not necessarily the case. I do not mean that when you have been given a promise, you must fight for it by yourself. I do not mean that when you are on the brink of a blessing, God will leave you high and dry. God is with you, He is for you, and as long as He is on your side, you cannot help but be victorious. God has an uncanny way of involving you to make miracles happen in your life. Sometimes He just asks you to position yourself correctly, and sometimes He asks you to fight. It all depends on the magnitude of the gift.

You have to fight for some promises because an enemy fights against your receiving them. That same enemy will also fight to take your gift once you have received it, so you must be able to appreciate what it takes to get the gift in order to keep it. Some promises have long-range consequences that the enemy would rather not have to address. Often a promise from God unlocks further blessings, and the blessings continue to multiply to the point that they spill over and bless others. Then those blessings can spill over to a community, a nation, and a world.

Exactly what kind of blessing did God intend to give Israel?

> It is a land filled with large, prosperous cities that you did not build. The houses will be richly stocked with goods you did not produce. You will draw water from cisterns you did not dig, and you will eat from vineyards and olive trees you did not plant . . . . For the LORD your God is bringing you into a good land of flowing streams and pools of water, with springs that gush forth in the valleys and hills. It is a land of wheat and barley, of grapevines, fig trees, pomegranates, olives, and honey. It is a land where food is plentiful and nothing is lacking. It is a land where iron is as common as stone, and copper is abundant in the hills. *Deuteronomy 6:10–11, 8:7–9*

The Israelites were going to receive these blessings upon taking possession (a war term) of Canaan. Everything they left behind in Egypt and more would be theirs upon entry into Canaan.

How easily can someone walk in and take what you have spent a lifetime building? How easily can someone walk in and take what has been in your family for generations? Let us say that your ancestors bought acres of land, with a house and everything needed to sustain a family and to make them wealthy. The fertile land produces grains, fruit, and vegetables. You have all sorts of livestock; you lack nothing. The city where your land is located is well fortified and secure, built by men of generations gone by. Let us say that God then decided to give all of that to strangers. It is not theirs and they did not build it. Would you allow someone to walk in, take up residence, and take over your property without putting up a fight? People will fight to their death for family, land, and country. If an enemy managed to prevail against you and take what you felt belonged to you, would you not regroup and mount a counterassault to reclaim what you felt was rightfully yours?

God did not share the whole plan with Israel concerning Canaan. Had He done that, He would have had difficulties convincing Israel to leave Egypt. If God had shown her the full picture, she would have said, "Why should I leave the comfort and familiarity of my desperately horrible life where I am living as if I'm less than human, only to walk through uncertainty in the wilderness and into a land where I have to fight and possibly die?"

God told her about the blessing He was taking her into, but He did not tell her how she was going to receive the blessing. Given the magnitude of the blessing God was giving Israel, it did not occur to her that she would have to conquer the people of Canaan in order to possess it. She thought that all she had to do was show up, walk into the land, and knock on doors, and the people of Canaan would graciously open their homes and receive her. She did not know that she would have to fight, resist, and deny the claims of the current occupants to the land. God did not tell her because He did not want her to be discouraged. God was building Israel up to take Canaan. He planned to reveal His plan gradually, in stages, one experience at a time.

Step by Step

God purposely did not take the direct route into Canaan because Israel was not ready. In order to enter into the promises of the Lord, you have to fight. If you have no strength to fight, receiving the promises will be difficult, if not impossible. This was true in the case of Israel, and it is still true in the life of every believer who has received a promise from the Lord. In the wilderness, the Lord had to prepare Israel for battle, but immediately following her release from slavery was not the time to take her into battle. She was tired, discouraged, and vulnerable. That was not the time to engage in a battle; she did not have the energy to fight. She needed rest and recuperation. Although she was physically capable of fighting, she was not emotionally and spiritually able. Israel had just left slavery, where she had developed a defeatist mentality.

If you have been beaten down all your life and taught that resistance is futile, you will not fight. When you encounter resistance, you will give up. Discouraged, depressed, and broken people will take the path of least resistance. "If I have to fight, it is better to stay where I am because I do not have the strength to fight; I have no fight left in me."

> When Pharaoh finally let the people go, God did not lead them on the road that runs through Philistine territory, even though that was the shortest way from Egypt to the Promised Land. God said, "If the people are faced with a battle, they might change their minds and return to Egypt." So God led them along a route through the wilderness toward the Red Sea, and the Israelites left Egypt like a marching army. Exodus *13:17–18*

God was angry with the Amalekites and had a personal score to settle with them because they attacked Israel when she was vulnerable and was not in a position to defend herself. God was cocooning Israel in the wilderness. He had taken care to avoid hostile territories so that Israel would not get discouraged, only to have the Amalekites ambush Israel and foil His plans. God was trying to shelter and protect Israel; He was trying to nurse her back to health. He was trying to restore her dignity and remove the shame of slavery from the psyche of the Israelites. He was trying to restore self-worth to a broken, hopeless people. He was trying to strengthen and rejuvenate Israel.

Although Israel was free for the first time in four hundred years, she carried a lifetime of scars and a defeated slave mentality. Sometimes wounds run so deep that only God can heal them. Slavery had broken Israel's spirit.

> The spirit of a man will sustain his infirmity; but a wounded spirit who can bear? *Proverbs 18:14, KJV*

Only God can heal wounded hearts and broken spirits. Israel was fragile, vulnerable, and under pressure, and for people under pressure, everything is a big deal. Any pressure added to a system already under maximal pressure, no matter how slight, has a greater impact than if it is added to a system under minimal pressure. Things that would not normally cause a stir in the average person become mountainous to people under pressure.

Because tomorrow is not promised, uncertainty makes people with a slave mentality live only for today. Such people view themselves as inferior to the rest of humanity and undeserving of the good things in life. They are comfortable with hardship because it is familiar, and they cannot imagine a life of ease, comfort, and abundance. Slaves have been treated as if they are nothing and have nothing to offer. They are programmed to believe that they are powerless to control their destiny. Life happens to them instead of their making life happen. They cannot appreciate their intrinsic value or the value of others like themselves. People with a slave mentality believe life is cheap. They squander everything they have, for fear that it will be taken from them. People with a slave mentality settle for scraps and shun goodness and abundance because they feel undeserving.

There comes a critical time when a wounded spirit can be set on the road to recovery. At this point it is important to establish trust. If anything negative or discouraging happens before trust is established, those people become unrecoverable. Once you reach that point with God, you cannot walk any further with Him. It takes trust to walk with God and to allow Him to accomplish the impossible in your life. It takes trust to suspend your will and your plans in order to accept God's plans. It takes trust to believe that He has a better plan for your life and knows what is best for you. However, if God reaches a point where He determines that you are the biggest hindrance to your own blessings and that He can accomplish nothing through you, you are indeed hopeless. When a man loses his ability to trust God, nothing miraculous can be accomplished. (At that point, the miraculous would be restoring faith where doubt and unbelief reign.) Israel reached that point with God, and all He could do with those dispirited people was to spend their lifetime taking them through the healing process. He could not fulfill His promise through Israel because no matter what He did, He could not gain their trust.

You set the limits on yourself by setting limits on God, but the converse is also true. You set limits on what God can accomplish through you by the limitations you place on yourself. When human beings determine God's capabilities using human standards, they place limitations on God. God can do abundantly more than we can ask for or imagine. Israel limited God by the limitations she placed on herself. What God needed Israel to do was use her ability to cooperate with what He was trying to do. When Israel determined that she could not accomplish what God had said she could accomplish, she limited what God could accomplish through her. Although God is omnipotent, He can only accomplish as much in and through you as you allow. Israel had set limitations on herself that God could not overcome. God spends more effort to get humans to catch His vision, to change attitudes and thoughts, and to get cooperation than He does on the miracle itself. The greatest miracle, then, is getting human beings to remove the mental stops. Take your foot off the brakes.

I'm Going to Bless Somebody: If Not You, Then Who?

Israel's rebellion, resistance, and obstinacy flabbergasted God; it was more than He could stand.

I am going to bless somebody. I am going to honor my word if it is the last thing I do. More is at stake here than you receiving a blessing; my word is on the line. I promised your ancestors and they believed me, and I intend to make good on my promises. If not you, then who? If you choose to forfeit my blessings and refuse to allow me to honor my word, I will find someone who will jump at the opportunity to be blessed. I will find someone who will appreciate what I am trying to do. I will find someone who will let me be who I am. If you refuse to be the channel through which my blessings flow, then I will find another.

> But surely as I live, and as surely as the earth is filled with the Lord's glory, not one of these people will ever enter that land. They have seen my glorious presence and the miraculous signs I performed both in Egypt and in the wilderness, but again and again they tested me by refusing to listen. They will never even see the land I swore to give their ancestors. None of those who have treated me with contempt will enter it. . . . As surely as I live, I will do to you the very things I

> heard you say. I, the LORD, have spoken! You will all die here in this wilderness! Because you complained against me, none of you who are twenty years old or older and were counted in the census will enter the land I swore to give you. The only exceptions will be Caleb son of Jephunneh and Joshua son of Nun. You said your children would be taken captive. Well, I will bring them safely into the land, and they will enjoy what you have despised. But as for you, your dead bodies will fall in this wilderness. And your children will be like shepherds, wandering in the wilderness forty years. In this way, they will pay for your faithlessness, until the last of you lies dead in the wilderness. *Numbers 14:21–23, 28–33*

When you refuse to walk in faith, you block God from being who He is; you block Him from being God. Lack of faith is rebellion, because faith is more than just mental acquiescence. Faith is made up of two components: belief and God-directed action. If you believe a thing, you act on it. Lopsided faith is when one of the components is missing. Either you believe the information you have received but do not act on it (as when God told Israel to go into Canaan and she refused) or you act upon presumption (you act on something for which you have been given no information or authority). For instance, when the Israelites heard God's decision, they were sorrowful and regretted their sins. They decided to cooperate a bit too late; "We will go and conquer the land!"

> But Moses said, "Why are you now disobeying the LORD's orders to return to the wilderness? It won't work. Do not go into the land now. You will only be crushed by your enemies because the LORD is not with you. When you face the Amalekites and the Canaanites in battle, you will be slaughtered. The LORD will abandon you because you have abandoned the LORD." But the people pushed ahead toward the hill country of Canaan, despite the fact that neither Moses nor the Ark of the LORD's covenant left the camp. Then the Amalekites and the Canaanites who lived in those hills came down and attacked them and chased them as far as Hormah. *Numbers 14:41–45*

Israel's failure teaches three things that are extremely important when you have a promise from God. First, if you have a promise from the Lord, protect it. Be extremely careful about who you share information with concerning your promise. You may find that you cannot share it with anyone, because no one has the same faith you have, nor does everyone around you necessarily care to see you receive the gift. The only way you will ever know how people really feel about you is to wait to see how they react when you are about to be blessed. They may cause you to abort the promise by their lack of faith, or they may intentionally try to discourage you because of their envy. God gave *you* a promise, not them, and He only requires *you* to believe it. You do not have to convince anyone else of God's promise to you, nor do you have to wait until others are on board before you receive what God has in store for you.

Second, now that we understand that faith is belief and action, we know that it is important not only to trust God but also to do what He says. It is critical that you continue to follow His instructions so that you can obtain the blessing. Determine in your mind that no matter what it looks like, you are going to do what God tells you to do, even if it means that you have to die trying to receive the blessing. It is better to die trying to see a promise fulfilled than to live a lifetime of regret. You have to fight to make God's blessings and promises happen in your life. You can go as far with God as you are willing to go.

Last, words are powerful. Make sure that what you say is in agreement with what God is saying. Speak those things that are not as if they were. You may not yet have what God says He's going to give you, you may not see what God sees, and you may be miles from where He says you are going to be, but keep rehearsing what He says. You will have what you speak, and even if you do not have a specific promise given to you directly from God concerning your life, all the promises that He has made to mankind are available to you. Those promises are found in His written word, and all of God's promises are "yea" and "amen." Should you choose to take God up on any of His promises, start by rehearsing His promises. Your words are powerful!

If you do not walk in faith, there are consequences. For Israel, it meant spending the remainder of her life going through a pain management program in a recovery room. She could not enter into God's promise. Certain blows can occur in people's lives that rock them to the core and make them question everything. There are situations that can make you feel as if all hope is gone and your destiny has been lost, but you must decide that you will not allow that situation to continue wreaking havoc in your life. Develop a fighting mentality that tells the devil that you refuse to let any situation crush you. If you spend the rest of your life licking your wounds, you give more power to the situation than it should have had.

Take-home message: We live by our words. Our words are powerful and have the power to shape our destinies. The power of life and death resides in our mouths.

3.

Do or Die in the Wilderness

The stint in the wilderness was supposed to be short. An extended stay was not part of the plan, but God took full advantage of the time to prepare the Israelites for life in Canaan. He sentenced Israel to the wilderness for forty years as a result of the forty-day exploration by the scouts. Israel's lack of faith put her in a holding pattern. God used the wilderness to accomplish many things.

> Because the men who explored the land were there for forty days, you must wander in the wilderness for forty years—a year for each day, suffering the consequences of your sins. You will discover what it is like to have me for an enemy. I, the LORD, have spoken! I will do these things to every member of the community who has conspired against me. They will all die here in this wilderness!
> *Numbers 14:34–35*

God's Use of the Wilderness

God used the wilderness to kill old resistant, rebellious thought patterns, attitudes, and habits. The only way He could accomplish this was to wait until either the people who possessed those attitudes died or He sped up the process. God chose to wait until the men of fighting age died because He needed fighting men who would trust Him and work in concert with Him. God will put you in the wilderness until He can rearrange your thinking. You will stay in the wilderness until the old obstructive thought patterns that prevent you from walking in His promises die, because thoughts translate into actions. Who decides when obstructive attitudes will die? You and God; it is a collaborative effort. The sooner you cooperate and get with God's program, the sooner God can work to change your attitude and situation.

> Moses continued, "Then the LORD told us to cross Zered Brook, and we did. So thirty-eight years pass from the time we first arrived at Kadesh-barnea until we finally crossed Zered Brook! For the LORD had vowed that this could not happen until all the men old enough to fight in battle had died in the wilderness. The LORD had lifted his hand against them until all of them had finally died." When all the men of fighting age had died, the LORD said to me, "Today you will cross the border of Moab at Ar and enter the land of Ammon."
> *Deuteronomy 2:13–19*

How close was Kadesh-barnea to the Zered Brook? It was as close as you are to the blessing that God has for you.

What a precious gift God extends to a person or a race of people when He chooses to reveal Himself. Another lesson in the wilderness was getting to know God, learning how to be in His presence, and learning how to follow Him. *Let's get acquainted, I want you to know me. I want you to know me so that you will never accept a substitute.* God gives you the opportunity to know Him personally so you will know that He is God. When you get the real thing, you will not be fooled by substitutes. No one can sway you about God's existence or who He is when you have had a personal encounter with Him. When a counterfeit spirit shows up claiming it is God, you will know better.

God was up close and personal with Israel, revealing Himself to her so that they could get to know one another. No other nation could claim that God had personally rescued them from another nation with a great display of power and had spoken to them from fire and from heaven. He had established an undeniable track record with Israel, proving His love and establishing that He alone was God without substitutes. There is nothing greater, nothing sweeter or more precious on this Earth than knowing God, being with Him, and obeying Him.

The only thing equal to being around God and knowing Him is learning how to follow Him. This is also a gift He gave Israel in the wilderness. It is not natural for people to follow God, because the enemy of God has tricked humanity into believing that it is not only possible but also necessary to live life independently of God, the Creator of life. God sees everything, and we are blind compared to Him. Therefore, there is a natural conflict between the mind-set of God and that of humanity. We do not think the same way God does, because we do not see everything God sees. Flawed perception leads to flawed thinking, which results in flawed behavior. It is a gift to learn to trust and follow God.

God spent the forty years in the wilderness training Israel to follow His lead, just as He had trained her ancestor, Abraham. Because Israel contributed to the construction of the Tabernacle, she was rewarded with God's presence. Once the construction was complete, a cloud covered the Tabernacle, and Israel began to recognize God's presence, which took the form of a cloud above the Tabernacle by day and a pillar of fire by night. When the cloud settled in a place, Israel set up camp, and when the cloud lifted, Israel broke camp and moved. By obeying the instructions God gave through Moses, Israel learned to obey God. Learn how to follow God and you cannot fail.

God used the wilderness as a place of discipline to test Israel's obedience. The wilderness was a barren land that was not designed to support life; it was uninhabitable. There were no resources, no vegetation, and no water. It was arid, scorching, nonfertile, hostile, and dangerous. Only the meanest, toughest, most ill-natured creatures, such as scorpions and poisonous snakes, claimed the wilderness as home. God used that setting to sustain Israel by His power and to discipline her. There was no way to survive in the wilderness without His power; human ingenuity was no match for the barren desert.

In the wilderness, Israel found herself in a do-or-die situation. She either obeyed God, followed His lead, and lived, or she disobeyed God, followed her own path, and quickly died. There were no other options. The margin for error was null; there was zero tolerance. God gave Israel a crash course in obedience to benefit her, and only those who learned to obey God survived. In that way, God broke her self-reliant attitude and taught Israel to depend on Him. He was her source of life, and He taught the Israelites the importance of His words to their immediate survival. It is not food and water that sustains a people, but every word that proceeds out of the mouth of God.

> Remember how the Lord your God led you through the wilderness for forty years, humbling you and testing you to prove your character, and to find out whether or not you would really obey his commands. Yes, he humbled you by letting you go hungry and then feeding you with manna, a food previously unknown to you and your ancestors. He did it to teach you that people need more than bread for their life; real life comes by feeding on every word of the Lord. For all these forty years your clothes didn't wear out, and your feet didn't blister or swell. So you should realize that just as a parent disciplines a child, the Lord your God disciplines you to help you. *Deuteronomy 8:2–5*

If you are going to come out of a difficult situation alive, it takes obedience. It is imperative to obey God in order to survive the wilderness, but you must fight your way out before you can enter the Promised Land. To move to the next higher level, your thought processes and attitudes about fighting must change.

There were two attitudes that God had to imprint on the minds of the Israelites. First, without struggle, there can be no progress. It takes effort to move to a higher level, and once the higher level is attained, it takes effort to stay there. Second, change requires resistance, struggle, and the expenditure of energy. The Lord joined forces with Israel to create assured victory. That is an unbeatable combination.

A Successful Track Record

Since it is not enough to develop a fighting mentality without actually fighting, God led Israel through a couple of practice drills. He deliberately chose strategic battles that would be similar to what Israel would face when she entered Canaan. He wanted her to understand through firsthand experience what it meant to attack, conquer, occupy, and possess. Although God declared Israel's victory before the battles were actually fought and won, that did not exempt her from having to fight. Israel had to expend effort fighting to achieve victory. God gave Israel the assurance that her active resistance against her enemies would gain her victory, but there can be no victory without a fight. Predestined victory does not give people a license to be passive. Even though people have been declared the victors, if they do not fight, how can they claim victory?

God used two battles as a prelude to Israel's future success and victory. He established a track record with Israel on the east side of the Jordan River to show her what He would later do for her on the west side. With God as her Warrior and Moses as her commander, Israel defeated King Sihon of Heshbon and King Og of Bashan. In those two battles, Israel completely annihilated the people of both nations, defeated fortified cities with high walls and barred gates, conquered unwalled villages, and defeated King Og himself, who was the last descendant of the Rephaites and stood at least ten feet tall.

Reports of Israel's conquest of those two kings caused other nations to fear Israel. The Rephaites were a powerful race of giants. Some believe that their ancestry could be traced to the union of nephilim (angels who had left their former estate, better known as demons) and human women. Their union produced a race of people possessing superhuman stature and strength. Victory in those battles sent a clear, unmistakable message that no one could resist Israel and her God. When other nations heard that Israel had defeated those two nations, they were terrified of Israel because those two nations were indomitable.

God was trying to instill the attitude of Caleb and Joshua in all the Israelites. God developed a track record with Israel through the things He accomplished in her life. When Israel walked into overpowering situations, He wanted her to realize that past victory with Him was an indicator of future success with him.

I need you to agree with me and to work with me and I need your cooperation, but I want you to realize that I am fighting for you. Judge the situation by my ability, not yours. Here is how this will work: I need you to fight against the inhabitants of the land I am giving you. I will multiply and magnify your efforts by sending my angelic warrior troops (hornets) to fight alongside you, assuring you of victory. In this way you cannot fail. They may be more powerful, but I (God) have all power!

If Egypt is too much of a distant memory, think of what I have done for you lately. Think about how I displayed my power in recent battles to give you victory. You faced fortified, walled cities, giants, and people who were stronger and had the resources to defeat you. You were no match for them and your strength was not enough to conquer those people, but I took up the slack. In the same way, I will do this to the people of Canaan that you now face.

I will go before you to initiate the battle. I will roar against them like a devouring fire. In this way, I will weaken their defenses so that when you cross the Jordan, you can act as the clean-up crew. I will hand your enemies to you on a platter. I will not forsake you, nor will I fail. I am with you; I have assigned Joshua to lead you. Show no fear but be strong and very courageous. I will repeat what you have seen me do to kings Sihon and Og. The nations say, "Who can stand up to the Anakites?" but they will begin to say, "Who can stand up to Israel and who can resist the irresistible power of her God?"

You are no match for the things you face, but then again, you never have been, and I have brought you through insurmountable odds. Keep that in mind as you face your present circumstances.

God's action to expel the people of Canaan and replace them with the Israelites was not unique. God had established a precedent of replacing races of people with another race. He had given Esau's descendants, the Edomites, all the hill country around Mount Seir as their property, displacing its previous residents, the Horites. God had given Ar, a land that had previously been inhabited by the Emites, a powerful race of giants, to Lot's descendants the Moabites. He had given Lot's other descendants, the Ammonites, the land of Ammon, replacing its former owners, the Rephaites, who were also a race of giants. God had given Gaza, a land previously held by the Avvites, to the Caphtorites.

As Good as It Gets

God expended much energy and effort to prepare Israel for life in Canaan, and when He had finished her teaching and training, He had to resign Himself to the fact that the people were as good as they were going to get. *I know that you are a rebellious, stiff-necked, and incorrigible people, but I am going to take you into the blessing anyway. If I wait until I have developed perfect people, I'll never fulfill my promise.*

I am not naïve. I already know how Israel will turn out after I have fulfilled the promise I made their ancestors. Once you are in the land of abundance, prosperity will cause you to grow arrogant and you will snub me. You will despise and reject me, preferring to worship other gods. Israel's behavior will bring about her own destruction. I am telling you this in advance as a testimony against you. I know more about your heart than you do, for the human heart is desperately wicked. Only I know the great evil you are capable of, and yet I love you. I choose to bless you in spite of what I know. You are a rebel.

It is a message of hope for sinners. God does not sweat the "small" stuff. He embraces you and all your imperfections. You have done your best, and your best is not good enough, but God will look beyond your faults and meet your needs. Let's go into the Promised Land!

God's last dictation to Moses before his death on Mount Nebo was a song that prophesied Israel's future. It was a song to share with Israel that would later serve as a witness against Israel for her unfaithfulness and as a testament to the faithfulness of God. God took Israel to court, with a jury comprised of heaven and earth, to try the civil case of God versus Israel.

The opening statement: I will defend the name of the Lord. He is glorious, He is the Rock, and His works are perfect. Everything He does is just and fair. He is a faithful God who does no wrong. He is just and upright. Israel acted corruptly toward God. She is deceitful and twisted. She repaid God, the One who made and established her, with evil. Israel belonged to the Lord. He found her in the desert land, an empty howling wasteland. He surrounded her as his most precious possession. Israel slept on His chest. He tucked Israel into His bosom. He carried Israel by Himself over highlands. He fed her from the crops of the field, the honey from the cliffs, the olive oil from the hard rock, the curds from the herd, and the milk from the flocks. He fed Israel with the choicest rams and goats from Bashan, the best wheat, and the finest wine, but Israel became fat, spoiled, and unruly. She abandoned God and made light of Him. She forgot that without Him, she would not have a life. She stirred up His jealousy and provoked Him to wrath by worshiping foreign gods. She offered sacrifices to demons, nongods, gods she had not known before, and gods her ancestors had never feared, while neglecting the God who gave her birth.

Take-home message: You determine when you will come out of the wilderness by how quickly you release flawed thinking in exchange for the mind of God.

4.

The Man God Spoke With Face to Face

Moses was a man who maintained a constant line of communication with God. In turn, God loved Moses and spoke to him face to face. They shared the rarest and most precious of relationships: God in love with a man and a man in love with God. There are only a few accounts of such relationships in the Bible, so when we find them, they are noteworthy. There is nothing more precious on this Earth than spending a few minutes with God, yet Moses spent at least eighty *days* in uninterrupted contact with the Lord. God leaves you wanting more of Him because it is such a sweet, indescribable experience to be with Him.

The Oneness of Moses and God

Moses made an unorthodox request: "I need to look upon the One whom my soul loves with loving eyes. I already know your personality and you are beautiful. I know your ways and your character and I could recognize your presence anywhere without ever seeing you. I have experienced you spirit to Spirit. However, I feel as though I am missing part of you; I feel as though you are hiding something from me because you have not let me see you with my own two eyes. I need you to complete the picture for me. I need to put a face to your name. Reveal yourself to me. I need to see the love of my life." God approved Moses's request, even though no man had ever looked upon Him and lived. God revealed only as much of Himself as He could so that Moses would not die in the process. *I want you to see me, I want to give you the whole picture. I am not trying to hide from you. I want you to know who I am.*

A well-developed relationship creates a new organism that is hidden from ordinary view. The parties within the relationship adopt certain roles; they function automatically and in concert without thought. They have created a oneness that obliterates individualism. Occasionally observers will get a glimpse into or snapshot of the inner workings of the relationship by watching the pair in action. However, an observer can never have the complete picture, because the organics of the relationship have developed over time, in private, and without outside observation. Frankly, relationships are private and only the two who have invested their time and energy in building the relationship have a right to know what is going on. Outsiders have no way of knowing the intricacies and etymology of the relationship. It is impossible to know what has transpired for them to reach the level of intimacy they share; it is impossible to know what understanding the two have of each other that causes them to respond the way they do. Because of the way they develop, relationships have a natural mystique.

Moses and God invite us to observe the mechanics of their relationship from time to time by some of their recorded interactions. Because relationships are intimate and developed in private, an up-close glance causes people to want to cover their eyes; they see something that was not meant to be observed—indeed, something they do not deserve to watch. The relationship between Moses and God was personal, deep, and intimate. Moses fulfilled a longing in God that we all have as human beings. He satisfied God's desire to be known, loved for who He is, and accepted without condition.

They created a oneness where each not only had the other's best interest at heart but also understood and respected the feelings of the other. They had such an intimate relationship that when Israel rejected God, God pleaded with Moses to let Him destroy the Israelites and start all over with him. *I can create a powerful nation through you.* "If you love me," Moses said, "stay with your people and honor your covenant with them. We will not leave without you." When God was so frustrated with Israel that He was tempted to wipe them out, Moses provided the voice of reason to prevent God from ruining his reputation and making a regrettable mistake. "I understand that you are hurting because they have rejected you, but they don't know any better. And you are responding out of emotional pain. It would be easy for you to give up and walk away, but do not take the easy route; don't do something you will later regret. I know that you love them, and I love what you love. If you can find no other reason to stay, stay because you love me."

They developed a oneness where each felt the other's pain, so that an attack on one was the same as attacking the other. When God wrote the Ten Commandments on the tablets the first time, Moses broke the tablets in anger when he learned that Israel was practicing idolatry in the camp. When the people of Israel challenged Moses's authority, God was furious. *I trust Moses with everything I have. I am comfortable talking to him, and I am not afraid to be myself around him. He belongs to me, and if you touch him, you will answer to me. Ours is a relationship that surpasses the normal relationships I have with prophets.*

We are intimates. When you attack him, it is the same as attacking me. They each had a visceral defensive response to the injuries the other suffered, and they defended and protected one another because they were passionate about each other. Moses and God shared the same Spirit.

> Now listen to me! Even with prophets, I the LORD communicate by visions and dreams. But that is not how I communicate with my servant Moses. He is entrusted with my entire house. I speak to him face to face, directly and not in riddles! He sees the LORD as he is. Should you not be afraid to criticize him? *Numbers 12:6–8*

God accomplished great things through Moses because they were unified in purpose. When God gave instructions on how to create a well-ordered society, Moses carefully followed them and instructed Israel to do so as well. A healthy society needs God at its core, and God established dietary, health, property, and civil laws through Moses. *If you follow my instructions you will be prosperous, because they are designed to give you a full, long life.*

Many of the property and civil laws God gave Moses have been incorporated into the American judicial system. For instance, every person is presumed innocent until proven guilty by trial. A person cannot be convicted solely by virtue of one person's testimony. Property owners are accountable if other people are injured on their property. If an animal with a historically bad disposition kills someone, the owner is accountable and the animal is put to death. The responsibility of implementing God's regulations and settling legal disputes was given to the Levites. There were a common court, a higher court, and the highest court, presided over by the high priest, and his rulings were final.

The Israelites experienced strong spiritual leadership under Moses in the wilderness. Moses was a true servant leader, a man in authority while under authority, and he never thought about personal gain. He submitted to God's desires. When someone challenged his authority or questioned his actions, Moses presented the situation to God and allowed Him to make the decision instead of attacking his challengers.

Moses was the mediator between God and His people. Each time the Israelites sinned against God, it was Moses who interceded on their behalf. When the people complained about their living conditions, it was Moses who went to God for a solution. He was selfless and always had Israel's best interests in mind. He was more concerned about the welfare of those he served than about his own personal benefit.

Those who love God more than they value their own lives and have an amazing relationship with Him tend to accomplish great things for God. They accomplish so much for God because they are out to please Him. They become His hands and the vessel of honor through which He works. Their will is to do what God desires. "Anything, God, you name it and I'll do it."

God's Requests

God desired a relationship with His people, and Moses facilitated it. The first thing he did was to prepare Israel for a one-on-one encounter with the Lord following God's instructions. God instructed Moses to sanctify them in preparation for a meeting with Him. Moses told the Israelites to purify themselves by bathing, putting on clean clothes, and abstaining from sex in preparation for their momentous encounter with God. He instructed Moses to keep the people at a distance from Mount Sinai so they would not die in the encounter with Him. *Guard my holiness, Moses, and protect the people. No one is to get too close to Mount Sinai. If they do, they'll die.*

Later, the Lord gave Moses plans to build a place so He could permanently live with His people. God gave Moses plans for the Ark of the Covenant, the priestly garments, and the Tabernacle. He told Moses what materials would be necessary to make the Tabernacle and then instructed Moses to invite the people who were willing to give those materials as gifts. God appointed Bezalel and Oholiab, men who were gifted with creative skills and the ability to teach others, to do the work, to supervise volunteers, and to complete the project.

Moses built the Ark of the Covenant and the Tabernacle according to God's blueprints. He then established the order according to God's direction. He installed the tribe of Levi as the servants of the Lord and gave them a list of specific duties. Once the project was completed, the glory of the Lord filled the Tabernacle.

> Then the cloud covered the Tabernacle, and the glorious presence of the Lord filled it. Moses was no longer able to enter the Tabernacle because the cloud had settled down over it, and the Tabernacle was filled with the awesome glory of the Lord. Now whenever the cloud lifted from the Tabernacle and moved, the people of Israel would set out on their journey, following it. But if the cloud stayed, they would stay until it moved again. The cloud of the Lord rested on the Tabernacle during the day, and at night there was fire in the cloud so all the people of Israel could see it. This continued throughout all their journeys. *Exodus 40:34–38*

As a reward for giving their time, talent, and treasure and for fulfilling God's request, He gave Israel His presence, guidance, provision, and protection. What more could a human being want? If you desire God, do not go to Him empty-handed. Give God what He requests. It is an act of faith and worship to give God what He asks for. Start by giving the greatest gift you possess, yourself.

Moses taught the Israelites to please God by commemorating His accomplishments in their lives. The Passover celebration reminded Israel that God had spared her when He saw the blood on her doorposts in Egypt. The Festival of Unleavened Bread commemorated their deliverance from Egypt, when the Israelites had to make bread without yeast because there was no time to wait for their bread to rise. The Festival of Harvest was a time to celebrate the first crops of the harvest by giving God His portion first. Fifty days later, Israel brought grain representing the first of the later crops. The Festival of Trumpets was celebrated with loud trumpet blasts to celebrate a day of complete rest. Nine days later, the Israelites used the Day of Atonement to wash the slate clean through fasting and humbling themselves before the Lord. Finally, the Festival of Shelters was a reminder that their ancestors had lived in shelters when God delivered them from Egypt. Moses also taught Israel about the various sacrifices and how they could be used to worship God.

Celebrate God in the way He chooses and in the place He chooses to be celebrated. *Celebrate that I fed you when you were hungry. I made the sun shine and I sent the rain to produce bumper crops. You planted, and I gave the increase and blessed your efforts.*

The greatest gift any human being can give is to teach another person how to recognize God, please Him, connect with Him, and make Him a permanent part of their life. Moses was a great man because He taught Israel how to connect with God and he facilitated their relationship.

If Moses Could Turn Back Time . . .

Moses's purpose was to lead Israel out of bondage, through the wilderness, and into the Promised Land. Their extended stay in the wilderness was not God's original intent. As a matter of fact, many things that happened in the wilderness were not intended. In the wilderness, Moses's destiny was forever altered. He lost the privilege of leading the Israelites into the Promised Land, and he lost the opportunity to fully experience God's promise. He suffered great personal loss, the biggest loss of his entire life.

Moses was an extremely humble man, but he was a man nonetheless, and every man has limitations. Eventually he grew tired and frustrated with the constant challenges to his authority, the complaints about his leadership, and the threats against his life when things were not going the way the Israelites thought they should. Every time things went wrong, even things out of his control, the people blamed Moses.

People often fail to realize that the person leading them is just as human as they are, and the expectations they have for their leader are often unrealistic. A regular person can live a billion lifetimes without ever experiencing 1 percent of the assault and abuse that a leader experiences in one lifetime. We expect leaders to be thick-skinned and to handle pressure with poise and dignity. We expect them to be superhuman, and if a leader explodes under stress, their followers are surprised and wonder why they are so riled up. The expectations we have of leaders are truly remarkable.

Moses could have unleashed his fury on the Israelites many times, but he did not, even though the complaints never seemed to end. The "why did you bring us out here to die, we could have done that in Egypt" was getting old. Finally, in one unguarded moment, Moses let his frustration show and it cost him his destiny.

It was at the waters of Meribah, the place of arguing, in the wilderness of Zin, where Moses and Aaron watched their hopes of entering the Promised Land gush away. If there were more than six hundred thousand men above the age of twenty who left Egypt, there were at least two million people in the Israelite camp. Just meeting the basic needs of such a large group was a daunting task and a constant source of contention. Every time there was a lack of bread, meat, variety, or water, the people complained. They reminisced about their slave days in Egypt, when they had all the food and water they wanted. In their minds, it was better to be well-fed slaves than hungry free people.

When the Israelites reached the parched wilderness of Zin and found there was no water, a feverish, riotous rebellion ignited. They blamed Moses and Aaron, accusing them of leading them into the wilderness to die. Some people even wished for death. The situation at Meribah was explosive, and the people threatened to kill Moses and Aaron. Moses was under the gun, desperate for a solution that would satisfy the people and save his life. Moses and Aaron fell prostrate before the Lord, asking for help.

> Then the glorious presence of the LORD appeared to them, and the LORD said to Moses, "You and Aaron must take the staff and assemble the entire community. As the people watch, command the rock over there to pour out its water. You will get enough water from the rock to satisfy all the people and their livestock."
>
> So Moses did as he was told. He took the staff from the place where it was kept before the LORD. Then he and Aaron summoned

> the people to come and gather at the rock. "Listen, you rebels!" he shouted. "Must we bring you water from this rock?" Then Moses raised his hand and struck the rock twice with the staff, and water gushed out. So all the people and their livestock drank their fill.
>
> But the LORD said to Moses and Aaron, "Because you did not trust me enough to demonstrate my holiness to the people of Israel, you will not lead them into the land I am giving them!" This place was known as the waters of Meribah, because it was where the people of Israel argued with the LORD, and where he demonstrated his holiness among them. *Numbers 20:6–13*

If Moses were able to turn back time, he would have done some things differently. Moses was irritated and under extreme stress as he carried out the instructions of the Lord, but he went too far. Instead of commanding the rock to release its water, he railed at the people and then struck the rock twice. Moses rebelled against God's instructions and failed to demonstrate God's holiness to the Israelites, and it cost him dearly. God instructed Moses to strike a rock at Rephidim to get water, but God was doing a new thing at Meribah. God cannot be placed in a box and restricted to formulas. In order to walk with God, one must be flexible, because God changes His mode of operation to fit the situation.

Every time the people complained about lack of provisions, they were really asking the Lord, "Are you going to take care of us or not?" Moses's actions at Meribah gave the Israelites the impression that God was frustrated with meeting their legitimate needs and made them wonder if they would have to wrestle with an angry, irritable God every time they needed His help. (It does not strain God to meet your needs.)

I don't want the people to think that I am grudgingly fulfilling their needs. I also don't want them to think that I don't want to take care of them or that I don't have the power to meet their needs.

A private discussion with the Lord about the frustration and stress of leading the people would have done more good to effect change, but Moses was not thinking rationally and did not think things through. Who does in a crisis? Moses had had a heated discussion with God earlier about the strain of leading the Israelites, and God had relieved his burden.

"Your people are weeping and I feel guilty and inadequate. Every day is a crisis, for when supplies are low, they cry out. Things are tense, and I am tired of living with the strain and stress of this situation. Lord, if you love me, why are you treating me so badly? What have I done to deserve this burden? Am I their father? Am I responsible for providing meat for them? It is impossible to meet the staggering needs of Israel even with our resources. All our livestock and every fish in the sea would not be enough to meet their needs. I cannot bear this burden alone; it's too much responsibility for one person. I would rather die than to continue living life like this. God, have mercy on me." Taking pity on Moses, God took some of the spirit He had given Moses and gave it to seventy men so Moses would no longer have to carry the burden alone.

Under duress, Moses misrepresented God at Meribah, and it cost him his chance to lead the Israelites into the Promised Land. It was the first and only time Moses had failed to do exactly as God instructed, and it was the first and only time he had misrepresented God. Although Moses lost his ticket into the Promised Land, it did not change God's plan to take the Israelites in. Because leaders are held to a higher level of accountability, it is entirely possible for people to be blessed while their leaders suffer loss and deprivation. The key to avoiding personal loss as a leader, then, is to make certain you understand God's instructions and do exactly what God says to do.

Moses had the kind of relationship that God desires with every human being. When you are in a relationship with God, He always leaves you wanting more. Moses spent eighty wonderful days in the presence of the Lord on Mount Sinai. Moses asked to see God's glory, and it was granted. Moses spoke face to face with God. Moses had the kind of relationship with God that all people should aspire to have.

However, as Moses neared the end of his life, he said, "God, I'm just beginning to see your power. I am beginning to see a side of you I have never seen; it's as if I've never known you. There is so much of you to explore; please grant me permission to go further with you. Please let me go where no man has gone before. Let me know you. Let me go and see the place you prepared for Israel." God allowed Moses to see the land He had promised Israel, but He would not let him enter.

You can never know God completely, even if you spend a lifetime in His presence, and you can never exhaust exploration of Him. How unsearchable are His riches, and His ways past finding out. Modern man believes that space is the final frontier, but God is the *inexhaustible* frontier. It is not that God is trying to hide Himself; it is just that it would take an eternity to explore all His levels. A life given to exploration of God would be a lifetime well spent.

Take-home message: The greatest gift any human can give another is to teach them how to recognize God, how to please Him, and how to enter into His presence.

5.

By the Book

Moses died in full strength, leaving Israel in the capable hands of Joshua. God had groomed Joshua so that when the time for the changing of the guard arrived, the leadership baton would be passed smoothly. No leader who has a heart for the people is concerned with his legacy or how history will record his name; he is not a glory hog. He is concerned about making sure the next leader will continue to care for the people's welfare. Good leaders produce future leaders capable of carrying on their spirit of servanthood.

Establishing Joshua's Credibility

Joshua had been Moses's personal assistant since his boyhood. He was on Mount Sinai when God gave Moses the Ten Commandments for the first time. It was one of the few times when it was significant for a man to claim that he had been with a powerful person. Mount Sinai and everything on it were hallowed by the very presence of God. The grass, the trees, and even the insects and dirt were hallowed, so any man who was on Mount Sinai that day was especially hallowed. Holy, Holy, Holy is the Lord!

Joshua was with Moses when he went out to the Tent of Meeting outside the camp. Anyone who wanted to consult with the Lord went there. While Joshua served Moses, he also developed a personal relationship with the Lord. He was not with Moses just for the sake of being able to say, "I was with Moses." God was letting Joshua get acquainted with Him because he would one day lead Israel in Moses's stead.

Moses often corrected Joshua's misguided attitudes about leadership. Healthy leaders strive to duplicate their leadership in others. They understand that the duplication of their leadership (their ministry) multiplies the benefit to the people they serve. Hoarding the glory limits the effectiveness of a leader because one person can only do so much.

Like Moses, Jesus was frustrated because He and His disciples were giving 200 percent, yet Israel's need was still greater. The harvest is ripe, but the laborers are few. Pray for the Lord of the harvest to send more laborers. Jesus Himself recognized His limitations, which is why He told His disciples that it was to their benefit that He go away so He could release the Holy Spirit, the Comforter who knows no boundaries and no limitations, thereby multiplying His efforts.

The Holy Spirit is not limited by space and time as humans are. The Holy Spirit made it possible for Jesus's disciples to preach in the outermost parts of the Earth. The Holy Spirit can manifest in India, causing a revival, creating a stir among tsunami survivors, or in the last pew of a church on 57th and Park Streets, all at the same time. The Holy Spirit is undiluted, so His full magnitude and power is always available wherever He manifests.

Moses was so exhausted by ministering to the Israelites that he began to lose his effectiveness. He begged God for a reprieve because he knew that he could no longer continue to carry Israel alone. God told Moses to summon seventy leaders so He could anoint them. Only sixty-eight of the leaders summoned met with Moses while the other two remained in the camp for some reason. When Moses did as he was instructed, God put a portion of the Spirit that had been on Moses onto the men. When He did this, the men present began to prophesy. And although the two other appointed men were not present with Moses when God poured out His Spirit, they also began to prophesy at the same time. Someone who saw the two men prophesying ran and told Moses what the two were doing. When Joshua heard the report, he insisted that Moses make them stop. To this Moses replied, "My son, are you jealous for my sake? I wish that all of God's children would prophesy." Don't be a glory hog; there is too much work to be done!

There is a day coming when God will pour out His Spirit upon all flesh. Old people will start to dream again, and young people will catch God's vision and no longer live aimless lives.

Joshua was the commander of Israel's army during Moses's leadership, and he was one of the twelve spies who went to Canaan. God taught Joshua warfare under Moses's leadership. Joshua led the troops on the battlefield during the battle with the Amalekites in the wilderness while Moses was on the mountain, holding up his staff and securing Israel's victory. Joshua and Caleb were the only two spies who gave a faith report about Canaan. God did not want a passive man who would avoid a fight at all costs. The kingdom of God suffers violence, and the violent take it by force. God did not need a man who would use "Well, if it be the Lord's will" as an excuse for lack of opposition and aggression. God developed a man with a fighting mentality who would use human ability in warfare but understood that victory ultimately would come from God's ability.

On the last day of his life, Moses transferred the Spirit that was upon him to Joshua by the laying on of hands. God endorsed Moses's replacement, and the people received him. Moses, who always looked out for Israel's best interests, asked the Lord to replace him with a man who would lead Israel into battle. Moses understood the needs of the people, and he knew that the next phase of Israel's life would require warfare. God instructed Moses to lay his hands on Joshua bar Nun (Joshua son of Nun) to transfer the Spirit and his authority and to present him to the priest Eleazar in front of the community of Israel. In so doing, Moses commissioned Joshua to take the helm.

Joshua would not have the same kind of relationship with God that Moses had. God addressed Moses directly, face to face, but He decided to make His will known to Joshua through the priest by casting lots (using the Urim and Thummim). This action established a precedent for future kings of Israel. Although this was the plan, God did not adopt it at the outset of Joshua's reign, because Joshua needed God's assurance. Joshua had the monumental commission of leading Israel into Canaan. Joshua had to provide the kind of leadership of a warrior, not a tour guide. He could not just walk into Canaan and say, "This land is your land, this land is my land, from the Negev Desert to the Lebanon Mountains, and from the Mediterranean Sea to the Euphrates." He had to fight his way into Canaan and take the land from the current inhabitants and possess it. Conquering the people of Canaan was a daunting, debilitating task. Therefore, God had to encourage and admonish Joshua. *Be bold and valiant in the task before you.*

> No one will be able to stand their ground against you as long as you live. For I will be with you as I was with Moses. I will not fail you or abandon you. Be strong and courageous, for you will lead my people to possess all the land I swore to give their ancestors. . . . I command you—be strong and courageous! Do not be afraid or discouraged. For the Lord your God is with you wherever you go. *Joshua 1:5–6, 9*

God chose Joshua as Moses's successor and gave Him authority so Israel would receive and respect him. God had Moses lay hands on Joshua to transfer His Spirit in front of all Israel. This let the people know that Joshua was not only Moses's choice, but more importantly, he was also God's choice. What is authority without substance? If you have authority but no power to back it up, people will lose respect for you, so God decided to substantiate Joshua's authority.

The River Jordan was overflowing its banks when God told Joshua to command the Israelites to cross it. The priests carrying the Ark of the Covenant went first, and as soon as their feet touched the water, the water piled up in a city called Adam while the water below that point emptied into the Dead Sea until the riverbed was dry. It was as if a glass wall had been placed upstream to prevent the water from flowing beyond that point. Then the Israelites crossed the river on dry land near Jericho, the same way they had gone through the Red Sea when Moses led them out of Egypt. The priests carrying the Ark of the Covenant stayed in the River Jordan until all had crossed, following the instructions God had given Joshua. Then Joshua commanded the priests to come out of the river, and as soon as they did, the waters of the Jordan flooded back into the riverbed. God used the exercise to establish Joshua's credibility and authority before Israel.

Victory Requires Obedience

Lessons learned at the beginning of the march against Canaan set the tone for the remainder of the campaign. The walls of Jericho came tumbling down because God made it happen. During the battle at Jericho, God instructed Israel not to take anything that was set apart for destruction. Everything made from silver, gold, bronze, and iron was sacred to God and had to be brought into his treasury. All of Israel would suffer if one person violated those instructions. As it turned out, one of the Israelites, Achan, did violate the command.

When Israel went to the next town, Joshua sent a few thousand warriors, but the people of Ai defeated Israel, causing her to retreat. Ai was a small town that could easily be defeated. The Israelites had not lost a battle since they had entered the wilderness, and they should have been able to defeat Ai without divine assistance, so that loss caused them to lose courage. Joshua and the leaders fell on their faces before the Lord, crying out to Him for an explanation for their defeat. Joshua used one of Moses's tactics with the Lord.

> LORD, what am I to say, now that Israel has fled from its enemies? For when the Canaanites and all the other people living in the land hear about it, they will surround us and wipe us off the face of the earth. And then what will happen to the honor of your great name?
> *Joshua 7:8–9*

God told Joshua that one of the Israelites had violated His command, causing their enemies to gain the upper hand.

I am fighting against you as a result; I am not on your side unless you remove what I claimed for myself to set apart for destruction. Tell Israel to purify herself and

I will reveal what is hidden. You cannot win until you get rid of sin.

Righteousness exalts a nation, but sin is a reproach to *any* nation. Sin caused those destined for victory to suffer unintended defeat, lose courage, tuck tail, and run. Israel suffered the loss because one person had brought a curse on the entire nation by violating God's command. The morality of a nation and its troops at war determines the outcome on the battlefield. You cannot defeat your enemies until you address and remove sin from your own ranks. The leaders of Israel fell on their faces before the Lord to identify the problem, and then they followed His instructions to resolve it. This is the protocol for any nation seeking restoration with God. It was good that Israel learned that lesson up front, because from that point forward Joshua and Israel followed instructions. It took obedience to survive the wilderness, and it would take obedience to receive the promise. Because of obedience and cooperation with God's words, Israel became a stunning success.

> Then if my people who are called by name will humble themselves and pray and seek my face and turn from their wicked ways, I will hear from heaven and will forgive their sins and heal their land.
> *2 Chronicles 7:14*

God advised Joshua to obey the teachings He gave to Moses if he wanted to continue to be successful. God set another precedent with the advice He gave Joshua, because it was the same advice he gave to the kings of Israel. Fortunately for Israel, Joshua was a no-nonsense, by-the-book kind of person. He followed the rules God gave to Moses as well as God's direct instructions. When God told Joshua to circumcise the entire male population because those born in the wilderness had not been circumcised, Joshua did it. God also gave Joshua strategic instructions about the battles, and when Joshua obeyed, Israel gained the victory.

It was important not only for Joshua to be a by-the-book type of leader, but he also had to have by-the-book kind of people. He led by example and taught the Israelites God's words. People can live by the word of God only when they are confronted with it. It is only when a whole society (from the leaders to the people) is living in cooperation with the word of God that it can experience success, prosperity, and victory. When a society refuses to teach people about the consequences of their behavior, avoids holding its people accountable for their actions, and teaches its people not to blame themselves for their crimes, it produces a hurting, unhealthy, and broken society.

Joshua gave Israel an ultimatum: since everyone has free will, he asked the people to decide whether they would live according to God's will or according to their will. At Mount Ebal, he read the Book of the Law to all the people of Israel (ordinary citizens, foreigners, and leaders), confronting them with the word of God because no one was exempt. Joshua presented them with every command Moses had ever given, along with the consequences: blessings for those who decided to follow God's words and curses for those who decided against them. He asked everybody to make a choice, because each person's individual choice had the power to affect the entire Israelite population. He set up a dividing line, because Israel as a whole could not afford to be dragged down by the sins of one person or group of people. "Either you are with us or against us. We cannot afford to have anyone sabotaging us because of their sinful lifestyle. I acknowledge and respect your choice and your free will. I will respect whatever decision you make, but let me caution you, should you choose to sin, I am separating you from those who choose blessings by following God's words."

We teach people the importance of voting and tell them that one vote can make a difference. Each vote is a decision, and one person's decision to live or not to live according to the word of God affects the direction of the entire society. Therefore, each individual in a society is important and powerful because of the lifestyle choices they make. Their choice can benefit or bring calamity to society. In order for society to turn around, it must begin with me and you. Change the world by changing yourself. We must adopt the same attitude toward sin in ourselves and in our society that Israel finally had to come to grips with. Unchecked sin not only affects the person who sins, it adversely affects their entire society. How can we experience God's full blessings when our society supports sin?

When the tribes of Reuben and Gad and half of the tribe of Manasseh moved into the land of Gilead, they built an altar. As you recall from Chapter 1, it was a capital offense to offer sacrifices anywhere except at the Tabernacle, and only priests could offer those sacrifices. The Lord forbade separate altars in order to prevent sacrifices to demons. The other tribes of Israel went into an uproar because they thought the people in the land of Gilead were practicing idolatry. The rest of Israel understood that each individual's actions could bring God's favor or ignite His anger, which would result in societal punishment. The rest of Israel refused to suffer for sins of the Israelites living in the land of Gilead. They were prepared to wipe out the inhabitants of Gilead in order to prevent calamity from God.

> When they arrived in the land of Gilead, they said to the tribes of Reuben, Gad, and the half-tribe of Manasseh, "The whole community of the LORD demands to know why you are betraying the God of

> Israel. How could you turn away from the Lord and build an altar in rebellion against him? Was our sin at Peor not enough? We are not yet fully cleansed of it, even after the plague that struck the entire assembly of the Lord. And yet today you are turning away from following the Lord. If you rebel against the Lord today, he will be angry with all of us tomorrow. If you need the altar because your land is defiled, then join us on our side of the river, where the Lord lives among us in his Tabernacle, and we will share our land with you. But do not rebel against the Lord or draw us into your rebellion by building another altar for yourselves. There is only one true altar of the Lord our God. Didn't God punish all the people of Israel when Achan, a member of the clan of Zerah, sinned by stealing the things set apart for the Lord? He was not the only one who died because of that sin."
> *Joshua 22:15–20*

No one is an island and no person lives unto themselves, even those who actively practice isolationism. My sins affect you, and your sins affect me; the consequence of sin is death. When we observe sin in ourselves and our society, we must work vehemently to eradicate it as if our very lives depended upon it, because they do. What would you do to spare your life or the lives of your loved ones if you knew that your actions would mean the difference between life and death? When observing the sins of others, we cannot turn our heads and look the other way as if to say, "That's not my problem," any more than we can tell others that it's none of their business what we do in our own private lives. We must demand accountability. We must fight against our own sins, and we must fight against sin promoted and condoned by society, because our lives are hanging in the balance.

Most of us walk around in denial about the shape our society is in. We do not want to admit that something is terribly wrong, and that we had a hand in creating the situation. We are too proud to admit that we have done wrong, and our pride causes us to remain in a decimated state. No one wants to admit that we have followed the social theoreticians into a ditch. We are angry, miserable, poor, blind, and naked because of the choices we have made in our lives, but we are the sum total of every choice we have ever made. Doctors want us to believe that a miracle pill will magically erase all the accumulated consequences of the bad choices we have made, but maybe you *should* feel bad if feeling bad will cause you to examine yourself and cry out to God for change. Godly sorrow leads to repentance.

Every day there are news reports about increasing rates of obesity and of drug and alcohol abuse in our country. Could it be that these abuses are the result of all the pain we are feeling inside? Is it possible that we use these "crutches" as mind-numbing techniques to dull the pain? Could it be that our sins have immobilized us to the point where we no longer enjoy life? For some it is all they can do just to put one foot in front of the other.

Our society is morally and spiritually bankrupt, and we are feeling the aftershock. Children are hurting because of the poor decisions their parents have made. We are financially bankrupt. Our economy is propped up with toothpicks. It's only a matter of time before the manipulations of financial magicians and genies lose the power to keep us from crumbling financially. Is anybody, other than me, tired and worn out? Is anybody willing to admit that something is terribly wrong and that changes need to be made? Is anyone longing for a change and willing to give God of all creation a try?

> So now today we are slaves here in the land of plenty that you gave to our ancestors! We are slaves among all this abundance! The lush produce of this land piles up in the hands of the kings whom you have set over us because of our sins. They have power over us and our cattle. We serve them at their pleasure, and we are in great misery.
> *Nehemiah 9:36–37*

"Lord Jesus, have mercy on us. We have made a mess of things. We have fallen, and we have no power to get up. Please, Father, we invite you into our society. We admit that we have sinned and we long for reform. We long for the peace that comes after You have washed our sins away. Blessed is the man who is not charged for his sins. We humble ourselves and repent. We turn from our wicked ways. Please hear us and heal our land. Be our God and let us be your people."

Since we already know the consequences of living contrary to God's words, we should explore what our society could be if it lived in alignment with God's words. The nation that decides to live according to God's laws can expect victory over its enemies, accompanied by the wealth of its enemies, and peace from its enemies.

When Joshua and Israel set out on their campaign, many nations allied themselves to fight against Israel. On three separate occasions, three alliances were formed against Israel, with a collective power that was more than enough to wipe Israel off the face of the planet. Those alliances were stronger, had better resources, outnumbered the Israelites, and frankly, from a human perspective, were the favorites. However, because Israel decided to live by God's rules and to follow His instructions, God fought for her, giving her spectacular success. God gave Israel victory by fighting for her using a number of tactics, including "hornets," panic attacks, and hailstorms.

Israel acquired the wealth of the enemies God conquered for her. When Joshua honorably discharged Reuben, Gad, and the half-tribe of Manasseh, he blessed them and told them to share their wealth with their relatives. The last gift God gave Israel for her faithfulness was peace. The benefits of living in alignment with God's word far outweigh the consequences of living without Him. Considering the benefits, what kind of madness would cause a nation to live contrary to the word of God and to live irrationally?

Exercise Your Faith Muscles

Joshua tried to prepare the people for his departure. There was no understudy to replace Joshua, so he tried to teach the Israelites to exercise their own faith to obtain what had already been given. As Joshua grew older, a large amount of territory earmarked for Israel still remained unconquered. God planned to drive out the inhabitants so Israel would have a special inheritance.

Joshua divided both conquered and unconquered lands among the tribes of Israel by casting lots. Since he knew he would not be around much longer, he began shifting the responsibility of conquering and possessing the land to the tribes. When descendants of Joseph complained about not having enough land, Joshua told them to clear the land of the Perizzites and Rephaites. "The land is yours just waiting for you to take possession of it, go get it." However, instead of following Joshua's advice, Joseph's descendants complained that the inhabitants of those lands were too strong.

In a way, the Israelites were acting like many Christians do today. When they ask God for something, they sit back and wait until it appears rather than going out to work for it. Many Christians take a passive approach when it comes to receiving the blessings of God and tend to want others to exercise their faith to obtain the things that are most important to them. They expect things to appear magically. This is why untold blessings have slipped through the fingers of believers.

Joshua was frustrated because the Israelites were displaying a passive attitude, even though they understood that just because a thing was promised it did not mean they would not have to expend effort to receive it. Assured victory is no victory at all unless a fight takes place. What are you waiting for? When will you lay claim to the blessings God has promised you?

> But there remained seven tribes who had not yet been allotted their inheritance. Then Joshua asked them, "How long are you going to wait before taking possession of the remaining land the LORD, the God of your ancestors, has given to you?" *Joshua 18:2–3*

Those who consistently receive gifts from the Lord and see His promises fulfilled understand that they must exert effort to receive God's gifts. Those who fight for gifts receive them. The kingdom of God suffers violence, and the violent take it by force. Jacob (Israel is the name the angel of the Lord gave Jacob and it means one who prevails with God and man) displayed the type of character that God expects all Christians to have. Jacob wrestled with the angel and refused to let him go until the angel blessed him. In God's economy, there is responsibility on the part of both the giver and the recipient. God expects the recipient to actively pursue and take the gifts they are entitled to.

When God says He has given you a gift and it is not yet yours, He expects you to pursue that gift, and He will multiply your efforts, guaranteeing your victory. How many gifts have slipped through our fingers because we did not understand that God does not just hand things to us? How many gifts have we left lying on the table?

Joshua gave Caleb unconquered territory, and Caleb fully understood that he had to use his faith (belief and actions) to conquer the land and make it his. Caleb knew what was promised, asked for it, understood what it would take to obtain it, and then fought for it. Joshua expected all the tribes of Israel to respond like Caleb, just as God expects Christians to respond the same way to get the blessings He has promised them.

> "So I'm asking you to give me the hill country that the LORD promised me. You will remember that as scouts we found the Anakites living there in great, walled cities. But if the LORD is with me, I will drive them out of the land, just as the LORD said." The LORD instructed Joshua to assign some of Judah's territory to Caleb son of Jephunneh. So Caleb was given the city of Arba (that is, Hebron), which had been named after Anak's ancestors. Caleb drove out the three Anakites—Sheshai, Ahiman, and Talmai—descendants of Anak. Then he fought against the people living in the town of Debir (formerly called Kiriath-sepher). *Joshua 14:12 and 15:13–15*

Joshua's Final Address to the People of Israel

The best thing about you, Israel, is that you have God of all creation on your side. What makes you special and unique is God. He took an interest in you, esteemed you, and removed the shame of slavery. He protected you, provided you with the best of everything, gave you wealth, and fought for you. He made you powerful. He has made you what you are today, and without Him there would be no you. God is the best thing you've got going for you. You do not have bragging rights unless you brag on God, because He did everything that has been accomplished in your life. God has given you everything you have. God has distinguished you. You have been successful because of your love for Him and your obedience to Him. Therefore, guard your relationship with Him at all cost. Forsake all, but do not allow anything or anybody to come between you.

> So be strong! Be very careful to follow all the instructions written in the Book of the Law of Moses. Do not deviate from them in any way. Make sure you do not associate with the other people remaining in the land. Do not even mention the names of their gods, much less swear by them or worship them. But be faithful to the Lord your God as you have done until now. For the Lord has driven out great and powerful nations for you, and no one has yet been able to defeat you. Each one of you will put to flight a thousand of the enemy, for the Lord your God fights for you, just as he has promised. So be very careful to love the Lord your God. *Joshua 23:6–11*

Do not fool yourself into thinking that you are somehow worthy of God's love and affection and that your personal attributes make you special. Do not think for one moment that you have immunity and freedom to do whatever you want just because God loves you. That would be a big mistake. The moment you adopt that attitude, the God who has blessed you will be the same God who destroys you.

> But if you turn away from him and intermarry with the survivors of these nations remaining among you, then know for certain that the Lord your God will no longer drive them out from your land. Instead, they will be a snare and a trap to you, a pain in your side and a thorn in your eyes, and you will be wiped out from this good land the Lord your God has given you. But as surely as the Lord your God has given you the good thing he promised, he will also bring disaster on you if you disobey him. He will completely wipe you out from this good land he has given you. If you break the covenant of the Lord your God by worshiping and serving other gods, his anger will burn against you, and you will be quickly wiped out from the good land he has given you. *Joshua 23:12–13 and 15–16*

Today you are in the Promised Land, and you must decide how you will live. There are four ways you can choose to live: You can adopt the customs of your people beyond the Euphrates, you can live by the customs of Egypt, you can adopt the customs of the people living around you, or you can choose to serve the God who has been with you all along and brought you into this great land. It is your choice, but only the last way leads to life, abundance, and the path of blessings. The others lead to death. Choosing to serve God and living for Him is not the easiest path. It will take your mind, your will, and everything else you have. However, it is the most rewarding path. Choose today whom you will serve and how you will live, because it will determine the direction of your life and the life of this great nation.

Take-home message: No man is an island when it comes to sin.

6.

Unconquered Surveyed Lands

Joshua led Israel as she fought her way out of the wilderness and into the Promised Land. During his campaign thirty-one kings were conquered, and their territory and possessions became Israel's reward. Under his leadership, Israel drove out many of the inhabitants of the land of Canaan, which God had promised to Abraham's descendants. Just the mention of Israel's name struck immobilizing terror into the hearts of her enemies. The enemies of Israel lived in constant dread of attack by Israel and her God. Her reputation preceded her.

Israel had the distinction of having a God with irresistible power. Her God had performed great miracles and accomplished many exploits on her behalf. Anyone who was an enemy of Israel became an enemy of God. Neither the strongest alliances nor the most sophisticated weaponry could defeat Israel. Many times the Israelites did not even have to fight. They just showed up, and the enemy nation became so petrified with fear that they began to kill one another. Israel had a glorious reputation because of her God. How, then, did this powerful, indomitable nation begin to get spanked by surrounding nations?

Communication Gap

Joshua surveyed Canaan and assigned land to all tribes but left many of those land assignments to the tribes of Israel to conquer. The tribes were responsible for conquering the land allotted to them and for taking possession of it without Joshua's assistance. Some tribes, such as Judah, Simeon, and Joseph, had success in conquering the lands assigned to them. The tribe of Simeon experienced success when they allied themselves with the tribe of Judah, but eventually all tribes, including Judah, began to fail miserably. Judah failed to drive out the people living in the plains because they had iron chariots. Benjamin failed to drive out the Jebusites living in Jerusalem. Ephraim failed to remove the Canaanites living in Gezer. Zebulun failed to drive out the Canaanites living in Kitron and Nahalol. Naphtali was similarly unsuccessful in routing the people of Beth-shemesh and Beth-anath. The Amorites refused to let the tribe of Dan come into the plains. Manasseh and Asher had similar failures. For a people who were guaranteed success, the Israelites were suffering massive failures. In the past, they only had to show up in order to gain victory. They were God's "clean-up crew." One Israelite could put a thousand enemies to flight. How did they go from such stunning success to such widespread failure, from invincible to vulnerable?

The answer would have been obvious to all Israelites who witnessed the battles of Jericho and Ai. Joshua's cohorts knew from experience that the entire country would suffer defeat on the battlefield for one person's sin. In the battle of Ai, Israel could have fought without God's assistance and still gained victory had it not been for the sin of Achan. Those who fought in Joshua's campaigns knew how critical it was to be obedient and to keep their covenant with God. They knew that their success in battle was not a result of personal skill, warfare acuity, or sophisticated weaponry. God was their champion in battle. They also knew that if they failed in battle, sin was in the camp and that they must fall on their faces before the Lord so He could identify the problem and present its resolution. However, the new group did not have the benefit of that experience. They thought they could continue to enjoy victory even with the stain of sin on their uniforms. They thought they could enjoy the benefits of covenant without upholding their end. That was why the angel of the Lord went up from Gilgal to Bokim bearing a message for the Israelites.

"I fought for you, and that's why you enjoyed cosmic success in the past. I made a covenant with you, and I promised never to break my covenant as long as you did your part. All I asked for you to do is to be faithful to me, which meant worshiping me exclusively, not making covenants with the remaining inhabitants, and exterminating the gods of the people along with their images and altars. There is no longer a distinction between you and the inhabitants of the land. You have broken covenant with me and you are as much an enemy to me as they are. How fair would it be for me to punish the inhabitants for their unfaithfulness and sins by destroying and uprooting them from the land when you are as sinful and unfaithful as they are? My hands are tied. Therefore, I am no longer obligated to fight for you. I will not drive the people out, and they will be your nemesis, your Achilles heel. They will drag you down, sap your strength, and keep you from fulfilling the destiny I had planned for you."

The Israelites served the Lord throughout the lifetime of Joshua, Eleazar, and the tribal leaders who outlived them—those who had witnessed and experienced all the great things the Lord had done for Israel. After that generation died, another generation grew up that did not acknowledge the Lord because they did not remember what He had done for Israel, nor did they have personal experience with Him.

During the period of the judges, the word of God failed to be communicated to the people; there was an information gap. Joshua was not there to remind the people about the Lord their God. No one rehearsed God's history in Israel, and no one explained His covenant to them. Failure to communicate the word of God caused a society to cast off all restraint, run wild, and perish. Israel reverted to her old ways of idolatry because the worship of the true and living God had not taken root in her heart. The Lord God was angry because not only had He delivered Israel from Egypt, provided for her every need, directed her, and protected her in the wilderness, but He had also defeated her enemies, ejected the prior occupants from their land, and placed Israel in a place that was already developed. She forgot the one who had so meticulously cared for her every need, not allowing the slightest detail to slip. She forgot the ostentatious display of His protecting power and His love for her. She forgot Him, the love of her life. How astonishing and mind-boggling!

However, it is not that incredible, is it? Before anyone mounts a high horse, we can examine ourselves and see the same pattern. God so mightily saved you from destruction, reaching down into the quagmire and pulling you out. Death was all over you; you croaked death, and you wreaked fumes of death. You were in the discard pile marked *Destruction*. You had been passed over many times, and you were on a conveyor leading to the incinerator. You were not even fighting for your life; you lay limp, resigned to die. You edged closer and closer to the flame, so close that you could feel the heat. All of a sudden, out of nowhere, the mighty hand of Jesus reached down and grabbed you. He cleaned you up and made you better than you were before. He adored you and smothered you with His love. He treated you so tenderly, like a thing of inestimable value. Oh, how you basked in His love, how you flourished! You frolicked, splashed, and dived into His loving embrace. As time went on, you began to take His love for granted, thinking that you deserved it and had a right to His love. You acted as if you were doing Him a favor by being His. Eventually you took yourself out of His arms. You walked away, thinking that you could make it on your own. You had that proud I'll-show-you look on your face as you glanced back at Him. You had a look of defiance and belligerence. You forgot that without Him you would not have a life.

God intentionally left lands unconquered in the Promised Land for several purposes. First, on a practical level, Israel's population was not large enough to fill the entire territory of Canaan; if God had removed all of

Canaan's occupants, wild animals would have taken over. Second, He wanted to test the Israelites to see if they would obey Him as their ancestors did. It took obedience to survive the wilderness, and it took obedience to enter the Promised Land. Obedience was required to live peacefully and to experience greater blessings in the Promised Land. Obedience is the key to seeing miracles and living victoriously. God honors His covenant with a nation as long as that nation does its part.

Finally, God left the Philistines, all the Canaanites, the Sidionians, and the Hivites in the Promised Land to teach warfare to generations of Israelites who had no experience in battle. One must fight to obtain and to keep the promises God has given them. One does not fight God to get Him to fulfill His promises; one fights alongside God to receive blessings. One fights against those who would deny the blessings God has in store for them. A life of ease, devoid of personal challenges and struggles, is a life that will not seek God. If you never face problems bigger than you can solve, you will never seek God, who is bigger than your problems. God designs challenges for each life to cause a person to turn to God. Some believe that avoiding challenges and conflicts leads to peace, but it actually leads to stunted growth. True growth, reaching your maximum potential, and peace come by embracing challenges and conflicts. Progress comes through struggle.

Two-Timers, Beware

Israel discontinued her quest to conquer the surveyed unconquered territories because she had broken her covenant with God. God was the only reason she had succeeded, so it was pointless to continue offensive assaults if He was not going to back her up. No one should take on giants with unresolved sin in their life. The best thing to do at a time like that is to stay before the face of the Lord in repentance. Grieve about the sin and earnestly seek forgiveness, deliverance, and resolution. No one can afford to have unresolved sin in their life. Seek resolution quickly. People are in their most vulnerable state, with the potential for great losses, when sin goes unresolved.

Although Israel mourned the loss of God's favor, her mourning did not produce the proper change in behavior. Her grief did not lead to repentance. Instead she became worse. Maybe she figured, "What's the use? Since I have already lost His favor, what more do I have to lose? I might as well do whatever I want." Israel abandoned the Lord, the God of her ancestors, who had brought her out of Egypt. Some kind of sickness or madness overtook her; she had a crazy lust for worshiping the gods of the people around her. She was not slowly lured into worshiping other gods, she eagerly sought after them. She intermarried with the remaining inhabitants of the land. She abandoned the Lord to prostitute herself with Baal and the images of Ashtoreth. She continued to break her covenant with the Lord. With each passing moment the depth of her sin engulfed her. God showed Israel that she could not worship idols and shower her affection on them and expect His protection.

You want my blessings, but you don't want me. I can't stand your two-timing ways. You can't live in defiance to me and expect me to condone your behavior by continuing to bless and keep you in peace. You've got plenty of enemies straining at the leash to get a piece of you.

Thus, He used Israel's enemies as an instrument of discipline to remind Israel how far He had brought her. Israel was in a precarious predicament because her enemies surrounded her, and God was the only force keeping them at bay. Israel could not afford to infuriate God or to have God as an enemy. Unfortunately, she did not realize this until God handed her over to her enemies, who stole her possessions. He sold her to her enemies and she was not able to resist them. Every time Israel went to battle, the Lord fought against her, bringing defeat, just as He had promised. There may have been some battles that Israel would not have lost had it not been for the fact that God was assisting her enemies by fighting against her in the same way that He had assisted Israel against the nations He removed from the Promised Land. Israel was no longer in control, because she was not favored. Her God had abandoned her, making her vulnerable. Her enemies did not fear her, because she was no longer a force to be reckoned with. Israel took a defensive posture, cowering in retreat and no longer attacking.

God allowed Israel's enemies to rule over her. Her enemies dominated her and treated her cruelly, showing no mercy. Enemy oppression caused the children of Israel to travel on side paths instead of main roads to avoid enemies. She also abandoned her villages. Those who did not manage to hide livestock and produce from the raiders starved. Israel was cowering in caves, hungry, terrorized, and broken. When overpowered by enemies, she remembered the one she had forgotten. It is far better to suffer God's wrath directly, because He will relent, than to be under the cruel, unrelenting, merciless hand of man. Israel cried out, "Lord God of Israel, save us." (How many lumps must you take before you cry out, "Lord have mercy, forgive me, I have been wrong"?)

> The Israelites were in great distress. Finally, they cried out to the LORD, saying, "We have sinned against you because we have abandoned you as our God and have served the images of Baal." The LORD replied, "Did I not rescue you from the Egyptians, the Amorites, the Ammonites, the Philistines, the Sidonians, the Amalekites, and the Maonites? When they oppressed you, you cried out to me, and I

> rescued you. Yet you have abandoned me and served other gods. So I will not rescue you anymore. Go and cry out to the gods you have chosen! Let them rescue you in your hour of distress!" But the Israelites pleaded with the LORD and said, "We have sinned. Punish us as you see fit, only rescue us today from our enemies." Then the Israelites put aside their foreign gods and served the LORD. And he was grieved by their misery. *Judges 10:9–16*

You are taking advantage of my love for you. You know how to touch my heart; you know how to manipulate me. I cannot resist your tears; I cannot stand to see you suffer. I cannot harden myself to your pleas for help; I cannot sit by and do nothing when you cry to me for help. So I help you, even though I know this is not going to draw us closer. It will not be the last time I come to your aid. You will not stay by my side; you are using me. What kind of madness has befallen me? You don't appreciate anything I have done for you and the thanks I get is that you turn your back on me. You use me when you are in a bind; as soon as I get you out of the bind you reject me and want nothing to do with me. Those who you have chosen to worship should deliver you. Where are they? You are in this situation because you rejected me, and now you have the audacity to ask me to help you.

God is merciful, for even though He was disgusted and fed up, even though He had been rejected, and even though He knew that Israel would reject Him again shortly after He delivered her, He assisted her. He was grieved by her misery. He could not bear to see her suffer, so He relented. He sent her help, although He knew that she would not be loyal to Him.

Deliver Me from My Enemies

The Lord took pity on Israel because she was burdened by oppression and suffering. God relented by sending judges or deliverers to rescue the Israelites from her enemies. The deliverers defeated or put her enemies at bay. Whenever the Lord placed a judge over Israel, He was with that judge and rescued Israel from her enemies throughout that judge's lifetime. Once the judge died, Israel not only reverted to her old ways of idolatry, but she also found more gods to worship to satisfy her insatiable, growing appetite, completely abandoning God. Restraint will either diminish or increase the appetite for something. In Israel's case, her appetite for unfaithfulness grew, so she added more gods to those she already worshiped. Like a teeter-totter, the Israelites went back and forth, drawing near to God and then casting Him to the side. It was a time of spiritual stagnation and defeat.

Repentance should lead to a complete improvement in behavior in which sinful habits and actions are abandoned. Israel's sorrow, however, grew from the consequences of her behavior. She was sorry about the consequences of her actions, but she had no remorse about the actions themselves. Israel had the kind of "repentance" that wanted God to get her out of a bind (the consequences of her behavior) but not the kind that corrected the behaviors that had led to the consequences she hated. Once out of the bind, she felt she was free not only to continue the behavior that had gotten her into the messy consequences, but also to turn away from the path of her ancestors, who had walked in obedience to the Lord's commands. Israel reverted to her corrupt ways, behaving progressively worse than those who had lived before her, refusing to give up her evil practices and stubborn ways. She lived with the inhabitants of Canaan, intermarried with them, and worshiped their gods. Israel forgot that she was married to the Lord. *How do you forget our history after all we have been through together?*

God had a problem with Israel because He had earned the right to the love, affection, adoration, and praise that Israel showered upon other gods. He had brought her out of slavery, had made her His own possession, and He had become hers. Without His care and His sustaining power in the wilderness, Israel would have died. Then He took her into an established land with everything she needed and could ever want. He provided twenty-four-hour protection from her enemies. He showed Israel His love by the things He did for her. Withholding nothing, He loaded her down with lavish gifts. He anticipated her needs so that she lacked nothing. The gods she prostituted herself with had not done a thing for her, but Israel took the gifts God gave her and gave them to other gods, gods who took and never gave. Israel gave the affection, adoration, praise, and worship that God had earned to gods who had never lifted a finger for her and would not love her back. The gods Israel worshiped and bowed to did not love her, and never made such a claim, and they would do nothing for her, even if they could.

You do not even know the meaning of love. You do not know how to recognize love, even though it is staring you in the face. Love is about giving, being faithful and committed to the well-being of the one you are in covenant with.

What kind of sickness could cause someone to trample on the One who loves and trot to the one who does not love? Where did Israel's definition of love become distorted? Was it low self-esteem or plain madness?

Cursed While Living in the Place of Blessing

Unholy alliances are the most effective killer of god-fearing people. It is important to choose relationships wisely, and prayer is the key. A study of King Jehoshaphat will show how unholy alliances and good intentions can destroy. God would not have minded Israel's intermarrying with the inhabitants of the land if they had been righteous. He knew that when people get tangled in love, they do whatever it takes to please their spouse. They compromise and lower their standards. He understood that the hearts of his children would be drawn into idolatrous practices because these were an integral part of their spouse's lives. For the very same reason, He warns believers today not to be unequally yoked with unbelievers.

Although this subject will come up again later, it is good to introduce it here. It is entirely possible to be in the promise yet living an accursed life. It is possible to be in the place of blessing yet suffering from the curse of sin. The roller coaster of sin takes you up and down, so that you never reach the potential that God has for you and you never make any progress that is not lost as a result of sin. Today, people who have obtained salvation without internalizing change will find themselves living an accursed life in the place of blessings. God required Israel to enter into the blessing with a changed way of living. He taught her His expectations, He taught her how to live, and He trained her to obey Him. He spent a great deal of time telling her what pitfalls to avoid. He even told her why she was replacing the people of Canaan so she would know what to avoid. For more than four hundred years, Israel teeter-tottered in her relationship to God. Sin put her in a holding pattern and threw her on a downward spiral. It is a tragedy for a nation or an individual to share Israel's testimony. Israel lived in the Promised Land, the place of God's blessing, yet she could not enjoy the benefits because she behaved worse than the inhabitants that God had ejected from the land. The Promised Land was supposed to be a place of blessing, but it became a place of suffering as a result of unresolved sin, unholy alliances, and failure to shun ungodly customs.

Just as Israel discovered that embracing the customs of the Canaanite society, intermarrying with them, worshiping their idols, and holding on to old personal habits caused them to suffer while in the Promised Land, today's believer in the kingdom of God must live according to the instructions of God or suffer as an evildoer in the place where they should be blessed. Today's believer must let old habits die, correct their conduct, shun ungodly societal customs, and avert unholy alliances in order to experience blessings in the kingdom of God. There is no immunity in the Promised Land when you are living like the child of the devil.

> Do you think that God will judge and condemn others for doing them and not judge you when you do them, too? Don't you realize how kind, tolerant, and patient God is with you? Or don't you care? Can't you see how kind he has been in giving you time to turn from your sin? *Romans 2:3–4*

No Rules, Just Right

The period of the judges was riddled with many examples of a society gone mad. Little benefit would result from examining each incident. However, the situation surrounding Gideon demonstrates the extent of Israel's bondage to idolatry and how warped her sense of values was because she shunned God.

Driven to feed her addiction to idolatry, Israel would worship anything she could find. God fought and defeated the Midianites through Gideon to relieve Israel from their oppression. Israel wanted to make Gideon their ruler and to establish a dynasty in Gideon's family, but Gideon refused because he understood that the motive behind Israel's offer was to supplant God.

> I will not rule over you, nor will my son. The LORD will rule over you!
> *Judges 8:23*

Gideon requested that they each give him one golden earring that they had collected from the fallen Midianites. They gave Gideon more than forty-three pounds of gold, and he used it to make a sacred ephod and then placed it in Ophrah, his hometown. To his horror, Israel began to worship the ephod, causing a snare for Gideon's family. Israel had a voracious, insatiable appetite for idolatry, from which she desperately needed deliverance.

Gideon had seventy-one sons, and one of his sons, Abimelech, was the son of his concubine. After his father died, Abimelech decided that he should be king even though his father had refused the dynasty the people had so graciously offered. Since Abimelech was not a legitimate son, he decided that he had to obliterate all who had a legitimate claim to the throne by killing all of his half brothers. Those who participated in the plot did not see any wrong in Abimelech's ambition, and no one lifted a finger to prevent the murders. The people of Shechem and Beth-millo made Abimelech their king. God brought justice to the situation, but the fact that the people allowed such a travesty of justice to occur shows that their sense of right and wrong was severely warped.

For nearly four hundred years, Israel lived in defeat because she rejected God. The period of the judges was one of regression, a time of failure. The extent of evil in Israel was great. It was a sad testimony that the once-mighty Israel was cowering in retreat. She lost territory she had previously conquered. In a single word, the reason she lost territory was *sin*. She sinned worse than the original inhabitants God had driven out of the land for her. She broke her covenant with God by making treaties with the surrounding people, she gave her sons and daughters in marriage to the remaining inhabitants, and her children worshiped their gods. Israel did this evil because she forgot the miracles God had performed for her; she had selective amnesia. She did not have a spiritual leader holding her accountable and teaching her God's requirements, so she did what seemed right. When God's words are not taught, there is no standard, which leaves everyone to their own devices. Moral relativism dominates; "no rules, just right." Israel had the same relativistic morality that we have today. No standards, no absolutes, no rules, it's your thing, do what you want to do. The Israelites agreed upon one thing, however, and that was the denial of God's involvement in their lives.

> I prayed, "O my God, I am utterly ashamed; I blush to lift my face to you. For our sins are piled higher than our heads, and our guilt has reached to the heavens. Our whole history has been one of great sin. That is why we and our kings and our priests have been at the mercy of the pagan kings of the land. We have been killed, captured, robbed, and disgraced, just as we are today." *Ezra 9:6–7*

The evil that Israel involved herself in was not confined to the people at large; it also affected the church, the Levites. An examination of David's descendants shows that society's spiritual failure and unfaithfulness could be attributed to the moral decay in the church that was supposed to provide spiritual leadership. The administration of Eli and his sons accurately represents the broken-down condition of the church.

Take-home message: It is entirely possible to live an accursed life in a place that was meant to be a blessing, as a result of unresolved sin.

7.

Lame Church, Maimed Society

What a privilege and an honor it is to be chosen by God to be His minister! You get an up-close look at the Creator of the universe and get to enjoy the nearness of God. Nothing else compares to being around God. It is so sweet that you do not want to leave. He will be with you personally and call you His friend. What adventures He will send you on, and what great things He will accomplish though you! You have the awesome privilege of knowing Him intimately, knowing His likes and dislikes. You learn how to please Him. You can spend a lifetime exploring God without exhausting His vastness. He transforms your thinking and your behavior because you see things from His perspective. Since His ways are not our ways and His thoughts are not like ours, you will have a level of knowledge that exceeds that of the most learned men. You are His tool, His vessel, the one He works through. Father God, how special and oh, how sweet!

The Levites enjoyed such a tremendous privilege. God chose them from among all the people of Israel to be near Him, to serve in His Tabernacle, and to stand before the people to minister to them. The priesthood, a special class within the Levite family, was given a special gift of service. The priest was responsible for the Tabernacle and everything associated with it, and was the only one allowed to handle the sacred services associated with the altar and everything within the inner curtain (the Holy of Holies).

The Levites received an inheritance not given to any other tribe of Israel. The Lord declared Himself to be their inheritance and their share. *Whatever is mine is yours.* A portion of the gifts specially set apart for the Lord also belonged to the Levites. There was a marriage between God and the Levites. He chose them to serve Him and His people, they gave their lives to attend to Him, and in return, God gave everything He had.

The Vulnerability of God's Servants

What an outrageous, monstrous proposal! Certainly the Levites got the better end of the arrangement, no matter how you look at it. They got to operate in the supernatural and the miraculous. They could be with the One who created the universe and everything in it, explore Him at whim, serve Him, learn how to please Him, have access to Him, and to top it all off, God took care of their needs. Hot dog! You mean to tell me that I get to do the one thing that I want to do most, and God will provide for me because I'm doing it? I should be paying you. What an incredible arrangement. Where do I sign up? Imagine the Lord being your inheritance. What more could you want, what more could you need? More than the things He gives, God gives Himself. How much more wonderful could it be?

Excuse me for getting all starry-eyed over such a proposal. Of course, there is a price to pay. Serving God can be as dangerous as it is rewarding. God has standards that must be adhered to, and He has His own way of doing things. If you learn those ways, all will go well for you. However, if you have a rebellious nature or honor others above God, you will have a hard row to hoe. For the priests, mistakes could cost them their lives. In the words of Eli, the high priest during the time of Samuel, "If you sin against another person, God can mediate for the guilty party, but if you sin against the Lord, who can intercede?"

God's servants are in that same position. Who stands between you and God when you sin against Him? Who mediates? Who do you turn to? You are so close to Him, beholding His face, you are like an angel who stands before the Lord, awaiting His command. When you are personally accountable to God for executing His commands, what excuse can you give for not doing exactly as He says? There can be no misunderstandings, because God gives direct commands to His servants. Being a servant of the Most High is a rewarding opportunity, but it can also turn into a dangerous situation when a servant is disobedient, respects others above God, or is bound by unresolved sin. God will address those sins directly; there is no middleman.

Who prays for you, who intercedes, who begs God for mercy on your behalf? When you sin against God, you feel like a dirt ball, and you fear being in His presence. Because you have been so close to Him, you have seen Him display His anger, and you do not want to be the recipient of that. No human can withstand God's wrath. You are ashamed and afraid because of your unresolved sin. You see no way out; you feel trapped. You feel as though you are compelled to sin. You hate your sin and the bondage, but you cannot control what you do. You hate the fact that you have betrayed God and have broken His heart. You no longer feel worthy to serve Him or His people. You just want to walk away, resigning your position. Taking a sabbatical would be the best thing to do, but you have obligations. There is a way of escape, as we will later learn from David's example.

There is no one to turn to when you sin against God. Everybody looks at you as if you are a spiritual giant who could not possibly have any irresolvable sins, but to whom does a wounded giant run? If they only knew the problems you face. You feel trapped because you cannot reach out for help. If you share the things you are facing and the terrible things you are doing, people will reject and ridicule you, calling you a hypocrite. Your pain, that sensitive spot that you have tried so desperately to cover up because it hurts so bad, would be intensified if the truth were exposed. You have to be on guard at all times; you cannot risk exposure. Christian folks, bless their hearts, are always sniffing for wounds to expose.

What would be the difference between crying out for help and having a vicious media expose you or having jealous people within the Christian community who are eager to participate in your downfall bring you down? The outcome would be the same. You would lose your credibility and your ministry. You would be the butt of jokes, the topic of conversation at dinner tables around the world, criticized from pulpits, rejected by the Christian community, and sliced up by the media for months (or even years).Your downfall might even be worthy of a movie satirizing your struggles. You could not bear to see people exploit your pain. No, you could not do that. You could not face that type of retribution, so you decide it is best to bide your time. "O God," you desperately groan, "please save me." You give altar calls, all the while desperately wishing you could run to the altar yourself, but how would that look? It just would not do to have the preacher knocking people down trying to get to the altar.

To J.S. and to ministers of God who have fallen: Please forgive me for failing to pray for you. I watched you on television on Sunday mornings before church when I was in high school. How wonderfully God used you. You were a man with a message, on fire for the Lord. If I had only known then what I know now. I understand exactly the precarious position you were in.

However, something good has come out of this. I no longer take for granted that my own pastor sometimes faces precarious situations that he cannot share with his congregation. I no longer take for granted that he may find his back up against the wall, not knowing which way to turn. There may be times when he will have a "falling out" with God that causes his advocate to become his adversary. I know my own pastor is vulnerable, and I pray for him when I wake up in the middle of the night. I spend days interceding for him. I pray for him and other servants of the Most High. Your tragedy and our loss has become a wake-up call for the Christian community. We have failed to protect God's servants, and though some have felt that it was right and just for a man or woman of God to fall, these people have failed to realize that when *you* fail, we all suffer a wound in the universal body of Christ. We must guard God's servants with prayer. Sir, if I may be so bold, may God deliver you completely from bondage. May He keep you from the snares of the wicked one. May God restore you, mighty warrior. May he use you now more than ever before. This is my prayer for you today.

Deaf Ears

Near the end of the Judges era, the Levite priesthood, which represented the church, suffered from corruption. The church is supposed to draw people to God, not away from Him. Nothing represents the moral breakdown of the church better than the situation surrounding Eli, the high priest, and his sons, Hophni and Phinehas. They were corrupt, and their corruption was a stumbling block to the people. The godly people avoided the Tabernacle, stopped giving sacrifices, and stopped doing things to please the Lord. Eli's sons were scoundrels and did not respect the Lord or the responsibilities entrusted to them. They sent their servants to get their portion before the meat of the sacrificed animal had been boiled and the fat consumed on the altar before the Lord, taking their portion before God received His. People protested because they knew the fat had to be consumed first to validate the sacrifice, but the servants of Eli's sons threatened to take the offering by force if the people put up resistance.

Hophni and Phinehas also seduced the women who assisted at the entrance of the Tabernacle. Woe unto you if you use the authority God gave you to take sexual advantage of people. God desired a relationship with His people and used the church to facilitate that relationship. The church's corruption was a stumbling block to God's relationship with His people because it blocked the rehabilitation of God's people. If the church was unhealthy, how could it fulfill its role of producing a spiritually healthy society?

High priest Eli followed the Lord; he knew the voice of the Lord. The special relationship he enjoyed with God was evident when he prayed for Hannah. Elkanah, a Levite, had two wives: Hannah and Peninnah. Peninnah had children, while Hannah had none. Every day Hannah was reminded of her inability to have a child. Each year, when Elkanah and his family traveled to the Tabernacle, he presented his sacrifice and gave his wives and children a portion of the sacrifice to give to the Lord. Peninnah used the opportunity to tease Hannah, just as the circumstances of life have a way of teasing and tormenting us when we lack the things we want and need. Peninnah's cruelty reduced Hannah to tears and caused her to lose her appetite.

Hannah sobbed deep, bitter tears as she prayed for a son at the Tabernacle. Her prayer was nonverbal. Her lips moved, but her voice did not give utterance to the words she spoke. It is a good thing that God hears both silent prayers of the heart and verbalized prayers. Eli saw her lips moving but heard no sound, so he assumed she was drunk and scolded her for coming before the Lord in that condition. Sometimes when we observe behavior in others, we try to interpret their actions without knowing the motivations behind them, but only God knows the heart and can deal with all of its complexities. Hannah explained to Eli that she was pouring out her heart before the Lord, and that she was not an irreverent woman. Once Eli understood her situation, he prayed that the Lord would grant her request.

Hannah was bubbling with joy and got her appetite back. Elkanah later slept with Hannah and in due time she had a son she named Samuel, "asked of God." God had honored her request because of Eli's appeal in her behalf. Hannah had a bubbly, bouncing baby boy. He was beautiful and perfect, and he was a little angel. Hannah had prayed, fasted, given, and wept bitterly before the Lord many times in the barren years before she had Samuel. The only thing that changed was that she finally obtained the agreement of Eli, the high priest, and that agreement produced results. That incident demonstrated that Eli had special favor before the Lord. It was part of his responsibility as high priest to bless the people.

Hannah promised God that if He gave her a son, she would give him back to the Lord; he would be God's servant for life. Hannah honored her commitment, and we would all do well to follow her example. She made a vow when she was in a crisis, and then she kept her word when the crisis was over. It was difficult to give away the one thing she had wanted the most, but Hannah took pleasure in the satisfaction of finally validating her womanhood by experiencing the indescribable, miraculous beauty of bringing life into the world.

Every year thereafter, when Hannah and Elkanah went to the Tabernacle for their yearly sacrifices and to visit Samuel, Eli blessed them again, saying, "May the Lord give you other children to take the place of this one she gave to the Lord" (1 Samuel 2:20). The Lord gave Hannah three sons and two daughters. God is the great equalizer. He makes the poor rich and the rich poor. He lifts the poor from dust and ashes and treats them like princes, placing them in seats of honor. Eli had a positive impact in Elkanah's family. Eli had influence with the Lord, and the Lord honored his requests.

When Samuel heard the voice of the Lord for the first time, it was Eli who taught him to identify God's voice and to respond to Him. Little Samuel wore linen ephod, just like the priests. He was a spiritual leader in training who grew up in the presence of the Lord. As Samuel served Eli in the Tabernacle, he not only grew physically, but he also continued to gain favor with the Lord and other people. In those days, messages and visions from the Lord were scarce. God gave Israel the silent treatment because of her sins and because she constantly rejected him.

One night, however, Samuel heard someone calling his name. He thought it was Eli. God called him three times, and each time Samuel ran to Eli. The third time, Eli said, "Go and lie down again, and if someone calls again, say, 'Yes, LORD, your servant is listening'" (1 Samuel 3:9). This represented a changing of the guard, so to speak. Samuel served God indirectly by serving Eli, but when God addressed Samuel directly, He was essentially saying that Samuel would serve Him directly from then on. Samuel learned to identify and respond to the voice of the Lord because of Eli's experience.

It would stand to reason that if Eli recognized the voice of the Lord and had such influence that he could speak blessings into the lives of others, he had a relationship with the Lord. Eli's relationship with the Lord should have caused him to honor the Lord above everyone else. Unfortunately, he favored his sons more than he feared God. The people complained to Eli about the wickedness of his sons, making him fully aware of the problems. If the people are complaining about wrongdoing in the church, you have a real problem on your hands, because correction usually comes from the pulpit. However, when people are complaining about the wrongdoings of their leaders, those leaders become a stumbling block to the spiritual growth of the people. Instead of disciplining his sons for their sins and corruption, Eli just smacked them on the hand and said, "No, no, don't do that."

If the problems associated with Eli's sons had been a one-time event, Eli's actions would have been appropriate, but they were persistent problems stemming from deep-seated attitudes that could not be adjusted by reprimands. Eli should have relieved them of their duties since they did not respect the Lord and acted as if they were doing God a favor by being His priests. God was the priests' inheritance; He made provision for them by assigning them a portion of the sacrifice, but Eli's sons took for themselves what God had reserved for Himself. Eli's sons felt that they were more deserving of the offerings the people gave to God than God was. They acted as if God owed them something. The problem that can arise with privileged people is that they grow up with a sense of entitlement, feeling as if everybody owes them something.

Eli knew what God expected and had the authority to correct wrongs, but he did nothing to fix the problem. Although Eli was not personally involved in the actions of his sons, he was responsible. He was the high priest, which made him accountable for whatever happened in the Tabernacle, and it was his responsibility to make sure things operated according to God's desires. Eli did not seduce women, nor did he take part of the sacrifice that was reserved for God, but he did benefit from the corruption of his sons because he ate the meat that had been taken before it was properly sacrificed.

When you are a leader, there may be no personal connection between you and the sins of the people who assist you, but once you are aware of the problems and fail to correct the issues, you are as guilty as the people committing the sins. The actions of your assistants reflect upon you. If your leadership position is jeopardized by the mistakes of subordinates, and if your ministry's reputation is suffering because of your assistants, you must do all you can to correct the situation or remove them because, at the very least, it is a matter of self-preservation.

Since the complaints of the people fell on deaf ears, God decided to send a prophet to confront Eli directly.

I want you to see things from my perspective, and maybe you will understand how I feel about the way you have handled the problems in the Tabernacle. It is my hope that you will resolve the problems. I exalted your family above all the families of Israel when I revealed myself to your ancestor, Aaron. I chose you from all the tribes of Israel to be my servant. In return for being my servant, I made it my personal responsibility to take care of you, giving you the best that Israel had to offer. I favored you, I honored you, and I exalted you above all others, giving you a privileged status. Why do you disrespect me by spurning my gifts? Considering all I have done for you, don't I deserve to be number one in your life? At the very least, I deserve your undying loyalty. Why do you honor others over me when they haven't done a thing for you? I've given you the best and you act like my best isn't good enough, because you have taken what I reserved for myself and grown fat.

I can't let this go on. I am not obligated to honor those who despise me. I cannot tolerate the sins of the priesthood, because they are detrimental to my people. If you fail to correct the problems plaguing the priesthood, I will have to take matters into my own hands, and that will be disastrous for your family. I loathe having to retract the priest dynasty I promised your family. In order to still honor my promise, I will wipe out your family so there will be no one to serve as my priest. The members of your family will die prematurely; no one will live out their days. Those who survive will suffer from depression as they watch their children die violently. Your family will be impoverished, because prosperity will avoid you. Your family will beg my new priest for money, food, and jobs. Both your sons will die in the same day to signal that I will do what I have said.

God warned Eli through the prophet, but Eli did not heed the warnings and went about business as usual. It is ironic that the person who taught

Samuel to recognize the voice of the Lord was also the subject of God's first conversation with Samuel. By that time, God had determined that Eli would not correct his sons, which forced God to fulfill the threats He had made concerning Eli's family. God dropped a bombshell on Samuel about Eli and his sons.

I am going to carry out my threats against Eli and his sons. I will shock the socks off everyone. I've warned Eli repeatedly, but there has been no improvement. Eli's lack of humility and failure to correct wrongdoing over an extended period of time has led to an unpardonable state.

Samuel probably did not sleep the rest of the night, because he had met God for the first time and because of what God told him. Samuel experienced the awkwardness of being a prophet—sometimes you have to relay hard messages. Samuel told Eli exactly what God had said, but Eli just yawned and said, "It is the LORD's will. . . . Let Him do what he thinks is best" (1 Samuel 3:18).

God had warned Eli through prophets before, but He had not carried out his threats, so Eli viewed the message God gave Samuel as another empty threat. Eli's ho-hum, lackadaisical attitude was maddening. He did not realize that God had not followed through with His past threats because He was giving Eli the opportunity to resolve the problem. God is merciful, and His warnings are meant to bring correction. God gave Eli time and space to repent and correct the situation.

When God convicts a man, that man can either receive correction with humility and repentance or he can refuse to resolve the issue and bring about his own condemnation. What God desires is repentance; He prefers that a man correct himself. God does not stand around waiting to clobber a person for their flaws and errors. He does not take pleasure in the death of an individual. God is long-suffering and merciful, but there comes a point of no return after He has continually warned a stubborn man when repentance becomes futile. When a man cannot be forgiven by sacrifices and offerings, it means he has hardened his heart by repeatedly refusing correction. God convicts a man first, giving him time to resolve the problem, but a stubborn man condemns himself by his refusal to change, his refusal to repent.

When a man repeatedly refuses to make a correction, God is forced to correct the situation Himself. Eli's repentance was crucial because he was the highest spiritual leader in the land. The church was the last hope for reforming the nation; if the church was corrupt, the nation did not stand a chance. The church is, and should be, the vehicle for moral improvement in society and is responsible for addressing societal ills. If God's ministers are not working in concert with Him, they are frustrating His goals. If the highest spiritual officers are morally corrupt, how can the people ever hope to come to God? Corruption infected the ranks of the priests, and their corruption did not help reform the hearts of an idolatrous nation. The priests were a liability to God's cause, so He had to minimize their role in society temporarily until He could revamp the priesthood.

No Weapon Formed Against Me Shall Prosper

To get a better feel for David's society, let's look at another testimonial about the attitude of the people and the priesthood. Israel was constantly wavering in her loyalty toward God. She served God when she was in trouble but rejected Him when she did not feel threatened. The Israelites went to war with their constant nemesis, the tool of God's correction, the thorn in their flesh, the Philistines. The Philistines were descendants of the Caphtorites, and their ancestor, Mizraim, was a son of Ham. They slaughtered four thousand Israelite soldiers in one day.

The people of Israel were alarmed and inquired of their leaders as to why the Lord had allowed such a defeat, but their leaders could not provide an answer, since they were in a spiritual quandary themselves. Since they could not produce an answer off the top of their heads from knowing God's words, they should have asked God directly, but they were on bad terms with God themselves, and He would not respond to their inquiries.

God left them to their own devices. It did not occur to them that they were responsible for their defeat. Could worshiping other gods and following the practices of the former occupants have had anything to do with it? Instead of waiting for a response from the Lord, they decided that God was a mere amulet, an Aladdin's lamp, a charm, a genie at their command. "It doesn't matter that we don't live right or regard you. Just come down here and defeat our enemies—be our puppet on a string."

That proved to be a disastrous and costly position to take, yet that same attitude is prevalent among Christians today. Many go around singing, "No weapon formed against me shall prosper." That is true for one who is living according to the mandates of God, but it is not true for a defiant Christian in willful opposition to the Lord. We remember the promises of the Lord and forget that there is a covenant attached. God will do x, y, and z when you do a, b, and c. If you don't fulfill your part of the covenant, you cannot expect God to do His part.

The most brazen thing to do is to be deeply engrossed in sin and completely rebellious toward God and then demand that He defend you (no, what you need is mercy). You got yourself into your mess by not obeying Him, and the last thing you want to do is face an enemy when you are vulnerable to defeat because you are a sinner. The best thing for you to do is to withdraw from as much activity as you can, get on your face before God, plead for mercy, and ask Him to deliver you. The Lord will not despise a broken heart and a contrite spirit, but He resists the proud. It is not the time to take on giants. The past victories you enjoyed were completely due to the fact that you found favor before the Lord and He gave you victory. Therefore, if your relationship with the Lord is in jeopardy, humbly seek restoration posthaste and with all diligence.

The Israelites tromped out to the battlefield against the Philistines with the Ark of the Lord carried by Hophni and Phinehas, of all people. When the Ark arrived in the camp, they were so elated that they made the ground shake. "Nooooo weapon formed against me shall prosper, this is my promise from the Lord," they sang with much jubilation. They were so cocky and confident of victory because the Ark of the Lord was in the camp. The camp reverberated with their premature victory dance, and that reverberation could be felt in the Philistine camp. The Philistines were puzzled and frightened by the jubilation. It sounded as if a mighty army were coming against them. What's all the uproar? This does not sound like an army that is about to get spanked! Instead of being afraid, Israel was strutting her stuff, celebrating victory.

Ordinarily, that would have been the proper response to the Ark of the Lord, because His glorious presence secured victory. Even their enemies knew that the God of Israel would cause their defeat. Unfortunately, Israel failed to realize that she had created an enemy in God because of her idolatry. She caused her own demise because she had angered the Lord and created an enemy instead of an ally. If she had gone into battle without the Ark, the slaughter would not have been as massive. In the earlier battle, Israel had lost only four thousand men, but when Israel brought the Ark of the Lord into the camp, she lost thirty thousand men. The slaughter was great because the Lord was fighting against them as well as giving the Philistines indefatigable strength.

God's correction of Eli's priesthood began on the battlefield that day. The deaths of Phinehas and Hophni during that battle signified that God would carry out His threats concerning Eli's descendants. The Philistines captured the Ark, and when word of Israel's terrible defeat and the capture of the Ark reached Eli, he keeled over. His pregnant daughter-in-law went into labor prematurely when she heard that the Ark had been captured and that her husband, Phinehas, and her father-in-law were dead. She named the child Ichabod, "God's glory is gone" or "Where is the glory," and then she, too, died. The premature deaths that God had promised Eli had begun.

God purged corruption from the Tabernacle because Eli and his sons had proved to be a liability to God's cause. God desired fellowship with His people, but Eli and his sons had discouraged the few godly people remaining in the idolatrous nation. Eli and his sons died as a result of their violations. God held Eli accountable, although he was not personally involved in the sins of his sons, because everything that happened in the Tabernacle was under his supervision. His weak stance toward his sons' sins did nothing to correct them, and evil thrives when good men do nothing. From the reign of Saul to the reign of Solomon, God fulfilled his threats against Eli's family.

God Is Holy

The way the Philistines initially handled the Ark of the Most High shows that they regarded God as little more than another powerless god. To conquer a people was to conquer their god since their god was not strong enough to protect them. The Philistines knew that the God of Israel was very powerful, because of the effort it took to defeat Israel. The God of Israel had a reputation that preceded Him. He was one god they wanted to keep, and though they believed that He was not as powerful as Dagon, they knew He could enhance them and could become an asset once they learned to harness His power. It seems that we are always looking for a god we can control, not one to which we have to relinquish our control.

While the Israelites were suffering from selective amnesia about God, the Philistines quickly developed a healthy respect for the Lord, and they quickly learned that the God of Israel was *not* just another god. Even Dagon fell down and worshiped Him. The Philistines had to correct Dagon's view of himself, so they lifted him up from the worshipful prostrate posture he had assumed. Dagon made another self-assessment and decided he had no power or authority that was not given by God.

God's power began to explode against the Philistines. People began to develop tumors, rats overtook them, and death and destruction overwhelmed them (there is a connection between viruses carried by rats and the tumors humans develop when they are plagued by them). The Philistines began to scream out in anguish.

God's presence will either bless you or judge you, and the Philistines quickly identified God as the source of their calamity. They decided not to be pigheaded like the pharaoh whose stubbornness had cost him his life and ravished his country during Israel's departure from Egypt. They sent the Ark of the Lord to Gath, where people of all ages immediately began to be afflicted with tumors. They then sent the Ark to Ekron, but before it had even arrived, people began to die, and others were inflicted with tumors, so the people of Ekron begged for the Ark to be sent back to Israel. The Lord sent plagues upon the Philistines for the entire seven months He was with them. They finally sent the Ark back to Israel, along with five golden tumors and rats from the rulers of Ashdod, Gaza, Ashkelon, Gath, and Ekron as a guilt offering for their people. Apparently, they had a better perspective concerning fear of the Lord than the Israelites.

After the Ark of the Lord was returned to Israel, the Israelites experienced the same problems as the Philistines. Initially they handled the Ark properly. The Levites lifted it from the cart, placed it upon a large rock, and offered sacrifices and burnt offerings, but seventy men of Beth-shemesh died because they let their curiosity get the best of them by looking into the Ark. In desperation, they sent the Ark of the Lord to Kiriath-jearim, where it remained for decades.

National Depression

Everything that had made Israel great was gone. She was suffocating because she was cut off from God, and His departure caused Israel to feel defenseless and insecure. She experienced dreadful terror, realizing that it had been God's presence that had given her distinction above all other nations. She recognized that it was God, and God alone, that made the difference. He protected, provided, led, and guided her. Without God she was vulnerable to her enemies, and she mourned because God had abandoned her.

It is funny how the loss of a thing causes appreciation for it to grow. Losing a thing causes one to put things into their proper perspective. "When God is gone, our life, our strength, our *everything* is gone. How can we function? How can we breathe? How can we live without God? Without Him, we are aimless, directionless wanderers, unsure of which path to take, unsure of every decision. Our days are filled with uncertainty, and life has no meaning and no purpose without God. Our value was derived from Him, so we are fearful and anxious. Our life is gone . . . our God is gone."

In that day, messages from God were scarce and visions almost nonexistent, because Israel was estranged from her God. Since God had distanced himself from Israel, there was a drought of His word in the land of Israel. *Why should I speak when they don't listen anyway?*

Many people mistakenly believe that fighting (heated verbal discussions minus verbal and/or physical abuse) and conflicts are detrimental to a relationship and that peacefulness and smooth sailing means everything is okay. The most dangerous time in any relationship is when a point of silence is reached. In human relationships, silence is dangerous, but when God is silent, it can be deadly. Silence means a stalemate has been reached and negotiations have broken down. Silence means, "I give up and I throw in the towel, since there is no hope of recovery."

When God, who is boundless and limitless, reaches that point in a relationship, there is no hope left. God spoke this world into existence, and all of creation depends on His word. Silence from God should make rational beings fearful, since everything hinges upon His word. God's silence speaks volumes, and His silence should cause people to take a hard look within to find out what is causing the blockage of communication. How are your thoughts and actions offensive? What conflicts are occurring that you have refused to address? What is it that is creating a holding pattern in your relationship with God? God is vast but bound by the limitations humans place on Him by refusing to remove the resistances that impede His ability to take the relationship to the next level. *I can't go any further than you allow.*

In any troubled relationship, one person is usually trying to hold it together more than the other person. In the relationship between God and Israel, God was the one doing everything, even though things were not working out. God knew that Israel did not want anything to do with Him, but He still tried to communicate, because He was hopeful. God was trying to make His relationship with Israel work. *Although you think I have abandoned you, I'm right here.* Israel mourned the loss of God and finally realized how critical God was to her daily life. What would she do without God? She mourned because sometimes it takes losing a thing before you grasp its significance. God was gone; her life source had left her. She missed waking up to hear Him say, "Good morning." She missed His embrace. Flowers seemed dull. Birds sang off key. She lost her appetite; nothing tasted right. Everything was off balance; nothing was right. Everything that made Israel great was gone. Israel was depressed because of the Lord's absence. The love of her life was gone. She felt abandoned and forsaken by God, and Israel was ready to grab on to any hope and listen to any voice of reason that would lead her back to the One she desperately needed.

God usually has a new appointee waiting in the wings as a replacement when a leader anointed by Him dies. This was the case with Eli and Samuel, just as it had been with Moses and Joshua. God promised to replace Eli's family with a faithful priest who would obey and serve Him. Through His new appointee, He would establish a priestly dynasty. It seems as if God intended to establish a new priestly line altogether instead of using the other division of qualified priests. While Samuel was a Levite of the Kohath division, he was not from the priestly lineage of Aaron. Samuel was Eli's understudy, his replacement, and God trained him because He knew He needed to fill the gap. He groomed Samuel while he was serving Eli. Samuel served God by serving Eli.

One who assists the pastor is also a servant of God. It is entirely possible to serve God without dialoging with Him, without knowing Him personally. Samuel's training under the spiritual authority of his mentor, Eli, made it possible for his smooth transition to being under the direct authority of the Lord. In the same way, parents are mentors responsible for training their children to obey so that they, in turn, can submit to the direct authority of the Lord. There is something to be said for dedicating children to the Lord before they are conceived and training them to be godly children. God took His relationship with Samuel to the next level by communicating with him directly.

God was impressed with Samuel's development and knew that Samuel was a man He could trust, so He decided to communicate through Samuel. From that point on, God continued to dialogue with Samuel and to speak through him.

Samuel led Israel in spiritual reformation. If you want the Lord to return to you, show that you are serious about wanting Him back. Get rid of the obstacles that impede your relationship with Him. Determine to follow God and God alone. Fast and confess your sins before God. *If you want me in your life, seek me and I will let you find me.* Samuel's intercession and leadership restored Israel to a right relationship with the Lord. Samuel ministered to and admonished the people during a time of national mourning.

> If you are really serious about wanting to return to the LORD, get rid of your foreign gods and your images of Ashtoreth. Determine to obey only the LORD; then he will rescue you from the Philistines.
> *1 Samuel 7:3*

Israel complied and did as Samuel advised. She got rid of her gods, destroying the images of Ashtoreth and Baal. She fasted and confessed her sins before the Lord during a ceremony held at Mizpah, where Samuel prayed for her and became Israel's judge.

The Philistines heard that the Israelites were gathered before the Lord at Gilgal, and since they had briefly had the Ark of the Lord in their possession, they had a healthy respect for His power. If Israel turned to her God and tapped into His power, it meant they would lose their dominion over her. So while the Israelites were gathered at the ceremony, the Philistines mobilized an attack against them. When you take a step toward restoring God into His rightful position in your life, the enemy that enslaved you will fight to prevent you from making that commitment and from reconnecting. Israel begged Samuel to pray to God for help. Samuel offered a young lamb as a burnt offering and pleaded with the Lord for help, and the Lord did save

Israel that day. In fact, the Lord subdued the Philistines throughout Samuel's lifetime. Israel also regained lost territories near Ekron and Gath from the Philistines and enjoyed peace with the Amorites. The Lord's favor returned to Israel as a result of Samuel's intercession, along with peace, restoration, and reformation.

Take-home message: God convicts people and gives them space to repent, but people condemn themselves when they refuse to take corrective action.

8.

Rebels Without a Cause

Samuel served Israel all his life, and Israel benefited from his leadership. Israel made Samuel her judge, and the Judges period closed with him. For the rest of his life, Samuel traveled to various cities, such as Bethel, Gilgal, Mizpah, and Ramah, setting up court to hear cases and to issue judgments according to the wisdom of the Lord, and Israel fared well under his leadership. When Samuel had advanced in age, he appointed his sons as judges, but the people would not have it. They did not want to be under the authority of Samuel's sons, because those men did not carry their father's spirit.

The people of Israel were enjoying spiritual reform under Samuel's leadership, and their continued improvement depended upon righteous leadership. They were still suspicious of God and had a hostile attitude toward Him, but things were getting better. Their relationship with God was on the mend. Samuel intended for his sons to rule in his stead, but they were greedy and could be influenced by bribes to pervert justice. Unfortunately, the torch could not be passed to his sons. Israel demanded a king instead. Although it was valid for the people of Israel to reject the leadership of Joel and Abijah to avoid having another Hophni and Phinehas on their hands, God told Samuel not to take their insults and rejection personally, because they were really rejecting God.

The prospect of not having a central leader to defend her from her enemies caused Israel concern. Samuel had aged, and the time of his retirement was quickly approaching. The torch could not be passed to Samuel's sons, since good leadership required integrity, and there was no one else like Samuel on the scene who could continue his spiritual leadership.

Without Samuel's influence, Israel's semi-reformed status could not be maintained, and the people would return to idolatry. The worship of other gods had always created problems in Israel's relationship with God, and that troubled relationship would have left Israel vulnerable to attack. Israel wanted a savior to defend her against her enemies regardless of her spiritual condition. While Israel was justified in rejecting Samuel's sons, God identified the true motive behind their request for a king. It was a rejection of theocratic rule, a rejection of Him.

We Need a Leader We Can Control

Israel wanted to remove the problems associated with the adversarial relationship her idolatry had created with God. Her relationship with her idols had caused God to allow enemies to oppress her. Instead of crying out to God as before, however, she decided she could no longer depend on Him. Without the kind of leadership Samuel provided, it was inevitable that idolatry and sin would run rampant, and since that was the case, Israel felt she could not expect the Lord to defend her. She wanted the assurance that someone would defend her in spite of her sinful condition. Up to that point, it was God, and God alone, who had delivered her from her enemies. What she failed to remember was the many times God had defended her while she was deeply engrossed in sin. She forgot that God had sent deliverers when she cried out for mercy, even though she was serving Baal, Chemosh, and Ashtoreth. God was faithful even when Israel was unfaithful, but Israel figured that God's mercy would eventually expire. She had to be prepared for that eventuality, because once she went back to her lovers there could be no turning back.

"We just cannot please You. We can't live with You nor without You. We don't want Your direct control, Lord. We no longer want to be ruled by You. We want to be like other nations who are not accountable to You. Your standards are too stifling; they cramp us. Other nations seem to prosper without You, and so can we. Other nations worship other gods and get along just fine.

"You seem irrational and will not be satisfied with any type of worship we slap together. You ought to be satisfied that we acknowledge You at all. You should be satisfied with whatever we give You, like all the other gods. Why can't You be satisfied with our halfhearted devotion? We try to include You in our list of gods, but You want exclusivity—all or nothing. We are tired of our duplicity. We can't please You and still please all the other gods we serve. You are supposed to serve us like a genie, but You refuse to cooperate. You are so possessive and jealous that we are suffocating! You are subject to irrational outbursts, temper tantrums, and fits of rage; well, it's just uncivilized! We are tired of You. If we can't control You, we don't want You. We need a leader we can control, one who won't require so much of us."

It is true that you have rejected me from being your king. All along it has been me. I am the one who brought you out of bondage when you couldn't free yourself.

You cried out so desperately that you broke my heart. I had pity on you and did what no other god, and not even you, could do for yourself.

I remembered my promises to your ancestor, Abraham. I became your God and called you my special people. Even your enemies became my enemies. Anybody who had a problem with you had to talk to me. I have been protective of you. I would not let anyone harm you, and if you hurt, I hurt. I have been careful with you, tending to your every need. I miraculously provided for you in the wilderness. I gave you water when you were thirsty. I fed you when you were hungry. I gave you the best quality clothing—which did not wear out, even after forty years. I gave you the spoils of your enemies, and you did not have to fight to get them. I gave you health; you did not have a sickly person among you.

I guided you in the wilderness with a cloud by day and a pillar of fire by night; you were not directionless and aimlessly wandering about. I did not leave you lonely; I was with you every step of the way. If that wasn't enough, I gave you a land that was already established, homes that you did not build, and crops that you did not sow. I gave you the land I had promised, flowing with milk and honey. So tell me, though I've shown you nothing but goodness, what fault have you found in me that causes you to treat me so badly?

I am absolutely heartbroken and infuriated by your unfaithfulness to me; you have provoked me to jealousy. I just don't get it—have you heard of another god like me? Just what do these other gods offer that you find them so appealing? What is this madness? It's obvious that those other gods can do nothing for you, because when you get in a bind you always come running back to me. I have an undying love for you that compels me to love you even when you are ungrateful and turn your back on me. You break my heart and then grind it to powder when you chase down other, useless gods to give them the love and affection that rightfully belongs to me.

The other gods you serve don't even want you; you are throwing yourselves at them. The useless gods you serve don't love you like I do; they haven't done a single thing to demonstrate their love for you. As a matter of fact, all they have done is harm you. If the truth be known, you are not worthy of me. You don't deserve my goodness and my care, but you need it. I'll continue to show you goodness for my name's sake. Outsiders will look at our relationship and say, "He is a good, good God. There is no other god like Him, not even the one we serve."

It is because of my goodness that I will grant you the request you have made for a king. You have rejected my being your king, but that does not release you from your accountability to me nor does it release me from being your God. It does not break the contract I made with your ancestors. I'm still yours and you are still mine. This covenant cannot be broken, for it was made in blood, and that permanently attaches us; we are inseparable. The only thing that can nullify this contract is death.

You are sadly mistaken if you think that you don't need me anymore or that you can push me out of your life and still be successful and have business as usual. There will be no changing of the guards as you had hoped, in which the old administration will leave, along with its rules and ways of governing. No, you and your king must still respect, worship, and obey me. If you and your king will listen and obey me and follow all my ordinances and not rebel against me, then all will be well with you. But if you don't, you'll feel my heavy hand of discipline.

An Anticipated Request

God was not opposed to Israel having a king. In fact, He had made provision for such an occasion. What God was opposed to was the motive behind the request for a king. A king, in Israel's mind, would supplant God. God is usually not concerned about the things people request, as long as those things are not harmful and will not be used to replace Him.

> You will soon arrive in the land the LORD your God is giving you, and you will conquer it and settle there. Then you may begin to think, "We ought to have a king like the other nations around us." If this happens, be sure that you select as king the man the LORD your God chooses. You must appoint a fellow Israelite, not a foreigner. The king must not build up a large stable of horses for himself, and he must never send his people to Egypt to buy horses there, for the LORD has told you, "You must never return to Egypt." The king must not take many wives for himself, because they will lead him away from the LORD. And he must not accumulate vast amounts of wealth in silver and gold for himself. When he sits on the throne as king, he must copy these laws on a scroll for himself in the presence of the Levitical priests. He must always keep this copy of the law with him and read it daily as long as he lives. That way he will learn to fear the LORD his God by obeying all the terms of this law. This regular reading will prevent him from becoming proud and acting as if he is above his fellow citizens. It will also prevent him from turning away from these commands in the smallest way. This will ensure that he and his descendants will reign for many generations in Israel.
> *Deuteronomy 17:14–20*

Since this was written well over four hundred years before Israel's request for a king, it proves that God was not opposed to a king in Israel.

Taxes and a draft came with the installation of a king. God told Israel that there would be financial drawbacks to her decision. It would no longer be a voluntary decision to join the army; it would be mandatory. Some young men would become the king's bodyguards, some would become commanders, some would be forced into slave labor to plow the king's fields and harvest his crops, and others would make weapons and chariots for the king. Some of Israel's daughters would cook for the king and make his perfumes. The king would take Israel's best fields, vineyards, and olive groves for his servants. A tenth of all harvests and flocks would be used to support his staff. The king would take her slaves and her finest livestock for his use. The king would make the people his slaves, causing a severe financial burden to the people.

Israel ignored the warning and stubbornly insisted upon having a king, believing it was better to have a financial obligation than a moral one. "We'd rather suffer financially and live without restrictions than to live under costly oppressive moral standards." Financial obligations do not cost as much as moral obligations. Moral obligations cost you everything, including your way of living and governing yourself, on top of what they cost you financially. Rather than taking the time out to learn how to please God and how to do things His way, Israel wanted a king. They would rather be ruled by a man with the same limitations as them so they would not be expected to live according to a higher standard of holiness. They would not have to try to rise above the level of their leader. They rejected the leadership of God, wanting to be like the other nations. It did not matter to the Israelites that those other nations were not doing well nor that God was the one who was responsible for Israel's success, the one who distinguished her.

Up to this point, this book has been painting the backdrop for the emergence of David. If we do not understand the history of Israel and David's society, we cannot appreciate what he did for Israel. Israel was suffering from moral decline and spiritual prostitution. The Israelites suffered from selective amnesia; it was convenient for them to forget all the miracles God had performed on their behalf and to forget all the things He had done for them to prove His love. Failure to communicate Israel's history had created a nation that did not know God and a people that did not know how to be in a harmonious relationship with Him. The people had declined to such a level that they built shrines and altars to Baal and Ashtoreth next to the altar of God. God was just another god in their collection. And God had revolted, just as a betrayed spouse would if his or her unfaithful spouse brought a partner to bed while he or she was lying there.

In order to appreciate what it is like to have a righteous king, we must understand what it was like to have an unrighteous one. Saul started out on the right foot, but he did not end well. He achieved many victories but made some serious errors that cost him his dynasty, his destiny, the resident presence of the Spirit of God, and, ultimately, his life. We can learn a lot by examining the life of an unsuccessful person, what they did right and where they went wrong, in order to avoid our own nonproductive behaviors.

Samuel's Wholehearted Reception

Samuel arranged a feast for a guest of honor that God told him he would meet the next day. Samuel planned a public sacrifice and invited thirty special guests and set aside the finest cut of meat for the unknown guest of honor.

The circumstances of our lives are not happenstance. All the circumstances of our lives build and lead to a divine appointment. It was not coincidental, then, that Kish's donkeys went astray and that he sent his son, Saul, and a servant out to look for them. They traveled through the hill country of Ephraim, the land of Shalishah, the Shaalim area, and the entire land of Benjamin, and ended up in the region of Zuph, where the town of Ramah was located. They traveled farther than they had expected, exhausted their provisions, and still had not found the donkeys. They searched for so long that Saul's family started to worry more about them than about the donkeys.

Saul decided that it was best to go home, but his servant had another idea. They were in Ramah, where a seer or man of God lived, a man highly respected because of his accuracy. Everything he predicted came true, so why not ask him to tell them the location of the donkeys? The seer could have been in any of a million places, but he happened to be in Ramah that day.

As Saul and his servant reached the town gates, Samuel was coming toward them to climb the hill. God identified Saul as the one he had appointed to rule Israel when he approached Samuel. Saul asked him where the seer's house was. Samuel replied, "I am the seer! Be my guest and join me at a public sacrifice. Let's eat together. Stay with me tonight and tomorrow, and I will tell you what you want to know. Don't worry about the donkeys; they have been found. The hope of all Israel rests on your family."

Samuel took Saul and his servant to the great hall and placed them at the head of the table, honoring them above the special guests. Samuel instructed the cook to bring Saul the finest cut of meat that he had set aside for the guest of honor.

Saul's mind was reeling as he lay his head down that night. "The seer was expecting me. He received me graciously, seating me at the head of the table, giving me the finest cut of meat, and putting me up for the night. I am from the smallest tribe of Israel, and my family is the smallest family within that tribe. Why is this man treating me like, well, like a king? Samuel said he would tell me what I wanted to know, then told me my father's donkeys had been found. I came to inquire about the donkeys. What more could I want to know?"

God usually prepares a person for any appointment before he confirms it through a prophet, and judging by Samuel's statement, Saul may have had prior knowledge about God appointing him king of Israel. The next day, Samuel privately anointed Saul king of Israel.

As confirmation, Samuel told Saul how his journey back home would unfold. He would run into two men on the border of Benjamin at Rachel's tomb who were looking for him, because Kish was worried about him. Then, at the oak of Tabor, three men would approach. One would have three loaves of bread, another would have a wineskin, and the third would have three young goats. Samuel instructed Saul to accept two of the loaves of bread. Then, at Gibeah-Elohim, he would meet a band of prophets returning from the altar on the hill who would be prophesying and praising God. At that time, the Spirit of the Lord would overtake him, causing him to prophesy as well.

All the events transpired just as Samuel had said. When Saul ran into the prophets, the Spirit of God overtook him. He prophesied, and he climbed the hill to the altar. His friends were amazed because they had never seen that type of behavior from Saul, and it certainly was not a family trait. If a man wanted to be a priest, he had to have the right pedigree. He had to be born into the tribe of the Levites; in particular, he had to be a descendant of Aaron and without physical defects.

Although it is not always the case, preachers tend to run in families today, but if a person wants to be a prophet or if God chooses to make a person a prophet, ancestry is irrelevant. God can pour out His Spirit on anyone He chooses without regard to family background. The Spirit of God can come on a person and make something beautiful; He can change a nobody into somebody. God can do whatever you allow Him to do, which is good news for someone who grew up on the wrong side of the tracks. You may have been a hardened criminal with a bad reputation, but if you invite the Spirit of the Lord into your life, He can change you and turn you into a person you can be proud of.

It is also good news for someone who grew up on the right side of the tracks in a completely nonreligious family. Your family may never have set foot in a church for a baby dedication, Christmas, or Resurrection Day, and it may have been that way for generations, but you can invite the Spirit of the Lord in and experience a glorious change in your life. In a world where we place so many limitations on people and spend so much time putting up barriers to keep certain people out, it is nice to know that there is one place where no human can block you from going as far as you aspire to go. There are so many opportunities in God; you are the single determinant of how far you can go in Him.

A Cool Reception for the King

Samuel summoned Israel to Mizpah to present God's choice for their king. Samuel called the tribal leaders before the Lord, and the Lord chose the tribe of Benjamin via the Urim and Thummim. Each family of that tribe was presented to the Lord and He chose the family of the Matrites. When Saul, son of Kish, was chosen among them, he hid himself. *Here is your king—Saul, son of Kish—hiding behind the baggage!*

Saul appeared to be scared stiff, but anyone would have been staggered by being appointed to such an awesome post. Was it modesty or humility? Fear of inadequacy and feelings of insecurity can sometimes be mistaken for humility. Some took Saul's actions that day as a demonstration of fear. "Is this a joke? I mean, you have to be joking!" They questioned Saul's ability to lead them into battle to defeat their foes, and they rejected him as king and did not give him gifts. The Israelites had asked for a king because they wanted a hero, and as far as they were concerned, Saul would not do.

The criteria God used to select Saul had nothing to do with inner substance and training. His only distinguishing feature was his height. He was not selected on the basis of charisma, self-confidence, fearlessness, or courage. His qualifications were not listed. He was head and shoulders above everyone else. Besides his height, nothing distinguished him.

The pending invasion of King Nahash prompted the people to ask for a king. Israel wanted a defender with no strings attached; she wanted someone to defend her without taking the status of her soul into consideration. Therefore, one of Saul's first acts after his public introduction as king was to save Jabesh-Gilead from King Nahash's attack. King Nahash agreed to a peace treaty under the condition that he could gouge everyone's right eye out.

God was concerned about the Jabesh-Gilead situation. Although Israel had rejected Him, He did not abandon His people, because it would dishonor His name and because He loved Israel. Thus, He sent His mighty Spirit upon Saul, and Saul became angry. Without the Spirit of the Lord, Saul was passive, even-tempered, and laid back. He was definitely not a fighter, nor did he express strong emotions such as anger. The Spirit of the Lord changed everything, enabling Saul to feel and express anger and to exhibit a dramatically different personality.

Saul slaughtered two oxen, cut them into pieces, and sent them throughout Israel, saying, "This is what will happen to the oxen of anyone who refuses to follow Samuel and Saul into battle." Saul rallied the Israelite army and led them successfully in battle against King Nahash. He had a sensible plan that included deploying three detachments of troops and arriving before dawn, catching the enemy off guard in a surprise attack.

The victory sealed the people's acceptance of Saul. It was a good test run for God, proving that His Spirit could make the impossible possible. He could even accomplish victory through a weak but willing vessel. God uses the weak ones to confound the mighty. The battle demonstrated Saul's ability and humility, and quelled all opposition to his being appointed king. Saul correctly attributed the victory to God. A lukewarm acceptance turned into a wholehearted reception by the people. People approve of you as long as you do what they want you to do.

Samuel was a good man and a healthy leader. He was Israel's prophet, priest, and last judge. His sons were supposed to be next in line to serve Israel, but Samuel respected the wishes of the people. He did not begrudge Saul's appointment or try to block him in any way. He received Saul, God's choice, with open arms, wholeheartedly, enthusiastically, and without hesitation. In fact, he assisted Saul, and although the reins of leadership had shifted from him to Saul, Samuel continued to serve Israel as a priest and a prophet.

The measure of good leadership is whether people flourish under your leadership and whether they are left in a better condition than when you started. As he handed over the reins to Saul, Samuel addressed the Israelites. He asked them if he had ever harmed them in any way, because he wanted to set things right. No one accused him; in fact, they responded that he did not oppress them nor take bribes.

Samuel reminded Israel of what God had done for her and how she had been unfaithful. God had cared for her while she was deeply engrossed in sin. God had sent judges to rescue Israel from the hands of her enemies and to help her live safely. Although God was her king, she had rejected him in the face of King Nahash's invasion. God had granted her request and given her a king. In order for Israel to understand how God felt about being rejected, Samuel asked God to give Israel a visual illustration. God sent thunder and rain during the wheat harvest (something that never happened), and Israel became terrified and begged for Samuel's intercession.

It is a horrible feeling when you realize that you have broken God's heart and severely disappointed Him. The thing you want most at a time like that is to beg His forgiveness and to make sure that you never do it again. Be faithful unto God and do not turn your back on Him. God loves you. Go forward, leave the past in the past, go and sin no more.

A Manager, Not a Visionary

After the battle with King Nahash, Saul sent the majority of his army home, retaining fewer than 1 percent of them in active duty. He retained three thousand troops, keeping two thousand in his charge and sending the other thousand with his son, Jonathan. His actions signified that he did not expect trouble. He kept enough men to respond to attacks but not enough to launch offensive assaults on Israel's enemies. He intended to put out fires, not create them. By nature he was not a fighter; he did not intend to conduct offensive maneuvers. While Saul prepared for a peaceful, uneventful reign, he did not take Jonathan into account.

Jonathan led an offensive assault and defeated a Philistine garrison at Geba. Early in Saul's administration, it became obvious that Jonathan was a better warrior than his father. Jonathan was an offensive warrior and liked to stir things up, while his father was a defensive warrior who tried not to make waves. Jonathan was like the conquering Joshua. He did not sit back hoping his enemies would not attack, trying to figure out how to live harmoniously with them, and wondering if "we could all just get along." Jonathan was a challenger. He challenged the authority of the Philistines and their right to oppress Israel. He refused to accept business as usual. The Philistines' continued occupation and domination was unacceptable.

There are two types of leaders: one type manages while the other initiates change. A manager is most effective when trying to maintain a smooth operation, while a visionary is most effective when trying to overhaul a system. Saul was a manager, and Jonathan was a visionary. Jonathan was also a man of faith. He believed the God of Israel was not subject to human limitations and could gain victory with many or a few.

There is nothing worse to a captor than captives in revolt. The Philistines were angry about the attack, because it sent a message that Israel would no longer be nice or submissive. The Israelites had challenged the Philistines' right to control them, resisted domination, and forcefully taken back their land and authority. Any challenge to the authority of an oppressor brings strong resistance and retaliation. Saul reassembled the entire Israelite army and met at Gilgal. Saul's major concern was not that a great victory had been won when the stronghold at Geba was destroyed. His only concern was that the Philistines had been stirred up against Israel, and Israel would have to fight, something he loathed to do.

The Philistines assembled an army that would strike fear in the bravest, stoutest hearts. They had three thousand chariots, six thousand horsemen, and innumerable warriors. The entire Israelite army had only two swords, because the Philistines had banned blacksmiths in Israel to prevent her from making weapons. From a human perspective, there was no way Israel could expect to beat those odds. The Israelite army was terrified at the sight of the Philistine army and scrambled for cover, hiding in caves, holes, tombs, and cisterns. Some crossed the Jordan and hid in the land of Gad or Gilead. Others defected, because they wanted to be on the winning side. The Israelite army had numbered more than three hundred thousand, but when a final count was made, only six hundred men remained in the Israelite camp, and those who stayed trembled with fear, completely scared stiff.

It is entirely possible that God was using the terrible odds as a weeding out process for the Israelite army. If they became fearful enough over what they saw to turn and run, they were not supposed to be there in the first place. Maybe God was trying to get rid of them because fearful people are more of a danger to themselves and others than the enemy would be. It did not bother God that many Israelite troops fled. It did not make God nervous that only 0.2 percent of the Israelite army remained. In fact, it was to His advantage to have only a fraction of the troops left, because then they could not say that they had procured victory by their own strength.

Forfeited Dynasty

Saul lost his dynasty at Gilgal. Samuel had instructed Saul to wait seven days for him at Gilgal. Upon his arrival, he would offer the burnt offerings and peace offerings to get battle instructions from the Lord. It was the first time Saul had faced a crisis while waiting on Samuel. If you have not learned to wait upon God, what will you do when you are under stress? In crisis mode, it is amazing how urgent everything becomes. By the seventh day, Samuel had not shown up, and Saul's army was rapidly thinning. The enemy had already gathered at Micmash, ready for battle; a strike was imminent. Something had to be done immediately; the situation was dire and urgent.

Saul decided to offer the burnt and peace offerings himself to ask for the Lord's help. Samuel showed up right after Saul finished offering them and demanded an explanation. Saul explained why he had done what he did. "You didn't show up when you said you would, my troops were rapidly thinning, and the battle is imminent. Under the circumstances, in the wake of the battle, I could not lead my men out without asking for God's guidance. I was obligated to offer the offerings." Saul gave a plausible explanation; his actions seemed justifiable considering the circumstances. What should he have done? Samuel rebuked him sternly.

> You have disobeyed the command of the Lord your God. Had you obeyed, the Lord would have established your kingdom over Israel forever. But now your dynasty must end, for the Lord has sought out a man after his own heart. The Lord has already chosen him to be king over his people, for you have not obeyed the Lord's command.
> *1 Samuel 13:13–14*

Saul had a good idea but not a God idea. It was right to consult the Lord, but it was wrong to offer the peace and burnt offerings. Saul alienated Israel's army from God because he overstepped his authority. Saul offered strange fire to God, because he was not ordained to offer sacrifices. He acted outside of his authority, because it was the job of the priest to offer sacrifices. God appointed a family, the Levites, and within that family he chose the descendants of Aaron for the priesthood and specifically taught them what to do. When they were careless with the things of God, death was the correction. When you fail to respect that office, you fail to respect God. In the words of Eli, the high priest, "When you sin against God, who mediates for you?"

Samuel was God's replacement, because the Levitical priesthood was an incorrigible liability to God. Samuel was Israel's priest, prophet, and judge. It was Samuel's responsibility to offer the sacrifices. Saul's offense was of the same magnitude as that of Aaron's sons, Nadab and Abihu, when they prepared an incense offering improperly (strange fire) and offered it to God, an offense God punished by death. The fact that God did not kill Saul on the spot was an act of His mercy.

Saul had a legitimate issue and a valid complaint on his hands. The enemy was about to strike and Samuel did not show up when he said he would. The fundamental issue for Saul was what to do when God does not show up on time. How do you respond to a crisis when God is not operating on your timetable? What do you do when you are in a desperate situation and you need God's help immediately but He does not provide immediate assistance? The pressure of a crisis creates an intensely irresistible force; its urgency demands a response. Do you take matters into your own hands and go it alone? Do you fight for the sake of fighting because you feel you have to do something? Or do you realize that the matter is too great for you to deal with alone and no matter what you do, you cannot solve the problem without God's help? Saul was facing a crisis where he was overpowered and outnumbered. If he did not respond, he faced death. If he tried to defend himself in his own power, he faced death. The only real hope he had of coming out alive was God. When you analyze the crisis and conclude that there is nothing you can do without God, it is best not to move until God goes with you. It is easy to say but hard to put into practice. It is even harder for some to take that kind of advice, because we are "take-charge" people, finding passivity repugnant. God does not advocate passivity. He strongly encourages guided activity.

Offering the sacrifices caused unintended consequences for Saul. Samuel rebuked Saul for his actions, because they caused him to lose his dynasty. Saul's mistakes were bad enough to blow it for his descendants, but they were not so bad as to cause him to lose his destiny, his throne. For some, losing a dynasty or a legacy is not that bad, because who cares about the upcoming generation! Let the next generation take care of their issues; what is that to us? Evidence of not caring about the legacy we leave to the next generation is as much a problem today as it was during Saul's time. We think we make decisions in a vacuum, failing to realize that the consequences of our decisions will reverberate in the next generation. Children are left to clean up the mess their parents created.

Saul's actions jeopardized the entire army. Samuel came and went without offering the peace and burnt offerings and without giving the instructions of the Lord. The result of Saul's actions was the loss of God's favor. Although it was not Saul's intention, his actions jeopardized his life and the lives of his troops. Saul and his army had to forego God's blessing and instructions. They had to rely on Saul's ingenuity alone, which meant they were in a worse state than before Saul offered the sacrifices. Before Saul made the offerings, God's reputation was on the line. If something went wrong, it went wrong while they waited upon the Lord, but after Saul offered the sacrifices, his rebellion released God from any obligation and tied His hands. Nothing stops God like rebellion.

Being unequipped in battle can mean the difference between life and death. It is even more costly, however, to go into battle without God's guidance. Saul and his troops were unequipped without God. The army could not function without God's blessing and direction, for in His direction there is protection and victory. Saul's actions also alienated the Israelite army from God. The last thing anyone who is facing a battle needs is to be alienated from God. Turning God, who is an ally, into an adversary while facing enemies is dangerous. The memory of the slaughter at Ebenezer, where Israel lost the Ark of the Lord and where the Lord assisted the Philistines in battle against Israel, was still fresh. The Israelite army had not forgotten the heavy losses they suffered when God was fighting against them. They understood the importance of God's favorable presence in battle.

Saul's motive for offering the sacrifices was to ask for the Lord's help, but there were implied motives as well. Saul wanted to assuage the fears of his troops. He was trying to encourage the soldiers and influence them to stay put. The army had already sized him up as a weak leader and knew that following him could cost them their lives. If Saul could convince them that the Lord was on their side, they would stay. The only thing that can make a man stay and fight when his leader is inept is God. Sometimes people use "thus saith the Lord" to promote their own agendas, subvert the will of God, and win the support of their followers. Saul's actions, viewed from a different angle, make it appear that he was trying to influence his men to do things without the Lord's support and instruction. It appeared that he had God's endorsement and guidance, but he did not. When a person does this, it is a recipe for disaster for his followers. Saul tried to influence the men to go into battle with the illusion of having God's direction, support, and protection, but illusions are not enough when you are facing a real enemy.

Some people are content with having the pretense or illusion of God's presence without His actual presence. Having the pretense of God's presence is bluffing. When you are called onto the carpet, you suffer heavy losses because you have no support. Some operate with a fairy-tale, make-believe notion of God. With that mind-set, a person can write God's script; God is a puppet. Such people call the shots and are accountable only to the rules and standards they set. When you are not facing difficulties, you can get along fine with a fairy-tale god. When life does not present problems and challenges that have no solutions, a fairy-tale God is sufficient. It is all right if you want to have an ephemeral notion of God, but I cannot afford to live with fairy tales. My life is at stake; my life is real, and I need a real God. When I am in a mortal battle (and every battle is a mortal one; otherwise it is not worth fighting), I want more than a nice thought that God is with me. I want Him right beside me, leading and protecting. If you are on the battlefront, you need more than a fairy tale to bring you through.

Dangerous Opportunity

Saul was driven by circumstance rather than waiting on God. Is a crisis a crisis because you say so? Who or what determines when a person is in crisis mode? During the time that Samuel conversed with Saul, and even when they parted, the Philistines did not manage to attack. Although the Philistines surrounded the Israelite troops, they did not attack; it was as if they were being held at bay. In fact, during that battle, they never attacked. The situation looked ominous, but there was still time to do things God's way; there was time to consult him. Saul overreacted and allowed his anxiety to make his circumstances appear worse than they were. The crisis was meant to test Saul's faith and his ability to wait patiently before the Lord, even though he was staring death in the face. It was meant to test his ability to rely on God, regardless of the circumstances. If God sees your situation (and He does) and does not flinch, why should you? It is not a crisis until God says it is (and what is a crisis to God?). God has perfect timing and knows exactly when to act, what to do, and how much you can stand.

There is a pregnant moment in every crisis when decisions determine fate. At that moment the outcome is sealed by what you do next. It is during that time when the pressure becomes so intense that you feel you have to make a decision. Although it is difficult, try to be rational. Take a few deep breaths and listen; the answer is there. In fact, there are two answers. There is the answer that you may consider the well-thought-out plan and there is another voice telling you to do the opposite of what you intended. As you lean closer to activating the well-thought-out plan, the other voice objects even more loudly. What do you do? Which action do you take? Be still and resist the urge to act impetuously. Listen, and then do what you are told. Drop your plan in exchange for His.

Some define a crisis as a dangerous opportunity, when the outcome largely depends on how well you have learned to rely upon God. It is during a crisis that you learn to wait on God. Learning to endure crises and knowing how to conduct yourself comes from experience. A series of crises will build tolerance to the pressure of dire circumstances. You may fail miserably during your first few crises, but eventually you will build up faith, because great faith develops as a result of a series of intensified crises. A crisis is the best and worst place to learn how to depend on God. A crisis is the last place you want to find yourself if you have not learned to trust God, but perhaps it is the only place you can learn to trust Him. What a dilemma.

The problem with Saul was that he had not had enough crises in his life to exercise his faith in God and build him up to a point of facing a major crisis. He crashed and burned when he could not afford to; the stakes were too high not to know how to trust God. When you are in a position of leadership facing a crisis, the stakes are always too high not to trust God. The consequences of failure are magnified, because they affect not only you but also those following you.

Saul was a pragmatist. Some would call him a realist who believed that victory in battle was a numbers game that depended on human ability and superior weaponry. The decline in the numbers of his troops decreased the chance of victory and elevated his fears. The Israelite army had only two swords, and Saul was petrified by his inexperience in battle. Because Saul lacked experience with God, he had yet to learn that it was better to rely on God's ability than on human ability or the size of an army. Saul thought, as some other leaders mistakenly do too, that he had been put into a leadership role because of some special ability he possessed and that he had been left to fend for himself, but God wanted to use him as a conduit of His power.

Many times in Israel's history, only a handful of soldiers had fought and defeated well-equipped and well-trained enemy soldiers because God was Israel's defender. It is better to have a hundred Gomer Pyles and God's direction than a thousand Arnold Schwarzeneggers and Rambos without God's direction. The troops'desertion did not bother God. Instead, that served His purpose, because He wanted to demonstrate that He could garner victory without a multitude of soldiers. He did not want to create a situation where Israel would conclude that she could defeat her enemies solely by her own strength. *I am Jehovah Nissi. I am your defender!*

Israel already believed that she did not need God. If she had been victorious in battle without God, she would have taken the credit and said, "See? This proves that Israel does not need you, God." What Israel was striving for when she asked for a king was a life without God. If she could do that, she would dismiss God.

Take-home message: Learning to endure crises and knowing how to conduct yourself in them comes from experiencing many crises and achieving victories in them through God's help.

9.

Faith Is an Action Word

Lack of faith is a signal that you do not trust God; it is offensive and insulting. "Without faith it is impossible to please God" (Hebrews 11:6, KJV). Faith is comprised of two components: belief and God-directed action. Therefore, without believing what God has said and acting on it by doing what He instructs you to do, it is impossible to please God. "Faith without works [God-directed action] is dead" (James 2:20, KJV). According to that verse, incomplete faith is when you believe what God has said but fail to perform the God-directed action. Actions are controlled by fundamental beliefs. In one word, God-directed action is obedience. Belief in God's word is the seed and obedience is the fruit of faith. Another form of incomplete faith is presumption; when you act on something that God has not given you information on and then expect Him to cover your agenda, it is indeed "the Leap of Faith." Incomplete faith is sticky, because you can have information from God but act out of season. In other words, you have God's word and you either act too late or you get ahead of God and act too early. Faith is believing God's words and doing what He tells you to do when He tells you to do it.

The Need for Faith in the Body of Christ

While there is a need for pragmatism in the body of Christ, there is a greater need for people who operate by faith. Pragmatism is needed to root out a lot of the harebrained schemes people have used to deceive gullible believers out of untold millions. However, pragmatism is the enemy of God when human perspective is used to determine God's ability. The greatest need, inside and outside of the church, is for people who operate by faith.

In this life, those who have achieved greatness have done so by faith in God. Human ability is severely limited and those who depend on it will have some achievements but nothing compared to what they could have achieved through faith in the power of God. The great landscape of life presents humanity with complex problems and challenges that have no solutions. God can address issues that are impossible to resolve by human ingenuity, but God needs yielded vessels to operate through. Those who aspire to greatness will realize their goal by faith in God.

Faith in God is needed on an individual level in the lives of leaders and followers. No one should go into the battle of life solely on the basis of human ability and ingenuity, especially when so much is at stake and human life is on the line. It is costly to go into the battle of life without faith in God. Why should a man waste his life by following another man who is not following God? Every man is just as limited as the next. Since following one man can lead a man to ruin, a man is better off by himself, for at least he is responsible for his own fate. People can fail by themselves; they do not need help.

People want someone who can lead them to victory, and only a leader who follows God and operates in faith can do that. God does not need ability—after all, He gives it. What He needs is obedience. He needs people who will lead His children by following Him. Overwhelming victory depends on one's ability to obey God. Leaders who operate in obedience to God have the single most powerful tool in their arsenal. People will be blessed under their leadership.

God's army follows a commander who follows God. That army is unstoppable, indefatigable, and mighty. However, when a leader lacks obedience, major battles should be avoided until issues are resolved. Leaders in rebellion against God do more harm than good, and all their followers suffer. The consequences of the errors of a leader are applied exponentially to those they serve.

Never Mind

Saul and the army of six hundred men were at a standstill without the direction of the Lord. They gathered around a pomegranate tree at Migron, completely at a loss about what to do next, waiting for something to happen. When Saul should have been leading the way in battle (for he had one of the only two swords in the entire land of Israel, and he was the commander of the army), he stood still. Standing still is good when you have the favor of the Lord and are waiting on His advice, but when you have destroyed that communication channel, the crisis is still there and you have to think something up.

Saul's sin caused him to lose God's instructions. All he had to rely on was his personal ability. He knew it was not equal to the occasion and that he did not have the things he believed would make him successful, such as training, experience, weaponry, and numerous troops. His inadequacies caused him to fear that he did not stand a chance against the formidable Philistines, which is why he was at a standstill. Saul could not inspire his troops to take a step toward the enemy because he lacked personal ability and, more important, God's direction. The soldiers would not follow a man who was not following God and was fearful. Why should the army follow a man who was not following God? Nobody wants to be led by a fearful man. Fear can cause you to lose a battle faster than inability. The attitude of the leader sets the tone for the rest. The men smelled fear, tasted it, and were overcome by it.

Meanwhile, Jonathan and his armor bearer secretly left the huddled group and went to the Philistines' camp at Geba. He had to leave the Israelite camp without his father's knowledge because he knew Saul would have forbidden it. The fearful and faithless try to quench those of faith. There is never a shortage of faithless naysayers. It was faith in God that caused Jonathan to challenge the Philistines. He was not relying on the advantage of a sword or on his human ability. Jonathan was a risk-taking warrior. A warrior may do a self-assessment, find inadequacies, and still go into battle because he relies on the Lord's power. Jonathan's statement of faith was this:

> Perhaps the Lord will help us, for nothing can hinder the Lord. He can win a battle whether he has many warriors or only a few!
> *1 Samuel 14:6*

As a result of his faith in God, Jonathan inspired the Israelite army to fight. His faith inspired the men to bravery and heroism, something Saul could not do because of his paralyzing fear. Israelites who had defected repented and rejoined the battle with Saul. Jonathan's faith even inspired those who were hiding in hills and caves to leave their secure places and fight valiantly.

What an awesome victory God gave Israel against her nemesis, the Philistines, that day! Faith is contagious; fear and unbelief are deadly. Jonathan and his armor bearer slaughtered twenty men, causing widespread panic in the Philistine army. All confusion broke loose in the Philistine camp, on the field, in their outposts, and among their raiding parties. The Philistines even began fighting against themselves. Then an earthquake shook the ground, further adding to their confusion and terror.

Saul's lookout men began to report strange activity in the Philistine camp. The Philistines were pulling back like a receding wave. Amid the confusion, Saul called for Ahijah, the priest, who was wearing the ephod, so he could inquire of the Lord. Ahijah had been there all along before Jonathan left the camp and while they had respite, but Saul did not use that time to inquire of the Lord. He waited until the situation forced him to ask but then did not wait for a response. It is hard to pray when you are in a crisis. As in any crisis, it is difficult to calm your nerves enough to talk and then listen to God. All your energy and attention are focused on the problem. In your mind's eye, all you can see is the problem looming before you and your lack of solutions. You try to pray, but you just cannot take your mind off the problem long enough to have a conversation with God. Sometimes you are just speechless. It is hard to focus on God; you just cannot calm down. Even when God gives an answer, you cannot hear it.

> But while Saul was talking to the priest, the shouting and confusion in the Philistine camp grew louder and louder. So Saul said to Ahijah, "Never mind; let's get going!" *1 Samuel 14:19*

Although it did not start out that way, Saul began to develop an attitude that disregarded God. God's opinion and advice were not important enough to seek and wait for. Saul was driven by circumstance, not by the Lord's advice. He allowed the heat of the moment to force him to make hasty decisions born out of desperation, and the crisis began to snowball because of his hastiness, inexperience in crises, and lack of divine direction.

Saul issued a counterproductive command that hampered the success of his troops in battle and caused them to sin. Saul made them take an oath not to eat that day before evening, until he had had vengeance upon his enemies. Anyone who ate would be put to death. The soldiers were weak and dizzy from hunger, exhausted and fatigued from exertion, so they could not operate at their full potential on the battlefield. Still, the soldiers somehow persevered, in spite of their condition. Jonathan, unaware of his father's command, ate some honey he had found. One of the soldiers told Jonathan about the oath after he ate the honey.

It makes no sense to instruct grown men in battle not to eat. Where do they get the strength to fight? Saul's command caused the men to sin. When evening came, the men jumped on the battle plunder like a pack of ravenous lions, eating meat without draining the blood. Although Saul built an altar so the men could drain the animals' blood, that command demonstrated how his leadership hampered success.

Saul wanted to keep the momentum going and to continue to pursue the enemy all night. Consulting God was not a forethought, nor was it an afterthought. In the beginning of Saul's reign, traces of an independent, self-reliant attitude had emerged. When Saul finally consulted the Lord, at the insistence of the priest, the Lord would not answer because there was sin in the Israelite camp. On the one hand, they had been victorious because they had defeated the Philistines, but on the other hand, they were in jeopardy because of the Lord's silence. You can silence your enemies and you can silence the roar of this world, but God's silence is deadly. If He does not speak, no one can live. Everything that God created is dependent upon His word.

> But the priest said, "Let's ask God first." So Saul asked God, "Should we go after the Philistines? Will you help us defeat them?" But God made no reply that day. *1 Samuel 14:36–37*

But God did not answer—silence. Experience had taught them that God's silence meant there was unresolved sin. Saul investigated, but no one would tell him what the problem was. He cast lots to identify the offending party. Saul passionately vowed to kill the offender, even (or especially) if it was his own son, Jonathan.

What a vehement reaction toward sin—the sin of others, that is. Saul was willing to go to any length to address the sin because it was not *his* sin. It is easy to take a hard-nosed stance toward the sins of others. We take a hard, unmerciful stance toward other people's sins, then cry for mercy for our own. We browbeat others for their faults but take a passive, excusing stance toward our own. How quickly we condemn others instead of seeking restoration!

Saul wrote Jonathan's death sentence when casting lots revealed Jonathan as the offender. Jonathan confessed that he had eaten honey. Holding a person accountable for a command he was not aware of and for a vow he did not make seems unfair, but God considered Jonathan's action a sin. Saul was ready to kill Jonathan, but the men prevented him from killing their hero.

There was another reason that Saul was so enthusiastic about killing Jonathan. He had just lost his dynasty and needed someone to lash out at, and Jonathan was the one responsible for putting him in the predicament that had led to his loss in the first place. However, Jonathan bested his father twice. Saul's failure to exercise leadership had properly cost him his dynasty. Jonathan was a visionary, but in Saul's eyes he was a troublemaker and a loose cannon. Although he was responsible for accomplishing great victories for Israel, he forced Saul, who was a manager, into battles he would rather have avoided. A natural antagonism exists between visionaries and managers, but Jonathan should have submitted to his father's authority, because Saul held the highest position in the land. Since Jonathan was his son, Saul knew Jonathan's talents and temperament and could have harnessed Jonathan's ability to accomplish great victories without suffering personal losses.

It is imperative to have a manager and a visionary working *together* to create successful outcomes. Visionary leaders make poor managers, so having a manager at the helm with a visionary is a perfect arrangement. Managers naturally resist visionaries because it is their nature to maintain rather than to rearrange. However, having a manager at the helm may sometimes hinder progress when a manager has the power and authority to suppress a visionary. In such cases, it is better to have a visionary at the helm with a manager under their authority so the manager can help regain stability after the tumultuous changes the visionary has created. Good leadership requires the skills of both visionaries to create change and managers to reestablish stability to achieve victories.

Saul had the authority to make an oath that if violated would require the life of the offender. His oaths were so powerful that God honored them; God considered it a sin to disobey the king's oath. God supported Saul's proclamation, even though it was counterproductive. Why didn't Saul use God's power to command his army? God had his back, but Saul did not feel His support; all he felt was the heat of his army. Jonathan unknowingly violated Saul's command, and although it seems unfair, he was bound to the oath even though he was unaware of it. By rights, Jonathan should have been slain that day. The men prevailed against Saul in the deadlock over the issue, and it set a significant precedent.

There is a difference between authority and power. Authority is the right to make decisions and issue directives. Power is the ability to get things done and to enforce directives using rewards and penalties. Early in the reign of a new leader, an incident always arises that is a defining moment for the leader. It is a critical moment, because it identifies where the true power rests and sets the tone for the effectiveness of his leadership. If the leader issues a directive and does not enforce it because people overrule him, it means the leader has authority but lacks power. Therefore, his ability to exercise power erodes. It sets the tone for the rest of the leader's reign because the people know they can prevail against the leader in a deadlock. When the leader issues directives in the future that the people do not agree with, they will not obey. They know how to oppose the leader, they know that they can, and they will. Saul relinquished his power that day, even though he had God's support, when he failed to slay Jonathan, and it would come back to haunt him in the future and cost him dearly.

Fear of Men

Who could fault Saul for offering the burnt offerings? Anybody could have made that mistake. He was just trying to do the right thing. He was in a desperate situation—Samuel had not arrived when he said he would, and the

Philistines were advancing. Saul did not intentionally overstep his authority just to disrespect God, and God was merciful to Saul for that very reason, or perhaps God was merciful because of His love for the people of Israel. God had just given Israel a king, and the people would not have received it well if He had snuffed out Saul's life so soon after ordaining him king. Up to this point, Saul had demonstrated the natural fear that any human would have shown under the circumstances. A certain amount of fear is healthy and preserving. A careful examination of Saul, however, also shows that his fear was not just of death but also of men.

Even while leaders are enjoying success from a public standpoint, they can suffer great personal loss, depending on their mistakes. Mistakes and bumps in the road are to be expected at the beginning of one's leadership. While Saul lost his dynasty and a significant power struggle with the soldiers at Gilgal, what the nation saw was a man who had ousted the Philistines. Saul also fought against Zobah, Moab, Ammon, Edom, and Amalek. He accomplished great deeds, conquering those who had plundered Israel. Saul was a hero. The Israelites expected him to defend them against their enemies, and he did that. He enjoyed a measure of success during his reign. He was successful in battle because of the Spirit of the Lord. Saul was a success from a public standpoint, but he was a dismal failure from God's standpoint. While he won on the battlefield, he lost favor with God and suffered personal loss because he failed to obey God during key battles.

God had an account to settle with the Amalekites because they had opposed Israel when the Israelites came out of Egypt. Fewer than sixty days had passed when Israel arrived at Rephidim. During that time, she had wandered in the desert, questioning God's ability to provide for her. By the time Israel reached Rephidim, God had begun providing a daily regimen of manna and quail. God provided food that the desert would not yield. At Rephidim, Israel was suffering from thirst. Moses struck a rock at Mount Sinai by God's instruction and in the Lord's presence, and water gushed forth, quenching Israel's thirst. In addition to suffering from the anxiety that scarce and uncertain provisions created, Israel was emotionally exhausted. She was weary from years of oppression and in no condition to fight enemies. God could have led Israel from Egypt straight into Canaan, but He did not, because He knew Israel would encounter enemies and would have to fight. However, she was in no condition to fight, and the slightest opposition would have caused her to return to Egypt. God led Israel in a roundabout way because she needed time to heal, and what she needed most was ministry. God was trying to avoid battles to keep Israel from becoming discouraged. Any time anything went wrong, Israel questioned the Lord's intentions. That is why God was furious when the Amalekites, who were located along the Egyptian border, decided to launch an unprovoked attack while He was doing all He could to prevent Israel from going into battle.

No one seems to mind when you are in bondage; they are comfortable with your pain, tragedy, and hopelessness. Although they may not express it, they find your bondage agreeable, and some may even benefit from it. No one feels threatened by a person who is down and out. It is when you make a move to improve your condition that opposition arises and the truth comes out that people want to hold you back. While it may be true that you find out who your true friends are when you are down and out, you can also identify your fake friends when you are up and coming. When you are trying to reach a new level, people from whom you never would have expected such behavior begin to show their true colors and often present the greatest opposition, hoping to stop you from reaching your promise, your goals, and your freedom.

Overcoming oppression is not easy, because one must exert a force greater than the thing that dominates them. The last thing a person in that situation needs is added opposition. The last thing a person needs is to have to expend limited energy resources fighting unexpected forces. Only a coward would attack his enemies while they are recuperating because he figures that is the only chance he has to gain victory.

The Amalekites seized the opportunity to attack Israel while she was resting to prevent her from leaving slavery and to block her from entering the Promised Land and a life of blessings. The Amalekites fought Israel from sunup to sunset. But Israel suppressed the opposition because Moses held up his staff, at the Lord's direction, while Hur and Aaron upheld his arms. If you cannot help, do not block a person from their destiny and augment their misery. God thought that the Amalekites' attack was ugly, tactless, and unprovoked.

> Then the LORD instructed Moses, "Write this down as a permanent record, and announce it to Joshua: I will blot out every trace of Amalek from under heaven." *Exodus 17:14*

Moses exclaimed, "Jehovah Nissi the Lord, my banner, my defense!"

After Israel entered the Promised Land, the day finally came when the Lord decided to call the Amalekites to task. The forty years in the wilderness, the leadership of Joshua, and the period of the judges (more than four hundred years) had passed before the Lord decided to fulfill His word regarding the Amalekites. (God has got your day of blessing or the day he plans to judge your enemies scheduled on His calendar. He has not forgotten.) The Lord scheduled the day on His calendar and circled it in red, since it was important to Him. He anticipated the day of fulfillment, and although the promise had been long forgotten by others, God did not forget. The day of reckoning finally came, and He assigned Saul to such an awesome assignment.

God instructed Saul to completely destroy the entire Amalekite nation—its people and livestock. *Spare nothing!* Ordinarily, the spoils of war and the plunder belonged to the king and the soldiers. After a town was defeated, the king and his soldiers paraded the defeated king through the towns of his own country. Saul executed an excellent assault on the Amalekites by God's power. He mobilized the soldiers and killed all the Amalekite people and their animals as instructed—but with a few exceptions. Judging by these exceptions, Saul either failed to communicate God's commands or the men overruled Saul. The Amalekite situation was supposed to be different; the Lord wanted to settle a personal score. The Lord wanted to avenge Israel, to redress a wrong, and to fulfill His promise, and nothing short of the complete annihilation of the Amalekites would satisfy Him.

> Saul and his men spared Agag's life and kept the best of the sheep and cattle, the fat calves and lambs—everything, in fact, that appealed to them. They destroyed only what was worthless or of poor quality. *1 Samuel 15:9*

Having waited a long time to fulfill His word, God must have felt tremendous betrayal when Saul botched His plans. It was a bitter moment for God, and He was rightfully furious when Saul disobeyed His commands concerning the Amalekites. Saul had failed to show God reverence. Saul's disobedience showed God that Saul's priorities were misaligned. The Spirit of the Lord can turn a weak man into a great warrior and an ordinary man into a thing of beauty, but the Spirit of the Lord will not override a man's will. The Spirit of the Lord will not force loyalty from a disloyal man, because loyalty is a personal decision.

Lost Destiny

God was livid, because He was trying to settle an account that was long overdue and Saul had foiled His plans. God told Samuel what Saul had done and that He rejected Saul as king, but Samuel cried out all night for Saul when God told him the news. The next day, Saul was congratulating himself over his "success" when Samuel confronted him. Saul jubilantly claimed that he had executed God's command perfectly. Samuel asked, "Then why do I hear bleating sheep and lowing cattle?"

Saul tried to defend the actions of his men. He claimed that the men had spared the best of the sheep and cattle to sacrifice to God. But they had had no such intention, for if they had, they would have followed God's commands and automatically sacrificed to the Lord. Doing what God says is a sacrifice in and of itself. Nothing extra needs to be done if God's commands are followed perfectly.

The lack of compliance with God's instructions sent a message that having the plunder was preferable to pleasing God. It showed their belief that God was not worthy of receiving the best. "You can have the scraps, but You are not worthy of the choice goods; we will not let that go to waste. We deserve to enjoy this goodness more than You. We consider this stuff more valuable and important than You and Your need for justice."

> But Samuel replied, "What is more pleasing to the LORD: your burnt offerings and sacrifices or your obedience to his voice? Obedience is far better than sacrifice. Listening to him is better than offering the fat of rams. Rebellion is as bad as the sin of witchcraft, and stubbornness is as bad as worshiping idols." *1 Samuel 15:22–23*

Obedience is better than sacrifice. Listening to God is better than offering the fat of rams. Rebellion is witchcraft. Stubbornness is idolatry. The greatest thing a person can give God is obedience. Listening to God and doing what He says is the best gift a person can give. If you were a pauper with nothing to give the Lord except obedience, God would consider your obedience to His voice more valuable than a million dollars given to Him by a person who did their own thing. Samuel informed Saul that since he had rejected God and disobeyed what God told him to do, God had rejected him as king.

Every time Samuel confronted Saul about his wrongdoings, Saul always made excuses for his actions. It is the epitome of lack of humility when a person insists there was no wrongdoing, even when the facts suggest otherwise. During the battle with the Philistines, Saul made excuses as to why he disobeyed God and offered the sacrifices. When Samuel confronted Saul about the Amalekites, Saul insisted that he had done what he was supposed to do. He lied for the men, saying they intended to sacrifice the animals they kept. People generally avoid taking responsibility for their actions, and they blame others for their mistakes. Why would anybody take the fall for someone else's mistakes? What in the world would cause a person to defend and make excuses for people who disobeyed their orders when it is not in their best interest to do so?

After Samuel had confronted Saul about his terrible act of disloyalty, he got to the heart of the matter. Samuel addressed Saul's insecurity and lack of self-confidence as the root of the problem. The incident highlighted Saul's fear of men, his fear of social disapproval, and his succumbing to social pressure. After Saul finished lying about it, he admitted that he had disobeyed God's command because he was afraid of the men and did what they demanded. Saul finally admitted that the men pressured him to sin against God. Disloyalty to God, whom he could not see, did not seem as bad as suffering the retribution of the men, whom he could see. He failed to exercise the authority and power God gave him to rule the soldiers. Even at that point in Saul's reign, when he had won so many victories by God's Spirit, he still had not learned to trust God and to lean on God's support to control the soldiers. His insecurities, lack of confidence, and failure to trust God were problems that led to dire consequences.

> Although you may think little of yourself, are you not the leader of the tribes of Israel? The Lord has anointed you king of Israel. And the Lord sent you on a mission and told you, "Go and completely destroy the sinners, the Amalekites, until they are all dead."
> *1 Samuel 15:17–18*

I appointed you king and sent you on assignment with specific instructions. It was your responsibility to see that those instructions were followed properly. I hold you accountable for the people's sin; it was your responsibility to make sure that the men obeyed. Why did you let them run over you? Who is leading whom? Who is king, after all?

Saul would have obeyed the Lord had it not been for the influence of his men. Having prevailed over Saul in the past bolstered the army to overrule him again. Saul could not obey God because his obedience depended upon his ability to control his men, and he had lost that ability when he failed to win the power struggle over Jonathan during the battle with the Philistines. Failure to exercise power in the past had sealed his fate and cost him his reign. He was not fit to be king. The Lord was sorry He had made Saul king.

Saul had a weak personality and was not a leader in the truest sense, because he was easily influenced by others; he was a people pleaser. While you should surround yourself with wise men of experience and men with their finger on the pulse of God, you should not allow anyone to persuade you to go against God's commands. Men did not appoint Saul; therefore, it was not

Saul's responsibility to yield to the masses or to be governed by public opinion. It was not an election; it was an appointment by the God of the universe. Saul's focus should have been on pleasing God, because pleasing the One who had appointed him would also have benefited the people.

Saul's primary goal, however, was to please the people. If he could please the people and please God too, that would be a bonus! Somehow he got his wires crossed; he believed that he could secure his throne by giving the people what they wanted. "I am king and God is my subject" was his modus operandi. Saul knew right from wrong; he knew what God required, but when push came to shove, it was better to shove God out of the way and satisfy the people than to be loyal to God and lose the support of the people. The people wanted somebody they could manipulate into doing what they wanted, and they had found such a man in Saul.

A leader has to endure the criticism, rejection, and ridicule that come from taking unpopular stands. A leader must be accustomed to standing alone. You may not get invited to dinner or to the country club for golf. Your name may be run through the mud and you may be the butt of jokes, but that comes with the territory. You cannot please everybody, and someone will always feel that you should have done things differently. A leader who is appointed by God should strive to stand before God and hear "Well done, my good and faithful servant" because you pleased God, rather than, "Depart from me, you worker of iniquity; you did things that were not authorized" because you pleased men or yourself.

It was not Saul's inability that cost him the throne, because God overcame that. It was his disobedience and disloyalty to God. Saul lost his dynasty when he offered the burnt and the peace offerings at Gilgal, and God rejected him as king of Israel as a result of his disobedience and disloyalty in the battle with the Amalekites. Saul's relationship with God deteriorated over time through a series of disloyal and disobedient actions. God concluded that choosing Saul as king was a big mistake. The Amalekite situation was the last straw. *He constantly goes against me.*

One thing that was absent in Saul was true repentance and godly sorrow. He made costly mistakes and committed disloyal acts, yet he did not try to correct his behavior so he would not repeat the errors. He was flippant about his sins, acting as if they were so minor that admitting to them and offering a halfhearted request for forgiveness were enough to correct the situation. Saul did not grasp the fact that the Amalekite battle was not an ordinary one. He knew God had sent him to wipe out the Amalekites for their cruelty toward Israel, but he did not understand the battle's significance to God. The gravity of his sins did not seem to sink in. There was no fasting and mourning over his sins, and he never tried to set things right. He never sat before the Lord to mend the rift between them. He allowed his sins to accumulate unresolved, and his relationship with the Lord deteriorated to a point of no return. He lacked humility. He knew he was wrong but never took steps to correct the situation, even after he had admitted he was wrong.

Take-home message: Faith is believing God and doing what He says when He says to do it.

10.

Appearances, Appearances

After a victorious battle, the king, army commanders, family leaders, officials, priests, and people of Israel would celebrate the victory by worshiping the Lord. It was the proper response to give praise and honor to the One who had given the victory. Even though Saul lost his destiny, Israel did gain a great victory and could celebrate having one less enemy.

After Samuel told Saul that God had rejected him as king, Saul's only concern was maintaining the appearance that all was well before the people. Appearances were more important to Saul than reality. So he begged, whimpered, and pleaded with Samuel to forgive him of his sin and to go with him to worship the Lord. The only thing that made the people respect Saul was their belief that he was God's chosen. If Samuel, the man of God, refused to go with him, the people would know that God had rejected him, and they would reject Saul too. He would lose credibility, respect, and honor, and that loss was far more important to Saul than losing God's favor. Fame is an addictive beast for some; once tasted, nothing less will satisfy—that is, if you are the type of person, like Saul, who feeds off the honor and recognition of men.

People Pleaser or God Pleaser?

Saul was a superficial man who did only the things that would increase his popularity in the polls. His objective was to win acceptance by saying and doing the right things. He was out to please the people, even if it meant disobeying and snubbing God. He lacked substance and personal ability but his desire to succeed was strong, so he became a people pleaser who perfected the art of illusion. What he lacked in substance and ability he tried to make up for through social pleasantness. "Don't offend anybody, don't step on anybody's toes, don't make waves, and all will go well." This kind of thinking works in some situations, but it did not go over well with God.

Saul settled for the illusion that he had a good rapport with God because he was a people pleaser more than a God pleaser. He did not care about what was; he only cared about how it appeared to be. Saul wanted it to appear as if he respected God and as if God was still his confidant, because it was the politically correct thing to do. But in the truest sense, he did not care for God. In reality, he was just like the majority of the people who wanted nothing to do with God. "We want to enjoy the things You give, we want the blessings and protection You provide, but we don't want You. What we don't want is the high standards that you require us to live by." The laissez-faire attitude that said "Leave us alone and let us govern ourselves independently" was as much a part of Saul's psyche, his soul fabric, as it was of his contemporaries'.

Samuel refused to go to worship with Saul, for he also understood that to do so would be a public endorsement, hinting that God still accepted Saul as king. Saul could not afford to have Samuel leave him high and dry, so when Samuel turned to leave, Saul grabbed him in an effort to hold him back and force him to do his bidding, and in the process he tore Samuel's robe.

> And Samuel said to him, "See? The Lord has torn the kingdom of Israel from you today and has given it to someone else—one who is better than you." Then Saul pleaded again, "I know I have sinned. But please, at least honor me before the leaders and before my people by going with me to worship the Lord your God."
> *1 Samuel 15:28, 30*

Saul's actions confirmed that God had torn the kingdom away from him and given it to another. God's decision was immutable. Although Saul knew it, he pleaded with Samuel until he finally persuaded Samuel to go with him to worship God. Saul was in a desperate fight for his throne—his destiny. If the people did not know that he had lost his throne, then he had not. He wanted to maintain his position as king, but getting the crown and keeping the crown were two different things.

To be rejected from any leadership position is not as bad as being rejected from entering the kingdom of heaven and living with God for eternity. The best thing to do is just to resign quietly and be thankful for what you have *not* lost. Unfortunately, that is easier said than done. For once you have tasted power, enjoyed privilege, and received respect and honor from men, power is harder to relinquish.

Some will do anything, even kill, to maintain their position. Maintaining his position as king was a matter of self-preservation for Saul, for how can you live after your destiny is gone? Why do you breathe and what is the glory of living when you have no future? Samuel finally relented and went to worship God with Saul out of self-preservation, for if he had continued to refuse, Saul would have killed him.

If Saul had demonstrated a little humility, it could have influenced God to relent. If Saul had killed King Agag instead of Samuel, it would have been a step in the right direction. If Saul had demanded that the soldiers gather all the animals and everything else they had taken from the Amalekites and destroy it all, it would have been a sign of repentance. If Saul had publicly relinquished his throne without a struggle, it would have demonstrated that God's will was more important to him. If Saul had done those things, it would have shown that he cherished God more than his position. However, Saul did none of those things, choosing instead to manhandle the man of God and force him to publicly endorse Saul against his will. Saul's actions after being told that he had been deposed demonstrated his true nature and false humility, and that his "repentance" had been just a matter of convenience. His behavior showed that he was not sorry for what he had done, would not correct anything, and would try to forcibly oppose God's will. Any man who is more interested in position than in pleasing God is a dangerous liability to God's cause.

Samuel and Saul worshiped together for the last time that day. Then they went their separate ways, Samuel to Ramah and Saul to Gilgal, and their paths never crossed again on this Earth. Samuel mourned constantly for Saul because God had rejected him as king.

There have been political leaders on this Earth who have worn the cloak of Christianity while their behavior, edicts, and administrations have been glaringly anti-God. According to them, there is a difference between private convictions and public behavior. Yet people of God have flocked to these leaders, publicly endorsing them. This sends a wrong signal, making the public believe that God supports men who are against Him. It is one thing to minister to a repentant man to bring restoration, but it is something entirely different to placate men who redefine sin instead of repenting and whose only regret is that they were caught. It is just a publicity stunt; they are just using you, for if you tell them they have sinned and need to repent, no one will ever know your name. God will hold you accountable for misrepresenting His stand against them. You are a watchman and are required to warn the wicked of their sins. If you do not, the wicked will still die in their sins, but their blood will be on your hands. Are the whispers of publicity and meeting a famous person so important that you would rather suffer God's retribution? You pay a far greater price, my friend.

Since things turned out so badly, why did God, who is omniscient, choose Saul? In all His foreknowledge, could He not have known that Saul was a bad choice? Could He not have foreseen that Saul would turn out to be a sore disappointment? The answer lies in the fact that God often picks the most unlikely people to use as His instruments. They often have some type of deficiency from a human standpoint and are often weak. God does this because He can exhibit His power unimpeded through them and operate without interference through them.

For example, when a person who normally cannot put a complete sentence together delivers a speech that rivals the greatest orators of our time, you know that person is operating from a source of supernatural power, either from God or the devil. God is the greatest optimist ever, because He knows that if a weak person will rely on His guidance and obey Him, He can make them the envy of the strong. He can accomplish great feats through a person riddled with deficiencies, inadequacies, and weaknesses. All He needs is cooperation. He needs a yielded vessel, and becoming a yielded vessel is an act of the will. It all comes back to obedience. It would have been possible for God to work through Saul if Saul had, by an act of his will, obeyed God.

There is so much safety in obedience, in being under God's authority, and in doing what God says that it seems laughable that you would want to do anything else. If something goes wrong because of obeying God (and it will not), it is not your responsibility to fix it. Being under God's authority is so liberating that people should be knocking each other over to have that situation in their lives. The sad truth, however, is that few people develop the ability to trust God emphatically and to obey Him without question, because humanity is cursed with the belief that they can successfully live independently of God.

Most people who have achieved greatness did it by their obedience to and trust in God. Successful leaders operate under the authority of God and in obedience to Him. God never expected Saul, or any other leader He has chosen, to lead his people by human ingenuity. The epitome of self-destructive pride is when you realize you are deficient yet refuse to listen to sound wisdom and continue to operate in self-reliance. The wisest thing you can do is to realize that the task set before you is beyond your ability to accomplish and then to rely on God's help.

Saul's leadership backfired because he was cursed with the sin of disobedience and rebellion. Saul failed because he did not develop a dependence upon God. God needed a trained man at the helm. It is too late to teach obedience and trust when the situation demands that they already be in place.

Ichabod

When we view Saul as insecure and fearful, we can better understand—though not condone—his behavior. His timidity was evident when he was first identified as Israel's king. Fear inspired him to offer the burnt and peace offerings when Samuel showed up late to Gilgal. Saul could not inspire his men because he was fearful, and it was fear that caused him to succumb to the pressure of his men during the battle with the Amalekites. Fear was the overriding principle that influenced most of Saul's actions, even though the Spirit of the Lord could have superseded all his fears if Saul had allowed Him to do so.

The Spirit of the Lord is a compensating, equalizing force in a person's life. The Spirit of the Lord will cause a man to accomplish far more than he ever dreamed possible by himself. God helps human beings accomplish tasks that they alone could not do. He compensates for weaknesses and flaws and creates wholeness. The Spirit of the Lord will make you feel like Superman, only better. King David gives us a feel for what it is like to have the Spirit of the Lord upon you.

> For by thee I have run through a troop; and by my God have I leaped over a wall. For who is God save the Lord? or who is a rock save our God? It is God that girded me with strength, and maketh my way perfect. He maketh my feet like hinds' feet, and setteth me upon my high places. He teacheth my hands to war, so that a bow of steel is broken by mine arms. Thou hast also given me the shield of thy salvation: and thy right hand hath holden me up, and thy gentleness hath made me great. Thou hast enlarged my steps under me, that my feet did not slip. I have pursued mine enemies, and overtaken them: neither did I turn again till they were consumed. I have wounded them that they were not able to rise: they are fallen under my feet. For thou hast girded me with strength unto the battle: thou hast subdued under me those that rose up against me. *Psalm 18:29, 31–39, KJV*

There is protection in the Spirit of the Lord. He makes you feel pumped up and positive. He keeps a smile on your face, and makes you see even the worst situations only as opportunities. You are filled with an indomitable spirit and a "can do" attitude. Some people grow weary of your enthusiasm.

When God resides in a person, He completes them, but He adds so much more. Oftentimes people look to others to complete them, when God brings the ultimate completeness to a person's life. A person who has God's resident presence enjoys His security and protection. God's sweet presence comforts a person with warmth, joy, love, and indescribable peace. God's presence guides and directs a person to paths of blessing. God's presence assures a person, causing them to feel they belong. Once a person has God's resident presence and enjoys the fullness He brings, their resounding cry is, "More!"

Saul lost his dynasty at Gilgal. He lost his throne, his destiny, during the battle of the Amalekites, but he lost far more than that: he lost God. God withdrew His Spirit from Saul, and it was God that had made him great. God's Spirit had enabled Saul to win battles. God removed His glory and favor from Saul. If being anointed could not hide Saul's fears and insecurities and if the anointing was not a buoying force for him, imagine how terrifying it was when God withdrew and divorced His Spirit. When Saul lost God, he became a wreck.

God was the best thing Saul had going, so when God left, Saul again became an ordinary man with extraordinary insecurities. Once you have lived with the Spirit of the Lord and lose Him, life is terrifying, because your life unravels and you are left with all your deficiencies. You become unsure of everything you do, paralyzed because you do not know which way to turn. It becomes especially frightening when you have relied on Him so long that you do not know what it is to make a decision without Him, so you become indecisive. Your behavior becomes erratic, irrational, hostile, agitated, belligerent, and completely unbearable.

The absolutely worst thing that can happen to a person is to lose God's Spirit. It is better never to have experienced His resident presence in your life than to have Him and then lose Him. A terrible sense of agony overtakes you. If you have been accustomed to God's resident presence, the slightest distance from Him is enough to cause you considerable stress. If God leaves, He leaves you feeling vulnerable, scared, and naked. You lose your identity because apart from Him, you are nothing. (May God bless you with His sweet precious Spirit and may you never lose Him.)

After God's departure, He sent a tormenting spirit that filled Saul with depression and fear and turned him into a madman, a raving lunatic. The only thing that gave him peace was a skilled harp musician named David, son of Jesse, whose worship attracted God so that God caused the tormenting spirit to leave Saul for periods. Praise is warfare, and demons know it. Any time you find a person resisting praise and worship, saying, "It doesn't take all that," you know that person is bound, because it *does* take all that and more.

Saul had received a triple blow: God took His Spirit away from him; his normal fears and insecurities were exposed; and to make matters worse, God sent a tormenting spirit in His stead. Saul had become a paranoid, terrified, groveling, raving lunatic. Although God sent the tormenting spirit that filled Saul with depression and fear, He really did not need to do that, because the lack of His presence in Saul's life had a worse effect.

God Found a Man Exercised in Faith and After His Own Heart

God sent Samuel to anoint the new king He had chosen. Samuel was afraid to go, because if Saul had found out he would have killed Samuel. Samuel went to Bethlehem under the guise of making a sacrifice. He instructed the town's leaders to purify themselves and invited the family of Jesse to the sacrifice. Samuel took one look at Eliab and thought surely he would be the Lord's choice, but God had changed His selection criteria. God rejected all of Jesse's sons who were present at the sacrifice. He would no longer choose a man based on his physical appearance but would choose according to the content of a man's character, and He chose Jesse's youngest son, David. Samuel anointed him with olive oil, and the Spirit of the Lord came upon David.

During the battle at Elah, Saul and the Israelites met Goliath, the champion of the Philistines. A standoff occurred between the Philistines, who stationed themselves at Socoh, and Saul, who gathered the Israelite army near the valley of Elah. The two armies faced each other on opposite hills with the valley between them, and Goliath offered a remedy for the standoff. Only one man would represent each country in a hand-to-hand combat. The losing country would become the slaves of the winner. Goliath, their champion, issued that challenge, but none of the Israelites wanted to accept.

Before the Israelites left for the battlefront, they had a pep rally, shouting battle cries. The Israelites get an A for effort for trying to encourage themselves. But as soon as they encountered Goliath, they lost all their nerve and ran away in fright. Twice a day for forty days, Goliath taunted the Israelite army, and for forty days they ran away when they saw him, with Saul leading the pack. Saul had lost his dynasty, had been rejected as king, and had been stripped of the Spirit of the Lord God Almighty. Having been stripped of God's Spirit, he was only an ordinary man with mammoth fears.

This battle with the Philistines was the first time Saul had faced the Philistines without the Spirit of God. Even when he had God's Spirit, he would avoid the Philistines. Because he was immobilized with fear, he could not inspire his troops to fight. Leaders who radiate confidence inspire their men to greatness and heroism, while those who exude fear cripple their men and inspire cowardice. Even the rewards Saul offered, exempting the whole family from taxes and giving one of his daughters as a wife, were not enough to stir the soldiers into action. What good were Saul's gifts to a dead man? Really, no one minds dying for what they believe in (for God, their country, and ultimately the freedom of their family) but no one wants to die as a result of the incompetence of their leader, for then they will have died in vain. People want to be led by a leader who is courageous and has a winning spirit. Saul's men had properly sized him up, knowing it would cost them their lives to follow him.

Things changed when Jesse sent his son David to the battlefield to check on his brothers. David arrived at the Israelite camp just in time for action; the army was preparing to leave for the battlefront. They sang songs of victory and shouted about overcoming; battle cries rang out, and the ground shook. The mighty marching army strutted out onto the battlefield prepared to do business, assured of victory. David's adrenaline was pumping; he could hardly contain himself over the chance to witness God's army in action. The Israelite army lined up on the battlefield and faced the Philistines. Then Goliath came forth, ranted and raved against Israel, defied her God, and issued the same challenge he had issued twice a day for forty days. To David's shock, amazement, and horror, the valiant Israelite army tucked tail and ran away in fright. He was embarrassed to see that the Israelite army, which was assured of victory because the God of the Universe was on its side, would allow a heathen to cow and abuse them when before their arrival on the battlefront they had boasted about victory and bragged about tearing their enemy down. How could the Israelite army have so much power yet fail to avail themselves of it? There can be no victory without a fight.

> David talked to some others standing there to verify the report. "What will a man get for killing this Philistine and putting an end to his abuse of Israel? . . . Who is this pagan Philistine anyway, that he is allowed to defy the armies of the living God?" *1 Samuel 17:26*

David watched the standoff and was flabbergasted that the Israelite army would endure such defiance and insolence toward the God of Israel. He was not indoctrinated by Saul's vision, which was inspired by fear and served to immobilize the entire army. David volunteered to defeat Goliath. Since David had no training as a soldier, it was impossible for Saul to believe that he could offer Goliath a challenge. Many people are like that. They believe that if you were not trained according to their standards or if they did not see you develop, you are unqualified. It became painfully obvious to David that the army was in the condition it was in and could not muster up enough courage to fight because they were hampered by Saul's vision. So David listed the qualifications he believed would make him successful against Goliath. David brought a fresh perspective to the table that did not rely on human ingenuity. He envisioned an army led by God. With God at the helm, no one could resist His power, and nothing was impossible.

Saul consented and said, "And may the Lord be with you!" Under his breath he said, "For I won't." Although Saul depended on weaponry and human ability, David did not. David relied on God. When you realize that the battle is not yours, but God's, and you are simply His instrument of righteousness, you stop focusing on your ability or lack thereof and start relying on His ability.

David fearlessly and without hesitation ran toward Goliath, and he attacked with the confidence of a seasoned warrior. His bravery inspired the Israelite army to fight. The same army that just minutes before could not muster enough courage to even face the Philistines, much less fight, ran forward, attacked the Philistines, and chased them back to Gath and Ekron. The situation was strangely reminiscent of the scene Jonathan created when his act of faith inspired the Israelite army to fight valiantly and defeat the Philistines at Gilgal. Faith inspires, fear paralyzes.

The Best Rival Is a Dead Rival

The loss of the Spirit of the Lord not only caused Saul depression and fear but also heightened his insecurities. He was suspicious of anyone who demonstrated abilities better than his. He did not want to lose his popularity with the people and wanted to maintain his position as king. Saul was Israel's savior; he had accomplished many things for Israel during his tenure, and he believed that he deserved her admiration and respect. He had defended Israel against her enemies and had been successful in battle. How had a boy from nowhere quickly won the respect and admiration of Israel with only one battle? Why did women sing, "Saul has killed his thousands and David his tens of thousands"? Did they confuse the words of the song or was it a prophetic recognition that David would accomplish ten times what Saul had? Whatever the reason for the slight, it made Saul angry. Saul had lost his most important things to David: God and Israel's love. Even some of his children cherished David.

> This made Saul very angry. "What's this?" he said. "They credit David with ten thousands and me with only thousands. Next they'll be making him their king!" *1 Samuel 18:8*

Saul recruited David into the army and made him one of his personal armor bearers. He appointed David as an army commander and even made David one of his sons. David quickly scaled the upper echelon to Saul's inner circle. People recognized David as a greater warrior than Saul and could see that the Spirit of the Lord was with him. David quickly won the hearts of the people, and they regarded him more highly than Saul. David had attained a place of prominence in a very short period. From that point on, Saul kept a watchful, jealous eye on David and secretly tried to kill him, since the best rival is a dead rival.

When you have or have had the resident presence of God in your life, you immediately recognize His presence anywhere and in anyone. Saul recognized God's Spirit in David, which caused him to take note. Just as one feels jealous when they see their former spouse with another, Saul was jealous because God was with David. Saul secretly tried to kill David because God's Spirit resided in David. He grew to hate David because he was anointed; Saul could not stand the sight of David, so he banned him from his presence. How many people of God have tried to kill a person because they recognize the Spirit of God in that person's life?

Saul's actions were no different from what many people in power have done when they have discovered that a person under them is more advanced. They may not go so far as trying to kill their "rival," but out of self-preservation they do everything they can to kill the spirit of the person, to discourage them, to hold them back, to stunt their growth, to discredit them, to disgrace them, and to cause them to lose favor.

Saul sent David on assignments and into impossible battles he believed no one could survive. He wanted David to fail and preferably to die. If David failed, his popularity would crash and Israel would stop loving him. Saul deprived David of all the things he thought made a person successful in battle. He sent him out against the dreaded Philistines short staffed and ill equipped. He gave David tasks that he himself would not do, hoping David would die on assignment. However, his plans backfired because each time he tried to eliminate David in this way, David accomplished more and his fame grew. The more Saul pressed David, the better he performed, because God was with him. When his trickery and deception did not work, Saul began a more direct assault.

Because unchecked abuse always escalates, Saul began to assault David directly. David's growing popularity only increased Saul's paranoia, and he attempted to kill David on at least three occasions. By this time David was wary of Saul, and he avoided him as much as possible. One of the few occasions where David would be around Saul was when he ministered with the harp. Saul started to use those occasions to make attempts on David's life. When the tormenting spirit sent from God overwhelmed Saul, he threw his spear at David, trying to pin him to a wall, but David narrowly escaped each time. Although these assaults were more direct, Saul could blame it on the tormenting spirit, so it technically could not be considered *his* fault. He could claim that he had an episode: "The devil made me do it."

Saul tried to get inside David's mind to find out what motivated him so that he could use that knowledge against him. Since he had expressed enough hostility toward David to cause David to put up his guard, he had to find another way to get close to David in order to get to know him. He sent spies to relay his carefully crafted messages and report David's responses. Beware of two-faced, tongue-wagging gossips, because they are reporting everything you say to the "king," all the while pretending to be your friend and confidant. They are just trying to gather information to use against you. You can always tell that you have a mole, and you can identify the mole by the specific information the "king" has about your "private" conversations. Anytime a person cannot talk to you directly and resorts to these tactics, something is wrong. David thought, "If the king likes me so much, why doesn't he talk to me directly? Why does he keep sending his messengers?"

> Then Saul told his men to say confidentially to David, "The king really likes you, and so do we. Why don't you accept the king's offer and become his son-in-law?" . . . he replied, "How can a poor man from a humble family afford the bride price for the daughter of a king?" When Saul's men reported this back to the king, he told them, "Tell David that all I want for the bride price is one hundred Philistine foreskins! Vengeance on my enemies is all I really want." But what Saul had in mind was that David would be killed in the fight.
> *1 Samuel 18:22–25*

Saul was appalled to discover that not only Israel was smitten with David, but his own children were, too, so he tried to pull his children into his web of deceit against David. He spent a great deal of time trying to turn his children against David or use them to trap him. Saul's daughter, Michal, fell in love with David, and Saul used her as bait, asking only the foreskins of one hundred Philistines as bride price. David gave double what Saul asked, so Saul gave Michal to David. After David married Michal, Saul tried to use Michal to trap David in their bedroom, but she helped David escape.

Saul tried to infiltrate Jonathan and David's friendship in order to assassinate David, but Jonathan informed David of all of Saul's plans. Although Saul made it seem as if he were trying to preserve the throne for his progeny by killing David, his real concern was preserving his own throne.

Jonathan was a more skillful warrior than Saul. Although Jonathan would have been the next heir to the throne, Saul could not live with the fact that his son had more bravery, courage, and heroic deeds to his credit. In his new state of mind, with his fear heightened and insecurity in record proportions, he was green with envy. Saul viewed with suspicion anyone who demonstrated greater ability and was recognized as a better warrior by the people. They were his rivals; they were out to destroy him; therefore, they needed to be destroyed at all cost.

In earlier battles, Jonathan had challenged the enemy, confronted them, and forced Israel into battle, but Saul grew tired of it. He was tired of being forced into battles, because it exposed his inadequacies. Jonathan was the type to ignite a battle, while Saul was the type who would try to pacify an enemy to avoid a battle. During the battle at Micmash, Saul was eager to kill Jonathan for his transgression, motivated in part by his need to get rid of the troublemaker. Saul later made a second attempt on Jonathan's life. What would make you try to kill your own child?

As part of Saul's inner circle, David normally celebrated the new moon festival with him. However, since Saul had displayed open hostility toward him and had even attempted to take his life, David decided it was not in his best interest to dine with Saul. (Although you have God's protection, there is nothing wrong with exercising wisdom. You do not have to put yourself in harm's way to prove anything to your enemies. Be wise.)

David discussed the matter with Jonathan, and they decided to use the new moon festival to test Saul's intentions. If Saul became angry over David's absence, it was because he had intended to kill him. During the first day of the feast, Saul did not comment on David's absence, but on the second day, he asked Jonathan why David was not present. Jonathan told him that he had excused David to attend a sacrifice with his family. Saul hit the roof and accused Jonathan of protecting David.

> Saul boiled with rage at Jonathan. "You stupid son of a whore!" he swore at him. "Do you think I don't know that you want David to be king in your place, shaming yourself and your mother? As long as that son of Jesse is alive, you'll never be king. Now go and get him so that I can kill him!" *1 Samuel 20:30–31*

After that lovely outburst, Saul tried to kill Jonathan by throwing a spear to pin him against the wall. Why would you repeatedly try to kill one of your own children unless you were blind with envy? They say that blood is thicker than water, but perhaps jealousy is even thicker than blood.

It is a mystery how Saul continued to reign in this state of mind. He was a lunatic, completely mad, but he refused to give up his throne without a fight. To him, maintaining his throne was a matter of survival, so he began a reign of terror. He abandoned his attempt to appear as a God lover when he began to openly challenge and oppose God. Saul's reign took on a distinctly anti-God tone. He tried to strong-arm God into doing what he wanted Him to do. God's servants feared for their lives, because they knew that if Saul did not fear God, he would have no problem killing them. He opposed God by manhandling, killing, and chasing God's anointed. With each passing moment, Saul's sin grew deeper and deeper, beyond the point of no return.

Saul decided that he would no longer hide the fact that he was trying to kill David, since subtlety was not working. He had to take a more direct approach. Saul spent a great deal of time hounding David. God had anointed David, yet Saul made it a top priority to kill David to subvert God's will. At times, Saul used the entire Israelite army to pursue David (leaving all of Israel vulnerable) and on other occasions he used three thousand special troops. He justified his actions by lying to the soldiers, claiming that David was an enemy who was plotting to kill him. However, when David confronted Saul in the presence of witnesses, Saul admitted there was absolutely no justifiable reason, besides envy, that he treated David so badly and sought to destroy him at all costs.

David was the only person who effectively ministered to Saul. David was Saul's most faithful servant and a highly honored member of his household. Everybody knew that Saul was lying about David, and they knew that David had never committed a crime against him. David was a blessing to Israel, had a servant's heart for Israel, and defended her at his own peril. They knew that nothing but sheer hate, fear, insecurity, and envy motivated Saul. That raises the question of why Israel's army and entire Israelite communities cooperated with Saul's efforts. When one person focuses their entire being and their every waking moment on destroying another person, it should send warning signals, red flags even, to others to back away from that destructive person. Why did Israel support a leader who had clearly gone mad and was totally bent on destroying a person they knew was innocent? The answer was envy, hate, and fear.

David rose to a place of prominence in a short period, was successful at any task presented to him, and was anointed. David did not play politics and did not snub anyone to get where he was. Many in the army were miffed because they felt that David did not go through the proper channels and did not pay his dues; therefore, they adopted the spirit of Saul. They agreed with Saul on some level, even though they knew his charges against David were false. If they had disagreed with Saul and believed he was out of line, they would have thwarted his plan, because they had done so on at least two occasions before.

Although all Israelites benefited in one way or another from David, many secretly hated him. People have a tendency to hate successful, anointed people because they wish they were in their place. Those who harbor hate and envy toward successful and anointed people cooperate with destroyers, even when the person they are helping destroy has only blessed and esteemed them. Saul's heightened insecurities caused him to become more belligerent, since preserving his throne was a matter of life and death. Nobody wanted to cross Saul, because they feared for their lives. Those who thought Saul was pursuing David on false pretenses did not stand in Saul's way out of fear and self-preservation. People's motivations for supporting Saul were many, varied, and complex, but the result of their support was that Saul had the liberty to defame, trap, torment, and unjustly hunt an innocent man.

The attempts Saul made on David's life were many and varied. One event should be highlighted, however, for it demonstrates Saul's insanity. The only person besides David and Jonathan who had the guts to tell Saul that he was wrong in his pursuit of David was a priest named Ahimelech. Eli, the Levitical high priest, descendant of Aaron, had two sons, Phinehas and Hophni. Phinehas had at least two sons, Ichabod and Ahitub. Ahitub had Ahimelech and Ahijah, the priest that served Saul. When Saul discovered that Ahimelech had assisted David's flight, he sent for him and all his family, who served as priests.

> When they arrived, Saul shouted at him, "Listen to me, you son of Ahitub!" "What is it, my king?" Ahimelech asked. "Why have you and David conspired against me?" Saul demanded. "Why did you give him food and a sword? Why have you inquired of God for him? Why did you encourage him to revolt against me and to come here and attack me?" "But sir," Ahimelech replied, "is there anyone among all your servants who is as faithful as David, your son-in-law? Why, he is the captain of your bodyguard and a highly honored member of your household! This was certainly not the first time I had consulted God for him! Please don't accuse me and my family in this matter, for I knew nothing of any plot against you." *1 Samuel 22:12–15*

Although Saul's bodyguards could not see the wrong in hunting David, they flat out refused to obey Saul's command to kill the priests. However, Doeg, the Edomite, who was in Saul's service, had no such inhibitions and killed eighty-five priests wearing their priestly tunics. He then traveled to Nob, the city of the priests, and killed the priests' families—men, women, children, babies, and their livestock—for Ahimelech's "offense." Only one man, Abiathar, son of Ahimelech, escaped.

There is an insanity to sin that makes you shun reason. Otherwise, what kind of lunacy would cause one to do that? Saul was a madman, and it was clear that he no longer had the capacity to make rational decisions; nothing but blind jealousy and self-preservation guided him. Although Saul could not seem to get it through his thick head that touching God's anointed was a serious thing, David did. It is a serious thing to attack God's anointed, for in attacking them, you are attacking God, for whom you are no match. My God, Saul, my God!

The hard truth is that the slaughter of the priests was a fulfillment of God's promise toward Eli. God decided to remove Eli's relatives permanently from their position as priests for the unresolved sins of the priesthood. God had promised Eli that his family members would die prematurely. No one would live to a ripe old age; no member would live out their days; sadness and grief would be their lot as their children died violent deaths; prosperity would skip them; they would beg the new priest for food, money, and work; and as proof that God would do what He said, both Phinehas and Hophni would die in the same day. Phinehas, Hophni, Eli, and Phinehas's wife died in the same day. That was the beginning of the fulfillment of God's promise.

During Saul's reign, Eli's relatives still served as priests. Ahijah, the son of Ahitub and grandson of Phinehas, was the priest who served Saul during battles by consulting the Lord. God gave the tribe of Levi the distinction and honor above all the tribes of Israel to be God's ministers. The tribe of Levi had three divisions: Gershon, Merari, and Kohath. Within the division of Kohath were four subdivisions: Ishar, Hebron, Uzziel, and Amram. From Amram came Moses and Aaron. God chose Aaron from the subdivision of Amram to be his priest. Priests could come from the descendants of the four sons of Aaron: Nadab, Abihu, Eleazar, and Ithamar. Nadab and Abihu died in the wilderness for their sins, leaving Eleazar and Ithamar to continue the priestly line. Priests could come from two separate lineages, Eleazar and Ithamar. While both lineages could serve as priests, only one served as high priest at a given time. Eli and his relatives were of the Ithamar priestly lineage. God promised to wipe out priests from the Ithamar lineage, leaving the Eleazar lineage to serve as priests. With the Ithamar lineage eliminated, God could still fulfill the priestly dynasty covenant He had made with Aaron and thus his descendants would still serve as priests. The priestly family that Saul decimated was of the lineage of Ithamar. Without intending to, Saul fulfilled God's promise; he was led by an invisible hand to promote an end that was not his intention.

Saul's Last Battle—Lost Life

Samuel died, and the whole nation mourned him. Saul killed almost an entire family of high priests. The prophets of God with any inkling of sense avoided Saul like the plague. Saul banned all mediums and psychics from Israel. There was no one to whom Saul could turn to get an answer from God; his line of communication with God had been severed. In Saul's mind, God was not the only source of information, and if God would not respond to him, Saul would find someone who would. Saul was facing an impending battle with the Philistines and needed answers.

Saul disguised himself as a commoner and traveled by night to a medium at Endor. The medium called Samuel's spirit out of the Earth. Saul figured he could get around God's silence, because he had established a consistent pattern during his administration of "going over God's head." Samuel asked Saul what he expected him to do if God would not answer him. The primary reason God would not answer Saul was that he had made God his enemy during the Amalekite incident. Samuel informed him that he and his sons would be with him in paradise the next day. The entire Israelite army would be brought down in defeat. During his reign, Saul lost his dynasty, his reign, the Spirit of God, and his life because of his rebellion.

The main reason you cannot follow a faithless and sinful leader is that he brings disgrace upon his country, and innocent people suffer because of his sins. During Saul's last battle with the Philistines, his sons, Jonathan, Abinadab, and Malkishua, lost their lives, and many Israelite soldiers died as a result of Saul's sins. The Israelites in the Jezreel Valley fled from their towns when they saw that their army had been routed and that Saul and his sons were dead. Saul caused Israel to lose ground they had conquered. Saul alienated the people of Israel from God by his rebellion. Although Saul reflected the attitude of the people, his rebellion caused the people to suffer heavy losses.

If Saul had not sinned beyond the Amalekite incident, it would not have mattered, because that was the overriding reason God had handed him over to the Philistines. However, to that sin Saul added the sin of killing and hunting God's anointed. Throughout Saul's administration, he demonstrated that he was not concerned with what God wanted. In fact, he wanted to block God from getting what He wanted. Saul used the Israelite army to sin, for it was a sin to hunt David, God's anointed. All the time and effort that were expended hunting David could have been used more productively against the real enemies of Israel. In his final battle at Aphek, Saul died, and the Lord turned his kingdom over to David, son of Jesse.

Some say it is the final analysis that counts. What is written in the history books about a person's leadership is more important than any single faux pas or all the messy scandals. If we put Saul to the rigors of that standard, what can we conclude about his reign? He was victorious in battle, he defeated Israel's enemies, he defended her from those who plundered her, and he was her savior. However, he often left Israel vulnerable while chasing a fugitive who had defended Israel against her enemies in his stead, and with his death, he brought Israel's army down in defeat and caused Israel to lose territory. The repercussions of the mistakes in Saul's reign were also felt in his successor's reign. When we stack up his accomplishments against his failures, we must conclude that he left Israel in a worse state than when he began.

If you think your private life has no bearing on your public life, think again. If you think you can lie, take advantage of people for selfish purposes, act dishonorably in private, and not have that affect your public life, think again. Can both bitter and sweet water come from the same source? The question of how the people fared under your leadership will not be answered until all the lies have evaporated. What awaits them in the aftermath of your leadership? People who appear to have fared well economically will discover the moral decay left in your wake. They will find that they are militarily weaker than they have been in ages. They will know that when you fought against a nation to remove the heat of public scrutiny, you created a merciless enemy capable of incomprehensible cruelty. They will suffer the costliness of a low-living leader.

David's life presents a different picture when compared to Saul's. While Saul was a spineless people pleaser, bent on doing things his way and completely opposing God, David was a God pleaser. David's primary concern throughout his reign was to please God. When the wicked are in authority, the people mourn, and when the righteous are in authority, the people rejoice. Saul, David's predecessor, has been examined. The stage has been set to understand the state of Israel when David emerged. Now we can appreciate who David was and what he accomplished.

Take-home message: Any man who is more interested in position than in pleasing God is a dangerous liability to God's cause.

Part Two: The Making of a King

11.

Legacy of Faith

Judah left home, moved to Adullam, and married Bathshua—a Canaanite woman. Their marriage produced Er, Onan, and Shelah. When Shelah was born, they were living in Kezib. Er married Tamar, the woman his father arranged for him to marry. All of Jacob's children were forbidden to marry Canaanites or people of surrounding nations, because they were idolatrous. What is it about forbidden fruit that seems so appealing? God knew that if they intermarried with the people of Canaan they would also become idolatrous, which He was trying to prevent. *I want you to be happy, and it is my pleasure to give you good gifts, but I don't want to lose you in the process.*

> But Er was a wicked man in the LORD's sight, so the LORD took his life. Then Judah said to Er's brother Onan, "You must marry Tamar, as our law requires of the brother of a man who has died. Her first son from you will be your brother's heir." But Onan was not willing to have a child who would not be his own heir. So whenever he had intercourse with Tamar, he spilled the semen on the ground to keep her from having a baby who would belong to his brother. But the LORD considered it a wicked thing for Onan to deny a child to his dead brother. So the LORD took Onan's life, too. *Genesis 38:7–10*

Fighting for a Promise

If Onan produced Er's heir, the double-portion blessing that belonged to Er would belong to that child. That was unacceptable to Onan because it interfered with the amount of his inheritance. But it was okay for Onan to reap the benefits and the pleasure of sex without the sacrifice, responsibility, and commitment. If you are not willing to accept the responsibilities of sex, then you are not ready for sex.

Judah sent Tamar home to her parents, instructing her not to marry. He promised Shelah to her once he grew up. But he did not intend to honor his promise, because he had lost two healthy sons and the common denominator was Tamar. Maybe she was a "black widow" who killed her mates after intercourse. He blamed her for the deaths of his sons, and he was not about to take a chance with his last son, his only heir.

Many sermons have been preached that have been unfair to Tamar. Many are quick to brand her a whore, denigrating her character, possibly because men have preached the sermons. When a conflict occurs between a man and a woman, even if the woman is the victim, many derogatory names are hurled her way. The woman always bears the brunt of the conflict. A man can play a lot of dirty games and be fully culpable in the situation, yet people still tend to place the blame on the woman; it is an incomprehensible phenomenon. Tamar's story is no different.

Judah picked her as wife for his son Er, but God judged Er a wicked man and took his life. Tamar lost her husband through no fault of her own. Onan married Tamar, but he did not want to raise a child in honor of his dead brother; he refused to produce his brother's heir. He had sex with Tamar, benefiting from her sexual pleasures but denying her his seed. Onan used Tamar, and while she gave all she had, he took all she gave without giving in return. God saw the unfairness Tamar endured and corrected the situation by taking Onan's life. God is so amazing because He takes notice of the smallest details in the lives of those He loves. Judah had one son left, and he was not about to give him to Tamar, although he claimed he would. He had already lost two able-bodied sons, and he blamed Tamar. Judah cannot be blamed for that conclusion, because anybody with limited human vision would have concluded the same thing. He did not see what God saw. However, even though the full picture is given in the scripture, preachers today still do not seem to regard Tamar as a victim of men. They choose to overlook the suffering she endured at the hands of the men in her life.

Shelah grew up, and since Judah did not intend to give Shelah to Tamar, he did not call for her. Judah cheated her. If he had been an honorable man, he would have suggested that she get married instead of waiting years for Shelah. Judah punished her for the deaths of his sons, even though their deaths were not her fault. She stayed at home wearing widow's garments, making herself unavailable and saving herself for Shelah. The number of years she waited for Shelah could have been spent happily married with children from another man. She refused many suitors while waiting for the promise. By the time it became apparent that Judah was not going to give her Shelah, her suitors had all married.

She spent years longing for a child, waiting for the promise. She suffered shame and ridicule and was called an old maid. The wait was bitter, and it was hard to see her childhood friends married and with children. She was isolated, because she did not have anything in common with her friends. She could not relate to them, because she lived at home with her parents. The wait was long and arduous, but she knew anything worth having was worth waiting for. The more she thought about her future life with Shelah, the sweeter it became. She survived the wait through her hopes and dreams.

Once it was apparent to Tamar that she was not going to marry, she took matters into her own hands. Shelah had grown up, and Judah had not called for her. A desperate situation calls for desperate measures. She intended to make sure she received justice. "I have not wasted all these years for nothing! I will have the promise! I will not stand idly by watching my dreams go down the tubes! My dreams will not be shattered and dashed! I will not be robbed! I've been used one too many times! As long as I have breath in my body, I will see to it that the promise is fulfilled by any means necessary."

The indignation of her shattered dreams propelled Tamar into action. She looked for any opportunity to fulfill her destiny. An opportunity presented itself when she heard that Judah was going to shear his sheep. She met Judah in front of Enaim when he was on his way to Timnah. She exchanged her widow's garments for a veil. Judah, taking her for a prostitute, propositioned her.

It is difficult for a man who solicits a woman's services to maintain his honor. Whether she is or is not a whore is immaterial. The way a man approaches her speaks volumes about him. If she is a whore, does that give him license to treat her with any less respect than he would give his mother? A man who respects women and has a clean character will honor any woman, regardless of her nature, unless he has unclean tendencies himself.

Tamar was a shrewd woman, refusing to accept his word as payment. There was no time for playing the fool again, no time for mistakes. She made him give her his identification seal, cord, and walking stick as collateral for a goat he was to give her later as payment for her services. She had sex with him, then went home and changed back into her widow's garments. Judah tried to reclaim his pledges by sending his friend Hirah to make the exchange. Judah did not personally go to reclaim his property, because he wanted to protect his reputation and save himself the shame. The men of the village told Hirah that there were no prostitutes in the village, and rather than draw attention to himself by insisting there was one, he dropped the issue.

Months later, Judah discovered that Tamar, his daughter-in-law, had played the harlot and was pregnant. What righteous indignation arose in his heart! Hypocritically, he called for her to be mercilessly burned at the stake. "Justice must be served!" Often, those who scream the loudest and demand justice with vehemence for the sins of others are often guiltier than the ones they accuse.

> "Bring her out and burn her!" Judah shouted. *Genesis 38:24*
>
> When they were about to kill her, she identified the father of her child.
>
> "The man who owns this identification seal and walking stick is the father of my child. Do you recognize them?" Judah admitted that they were his and said, "She is more in the right than I am, because I didn't keep my promise to let her marry my son Shelah."
> *Genesis 38:25–26*

Judah had to confess to the undeniable. "I am to blame for putting her in this position because I failed to honor my promise to her, I deceived her." Although Judah made this confession, a barrage of degrading names was aimed at Tamar. Judah did not demand that they burn him at the stake for his role in the situation. No one questioned the fact that Judah had propositioned her. Judah had procured sexual favors from a woman who was not his wife, but no one lifted a finger to judge him, suggesting that his crime was immaterial. Judah's lack of integrity had created a desperate problem for Tamar, a problem she was determined to resolve, so why blame Tamar for taking what was rightfully hers? Why insult her for refusing to be further victimized?

God rewarded Tamar for knowing what she was entitled to, waiting for the promise, and stubbornly fighting for its fulfillment. She had a spirit that refused to be denied. God rewarded Tamar with a double portion: twins. Both of them possessed their mother's spirit. When the midwife was delivering the twins, one child stuck his fist out of the womb as if to say, "I am first, I am number one." The midwife tied a cord around his wrist, confirming that he was the firstborn, and therefore, the heir. Although Zerah did not come out first, he fought for it.

Perez was so named because of the two children he possessed a greater measure of his mother's prevailing attitude. Perez, the one who breaks out, the one who prevails, took the status of firstborn. He came out of the womb knowing that if something is worth having, it is worth fighting for by any means necessary.

Rahab—The Shrewd Negotiator

Joshua sent spies to the land of Jericho, where they were assisted by a prostitute named Rahab, who would later play a pivotal role in its defeat. Her statement of faith: "I know God has given you this land, that is why we are all afraid of you. I have seen the results of your God's efforts and I know that He is the Supreme God of everything."

She then asked the spies to save her life, since she had saved theirs. Rahab was a shrewd negotiator, saving the lives of her whole family in exchange for the assistance she provided the Hebrew scouts. She was the new Noah.

> "Now swear to me by the LORD that you will be kind to me and my family since I have helped you. Give me some guarantee that when Jericho is conquered, you will let me live, along with my father and mother, my brothers and sisters, and all their families." "We offer our own lives as guarantee for your safety," the men agreed. "If you don't betray us, we will keep our promise when the LORD gives us the land." *Joshua 2:12–14*

Rahab honored her part of the covenant when she harbored the Hebrew scouts and helped them escape. After the men had rested, she let them down by a rope through a window and told them to escape to the hill country, stay there for three days until the search was over, and then go their way. She gave them vital information about the search party's habits and the procedures of her countrymen.

> Before they left, the men told her, "We can guarantee your safety only if you leave this scarlet rope hanging from the window. And all your family members—your father, mother, brothers, and all your relatives—must be inside the house. If they go out into the street, they will be killed, and we cannot be held to our oath. But we swear that no one inside this house will be killed—not a hand will be laid on any of them. If you betray us, however, we are not bound by this oath in any way." "I accept your terms," she replied. And she sent them on their way, leaving the scarlet rope hanging from the window.
> *Joshua 2:17–21*

When Jericho was under siege, the only house left standing was Rahab's ark. Rahab's family was moved to a safe place near the camp of Israel, and her family was adopted into the family of Israel. Rahab, from Jericho, negotiated her way into the commonwealth of God by faith and married Salmon, a prince of Judah.

Ruth—Your God Is My God

Abraham's nephew, Lot, was the son of Abraham's deceased brother, Haran. When Abraham left Haran, he took Lot with him. Only Lot and his two virgin daughters remained after God destroyed Sodom and Gomorrah. Lot's daughters thought they were the last people on Earth. They thought they would die virgins and their dad's family line would end. They decided to get their father drunk and sleep with him to produce children. They both became pregnant by their father, and both daughters had sons named Ammon and Moab.

The Moabites were distant relatives of the Israelites. Nearing the close of the Judges period, there was a famine in Israel. Elimelech, of the tribe of Judah, took his family and went to Moab for a better life. Both sons married Moabite women. The move proved to be disastrous for the family because in time Elimelech and his sons, Kilion and Mahlon, died, leaving Naomi and his daughters-in-law widows. Ruth the Moabite was the widow of Mahlon. Naomi decided to return to her homeland. Naomi, unlike Judah, urged her daughters-in-law to go home to their parents and remarry. "I have nothing to give you." But Ruth refused to leave her.

> Don't ask me to leave you and turn back. I will go wherever you go and live wherever you live. Your people will be my people, and your God will be my God. I will die where you die and will be buried there. May the LORD punish me severely if I allow anything but death to separate us! *Ruth 1:16–17*

"You gave me your beautiful son, and he was a precious, precious gift to me. I will not abandon you in your time of need when you are down and out, and I will not discard you because you have nothing to offer me. Our relationship goes deeper than that. I will serve you because you are grieving and in pain; that's what friends do."

Ruth loved and served the emotionally distraught Naomi. In addition to their friendship, Ruth stayed with Naomi for the pleasure of adopting Naomi's God as her own. She did not care if she ever married again, as long as she could have God, and God rewarded Ruth for her loyalty and faithfulness.

A kinsman redeemer, called a go'el, has the power to buy back or redeem what a poor relative was forced to sell; they are a rich family member who steps in and takes responsibility for a relative who has encountered hard times. They buy back property the relative sold, and they purchase the freedom of a relative who has become enslaved to debtors. If a man dies and leaves his widow without an heir, the redeemer marries the widow and produces a son with her. Naomi had a kinsman redeemer who relinquished his rights to the next kinsman redeemer, Boaz. Boaz, of the tribe of Judah, married Ruth. Ruth came into the Israelite family by sacrificial faith.

When we examine the tapestry of David's life, we can see God's purpose in David's bloodline. The ancestry of David is composed of people who exhibited different levels of faith, giving him a great faith pedigree. Some of his ancestors were not born into the privilege and promise of the commonwealth of Israel; they entered into the commonwealth of God by faith. His family line includes Tamar, who knew what a promise was and refused to be denied. She had tenacious faith, the kind that stubbornly fights to turn a promise into reality against all odds. Judah and Tamar the Canaanite had Perez. Perez had Hezron. Hezron had Ram. Ram had Amminadab. Amminadab was the father of Nashon. Nashon was the father of Salmon. Rahab of Jericho had a shrewd negotiating faith, the kind that recognizes value, negotiates for it, and then honors a commitment in exchange for a promise. Salmon married Rahab and they had Boaz. Ruth had a sacrificial faith, the kind that recognizes invaluable treasure and gives up everything for it. Boaz married Ruth the Moabite and they had Obed. Obed was the father of Jesse. Jesse was the father of King David. David inherited a legacy of faith.

Take-home message: If you give nothing else to your children, make sure you give them faith.

12.

The Boy Who Would Be King

As a youth, David was a shepherd and performed many duties that shaped his character. The Lord used that time in David's life to help him develop skills he would later use as king, because He could not afford to have another liability like King Saul on His hands.

The Good Shepherd

Although we do not have complete details as to what David did as a shepherd, we do know that animals have a way of softening the soul and developing a servant's heart. You can determine your own character by the way you treat the weakest creature in your life. How do you treat the ones in your life that are dependent upon you? How do you treat the ones in your life that cannot speak nor defend themselves? The way you treat the weakest is a gauge of the healthiness of your soul, and judging by how David treated his flock, we can assume that he was a kind, gentle, sensitive, thoughtful, and peaceful person.

The primary responsibility of a shepherd is to sustain the life of the sheep. Many duties are involved in being a good shepherd. The shepherd leads but does not drive the sheep. He is not callous or insensitive to the needs of his flock, nor does he lead them down paths he has not first traveled. He gently leads them at a pace that is accommodating for sheep with newborns so none of his flock is left behind. He leads them to good pastures and beside still waters so the sheep do not exhaust themselves getting their needs met.

When the sheep are faring well, it is a reflection of the care a shepherd has provided. However, it is not enough simply to provide sustenance; emotional detachment and aloofness will not work. The shepherd must develop trust with his flock before they will follow him; they must know him so well that they recognize his voice, and they must believe that he always has their best interests at heart. The shepherd must know each animal's personality, likes and dislikes, and strengths and weaknesses. A shepherd needs to know who bleats and be able to interpret the bleat.

A good shepherd loves his flock and never treats them as if they are expendable. He will leave the flock to search for any sheep that becomes separated from the rest. Then, when the shepherd has found the lost sheep, he carries it close to his bosom, giving it warmth and security as he returns it to the fold. The shepherd rejoices when he finds and recovers the lost sheep. What the shepherd is willing to do for one, he is willing to do for all. A good shepherd does not abandon his flock in times of trouble and will fight for each sheep's life during a crisis. When the crisis has passed, the shepherd dresses any wounds his flock may have sustained and then goes about nursing them back to health. He will gladly lay down his life to save his flock, thereby letting his sheep know that he values their lives even more than his own.

David was passionate about the lives of the sheep; he was a shepherd who defended the sheep. When a lion or bear took a sheep, David did not say, "Oh, well, I lost one." Instead, he pursued the predator and literally took sheep out of its mouth and clubbed the predator to death if it challenged him. The animals David fought could kill a grown man. Yet David fought them on behalf of his flock. His training was intense, but it paid off later when he faced the challenge of being Israel's shepherd. God will use the challenges you face early in your life to benefit others in the future.

A Time of Separation, Demonstration, and Motivation

The life of a shepherd is often lonely. The Lord set David apart from family and friends so He could spend time training David, which was also the case with many other biblical leaders. God sent Abraham away from the comfort of his homeland and family to wander in unknown places. Moses ran from the pharaoh's house and into obscurity for years until God spoke to him. Jesus went into the wilderness for forty days. Paul was in the desert, separated from the disciples in Jerusalem while God trained him. God sets people apart and severs all other relationships so He can establish a one-on-one relationship with them, free of distraction.

During the separation phase, the training for each leader is tailored to the needs of the situation. Each leader is created for a particular season, and David was created for a season of warfare. Therefore, God used his time of separation to teach David warfare. God created mock battles that would be similar in degree to what David would face as the shepherd of Israel. A lion is the king of the jungle, and when a lion is on the move, he does not find challengers. A bear towers over a grown man and can kill him with a few swipes. God taught David to fight powerful animals so that he would face the enemies of Israel with impunity.

God put David into many situations where he was outmatched to remove David's dependency on his human abilities so he would learn to depend upon Him. God let David know that He considered it His personal responsibility to protect him. When David was beyond the help of others and could not help himself, God saved him. God demonstrated His power to protect David when he was in mortal danger and to assure David that He would never hesitate to save him. He established a successful track record of protecting David and helping him overcome insurmountable odds, and thereby earned David's trust. The Lord cut the cords of dependency on self, others, and family, then attached those cords to Himself. God was a shepherd to David while He trained him to be a shepherd.

From here on out, you can depend on me. I will send you to places where there will be no support from others and you will be outnumbered. I will be there to support you as you defend my people.

Knowing that you have God's full support and that your life is securely in His hands allows you to face challenges other people could not. David was not a daredevil, but he would do whatever it took to protect his flock. What challenge would you not take on, what battle would you not face if you knew (from prior experience) that the Lord would help you through it? God changed David's perspective, and as a result of God's training David saw the impossible as possible. People often view an individual like David as crazy because he does not have normal inhibitions. It was God's intention to develop a man who was motivated to tackle any challenge with the full assurance of His protection as he defended His sheep.

"God is with me in my storms, and that gives me comfort. I know He will not abandon me in the time of great distress. He has the power to deliver me from impossible situations, even from death, and He won't hesitate to do it. He is my protector, I trust Him with my life. I am not apprehensive or insecure in my relationship to Him; I am confident of His love and support."

God taught David not to make decisions based on appearance. God developed a giant-slayer mentality in David and trained him to face insurmountable odds with a full assurance that He would deliver him. It is difficult to face Goliaths unless you have faced giants in the past. When you have faced certain death and triumphed through the power of God, your perspective changes.

When you walk into a battle, don't size up your opponent's ability versus your ability. You'll never accomplish anything that way. But rather size up your opponent's ability versus My ability.

God esteemed David so that he could understand his value. Even in the midst of a complex universe, God took the time to care for David, and each time He did, He demonstrated that David was a person of value, thereby increasing David's self-esteem. God created a leader who did not need the affirmation of men; He created a man who was not insecure. People tend to develop contempt for those with high self-esteem who derive their value from God, because they cannot be controlled by public opinion. They label those people as cocky and arrogant. David had unbreakable self-confidence. It was important for God to develop this attitude in David. In God's eyes, it is better to develop a confident person than an insecure person who lashes out at those who are more advanced and caves in to peer pressure. It is better to have a man who will do what He says even if that means losing the respect and approval of others. God esteemed David so that he would put more emphasis on pleasing Him than on pleasing men.

I want to make sure you understand where your loyalty should lie. Whenever you have to determine where to place your loyalty, I take priority.

God preserved David's life on numerous occasions, which forged a bond that could not be severed. When God saves you from a near-death situation, He is communicating His love for you and forging a bond that is even stronger than the bond between a mother and her child. Every time God saved David's life, He was giving him life. God was the source of David's life, and the one who gives you life earns your undying loyalty and devotion.

For David and God, this was the beginning of a love relationship. Every time God saved David's life, He was saying, *I love you so much that I don't want to lose you. I will do anything to keep you around. I am not going to let the enemy wipe you out, because I need you.*

"I am confident of God's love and I know that He has my best interest in mind. I can trust Him in uncertain situations. God is my life, and my life belongs to Him. Were it not for Him, I would not be here. I would have died a thousand deaths were it not for His mighty hand of salvation. God is the giver and sustainer of all life. He is my life."

Praise Is a Natural By-Product of a Relationship with God

God knew David before He carefully tucked him into his mother's womb. He formed every fiber of his being and watched his development like a proud expectant father. Before David took his first breath on the Earth, God had recorded his entire life story. He was so intimately acquainted with David that He knew his mannerisms and how he would respond to any given situation.

God loved David and diligently pursued David, tracking his every move. At any given moment He was aware of where David was, because He ensconced him. He pursued David, because He knew David would love Him back. David was one of those rare individuals who would love God without degree. Therefore, He was head over heels in love with David and excited about him.

"Apart from you there is no me. If I stand, you stand. If I sit, you sit. If I move left, you move left. You hound my trail. You are all over me. Wherever I go, you are with me. You would go to the very depths of hell and back for me. I can't shake you even if I try, nor do I want to. I can't breathe without you; you breathe out and I breathe in. My soul longs for, pants for, and craves you. You are my heart, my soul, my life, my everything. How could I not love you?

"You are my joy. How I love being with you! I want more of you than I can possibly stand. I feel such sweet peace, warmth, and comfort with you. Your thoughtfulness, gentleness, and kindness blow me away. I am obsessed with you. I am passionate about you. My soul is in hot pursuit of you. I am jealous over our relationship. You are mine, and I am yours."

Praise naturally flows from a person who is in a relationship with God. God eagerly anticipated and prepared for David's arrival on the Earth. God initiated a relationship with David by pursuing him. He showered David with His love and care. He smothered David with Himself. He doted on David. He personally protected, challenged, and developed David. David received God's love and responded by loving Him back. God's pursuit of David caused David to pursue Him in return.

God created a close bond with David, and David expressed his appreciation for God. He genuinely praised God to show his love, appreciation, gratitude, and affection for God. When he sang, "God, you are my shield," he was speaking from experience, not simply singing something that sounded good. David did not put on a show so that he would be remembered as the man who praised God with all his might. He was not there as an entertainment piece. He did not sing and play for the sake of winning the accolades of men. His skill as a musician developed as an outgrowth of his worship to God. He never forgot all God had done for him, and he showed his appreciation consistently, even to the point of losing control and appearing ridiculous at times. David was not afraid to honor God before men.

"God, when I think of Your goodness, a shout wells up inside of me that I just cannot contain. It bursts forth like a volcano, my whole body quakes, and I begin to leap and dance joyously because of Your goodness. My joy swells like the ocean tides, and I bask and frolic in your love. God, I am excited about you.

"I am thankful, Lord, for the many blessings You have given me, and I want to let You know how much I appreciated Your comfort when my heart was heavy. When I was overwhelmed by circumstances and could not find words to express my pain, You heard my cry and You answered. I thank you because You were merciful and did not let me feel the full brunt of my sin. When I fell, You picked me up and wiped the dirt off. I thank you for all you have provided for me."

Skillful performance with misguided motivation only produces entertainment. Praise and worship are misguided if they do anything other than attract God. God is attracted to genuine heartfelt praise that is personally directed to Him. When He shows up, people naturally become reverent. This allows Him to minister to the people.

When a tormenting spirit from God came upon Saul, he turned into a raving madman. David played praise songs and attracted God. When God arrived, He caused the tormenting spirit to leave. David worshiped the Lord before the people of Israel, and once God was on the scene, the people naturally began to worship Him. Any time God can be tangibly felt, even the stoutest heart melts in adoration of Him. Who can stand in the presence of the Holy Creator with an irreverent heart? Who can resist praising the King of kings?

Family Tension Creates Emotional Distance and Removes Distractions

Since family relationships can be intense, God breaks those relationships that will hinder a person from the mission He has given them. God sometimes uses mistreatment by family members as a way to break emotional bonds and family influence. (It's difficult to go to Eritrea when you are a daddy's girl.)

The last aspect of David's training was perhaps the most undesirable of all—when those who should have embraced him rejected him the most. He was the youngest of the sons, and though the youngest is usually the most loved, that was not the case in David's family. When Samuel came to anoint the king that God had chosen to replace Saul, all of Jesse's sons were invited to the sacrifice with the exception of David. David was not even an afterthought. Had it not been for the fact that he was the one to be anointed king, David would have learned of Samuel's visit secondhand. I surmise that this was not the first time David was left out of family activities.

In a healthy family, a gifted child receives encouragement and support, but a gifted child favored by God is sometimes mistreated in an unhealthy family. When other family members recognize that a child has special abilities or is favored by God, they feel threatened and jealous, which causes them to belittle and mistreat the child to put them in their place and to discourage them. Some parents will even favor other children over the gifted child. The gifted child then becomes withdrawn and emotionally detached, developing a deep inward focus.

David's older brothers treated him with hostility. They were jealous because he was anointed king of Israel. They had recognized his ability long before he was anointed, though. He was discouraged, put down, and held back a lot by his brothers. As evidence of this, when David's father sent him to the battlefront to find out how his brothers were doing, his oldest brother, Eliab, heard David talking to the men and became furious, demanding to know why David was on the battlefield and not tending the sheep. He accused David of being dishonest and a prideful showoff.

To that David replied, "Now what? I was only asking a question."

Eliab reprimanded, belittled, and even slandered David. Confidence and self-assuredness are often mislabeled as pride and arrogance. Judging from David's response to Eliab, it was not the first time David had been reprimanded by his brothers, and they went into overkill to the point of discouraging him. The undertones suggest that David was often scolded for no reason and that he constantly had to justify his actions to his brothers. They wanted to hold him back and prevent him from fulfilling his destiny. They often misunderstood him and misinterpreted his intentions. However, David was a loner, accustomed to mistreatment, rejection, slander, criticism, and loneliness. He had the makings of a fine leader indeed.

God's Goal: To Create a Leader with a Certain Mind-set

God wanted to create a particular attitude in David. David's ultimate goal as a shepherd was to please the Father by blessing the sheep. In the words of Jesus, "My meat is to do the will of him that sent me, and to finish his work" (John 4:34, KJV).

David's sustenance came from doing what God had assigned him to do. His reward was to help others live fruitful lives. He received great pleasure and joy from knowing that he could be used to benefit and bless others. He was loyal, dedicated, and passionate about the welfare of others, esteeming others above himself. He put aside his personal ambitions in order to do what was best for his flock, even if it might cost him his life. He dedicated his life to serving others regardless of how they treated him. People did not need to know all the struggles he went through in order for them to get blessed. Recognition and appreciation were not his motivators. He was committed to the goal that was set before him—that of pleasing the Father. As long as his goal was to please God, he did not sweat the small stuff like betrayal, disloyalty, slander, false accusation, and envy.

Just as Moses and God shared the same Spirit, so did David and God.

When God is in an intense love relationship with a person, He blends His Spirit with theirs. That person begins to feel passionate about the things God feels passionate about. They hate what God hates, and His enemies become theirs.

Take-home message: God uses the ordinary circumstances of your life to help you develop the capacity to face future challenges.

13.

Falling Out of Favor with Saul

David brought a different perspective to the battlefield. His attitude was not entirely foreign to the Israelite army, but it had not been adopted by the masses. People generally will not rise above the level of their leader, and those who do surpass their leader will be discouraged and frustrated under that authority.

Trust God's Perspective and Watch Your Efforts Multiply

This brings us back to Saul's son, Jonathan, and his statement of faith when he and his armor bearer went against the Philistines at Geba: "Nothing can hinder the Lord; He can save with many or with only a few." It was that kind of thinking that caused Jonathan to step away from his fear and to respond in faith, which led to a great victory for Israel. God also developed a spirit in David that echoed Jonathan's, as evidenced by David's statement of faith:

> You come to me with sword, spear, and javelin, but I come to you in the name of the LORD Almighty—the God of the armies of Israel, whom you have defied. And everyone will know that the LORD does not need weapons to rescue his people. It is his battle, not ours. The LORD will give you to us! *1 Samuel 17:45, 47*

The same thing that paralyzed Saul's men was the very thing that propelled David to victory. Different people can look at the same situation and receive different messages, causing them to respond differently. Saul taught his men to rely on numbers, ability, and weaponry. He believed that if they could not match or exceed their enemy in these areas, the Israelites did not stand a chance of winning.

Goliath towered above Saul, who was himself head and shoulders above the Israelites. Goliath had been in the Philistine army since he was a boy. He was a seasoned veteran and an undefeated warrior. His experience at warfare was greater than the combined experience of many men. The weight of his weapons alone could stop a normal man in his tracks. So how could any man expect to overcome all of Goliath's assets? However, if the Israelites could have leveled the playing field by pitting ten of their finest against Goliath, perhaps they might have stood a chance, but those were not the terms. Even Goliath was insulted by David's weaponry, which he felt should equal his own.

> "Am I a dog," he roared at David, "that you come at me with a stick?" And he cursed David by the names of his gods. *1 Samuel 17:43*

On the battlefield, David stuck out his thumb and sized up Goliath. He determined that Goliath was about the same height as a bear, so he decided that he had a chance to be victorious. However, with the God of the Universe on his side, David was suddenly standing on a whole new playing field with Goliath. God gives you the upper hand over your enemies; He changes everything. As long as He is with you, you are guaranteed victory.

Most things when viewed from the natural standpoint seem impossible to conquer. Sight walking is so severely limited. In fact, when you rely solely on physical cues, you do not accomplish much. Over the centuries, people who have accomplished incredible things have taken risks. However, a person of God has an extra advantage over all the other risk takers. They have the advantage of having tapped into God. God knows all because He created everything. He has foreknowledge and knows what is about to happen before it happens. He is all powerful; nothing can resist His mighty hand. God's ways are not our ways, and His thoughts are not our thoughts. If you walk with God long enough, you will begin to see things from His perspective and not from your limited human standpoint. Great feats can only be accomplished when you trust the One who makes it all possible.

God had been preparing David for Goliath all of his life. How well David transferred the skills he had attained by facing bears and lions to his battle with Goliath would determine the effectiveness of God's training. Trained as a shepherd, David understood that it was the nature of a shepherd to protect his sheep. If something was out to destroy his sheep, it had to answer to the shepherd, and the children of Israel were the sheep of God. While the rest of the Israelite warriors cowered in fear because they estimated their human strength and found themselves lacking, David did not let his seeming lack of ability stop him.

David was not oblivious to the situation—he was aware of the risks and knew his limitations. But he also trusted God's unlimited ability. He did not let his inexperience in battle stop him. He did not consider himself inexperienced; he simply had not proven his skill to others. Maybe his experience did not exactly match the situation, but his skills could be adjusted to fit his current circumstance. David was also well exercised in faith, and God had established a track record with him. In the future, this David would face seemingly insurmountable odds from a human perspective and emerge victorious because of his reliance on God. Prior victories in insurmountable situations cause you to view challenges differently and make you willing to take more risks.

It should not seem odd that David took on Goliath, because he was simply doing what he had been trained to do. It would have been more unusual if he had not used his training or if he had used it improperly. God would have viewed it as a tragedy to have invested so much time and energy in David's life only to reap nothing in return.

The challenge for every person when moving from a personally tailored training regime to the implementation of that training arises during the *scale-up process*. That is when you finally put your training into practice in a real-life situation.

God did not actually need David to defeat Goliath. He could have just snuffed the life out of Israel's arrogant enemy. However, God chose the confrontation and prepared David as a vessel to demonstrate His mighty power. God needed somebody who would work with Him and not against Him—for how can two individuals walk together unless they agree? God could not accomplish anything through a person who opposed His will by unraveling everything He had built up. God had spent time training David to help him develop the skills he would need to face Goliath, but if David had decided to ignore that training and rely solely upon his own skills, the outcome of the battle would have been disastrous.

Applying personal ability without relying on God in underdog situations is an attempt to accomplish things independently from God. A person like that becomes a liability to the Lord's cause. It was the combination of God's presence and the training that assured David of victory. All David had to do was press the "Autopilot" button and relinquish his self-control to God Almighty. Let God use the skills that He has developed in you in the way He wants to use them and when He wants to use them. Then you can be assured that they are being used in the most effective way. God will multiply your efforts in amazing ways.

David was a shepherd boy with no experience on the battlefield. He did not have the kind of weapons his enemy used, nor did he know how to use what he had access to. He was facing a well-seasoned veteran who had never lost a battle. God often chooses the weaker ones of this world to confound the mighty. God chooses impossible situations and the most unlikely of people to work His miracles. He does this to demonstrate His ability, and He does not want anyone to be able to say, "It was through my own strength and skill that this was accomplished." God does not want anyone to be confused as to who actually performed the miracle.

The Lord gave Israel victory at Elah when David exercised his faith. Faith moves the hand of the Lord, and without faith, it is impossible to please God. David's faith in God mobilized the Israelite army to pursue the Philistines. He taught them that since the battle belonged to the Lord, they could bank on victory. All you need is the authority of God to pursue and defeat His enemies. Infectious faith or lack thereof will have an effect on those around you. David's infectious faith inspired many to do what they had never done before. David did not try to rely on his own strength and ability, nor did he seek to steal God's credit for the victory.

Soul Mates

Have you ever met a person who instantly made you feel as if you had known them all your life? The more you communicated with them, the more you realized you shared common experiences. True friends are kindred spirits; they are soul mates. In that light, is it any wonder that David and Jonathan became fast friends? After all, they shared the same spirit.

Jonathan had finally found a true comrade, someone who understood him. Jonathan felt suffocated under the weight of his father's faithlessness. He had to respect Saul's authority, even though his father tried everything he could to stamp out his faith. Saul could not bear a person who was led by the Spirit of the Lord, because those types cannot be controlled. He also hated Jonathan's offensive stance, but people who take the offensive are the true movers and shakers of this world. Nothing can dampen their spirit more than the wet blanket of pessimism and narrow-minded thinking, and the fact that his father wanted to kill him did little to bolster Jonathan's spirit. He was surrounded by fearful doubters, which took a toll on his spirit.

By the time David came onto the scene, Jonathan had become so discouraged that he had given up, since he had no one he could identify with. Jonathan would have slain Goliath himself, because he was not the type to back down from a challenge. The fact that he did not proves he was discouraged by his father. David revived Jonathan's soul and gave him the inspiration to carry on. David was a breath of fresh air.

The potential for developing a lasting friendship can be seen through certain signs at the outset of a relationship. First, you share similar experiences. You find that you take similar positions about various topics, but you also respect each other's differences. Second, you feel comfortable being yourself and being vulnerable with each other. You earn each other's confidence. Beware when a person is guarded or you feel the need to be guarded with them. When you extend your friendship and the benefits that come with it and the other person does not, you do not have a mutual friendship; what you have is a one-sided relationship where you have vowed friendship and received nothing in return but a dependent. Finally, each one lends resources to avail the other. Jonathan's love for David caused him to give David the very clothes and weapons off his back. He was basically saying, "My life for yours. I will not hurt you."

> And Jonathan made a special vow to be David's friend, and he sealed the pact by giving him his robe, tunic, sword, bow, and belt.
> *1 Samuel 18:3–4*

They made a covenant of friendship before the Lord, which meant that each of them would do whatever he could to preserve the life of the other. Little did Jonathan know that he would be called to honor that vow on at least two occasions by saving David from Saul. Since Saul was unsuccessful in killing David, and the Philistines could not kill him, Saul urged those closest to David to kill him, but Jonathan tried to mediate. "How has David ever harmed you? As a matter of fact, he risked his life for you. Don't sin against David now."

Saul vowed not to kill David, but he did not intend to keep his word. After Saul had made multiple attempts against his life, David fled to Samuel. Saul sent two sets of troops to apprehend David, but the Spirit of the Lord arrested them and they prophesied. Saul decided to go to Naioth in Ramah to seize David himself. While he was on his way, the Spirit of the Lord arrested him as well, and while Saul lay naked and prostrate, prophesying day and night, David fled.

Having nowhere to turn, David ran to his friend Jonathan. Jonathan was shocked to learn that Saul was still trying to kill David and agreed to help David in any way he could. They realized that Saul had hidden his plans from Jonathan because of their friendship, so they devised a plan to discern Saul's true intentions. There was a tearful departure once Saul's intentions became clear.

> Then David bowed to Jonathan with his face to the ground. Both of them were in tears as they embraced each other and said good-bye, especially David. At last Jonathan said to David, "Go in peace, for we have made a pact in the LORD's name. We have entrusted each other and each other's children into the LORD's hand forever."
> *1 Samuel 20:41–42*

Saul's animosity toward David sprang from insecurity and envy, and he eventually forced David to flee for his life. Saul hated David because he recognized the Spirit of the Lord in David, which caused David to be successful in any assignment. Saul sent David into the deadliest battles, reduced the number of soldiers assigned to David, and sent David on impossible missions. He simply did not grasp the idea that God's involvement in any situation made the odds favorable for David's victory.

Israel loved David because of his success, and his fame grew because he was the most successful officer against the mighty Philistines, attacking them with fury and causing them to retreat. David's fame spread beyond the borders of Israel, and people in other countries thought he was king, even while Saul was still alive.

A healthy person would have been glad to add a man like David to their staff, a man who made such a significant contribution to the team. But Saul was an unhealthy, insecure person, and he felt threatened by David and did not want him around. Saul tried to cause David to fail because he knew failure would cause him to fall out of favor with the people. When his plans backfired, Saul became determined to kill David, and it took multiple attempts on his life before David finally fled for good.

"I know that I am God's anointed and that He can and will protect me," thought David, "but this man will kill me if I stay." Even when God has your back, that is no excuse to be irresponsible and fail to exercise good judgment.

Take-home message: It is all a matter of perspective.

14.

Intensified Training of a Fugitive

To truly know a person, observe them when they are under pressure, for that is when they drop all pretenses and allow their true colors to shine through. Four aspects of David's character emerged while he was a fugitive. He consulted God, was a motivator, stayed focused, and repaid evil with kindness.

Living by Every Word That Proceeded Out of God's Mouth

When you are in a situation that forces you to learn obedience, you get much more focused. Challenges, crises, and obstacles teach obedience. Because there was no room for mistakes, errors, or misinterpretations, David learned to consult and obey the Lord. David was running for his life, and it was important to consult God and to wait for an answer, because one wrong move could have led to his death. David's time of flight was an exercise in faith. He had developed dependence upon God when he was a shepherd boy, and he had to continue to rely on God when the stakes were higher.

> Lead me in the right path, O Lord, or my enemies will conquer me.
> Tell me clearly what to do, and show me which way to turn.
> *Psalm 5:8*

While David was fleeing for his life, he went to Samuel to get instructions. From there, he met with Jonathan, and they determined that Saul intended to kill him. After that meeting, David became an official fugitive. His first stop was to visit Ahimelech, the priest, at Nob. David had an established track record of inquiring of the Lord through this priest. He had consulted God through this man while he was still in the king's favor as commander. Although Ahimelech was alarmed to see David alone, he helped him because of their past relationship and because David lied and told him that Saul had sent him on an urgent mission, leaving him no time to gather weapons or food. Ahimelech gave David Goliath's sword and the Bread of the Presence.

The entire exchange between Ahimelech and David demonstrated the function of the church. David consulted God for direction. Living without divine instruction is like living a stunted existence or not living at all. Every life is on a mission; therefore, every life needs God's direction. David obtained the sword to defend himself against the onslaught of his enemies. God's enemies are the devil and his minions, and because Christians are the children of God, the devil is their natural enemy. The church is the place where Christians can gather armor to withstand the fiery trials of the devil. Christians obtain the sword of the Spirit which is the word of God. David also received sustenance from the Bread of the Presence, which was equivalent to communion. Communion is critical to Christians because by partaking in communion, they become one with Christ Jesus.

The Bread of the Presence was placed before the Lord in the Tabernacle, which made it holy. In order for David to partake of the bread, he had to be purified. For a man, this meant not sleeping with his wife. For a woman, it meant that she abstained from sex and also that she was in a purified state (a specified number of weeks from childbirth or a specified number of days from menstruation). If the Bread of the Presence was holy, those who partook of it became holy. Jesus said He was the bread of life and that a person must eat His flesh and drink His blood for Him to be in that person and that person in Him. When you consume Jesus, He becomes a part of you. At the last supper, Jesus washed His disciples' feet to qualify them to partake of Him. Then He broke bread and told them to eat it because it was His body. After that He offered them wine and told them to drink it because it was His blood. He told them to do this often in remembrance of Him. Every time they ate the bread and drank the wine, they were communing with Jesus.

Communion is the renewing and reaffirming of the covenant Jesus Christ made with Christians. Jesus Christ is married to Christians. Through communion, you become a part of Him and He becomes a part of you. His eternal life flows through you and conquers your death. Communion is to the Christian what marital sex is to humanity.

Since it is true that we can tell a man by the associations he keeps, we can conclude that David was a man of God. He was accustomed to being around men of God. He gladly received these men and was comfortable with them. His closest associates were priests, prophets, and men of faith. He respected them and the advice they gave. David did not overstep his authority; he allowed priests and prophets to do their jobs. He did not run ahead of God, nor did he take any action without first consulting Him. He consulted God in all matters and then did what God told him to do. That is one of the reasons God loved David so much, because he was confident in David's obedience. What David missed most when he was running for his life was being around the people of God and being able to worship God as his soul longed to do. He missed the presence of the Lord. When you are in a crisis, it is difficult to hear the Lord clearly; you need God's representatives to help you.

Many fail in the ministry because they have no one of equal faith to go to when they are in trouble. We have a mistaken notion that a man or a woman of God must be able to walk alone because they are leaders who should have their finger on God's pulse, but they should also have men and women of like faith to lean on when they are in a time of crisis. If God was trying to teach David to walk alone (in the way it is currently taught in ministry) without the assistance of other men and women of God, He would not have allowed David to consult them nor would he have sent prophets to advise him. God was trying to break David's dependence on people who were not on the same spiritual level and could only provide advice from a human perspective. This is a fallacy in the ministry that must be cleared up, because if the enemy is successful at continuing the lie, he has successfully divided and conquered the body of Christ. If the enemy of the Lord can make you feel isolated, it will be easy to defeat you. There is safety in wisdom and counsel, although that does not mean you have it all yourself; you need to know where to get help.

David had a personal priest, Abiathar, who joined him at the cave of Adullam. Abiathar was the only one to escape after his family was massacred upon Saul's orders. He ran to David, and David vowed to protect him with his own life. He became David's personal priest, and whenever David inquired of the Lord, he did it through Abiathar.

From Down-and-Out to Up-and-Coming

Some four hundred others joined David during his time at the cave of Adullam. They learned to follow the Lord through David's relationship with God by imitating their leader. They won great battles and accomplished things they would not have were it not for David's leadership. Their talents and skills had been there all along, but Saul did not have the ability to harness them. People will not rise above the level of their leader. David was a person God developed, and that enabled him to pull others up. Outcasts were attracted to David because he was well acquainted with discouragement and rejection, and he was able to minister to them. He received them and taught them discipline, he encouraged and inspired them to become better men, he gave them purpose, he rebuilt their self-esteem, and he taught them responsibility.

As time went by, many warriors from the Israelite army defected to David because they wanted to be attached to a winner. People want to be attached to a person who is dedicated to winning and has a proven track record. If they were not warriors when they came to David, he developed them into warriors.

Nobody would fault David if he had licked his wounds and cried, "Poor me." However, though he was under stress, David took people under his wing and motivated them to be greater than they thought possible. He was a charismatic leader who inspired greatness in his men. He knew how to prosper in the face of discouragement and adversity and caused others to rise above their circumstances.

David's brothers and relatives also joined him at the cave of Adullam. It brought joy to his heart to finally have the support of his family. People who had once held him in low regard, his critics of the past, came to join his band and to lend their support. They came to respect his position because of all that he had gone through.

On a more practical note, David needed to protect his family. Saul knew that the best way to get to David would be to attack his family. If Saul did not respect the men of God, how could David expect him to exempt his family from his murderous intentions? There is nothing worse than the agony one feels when they are worried that the enemy will use their family as pawns. "Your conflict is with me, not with my family, so don't involve them in this."

It is difficult to effectively minister to others when you are distracted by attacks on your family. God had prepared David for the attacks, but it was hard for him to watch his family suffer, so he took his parents to Moab, where he put them under royal protection. David and his men also set up operations there, because Saul was not the type to take the offensive against his enemies, even if David was among them.

Loyalty to God but Betrayal from Men

Even though the one place you want to avoid most is the place where your life is endangered, that is often the very place that God will send you. The prophet Gad instructed David to leave Moab and go back to Judah. David and his growing band went to the forest of Hereth. Why would the Lord send David back to hostile territory? God uses such hostile places as places of blessing, and He used that opportunity to show David that He would protect him—even in the valley of the shadow of death. *Though the enemy surrounds you, I will not allow them to lay one finger on you.*

God had protected David while he was tending his father's sheep, and He would protect him while he was defending his own sheep. *I've always been with you, and I will not abandon you now.*

God also wanted to keep David in Judah so He could use Him to defend the children of Israel. When news of Keilah's plight reached David, he consulted God through Abiathar to ask God if he should go and help, and God said *Yes*. Although David's men had misgivings, they went. David had taught his men to make a sacrifice to benefit others, because it is better to give than to receive. David went to Keilah to defend the city against the Philistines, who were stealing grain from their threshing floors.

While David was clearing out the Philistines, word reached Saul that David was at Keilah, a walled city, so he mobilized his entire army to march there.

"Will Saul come?"

God said *Yes*.

"Will the men of Keilah really betray us to Saul?"

God said *Yes, they will*.

The second question showed that David was shocked to hear that the people of Keilah would reward him with betrayal when he and his men had risked their lives to defend them from the Philistines. They would use him, and then when they did not need him any longer, they would have no problem handing him over to Saul. Saul should have defended them from the Philistines, for he was their king, but Saul showed up after the Philistines had retreated! The people of Keilah had a warped sense of loyalty; to them it was better to show loyalty to a king who did not risk life and limb to save them.

David faced constant betrayal by his countrymen. The very people who should have shown loyalty because he had blessed them were the ones who betrayed him, but God was testing David because a true leader always needs to keep the big picture in mind. He does not look to the sheep for his reward. His goal is to please God by ministering to His people. As long as you please the Lord, you can look to Him to reward you.

While David and his men were staying at a stronghold in Ziph, the men of Ziph notified Saul of David's whereabouts and offered to capture him. The information led to a close call when David was in the wilderness of Maon. Only a rock (later named the Rock of Escape) prevented David and his men from being captured by Saul. Saul called off the search because he received word that the Philistines were attacking.

What I really need to know, David, is will you serve me faithfully even when those you serve attack you, speak evil of the good you do, and run smear campaigns? Will you serve me even when they stab you in the back and seek your life? Will you minister to my people even if they don't appreciate what you do? I'm good to the just as well as to the unjust. Servants who represent me need to adopt the same attitude. I need you to resolve, to bless, though they curse. Bless—will you do that for me?

The Big Setup

David had another close encounter with Saul, but the tables were turned and Saul was vulnerable to David. In the wilderness of Engedi, Saul entered a cave to relieve himself—the very cave where David and his men were hiding. David's men said, "Look, God has made your enemy vulnerable before you; here's your chance to avenge yourself!"

David saw the situation differently. He saw a chance to value his enemy's life and to repay kindness for evil, just as the Lord had told him to do. Killing Saul would have been justifiable, and no one would have blamed him; he could claim self-defense. David could have reasoned that if his men killed Saul, he could say it was not his fault and his hands were clean. But he could not stand idly by and allow someone to kill, because that would make him an accomplice. If he condoned the behavior, it would be no different from doing it himself. Had that scenario played out, God would have asked, *Who is the leader, anyway? Are you going to allow the men to rule you? If so, you are no better than Saul.*

David taught his men to respect the Lord's anointed and not to return evil for evil. If David had killed Saul or had allowed his men to do it, it would have established a precedent. If any of David's men had become discontented with him, that precedent would have taught them to settle the matter by slaying him. Instead of killing him, however, David cut off a piece of Saul's robe to prove that if it had been his intention to kill him, as Saul had always claimed, he could have done it.

David had a sensitive conscience and was quick to repent. He relied upon the Lord to right wrongs instead of taking matters into his own hands. It is not a sign of weakness to turn the other cheek. On the contrary, the opposite is true. It does not take much effort to lose control or to allow anger and rage to get the best of you. That comes naturally. Strength is demonstrated through restraint. Anger is an explosive tyrant that can cause tremendous destruction, and it requires great strength to contain an explosion. Greater is he who controls his own soul than he who takes a city.

Before his last confrontation with Saul, David had a conflict with Nabal in the wilderness of Maon that became the launching pad for the big setup. That conflict was pivotal, because it helped David solidify his resolve. If he would respect the "least of these," how much more important would it be to respect the Lord's anointed one?

Nabal was mean and dishonest. David and his men were good to Nabal's servants and would not allow anyone else to harm or take any of Nabal's property. When Nabal was shearing his sheep for a celebration, David asked Nabal for provisions. Nabal refused. "Who is David but a runaway servant?

Should I take food intended for my shearers and give it to a renegade band?" It was fine for Nabal to benefit from David's protection, but when David asked for a token of appreciation, Nabal gave unsavory commentary. He did not put up a fuss when the "outlaws and runaway servants," as he called them, protected his sheep. He did not hurl insults when they protected his property. David did not hear complaints when his men helped Nabal. But when they asked to share in Nabal's bounty, he did not know who they were. David lost his cool and blew his top. Nabal was as good as dead.

> A lot of good it did to help this fellow. We protected his flocks in the wilderness, and nothing he owned was lost or stolen. But he has repaid me evil for good. *1 Samuel 25:21*

Glory to God that He sent a sensible woman to counsel and speak wisdom to David's heart, which later would strengthen David's resolve in his encounter with Saul. A leader should not demand a blessing from those who benefit from their leadership. Do you bless people for the sole purpose of receiving a blessing, or do you bless because it is the Father's will?

Although David was a man who consulted the Lord in all things, this time he acted impetuously. While David and his men were on the way to slaughter Nabal and his men, a servant told Abigail, Nabal's wife, what had happened. She quickly gathered enough provisions to accommodate David's men. Then she went to David, bowed before him, and asked for his forgiveness. Abigail spoke prophetically, ministering and encouraging David, and God prevented David from taking vengeance into his own hands. God protected David from his enemies, and He would reward David with a lasting dynasty for his faithful service to the children of Israel.

Up to that point in David's life he had been innocent, but he was about to do something he would regret for the rest of his life. Abigail stopped David dead in his tracks. Despite all the betrayal, the false charges, and deception, there were still some people who were not fooled and would not join Saul's vicious manhunt. There were still people who knew David was a hero, though he was being treated like an infidel. Abigail was such a person, and she provided him with wise counsel to prevent him from sinning. "You don't have to take vengeance into your own hands. The Lord has protected you this far and He will continue to do so. Remain innocent; don't take matters into your own hands."

David lived in constant fear for his life, not knowing if each new day would be his last. He was discouraged by the lies and slander, and he was tired of defending ingrates. Although God did not allow David's enemies to touch him, He did nothing to stop the lies and betrayal, and He did not punish David's enemies for their sins. What do you do when God checks your every move but sits back when your enemies sin against you? You may want to right wrongs by taking matters into your own hands, but it is best to leave those matters to God.

The next day, when Abigail told Nabal what she had done, he had a stroke and became paralyzed; he died ten days later. David heard the news and immediately asked Abigail for her hand in marriage. Abigail, true to her nature, said, "I am willing to be a slave to David's servants!"

If you are under stress, your first inclination is to eliminate the thing causing the stress or to remove yourself from the situation. However, removing himself from the situation was not an option for David, because the Lord sent him back to Judah to test his resolve to respect Saul. When Saul was relieving himself in the cave, he was still protected, because after a period of time, his men would have become suspicious if he had not returned. They would have gone in to investigate, there would have been an untidy battle, and Saul's men would have had the upper hand, because David and his men were trapped in the cave. It would have cost David too much to kill Saul at that moment, so the Lord set up a tempting scenario that would decide the matter, once and for all. It would have been difficult to resist the temptation if David's heart had been set on retaliation.

Later, David and his men came across Saul and his special troops in the wilderness of Ziph. God had put all of Saul's men into a deep sleep. God set David up to see if the only reason he had first refused to attack Saul was because he was waiting for a more auspicious moment.

If I put your enemies into a deep sleep, leaving them at your complete mercy, will you value their lives? They won't fight back; you don't have to fear reprisals or suffer losses. If you kill them all, none can escape to tell others what you did. It is not hard to kill a sleeping man; sleepers don't resist.

David's men clamored with glee over their good fortune. There was the man who was causing them such turmoil and blocking David from the throne. The Lord was favoring David! David asked for volunteers to accompany him into Saul's camp, and Abishai went with him. When they reached the camp, Saul's men were circling him, but they were all asleep. Abishai offered to thrust a spear into Saul—"It will only take one blow and I promise I won't miss"—but David exploded with vehemence.

> "No!" David said, "Don't kill him. For who can remain innocent after attacking the Lord's anointed one?" *1 Samuel 26:9*

David knew that he did not need to lay a finger on Saul, because the incident with Nabal had been an example of what happened to his enemies.

Take-home message: Crises reveal, form, and shape character.

15.

Although You Treat Me as Your Enemy, I Will Not Treat You as Mine

Saul lashed out at David and made it his number one goal to kill him because Saul was an unhealthy and insecure person. Saul handled highly skilled and talented people by suppressing them and killing their spirits. He did everything in his power to destroy David's reputation, set him up for failure, malign his character, and falsely accuse him. Saul had no problem recognizing the strengths, abilities, and talents of others, but because he had reached the pinnacle of his own development, he could not capitalize on the strengths of others when their skills exceeded his. He viewed anyone whose skills exceeded his as a threat to his sovereignty, and he attacked them out of self-preservation.

Leaving Judgment to the Lord

During his last encounter with Saul, David asked sobering questions. First, he asked Saul why he was chasing him, what he had done wrong, and what his crime had been. Then he said, "If the chase is inspired by God, who am I to fight against the will of the Lord? Allow me to make amends with the Lord if I have done wrong. But if this is of your own doing, God will judge between us. From evil people come evil deeds. If you have no charge against me, you are hounding an innocent man."

Saul could offer no justifiable excuse as to why he was hounding David. David addressed the core of Saul's accusations, where he claimed that David was trying to kill him, and proved that they were unfounded. David had had two opportunities to kill Saul, but he did not. Saul had to grudgingly admit the undeniable truth that David had demonstrated greater restraint and strength of character in how he handled the situation with Saul. David had shown respect to God's anointed leader even when that person was unworthy of respect.

David affirmed a principle we would all do well to implement: Matters of abuse of authority are best handled by God, for leaders are accountable to God. You should adopt the attitude that you will bless those who curse you. You should exhibit great character and strength in how you handle them.

> The LORD gives his own reward for doing good and for being loyal, and I refused to kill you even when the LORD placed you in my power, for you are the LORD's anointed one. Now may the LORD value my life, even as I have valued yours today. May he rescue me from all my troubles. *1 Samuel 26:23–24*

God found that David was not motivated by retaliation, would not allow his men to influence him into wrongdoing, and would not allow his men to do wrong. Through it all, David maintained his innocence and allowed God to fight his battles. He did not allow pride to get the best of him; he did not feel he needed to save face. God defended David because he was innocent.

You are no longer innocent when you sin by retaliating against your enemies. I have defended you this far. Will you trust me to defend you now or will you take matters into your own hands? Am I not fit for the task?

When you are falsely accused and shamefully treated, God sits high and looks low. He sees your situation and will judge the right and punish the wrong. Even when David was chased by those who sought his life, he did not avenge himself. He allowed the Lord to handle the situation. As the ultimate test, God handed Saul to David on a platter, yet David refused to attack, respecting the Lord's anointed even though he did not deserve it. David trusted the Lord to protect and avenge him, so he repaid evil with kindness.

"You may think of me as a mighty warrior, but let me tell you the secret of my success. There is a warrior behind me who protects me. He is my rock, my shield, and my fortress. He is my high tower that saves me from violent enemies. When the tentacles of death had a stranglehold on me, I cried out to the Lord and He delivered me, for I have never relied upon my own strength. My strength comes from the Lord, and there has never been a plea my Father didn't answer. When the sound of my cries reached His ears, He moved heaven, riding on the swiftest wings; He roared thunders, confounding my enemies. He moved earth, and reached down, clasping me in His hands. He rescued me from powerful enemies who attacked when I was at my weakest point. He rescued me because of my innocence; I have followed His ways and maintained purity, and my soul relentlessly pursues Him."

Snuggling with the Enemy

David left Israel for a short time, but God needed him in Israel. God sent Gad to instruct David to move back to Judah. David hid in caves, strongholds, forests, and wildernesses. However, Saul knew of David's whereabouts because his countrymen betrayed his hiding spots. David swore he would not kill Saul or his family, and he honored his word. Although Saul had made similar promises, David came to realize that Saul's word was as good as mud, meaningless. For no sooner had he called David his son and praised him than he had his spear poised and ready to strike when the opportunity presented itself. David knew that Saul would continue to pursue him, so he decided to take a sabbatical from the chase. He felt like he needed a break, a reprieve. He was tired of the stress that comes from being hunted, tired of constantly living on the edge of danger. He was weary and worn out; he needed time to relax and regroup.

At one time or another, we have all said to ourselves, "God, I need a break, I need time out, time for my wounds to heal and to refresh myself so I can gain a fresh outlook on this tired situation. The stress has robbed me of my strength, so please just let me steal away for a while so I can pull myself back together."

David initially sought refuge with King Achish in Gath when he first became a fugitive, but Achish refused him, considering him a lunatic. At that time Achish's men mistakenly thought David was king of Israel, because David had successfully defended Israel from her enemies—a king's function. David had to think quickly to prevent his untimely death. He drooled on his beard and scratched on doors. Achish released him, because he had enough lunatics on his hands. It was a combination of street smarts and theatrics that saved David's life.

After David had been a fugitive for some time, he again sought refuge with Achish, this time with his growing band of men and their families in tow. By this time it was clear to Achish that David was a fugitive on the run from Saul. Achish received him, figuring that David would be his servant forever. He gave David the land of Ziklag in Gath, a city of the Philistines. And thus David accomplished his objective, for when word reached Saul that David had moved to Gath, he stopped hunting him. David and his men took up residence with King Achish. Imagine that, snuggling up to the enemy because it was safer than being around the people of God.

David and his men stayed in Ziklag for sixteen months. During that time, David continued to defend the children of Israel, obliterating the Geshurites, the Girzites, and the Amalekites so completely that no one could escape to inform King Achish of what he was doing. He continued the mission God had given to Joshua, which was to remove the original inhabitants of the land. David and his men also chased down bands of raiders who harassed the children of Israel, and when they returned to Ziklag with their plunder, King Achish would ask David where they had raided that day. David lied, using the street smarts he had inherited from Rahab, to convince Achish that he had invaded various Israelite towns. David's quick thinking saved him from retribution and helped him gain Achish's favor. Achish was convinced that the Israelites hated David so much that he would never be able to return to them, and David would be his servant forever.

David deceived Achish so well that the king trusted him enough to invite him to fight alongside the Philistines against the Israelites. David really put on a show for Achish. "Just let me at them, put up your dukes, put them up! Now my lord, the king, will see how bad I am." David danced in a fighting circle, throwing punches in the air. "You will see me in action. You just wait!" He seemed to be straining at the leash. "Hold meeee back!" No one could put on a finer act. David and his men gathered at the rear of the Philistine procession.

When the roll was called, however, the other Philistine leaders were not fooled by David's performance and did not buy David's act. They did not want David and his men to accompany them against the Israelites. They feared that David would turn on them in battle in an attempt to win King Saul's good graces. David pretended to be highly offended when the Philistines snubbed him. With his feelings crushed, he said, "Why, I don't know when I have ever been so offended and disgraced." Achish did everything he could to soothe any hard feelings David may have felt. Then he sent David and his men home to Ziklag. They were relieved that they would not have to fight against fellow Israelites. "Whew, off the hook!"

It was an audacious move for David to snuggle with the enemy. It was safer for him to snuggle with the enemy than to be around God's people. Of all Saul's commanders, David had been the only one who could whip the Philistines. Sometimes enemies who are well matched have a healthy respect for each other that causes them not to attack. An enemy is silenced when he realizes his opponent is just as strong as he is, and David's warrior prowess easily matched or exceeded that of the Philistines.

I Am Alone in This World

Every leader must come to terms with certain things in order to be effective, remain consistent, and survive the rigors of leadership. First of all, people who have benefited from your ministry may turn on you. Second, people only love you as long as you are a blessing to them, and when you cease to be a blessing, you will find out that you have low priority in their book. Third, when crises hit, people can be insensitive, treating you as if you are superhuman, devoid of the normal emotions mere mortals experience. Fourth, you can pour your time and energy into many lives only to find that when you are the one in need, none are willing or able to help you. And finally, you need a strategy to survive in such an environment: you need a strong relationship with God and at least one or two soul mates who are committed to your well-being and can minister to you.

It is difficult to accept the idea that the very people who are blessed by you are the ones who will try to destroy you, but a leader being used by the Lord must realize that it comes with the territory. As repugnant as this reality is, it must be accepted. What is even more difficult is when disloyalty crops up among people within your inner circle. You expect more from those you have taken under your wing and cared for. You have poured into their lives, mended their wounds, and set them on the path to recovery, in some cases made them much better off than before. It is difficult to understand disloyalty among your protégés, but you must be prepared for it. Knowing this up front helps take the edge off the bitter pill of disloyalty and betrayal.

Those who had benefited from David's leadership turned against him when the tide changed. After being discharged from the Philistine camp, David and his men returned to Ziklag to find that their homes had been burned to the ground and that someone had taken their wives, children, and livestock. The men David had taken under his wing quickly decided to stone him because things had gone wrong, as if it were his fault, not stopping to think that David had lost his wives, children, and property, too, and was grieving just as much as they were. They all experienced the same loss, but they thought David's loss was unimportant. They viewed him as a superhuman who was not affected by calamity in the same way as mere mortals. Stoning David would not have solved anything, but the men wanted a scapegoat. Calamity strikes of its own volition, and leaders should not be held accountable for things they have no control over. Moses experienced the same thing with the children of Israel in the wilderness. A leader's popularity rises when all is well and the people are blessed, and it falls when calamity strikes.

At times like that, leaders learn where they really stand with the people they serve. You are in a crowd of "supporters" who are only around you for what they can get. They do not care about you personally, and once they derive the needed benefit from you, they discard you because you are expendable. When a crisis hits, they attack you as if it were your fault. When you suffer from a personal crisis and turn to them for help, you can find no one. Not one of David's men stopped thinking about himself long enough to consider that David not only had suffered the same loss but also was in danger. Not one of David's men stood up in his defense or offered a helping hand. No one cared. It was an ugly picture to see, and it was enough to cause despondency, "I am all alone," thought David.

When you come to this realization, you must lay your head on God's shoulder and find solace in Him. Even if everyone deserts you, there is One who will never abandon you. As long as you have God, you will never be alone. Seek encouragement from the Father, just like David did. After he had rested in his Father's arms, he asked God if he should pursue the enemy to recover that which had been stolen. (After crying, seek resolution.) God told David to pursue the enemy and that he would recover all that had been taken. David encouraged his men to move forward and begin the pursuit.

Human beings are social beings, yet being a leader is a lonely job. Therefore, as a leader, you need a few quality friendships to sustain you. In quality friendships both people are knitted together in an unbreakable bond, and each has adopted a my-life-for-yours attitude. Both of you have developed intimacy and demonstrated trustworthiness by exposing vulnerabilities to one another. You can trust each other, knowing that neither will hurt the other and each will do whatever it takes to help. Each of you has the other's best interest at heart, is committed to the well-being of the other, and will not hesitate to minister to the other. Yours is a friendship that has withstood the test of time, where both of you have encouraged and supported one another. It is best for such friendships to develop naturally; however, you should pray to God to send such friends to you and you to them. Jonathan and David were soul mates who had a covenant friendship. When David needed a friend, God allowed Jonathan access to David to provide support and encouragement. Jonathan found David at his lowest points and ministered to him, and David had no fear that Jonathan would expose him to Saul.

It was fortuitous that David and his men came across a slave who had been left alongside the road. They revived the man, and he told them that he had become ill and had been left to die by his Amalekite master. He told David that the Amalekites had attacked, plundered, and burned several cities to the ground, including Ziklag. The slave led David to the Amalekite camp, under the condition that they would not return him to slavery. David caught the Amalekites off guard as they were celebrating their victory, and he and his men annihilated the Amalekites, recovering their families and all their property, and confiscating the plunder the Amalekites had taken from other cities. From that plunder, David gave gifts to leaders in Judean cities, pointing out that God had given them the victory.

David and his men then returned to Ziklag, each man lost in his own thoughts. Things would never be the same; there could be no turning back.

The men had made it abundantly clear what David meant to them. They would only support him as long as he was a blessing to them, but when he ceased to be a blessing, they would abandon him. David's men had revealed their true nature and could no longer hide behind pretense. The rift they had created could not be repaired, and their future together was uncertain. Then a ton of bricks dropped on them, ending their reverie.

When One Suffers, We All Suffer

While David reflected on what had transpired between him and his men and its many implications, they were reuniting with their families. But then news from the battlefield put an end to reverie and reunions. Israel had suffered a mighty defeat. Many Israelite soldiers were dead, Israelites had abandoned their cities, and Saul and his sons had died in battle.

While David was a fugitive, he did not assist Saul in battle. Even when Saul and David were on good terms, it was rare for them to fight in the same battles. Saul made a habit of sending David to battles with limited resources so that David would fail. Well into David's administration, Saul's supporters continued to blame David for Saul's death, claiming he had purposefully avoided the battle to cause Saul's death. However, based on the circumstances, it appears that God had orchestrated events to prevent David from defending Israel. If the Philistines had allowed David and his men to assist them in battle, David would have assisted Israel, as they feared. If David had returned to Ziklag to find normal circumstances, he would have asked God if he should assist Israel in battle. God had trained David to assist the Israelites regardless of their attitude, and He had trained David to respect His anointed king. God did not want David to be available to consult Him about the battle, because telling him not to assist Israel would have contradicted everything He had taught him. Although David rarely acted without consulting God, his training would have caused him to automatically defend Israel. However, it was God's intention for Saul to die that day, and He purposely occupied David so that he would not interrupt His plans.

David had a way of looking at the big picture, and he understood that Israel could not afford factions. If her enemies could detect internal strife and disunity, they could use that to bring Israel to her knees. There was no time to be distracted by personality clashes and personal preferences that would cause Israel to lose sight of the real enemy. Internal strife gives the enemy an open door that he can enter without resistance. Saul was the epitome of a body fighting against itself. Because of his lack of focus, he left Israel defenseless many times while he pursued David. There is no room for competition in the Lord's army.

If behavior speaks volumes about the attitude of the heart, what does David's mourning the death of Saul say about his heart? He did not rejoice over the demise of his oppressor. Although Saul had treated David as his enemy, David did not adopt Saul's attitude. "You may call me enemy, but I don't consider you my enemy. You may be my enemy, but we have a common enemy. When confronted by our common enemy, it is time to put aside our differences and unite."

On a personal level, David never considered Saul his enemy. Just because someone hates you does not mean you have to respond in kind. David was leery of Saul, but he did not allow his personal feelings to cloud his judgment. David could have rejoiced with a sigh of relief over Saul's death, but he mourned instead, because he understood that Israel had suffered a heavy blow. The loss of many warriors had weakened her defenses.

David said, "Today our nation has suffered a mighty loss and a great setback. Let us not report it in the cities of our enemy, for they will rejoice and give credit to their gods. They will laugh in triumph over us. Furthermore, now that they have weakened our defenses, they can attack us while we are vulnerable."

Just as Israel represented one nation under God, *we* are the body of Christ. That body is as diverse and wonderful as the human body. It is not simply your church, it is the local, national, and international church that makes up the body of Christ. The body of Christ has systems that specialize in certain functions. Although the functions are different, the overall goal is the same. When one system shuts down or is functioning improperly, the whole body is in jeopardy. When part of the body suffers defeat, the pain reverberates throughout the entire body. It is a time of mourning, not ridicule, when a believer or ministry falls. It is your responsibility to restore the fallen believer or ministry. It is just as ludicrous to rejoice when a ministry falls because of sin as it is to rejoice at the loss of your own foot. Why celebrate when you will have to hobble forever? Our goal is the same; therefore, we do not rejoice when part of the body crumbles. When you are in the same kingdom, you are on the same team; there is no room for competition. Let that be the first coat you shed when you join the body of believers.

Being a leader of God's people is not as glamorous as it seems. Many laypeople covet a leader's position without understanding the process it took to get there and the price they pay. When you look behind the scenes at all a leader has to endure, being a leader is not all it is cracked up to be. Why would any sane individual choose such a lifestyle? Leaders are chosen by God and prequalified by Him. They take up the cross and fully commit to God's call because they love God. They remain consistent in the face of intensive training (adversity), abuses of authority, betrayals, death threats, and a number of other untold atrocities, because they keep their focus on the prize He has set before them. Instead of being jealous of leaders and secretly anticipating their demise, you should feel empathy and pray for them.

> But sometimes I think God has put us apostles on display, like prisoners of war at the end of a victor's parade, condemned to die. We have become a spectacle to the entire world—to people and angels alike. Our dedication to Christ makes us look like fools, but you are so wise! We are weak, but you are so powerful! You are well thought of, but we are laughed at. To this very hour we go hungry and thirsty, without enough clothes to keep us warm. We have endured many beatings, and we have no homes of our own. We have worked wearily with our own hands to earn our living. We bless those that curse us. We are patient with those who abuse us. We respond gently when evil things are said about us. Yet we are treated like the world's garbage, like everybody's trash—right up to the present moment.
> *1 Corinthians 4:9–13*

God never intended for a person to lead His people based upon their own ability and strength, because He knew that would mean failure for His people. God's people are His own special possession, and He cannot entrust them to just anybody. He needs a person who wants to follow Him with their whole heart and would turn the hearts of His children back to Him. David was the embodiment of the kind of leader God was looking for, because he would do whatever God told him to do. God was confident that David would teach the children of Israel how to follow Him and would not try to steal His glory.

> The person who rules righteously, who rules in the fear of God, he is like the light of the morning, like the sunrise bursting forth in a cloudless sky, like the refreshing rains that bring tender grass from the earth. *2 Samuel 23:3–4*

God could not afford another Saul, who had been a severe liability to His cause. God would not appoint anyone who had not been thoroughly trained first. He pre-trained David as a shepherd so He could develop the traits needed in a leader. Then He put David through intensive training to help him make the transition from a shepherd of sheep to a shepherd of the children of Israel. God methodically took David through a series of faith-building exercises, and each lesson he learned in the preceding trial was applied in the next one.

David's love for God caused him to take an interest in what God loved. Out of his love for God he defended Israel, even though he was treated like an enemy of the state. Many who had benefited from David's ministry disclosed his whereabouts to Saul. Even in times of intense stress, David did not lose his vision and his sense of duty to God's people. He did not defend Israel to receive their admiration; his sole duty was to God. The way to remain consistent in service to God's people is to focus on who you are working for. God loves the unlovable and ungrateful; He blesses His enemies with His unfailing love. For the sake of His name, He is faithful. For the sake of God, hold to your duties and be faithful even when the people who benefit from your ministry are disloyal.

Take-home message: Focus on who you are working for and be consistent, even when the people who benefit from your efforts show no appreciation.

16.

Rocky Road to the Path of King

Jonathan was so positive, upbeat, full of faith, and healthy that it was a shame he had to die along with his father. Why did Jonathan have to suffer for the sins of his father? Why did anyone have to suffer for Saul's sins? In actuality, Jonathan's death was long overdue. He should have died when he broke the oath Saul made his men take at Geba, and although he was under a curse that was screaming for the death penalty, his death also prevented Saul's loyalists from declaring him king.

However, Jonathan's death was a shame, because he could have been a great asset to David. The two of them could have conquered all of Israel's enemies in their lifetime. They possessed the same spirit of faith and when combined with their ability, they would have been unbeatable. Jonathan would have had no problems taking a back seat to David. He would have been happy for the privilege of being David's constant companion. With Jonathan's death, David lost a true friend—and a true soul brother. He lost the only true friend he ever had besides God.

Last Respects

David eulogized Saul and his sons Jonathan, Malkishua, and Abinadab in "The Song of the Bow," in which he paid his last respects to his friend.

Your pride and joy, O Israel, lies dead on the hills!
How the mighty heroes have fallen!
Don't announce the news in Gath, or the Philistines will rejoice.
Both Saul and Jonathan killed their strongest foes;
they did not return from battle empty-handed.
How beloved and gracious were Saul and Jonathan!
They were together in life and in death.
They were swifter than eagles; they were stronger than lions.

O women of Israel, weep for Saul, for he dressed you in fine clothing
and gold ornaments.
2 Samuel 1:19–20, 22–24

Jonathan my brother, I mourn your loss most of all.

Oh, how much I loved you!
And your love for me was deep, deeper than the love of women!
2 Samuel 1:26

David was so generous in his praise of Saul that it is hard to believe he was talking about the same Saul who had spent years trying to take his life. However, he was using objective optimism—the kind of optimism that can put a positive spin on anything, telling the world that although Saul was his toughest critic and had been bent on killing him, he did have his good points. David refused to allow Saul's evil treatment to cloud his judgment.

The most touching part of the eulogy, however, was David's statement about Jonathan and the quality of their friendship. Theirs was not a homosexual relationship as some have claimed. It is possible to love a person dearly without sexual involvement.

Saul visited a medium at Endor the night before his death, and she conjured the soul of Samuel. Saul figured that since God was giving him the silent treatment, he would turn to Samuel for guidance, trying to reject God's authority and to establish his own. That was rebellion on the grandest scale. Independence and self-reliance are deadly in God's kingdom. A person who refuses to depend upon God or to obey Him is a liability to God's cause. When things are not done according to God's instructions, unintended defeat occurs and the enemies of God rejoice.

The spirit of Samuel informed Saul that both he and his sons would be in paradise the next day. Although the single act of conjuring the spirit of Samuel was not enough to cause Saul's death, it solidified God's decision, because it epitomized the self-reliant and defiant attitude that Saul had displayed throughout his career. That attitude cost the lives of Saul and his sons, his armor bearer, and many Israelite soldiers. It caused Israelites on the other side of the Jezreel Valley and beyond Jordan to abandon their towns.

When the Philistines discovered the bodies of Saul and his sons on Mount Gilboa the next day, they beheaded them, stripped them of their armor, transported them to Beth-Shan, and pinned them to a wall. They put Saul's armor in the temple of the Ashtoreths. The Philistines proclaimed Saul's death to the people, and there was much rejoicing in the Philistine camp. The men of

Jabesh-Gilead traveled all night to reach Beth-Shan, prepared to do whatever it took to get the bodies of Saul and sons. They had a reverence for Saul, because his first act as king had been to save them from the oppression of the Ammonite King Nahash. They took the bodies off the wall and transported them to Jabesh, where they cremated and buried them.

Not by Force but by Choice

David's rise to kinghood was not as smooth as it should have been. For David it was more like a rocky road than a smooth highway. After Saul's death, David and his men moved back to Judah, near Hebron, at the Lord's instruction, where Judah's leaders crowned David king without hesitation. David then invited Jabesh-Gilead to become his loyal subjects, asking the Lord to bless them for their faithfulness and promising to reward them for their loyalty to Saul. However, Abner bar Ner, commander of Saul's army, blocked David by proclaiming Saul's son Ishbosheth king over the rest of Israel. Abner embodied the spirit of Saul and wielded enough power to circumvent the will of God and the will of the people for a time, but later, when Abner was ready to hand Israel to David, his statements indicated that Israel had wanted David as their king all along. What do you do when it is clear to everyone else what God's will is and who God's choice is yet there is one person who decides that they want to impose their will over God's? Abner had been the only one preventing David from becoming king.

You know you have done your job as a leader when people begin to imitate you. When your people tackle insurmountable obstacles and kill giants, you know you have trained them to walk in faith and to rely on God rather than on their personal strengths. There is no greater reward than to train people to walk by faith and to watch them in action. It does not pay to keep people in the dark about the source of your victories. One day they might save your life because of the way you have trained them.

Many leaders try to protect their position by withholding information, viewing potential trainees as threats. They do not understand that we are all in the kingdom of God together and on the same team. It is far more effective to impart your spirit to those around you, thereby multiplying your efforts and training new warriors for the kingdom of God. Many are not afraid to trample demons, because they saw you do it.

Sibbecai, from Hushah, killed Saph, the giant. Elkanah, son of Jair from Bethlehem, killed the brother of Goliath. Jonathan, David's nephew, killed a giant with six fingers on each hand and six toes on each foot. Those people would never have attempted to fight giants had they not seen David do it first. David shared in their triumphs and benefited from showing his warriors how to perform great feats in the name of God. Their victories were his victories, and each was a victory for God's kingdom. Sir, you too share the victories of those you trained, because you are on the same team. They do great exploits to the glory of God because you taught them by showing them that the impossible is possible.

By the time of David's coronation in Judah, he had amassed a great army of more than a half million men. Many of those men had defected from the Israelite army during Saul's reign or immediately before Saul's last battle, because of his incompetence. The news Samuel delivered through the medium about Saul's impending defeat could not be suppressed, and many men deserted. When the Philistines marched against Saul during his last battle, many Israelite soldiers joined David to defeat Saul, but it was not God's plan to have David present during Saul's last battle.

Since Judah was the only tribe to embrace David as king, the men who joined David were ready to forcefully install him as king over all Israel. Ambidextrous archers from the tribe of Benjamin, Saul's relatives, joined David, as did warriors from Gad who were experts with both shield and spear. The weakest Gad warriors could each take on a hundred regular troops, and the strongest could challenge a thousand. Warriors from every tribe joined David.

David had a core of mighty men of valor. These men had become famous by the feats they had accomplished. For instance, Jashobeam and Abishai had once killed three hundred enemies each in a single battle. Benaiah, commander of David's bodyguards, had once chased a lion into a pit and, despite adverse weather, killed it. There were at least thirty other men of equal stature in David's army, all eager to forcefully make David king, and they marched to Hebron in battle array for that purpose. It is evident that had David wanted to take the throne forcefully over the entire nation of Israel, there would have been no stopping him. David's men were strong and well trained, and they were capable of taking the kingdom by force, but David would not force himself on the people. He patiently demonstrated his attributes and waited for an invitation. A shepherd does not force his way into the hearts of his sheep, he earns it. That is also the nature of God—He only comes into your heart when invited.

Civil War

Even though Saul used his army to hunt David, there was never a fight between David's and Saul's men. Saul's men would have fought fellow citizens, but God prevented that by keeping David abreast of Saul's plans. David and his men only fought Israel's enemies until Saul's death. However, one day, Abner decided to test David's men, thinking that if he could beat them, he would gain control over Judah. He proposed a hand-to-hand combat to Joab, the commander of David's army, and Joab agreed.

Twelve men from each army were chosen, and they killed each other, so twenty-four men lost their lives at the pool of Gibeon. But that was not enough to satisfy Abner's curiosity as to whether the Israelite army could soundly defeat David's men. The only thing that could be concluded from that skirmish was that the men were equally matched, and the two armies began to fight at that point. David's men soon had the Israelite army on the run and doggedly pursued them. Zeruiah's three sons, Joab, Abishai, and Asahel, were in David's army. Asahel, the youngest brother, could run like a deer, and he relentlessly pursued Abner and would not be deterred by Abner's repeated warnings, "Go away, chase someone else." Abner tried to shake him twice, but Asahel would not listen, and Abner was finally forced to kill him. Joab and Abishai then had a personal vendetta against Abner to avenge their brother's death.

Abner was responsible for initiating the clash among David's men and the Israelite army. When it became clear to Abner that David's men were more than a match for the Israelite army, he relented and shouted to Joab:

> Must we always solve our differences with swords? Don't you realize the only thing we will gain is bitterness toward each other? When will you call off your men from chasing their Israelite brothers?
> *2 Samuel 2:26*

The armies parted and went their separate ways. Abner's army had lost 360 men, while Joab had lost only twenty, including his brother, Asahel. Although the battle at Gibeon ended that day when the armies realized that the sword could only create bitterness, a long civil war continued between the loyalists of David and Saul. David grew stronger with each passing day.

If Abner had not slept with Rizpah, one of Saul's concubines, Judah would have remained separate from Israel. Although Abner installed Ishbosheth as king of Israel, he was really the one calling the shots. He believed he could do whatever he wanted without answering to anyone, not even to the man he had installed as king. When Ishbosheth confronted Abner about his indiscretion of sleeping with Rizpah, Abner became indignant.

Abner did not feel as if he had to answer to anyone, much less Ishbosheth, and in his mind, sleeping with one of Saul's women was not even worth mentioning compared to the loyalty he had shown Saul and his family. Abner was a powerful force to be reckoned with, and when Ishbosheth realized his faux pas, he dropped the issue. "Sure, Abner, just sleep with the entire royal harem, no problem." Ishbosheth realized too late that he was only king in name and not in deed. What do you do when the military commander is stronger than the king? You bide your time, bite your tongue, and try not to offend the army commander. However, that error eventually cost Ishbosheth his kingdom. Abner resolved to hand the kingdom over to David; he immediately met with the leaders of Israel and the tribe of Benjamin (Saul's people) to win their support.

> "For some time now," he told them, "you have wanted to make David your king. Now is the time! For the LORD has said, I have chosen David to save my people from the Philistines and from all their other enemies." *2 Samuel 3:17–18*

His speech confirms two things: everyone was aware that David was not only God's choice but the people's choice as well. Abner personified Saul because he knew it was God's will for David to be king but tried to thwart God's will. When he realized that he could not prevail against David's men or continue to oppose God, he went to David to unite the kingdom. Abner sparked a civil war, but he was smart enough to stop fighting when he realized he could not win. He intentionally created a conflict with Ishbosheth so he could surrender without admitting defeat or losing face. Ishbosheth gave Abner an excuse to do what he wanted to do all along—surrender.

Abner sent word to David that he was willing to negotiate and would assist in handing the nation to him because he had Israel's support, including the tribe of Benjamin. David insisted on getting Michal, his first wife, back as part of the deal, so Abner brought Michal with him when he went to Hebron. David received Abner graciously and threw a great feast, and the two men sat down amicably to discuss how they would reunite Israel under David's leadership. David welcomed a peaceful union of the nation of Israel, one without more bloodshed and casualties that would further debilitate Israel. David did not want to take the throne by force, as evidenced by his eulogy for Saul and those who had fallen in battle with the Philistines, and Abner was tired of fighting a losing battle.

Abner's proposal to bring Israel peacefully under David's leadership would have put an end to the fighting had it been consummated. But when Joab returned from a raid and heard that Abner had left in peace, he went to David and accused Abner of spying.

> When Joab was told that Abner had just been there visiting the king and had been sent away in safety, he rushed to see the king. "What

> have you done?" he demanded. "What do you mean by letting Abner get away? You know perfectly well that he came to spy on you and to discover everything you are doing!" *2 Samuel 3:23–25*

Addressing a king that way could cost a person his life, but Joab acted with impunity because he was a powerful commander and David's nephew. Joab went after Abner and killed him, not because he thought he was spying, but to avenge Asahel's death. Because Joab killed Abner before he could complete his mission, the unification of Israel under David's leadership was once again delayed.

What Am I to Do with You, Sons of Zeruiah?

When David found out what Joab had done, he was careful to absolve himself. He wanted the people to know that he had not received Abner in peace just to lure him to his death. David commanded Joab and his men to tear off their clothes, put on sackcloth, and go into mourning for Abner. David also mourned Abner's death, making a public statement in a funeral song:

> Should Abner have died as fools die? Your hands were not bound; your feet were not chained. No, you were murdered—the victim of a wicked plot. *2 Samuel 3:33–34*

David refused also to eat, even against the people's urging. By his actions, David proved to the people that he had not been responsible for Abner's death, but he also knew that his nephews, Joab and Abishai, were becoming a liability. He openly admitted that although he was the anointed king, Joab and Abishai were too powerful for him to control. His prayer was to let God repay them for their wicked acts.

Joab fearlessly addressed David as if he were a child because David did not have the loyalty of his men, which had been made clear at Ziklag. What he had was a group of men who would only stick with him as long as it benefited them. David's men could be persuaded to turn on him in a heartbeat. Joab understood the undercurrents in David's army and derived his power by exploiting that knowledge. Joab was not powerful because of his physical strength or prowess; he was powerful because of his influence. He could use the disloyal of the army against David.

Every leader has a defining moment in which their power and authority are tested, and David's moment was at Ziklag. However, David did not cave in to peer pressure during his encounters with Saul, nor did he allow his men to harm Saul. He rebuked his men without fear of disapproval, but Ziklag revealed that his men were opportunists. Although David had ministered to them, transformed their lives, and changed their fortunes, he did not have their loyalty. Loyalty, like respect, has to be earned. David did enough to earn their undying loyalty, but his men were disloyal. Disloyal opportunists can be bought if the price is right and will turn their backs when a better opportunity comes along. David had a situation on his hands that he could not control, for how do you teach loyalty? Either you have it or you do not.

David was aware of the predicament he faced with his men, and so was Joab, and Joab took advantage of the situation. Joab knew that he could disrespect David and murder with impunity because he could turn David's men against him. He was the true source of power in David's administration and was ruthless enough to use the men's disloyalty to his advantage.

While David could have maintained control over his disloyal people, he had one person who complicated matters by exploiting the problem to usurp his power and authority. Gradually relieving the disloyal people of their duties and replacing them with loyal people would have solved the problem, but it would have taken time. The time between Ziklag and his ascension to king of Judah was short. The civil war Abner ignited and his eventual death also left little time for David to address the problem properly. It takes time to accumulate loyal followers, and time was a luxury David did not have. Many criticize David for having a foreign court. Is it any wonder that he resorted to that?

When Saul failed to control his men and demonstrated that he was afraid of them, God asked him, "Who's leading whom? I made you king, and if you cannot control your men, you are not fit to be king."

The same applied to David. Relinquishing control over the army, regardless of the reason, jeopardized David's ability as king. He was supposed to be the ultimate commander of the army, and abdicating his authority would have future repercussions. It had already created a delay in fulfilling his God-given destiny, because Joab's actions caused Israel to question David's character. What price would David pay in his tenure for his nephew's military leadership?

Anyone who has been witness to or victim of a military coup can understand David's predicament. Revolutions all around the globe have been accomplished by the military. The military can be your greatest asset if it supports you—or your undoing if it turns against you. Joab was a person to be reckoned with, and as commander of David's army, he could use the soldiers to help or hinder David. What do you do when the commander of the military marches to his own drum and does not submit to your authority? Anything the army commander did was a reflection upon David, because he was the ultimate authority.

With a king comes his cabinet, and Joab was an opposing force in David's cabinet from the beginning. Joab did not start the civil war, but he perpetuated it, and killing Abner to avenge his brother's death did not help matters. Joab's way of "uniting" Israel caused bitterness and resentment in the hearts of the Israelites. Israel lost a key leader with the death of Abner. It left pockets of resistance in Israel, but an absence of war and strife can mean the discontented feel powerless to defend themselves. True peace can be achieved only when there is accord by choice, not by force.

Delays, Delays, and More Delays

Later, the smoldering bitterness that was born out of Joab's forceful tactics would find an avenue of expression to taunt David. With the king comes his sovereignty. The military's attitude was a reflection upon David, since the actions taken by members of an administration supposedly reflect the beliefs and attitudes of the leader. Joab's forcefulness caused people to view David with hostility. He was accused of usurping the throne from Saul, even though it was not true.

It is the lot of a leader to be misunderstood often. His actions are constantly under scrutiny, and his decisions are often misconstrued. David was bred as a shepherd; it is not in the character of a shepherd to lose sheep. David made it abundantly clear that he was not responsible for Abner's death. David did not sanction the civil war that ravished his nation and weakened her internal defenses. How can a nation divided against itself stand? What was not clear to the public was that David was not in control of his administration. The true power rested in the hands of Joab, and the actions of the military did not reflect David's sentiments.

When our fortunes are on the rise, it is natural to want to take relatives along, but relatives should be evaluated in the same way as outsiders for positions of authority. Some relatives are best kept at a distance when you take their character into consideration. Giving individuals a position simply because they are relatives can be detrimental. The problems David suffered in his administration were the result of having unqualified relatives on his staff.

Although David was a great warrior, he was not a ruthless man. Up to that point in his life, he had never harmed another Israelite. He had killed Israel's enemies in battle, but he did not kill people so he could take their position. Those close to him knew that, but the Israelites did not. They did not know that David could have killed Saul on two occasions but had refused to do so. They did not know about David's promise to Saul not to harm his family or about the pact between David and Jonathan. They did not know that a man wrote his own death sentence when he told David that upon Saul's request he had thrust Saul through with a sword at Mount Gilboa. They did not know that David had considered a person worthy of death for killing a king. David was not a cutthroat.

With Abner dead, Ishbosheth lost all hope, because Abner was the true power behind his kingdom. Ishbosheth had reigned over Israel for just two years when two captains of his raiding party seized the opportunity to take his life. When Baanah and Recab killed Ishbosheth in his sleep and brought his head to David for show and tell, they thought he would congratulate them by giving them high positions in his administration. After all, the tone of David's administration suggested that he was a cutthroat and would support such behavior.

It was obvious that those two men had not been under David's tutelage. David did not view it as good news. Instead, he took an entirely different view. "God defends me from my enemies. I don't need your help, or your way of doing things." Instead, David condemned them for killing an innocent and defenseless man, a king no less, in his own house on his own bed. David's response showed that Joab's actions were not acceptable and that nothing would have pleased him more than to remove Joab from power.

In the beginning of David's reign as king over Judah, he suffered from the bad press created by opposing factions in his administration. The civil war that Abner initiated and Joab perpetuated, and the murder of key people in Saul's administration (such as Abner and Ishbosheth), did little to bolster his public image. It left a bad taste in Israel's mouth. David did everything he could to absolve himself of the wrongdoings of his nephews and the other circumstances outside of his control, but he could not correct his public image.

In essence, the people of Israel said, "You want us to believe that you have nothing to do with those deaths and that the civil war that is ravaging our country is not your doing? You want us to believe that your nephews are unruly monsters that you cannot control and that they are going completely against your will? We would like to believe you, but if you put yourself in our shoes and view things from our vantage point, you will get a totally different picture. It looks as if you are a vicious man who will stop at nothing to take the throne. It looks as if you will kill those who oppose you and then hide behind your cronies to let them take the rap. It looks like you hire hit men to do your dirty work and then kill them before they can expose your dirty secrets. We are trying, with great difficulty, to believe that all the events that have transpired were merely circumstantial and coincidental, but it's hard to swallow for the rational observant mind."

Delays, delays, and more delays occurred each time a key man within

Saul's administration was killed, causing Israel to have deep reservations about David. It took five and a half years after Ishbosheth's death for all of Israel to receive David as king. The bad press and bad publicity served only to harm David and fuel false accusations. Those outside of David's administration found it a far stretch of their imagination to believe in David's innocence.

The people were saying, "We don't know you; we know about you. We know what people have said about your behavior, and the events surrounding your reign seem to support their assessments."

Although he was innocent of both Abner's and Ishbosheth's death, what were the people supposed to think? The death of key people in Saul's administration was convenient for David. There would always be lingering doubt about David's innocence. After all, Saul had publicly accused David of trying to kill him. The rumors and slander, coupled with the circumstantial evidence, caused many to conclude that David was a ruthless man and fueled hostility toward him.

However, after more than five years, the people of Israel finally crowned David king at Hebron, where he made a covenant with the leaders of Israel before the Lord and was anointed king of all Israel. When the wicked are in authority, the people mourn. When the righteous are in authority, the people rejoice. It was a day of rejoicing when David finally took over the helm of the nation of Israel. There was a great celebration, and the people feasted for several days, because the burden of having a wicked, sinful leader had been removed. The yoke of sin had been broken and the people could finally breathe free.

> For a long time, even while Saul was our king, you were the one who really led Israel. And the Lord has told you, "You will be the shepherd of my people Israel. You will be their leader." *2 Samuel 5:2*

However, it was nothing short of miraculous that Israel was ultimately able to separate fact from fiction and to arrive at a point where they could embrace David. With time Israel was able to discern a difference between David and people in his administration like Joab. It was a miracle that David became king, all things considered, since he faced a hellish future with Joab in tow.

Take-home message: Unholy alliances can delay your destiny.

Part Three: Pinnacle

17.

First Initiative as King

I will rely on God. I won't rely on my ability or past conquests. What I have, you have given me. The victories I have enjoyed were won as a result of you. You have given me victory over my enemies. I have not adopted the mistaken attitude that I can operate independent of you and remain victorious. I don't rely on a massive army or the ability soldiers possess. Lord, if we are to be successful, it will be because we consult and obey you. Lord, you have a different vantage point than I do. I only see in part, but you see the whole picture. You have hoards of mighty angels to do your bidding, effecting change wherever you send them, for they are disciplined and focused, and they exist solely to fulfill your orders. In your infinite wisdom, you spoke this world into existence. No one can resist your irresistible power. I am your creation. Everything I have and all that I am came from you. If I fail to consult you and do as you say, I'm not the only one who will suffer. The men in my army will suffer, and the people you have put under my charge will suffer."

Setting the Tone

After his coronation over all Israel, David's attitude set the tone for his administration. An immediate difference can be seen between Saul and David with David's first official act as king. While Saul was possessed with hunting down the Lord's anointed and subverting the will of God, David was possessed with pursuing God and making Him the focal point of the nation of Israel. David was consumed with bringing God and His glory to Jerusalem. David's first official act after his coronation was to bring the Ark of the Lord back to its proper place, something that was not a priority during Saul's administration.

> It is time to bring back the Ark of our God, for we neglected it during the reign of Saul. *1 Chronicles 13:3*

That proclamation showed that the motivation of David's heart was to be near God. You do not crave the nearness of God if you are an unrepentant sinner. Although Saul thought he could do without God, David knew he could not, and David's number one goal was to have the presence of the Lord for himself and for the people he governed.

David did not issue an "executive order" to bring back the Ark of the Lord, however. Although Israel needed God, David would not force God on them. He made a proposal to bring the Ark of the Lord back, and then left Israel to decide to receive God. It was important to do it that way, because God needs a welcome from each heart, not a grudging acceptance of his "intrusion."

I need permission to come into your heart. I will not force myself upon you.

Do you want God to be involved in *your* life? Do you see a need for God in your life? Are there situations in your life that could best be handled by God? If you want God to return, ask Him to come back.

> The whole assembly agreed to this, for the people could see it was the right thing to do. *1 Chronicles 13:4*

David summoned Israel to join in the monumental occasion of bringing God back. He assigned thirty thousand special troops to go to the house of Abinadab in Kiriath-jearim and retrieve the Ark. When they put the Ark on a cart, Abinadab's son Ahio was in front and his other son, Uzzah, was behind. The people celebrated exuberantly and danced wildly before God, singing and playing harps, lyres, tambourines, cymbals, and trumpets. They riotously, unrestrainedly praised God.

As they arrived at the threshing floor of Nacon, the oxen stumbled and Uzzah touched the Ark to steady it. Instantly the Lord's anger burst out against Uzzah, and he died on the spot. A hush came over the crowd as they came to a dead stop and terror gripped their hearts. David, perhaps for the first time in his life, was afraid of God, since he had never before witnessed the anger of the Lord directed against anyone.

The fear of the Lord is the beginning of wisdom. To fear the Lord means to recognize that He has all power and to realize that God is not a plaything or an ethereal idea but a Spirit. It is not just that God has the ability to end a person's life, because man can do that; it is that He can throw both body and soul into hell. Nothing can cause one to fear the Lord more effectively than directly observing His anger bursting forth against someone.

David and the rest of the Israelites got a lesson in fear of the Lord that day. They were all scared stiff, completely paralyzed with fear and highly motivated to find the nearest place to unload the Ark. They did not take it to the tent David had erected in Jerusalem but left it at Obed-edom's house in Gath, where it stayed for three months while David tried to figure out what had angered God. David was discouraged.

> David was now afraid of the Lord and asked, "How can I ever bring the Ark of God back into my care?" *2 Samuel 6:9*

Too Much Information

The Philistines felt betrayed and threatened when David became king of Israel. As a way to congratulate David on his new appointment, they decided to attack Israel. When David was in exile, during his time of flight from Saul, he had found refuge among the Philistines in Ziklag. King Achish had figured that David was so hated by his countrymen that he would have to stay and serve him forever, but when David became king, he felt betrayed and felt that David had spied on him during his stay.

David did have vital knowledge about the Philistines, their military tactics and weaponry, their supply lines, and their government. He had more information than the Philistines would comfortably want any of their enemies to know; they were vulnerable. Now that David was king, he could use that information to his advantage, so they determined to obliterate him, along with the knowledge he possessed. The key to any battle is information. The more you know about your enemy, the greater advantage you have. Intelligence information is more vital than sophisticated weaponry.

The Philistines made two attempts to capture David before he defeated them. David was well informed of the Philistines' approach, so he went into a stronghold. When they arrived, they spread out across the valley of Rephaim. As was his nature, David consulted God before initiating the battle. The Philistines were defeated at Baal-Perazim, and David honored the Lord for the victory. David was always excited to see the Lord act on his behalf and never tired of God's miracles. God's actions were not commonplace.

The Philistines returned for another confrontation in the valley of Rephaim. Again, David consulted the Lord, asking what he should do. God knew that the Philistines had prepared for the same frontal assault David had used in the last battle, so He instructed David to change plans. The Lord told him not to attack directly but to circle behind and then attack when he heard the sound of marching feet in the tops of the balsam trees. That would be his assurance that the Lord was moving ahead of him to strike down the Philistines. David did what God commanded him to do and struck down the Philistines from Gibeon to Gezer.

Although David was a mighty warrior and had a proven track record, he still consulted God before going into battle. David did not believe it was through his strength and prowess that he defeated the Philistines. He acknowledged that the victories were a result of God. It was not a passive victory where you stand back and do nothing. God used him as an instrument to defeat the Philistines. What a blessing it is to be used by God; it is an honor. Never forget that you are an instrument in God's hands through which He can accomplish great victories. David did not forget. He could accomplish more in the hands of God than he could by himself. You may be well accomplished and men may call you a success, but if you yield yourself to God Almighty, He can accomplish even greater works through you—greater than you could ever imagine.

I Crave God

While the Ark of the Lord was at Obed-edom's, everything he had was blessed. During that time, David combed through the Torah, God's instructions to Israel that He had dictated to Moses, to find out why God's anger had been aroused and how the Ark of the Lord could be transported safely. On an individual level, David was desperately possessive of God's presence.

"I want to know how to please you. Teach me, Lord. I cannot bear to have this separation between us. I long to be near you. I am hungry for you. How my soul craves you, like my body needs air. You have spoiled me with your presence, and nothing else satisfies. Please teach me what to do to continually stay with you."

David's love for God caused him to strive to give God what He wanted most, a place in the heart of Israel. David wanted to return the Ark to Israel, because God deserved to be the center of Israel's consciousness and restored to His rightful place in the hearts of His people. Obed-edom's house had been blessed by the presence of the Ark, so why should those blessings benefit only a few while the rest of Israel suffered deprivation as a result of God's absence?

Evoking the Lord's presence simply for the gifts He brings is a mistake. Delight yourself in the Lord, and He will give you the desires of your heart. First seek the kingdom of the Lord and His righteousness, and all other things will be added. God does not like exploitation any more than you do. He does not enjoy being used, in the sense that you want the gifts, blessings, power, and protection He provides but you do not want anything to do with Him personally. Enjoy God for who He is; experience the ecstasy of knowing Him and the thrill of exploring Him. That is the greatest gift you could possibly receive; anything else that comes as a result of your relationship with Him is a fringe benefit. Enjoy the giver of the gift more than the gift. It is an occasion of joy and celebration when God takes up residence in the life of a human being. Diligently seek the Lord, and you will be more than satisfied.

Most of the massive revivals in Israel were inspired by kings in David's lineage. David started a precedent by using God's words to reorder Israel, and he passed that legacy on to the kings in his lineage. God is not illogical, implacable, or mysterious. If you want to know how to please Him, He lets you know what He wants in His word. At any time, you always have at least two resources to let you know what pleases God. You have access to His word, and you can ask Him when the first resource is not at hand.

How badly do you want to please God? How far are you willing to go? What will you do when you find out that you are in direct disobedience of God's word? What will you do when something in your life is a clear contradiction to God's word? Will you say, "It's only a little thing" and then dismiss it? Or will you say, "God, I am ashamed because I have been in opposition to you" and repent? When you find something wrong in your life, will you expend every effort to eradicate it from your life? The answers to these questions will determine whether you have the makings of a reformer.

David's study of the Torah revealed that the Levites were not operating properly. The corruption of the Levitical priesthood was demonstrated when Hophni and Phinehas, sons of Eli, the high priest, were discussed. There had been a breakdown in the Levitical order, and they had not recovered. God always leaves a remnant, but on the whole, the Levitical order was in shambles. Only Levites were qualified to carry the Ark, because the Lord had chosen them to minister before Him. No one was supposed to touch the Ark, not even the Levites (carrying poles helped prevent that). The Levites should have known that, and had they been functioning properly, Uzzah's death could have been prevented.

Church Leaders' Conference

David's study of the Torah caused him to reorganize the Levites for the purpose of returning the Ark. David held a summit meeting for church leaders, high priests Zadok and Abiathar, and Levite leaders Uriel, Asaiah, Joel, Shemaiah, Eliel, and Amminadab. He knew that if he was going to make changes in the church, he had to start with the leadership. To go in the other direction (starting from the pew and working upward) is counterproductive.

David told the Levites that they were not leaders in name only but also in deed. He instructed them to purify themselves and to see to it that those they were responsible for followed suit. He summoned 860 priests and Levites and instructed them from the notes he had taken from the Torah. He instructed the Levites to carry the Ark, since God's glory was not meant to be borne on the backs of animals. God's glory is best expressed on men. To carry the Ark of God on the back of an animal was insulting and demeaning. Even demons prefer to take up residence in a human, only possessing other objects or animals as a last resort. David understood that the Lord's anger had burst forth because the Levites had not carried the Ark the first time.

David organized a parade in honor of the Lord, and the Levites were to carry the Ark on their shoulders by its carrying poles, according to the instructions God had given to Moses. The Levites purified themselves for the occasion. David ordered the Levitical leaders to appoint a choir of Levite singers and musicians to sing joyful songs, accompanied by lyres, harps, and cymbals, during the procession. Three men of the Merari clan directed the musicians, and accomplished Levite musicians were assigned to play the instruments. Heman, Asaph, and Ethan were given the task of sounding the brass cymbals. Zechariah, Unni, Eliab, and four others would play the lyres; Obededom, Jeiel, and four others would play the harps; and seven priests would blow trumpets before the Ark. Kenaniah was chosen as choir leader. Singing songs of woeful lamentation to the King of Glory was understood to be inappropriate. Excitement, enthusiasm, thanksgiving, and honor should be shown when the God of the Universe decides to make His presence felt in a tangible way. Just in case anyone intended to receive God with dirges, David composed a song for the Levites to sing in honor of God's arrival.

The Second Time—Better than the First Time

David was determined not to repeat the disaster at Kiriath-jearim. He had an organized plan to take the Ark of the Lord to the special tent he had prepared. He assigned guards to surround the Ark, more for the people's protection than for the protection of the Ark. He summoned all Israelites to Jerusalem, then issued these instructions:

> When we transport the Ark of God this time, no one except the Levites may carry it. The LORD has chosen them to carry the Ark of the LORD to minister before him forever. *1 Chronicles 15:2*

It was a parade without spectators; everyone was a participant. Army generals, the leaders of Israel, and David led the way to Obed-edom's house to take the Ark to Jerusalem. Upon their arrival, they made a path for the Levites who had been assigned to carry the Ark. Their outer garments, undergarments, and headdresses were made of fine linen, and their sashes were woven with gold thread and blue, purple, and scarlet yarn. Every inch of the base of the Ark was overlaid in gold. There were rings on each corner of the Ark for the carrying poles. The Ark's cover, made of pure gold, had two cherubim facing each other, looking down on the Ark with their wings outstretched to protect it. Four Levites positioned themselves around the Ark, inserted the overlaid gold poles, lifted the Ark, and carried it outside. Seven Levites blew trumpets before the Ark and led the procession toward Jerusalem, followed by four Levites carrying the Ark and four other Levites guarding it. Next came the choir, led by Kenaniah, all wearing fine linen. The musicians followed—a row of harp players, a row of men playing lyres, and bringing up the rear, the cymbal players. The choir sang to the accompaniment of the skillful musicians. King David wore a robe made of fine linen and a linen ephod. Army generals and the leaders of Israel brought up the rear of the procession. The people of Israel lined the roads as the procession went by and then followed them to Jerusalem, singing, shouting, and dancing. The scene was very different from the first time. When you take the time to do things according to the instructions of God, He will help you. Draw near to God, and He will draw near to you.

If you make a move in my direction, I'll let you find me. I'll make myself known to you. If you attempt to do things my way, I will bless you by assisting you.

God was finally given the reception royalty deserves. The second time, God was received reverently, because David had organized the parade in painstaking detail according to His conditions. After taking a few steps with the Ark and seeing that God was helping the Levites transport the Ark, David stopped the procession by sacrificing seven bulls and seven lambs. David and the people joyfully ushered in the presence of the King of kings. They danced with all their might and leaped for joy, and with great celebration, they took the Ark to the place prepared for it. The crowd was berserk and ecstatic with praise to God. God deserves riotous praise when He appears on the scene. They roared, "All praise to the God of Israel, the one who sits on the throne. We crown you with glory and honor!"

Let Everything That Has Breath Praise the Lord

David and the people were ecstatic that God had returned. David danced and leaped for joy with all his might as they transported the Ark. He was a sight to see, dancing and shouting out of control like a madman. He praised God as if everybody else had disappeared and he was alone before God. When Michal, his wife, looked out the window and saw him, she was embarrassed and ashamed, thinking David's behavior did not befit a king. However, God had chosen David to be leader of Israel, and David was madly in love with God, so he did not mind showing the joy he felt. After all, the love of his life had finally come to Jerusalem. There is nothing, and I do mean *nothing*, that can be compared to being around God. "God, I just want to be with you. Just to be close to you, that's my desire."

Because David unabashedly praised the Lord in front of all Israel, the people were blessed. People are either going to be blessed or embarrassed by the uninhibited way you praise the Lord. The way they respond to your praising God is an indication of the condition of their hearts. If their hearts are right, they will feel your joy and start praising God with you. If all is not well with their hearts, they will say, "It doesn't take all that" or "Don't you have any self-respect?" Overcome your critics by the word of your testimony.

Praising God is not a spectator sport. It requires the full participation of everyone in attendance. No one but you can praise God like you do, because you have your own frequency. No matter how many times God has heard, "Lord, you are my fortress," it sounds different coming from you. That is why you cannot stand idle on the sidelines of praise. If you fail to praise God, the rocks will cry out, testifying to God's goodness in your life. If you find yourself a spectator, it is an indication of the condition of *your* heart.

If you stand as an observer, filled with disgust and shame, the enemy of the Lord has you bound. The enemy of the Lord gets mad when God's creation praises Him, because he is covetous of that praise. God's enemy understands that praise has the power to set captives free. Satan, along with Gabriel and Michael, is one of the three most powerful angels. He is noted for his beauty and his extraordinary musical ability, from which he derives his power. No one understands the power of praise better than Satan, and that is why many in the Christian community are bound in the area of praise and worship.

There is nothing wrong with praising the Lord; all humanity should praise God for His goodness. While praise can be infectious depending on the condition of your heart, it is not meant for *you*. It is meant for God, regardless of how ridiculous a person may appear. Praise is thanking God for all the wonderful things He has done, for His involvement in your life, and just for being God. It is between you and God and has nothing to do with anyone else.

Once they reached the tent where the Ark would rest, they made burnt offerings and peace offerings to the Lord. David appointed Levites to lead the people in praise and worship. They asked God's blessing and gave thanks and praise to the Lord of Israel. Asaph and the Levites then performed the song of thanksgiving David composed, and David performed the priestly function of blessing the people in the name of the Lord, giving the people gifts of bread, raisin cakes, and date cakes. Emmanuel—God is with us. What joy and peace comes to every man and woman when God comes to dwell with humanity! In

God's presence, you feel a sense of belonging and know you are safe, secure, and loved. There are no words to describe how it feels to be around God. When you feel God, you want to savor the moment and make it last forever.

"O God, you are an absolute joy! The gift of your presence is so precious. God, you don't have to give me anything. Just come and be with me and wrap your arms around me. O God, let me feel the warmth of your embrace."

Revival

The second attempt to return the Ark was successful because David had studied the Torah to find out how to transport it. All of Israel participated. The Lord received a lavish welcome; the people joyously received Him. It was important to have the involvement of all Israel during the procession, not just the leaders. God had been shamefully escorted out of Israel and carried into battle for manipulative purposes, in the same way people use good luck charms. The people did not want God—they only wanted His blessings. He was an intrusion, a hindrance in their lives. A corporate welcome is good, but a heartfelt welcome on behalf of each individual is more important.

The significance of the procession was manifold. It was a public apology and an acknowledgment that all Israel, collectively and individually, had treated God shamefully. It was also an entreaty for God's return. "We were wrong in thinking that we could get along without you. We need you and eagerly await your arrival. We are hoping that you will do us the favor of returning." A reluctant welcome was unacceptable. God needed to know the people really wanted Him.

Are you willing to do what it takes to get me back?

It was an acknowledgment of God's holiness and sovereignty. "You are the true and living God, the Creator of the Universe, and none can compare to you. You are unique, complete in and of yourself, and without you nothing can exist. We recognize you for who you are. We come before you with fear and trembling, we have purified ourselves, we have prepared our hearts, we have prepared a place for you, and we have followed the instructions you gave Moses to receive you. Now that we have come to the realization of who you are, we would consider it an honor if you would allow us the privilege of your presence. We won't take you for granted."

The people of Israel enjoyed individual reform, national leaders experienced a reformation, and spiritual leaders experienced a resurrection from the dead. The nation experienced spiritual springtime. Joy, hope, and optimism abounded in the hearts of the people. They leapt with joy as the heavy weight of sin and death was lifted. Buoyancy spilled over as new growth and change inundated the people. God returned and brought restoration with Him. The people reconnected with God, tapped into His limitless power, and felt invincible. The only negative thought they had was, "Why didn't we invite you sooner?" Even the dimness of this thought was elucidated by God's glorious presence. Forget the past and move on to new beginnings.

24/7

There is nothing worse than people operating at a lower level than their God-intended purpose. In the past, the Levites had been used by the Lord to accomplish great things, but God put the Levites out to pasture because of their corruption. They had caused the people to stumble by not holding the banner of righteousness high. They could not lead the nation to repentance, because someone needed to lead *them* to it. They would no longer be an idle class of has-beens. If you are going to turn the heart of a nation back to the Lord, you must first rehabilitate its godly spiritual leaders, and David began rebuilding the Levitical order by holding Torah seminars. He instructed them about purifying themselves, told them what garments they were to wear while ministering before the Lord, and assigned them tasks in accordance with the Torah. He re-instituted the daily sacrifices. He used his ability to restore people to their purpose, to reconstruct this group. He brought organization and discipline back to a group that had been out of order.

David restored the order in the house of the Levites according to God's original intentions after the Ark had been returned. He instructed Asaph and the Levites to continue to minister regularly before God, doing whatever needed to be done, organizing the worship of God in a way that had not been seen before. David appointed men to give thanks to God through songs and instruments. Levite musicians were relieved of all other duties in order to minister to the Lord in music 24/7. Zadok and his fellow priests were stationed at Gibeon to minister before the Lord. Regular burnt offerings were made morning and evening on the designated altar according to the instructions the Lord had given to Moses.

David was just the kind of man God was looking for. He made room for the presence of the Lord, because he was a man after God's heart. God needed a man who would restore Him to His rightful place and who would lead His people back to Him, not away from Him. God needed someone to remind the people of His goodness and faithfulness. He needed to provide an example of what He would do for a person who would trust and obey Him. David was consumed with God, head over heels in love with God. He fought against God's enemies, defended Israel, and prepared a special place for God to dwell among His people.

"Because of my love for you, Lord God of Israel, what is important to you is important to me. Your enemies are my enemies. I despise what you despise. I will fight for your honor. I love what you love and take a special interest in the things that interest you. I champion your cause. I just want to make you happy; I want to please you. I'm passionate about you. I want you to know how much I love you and how I long for you. Wherever you are, I want to be. I want to do everything I can to prove my love for you."

Take-home message: Draw near to God, and He will draw near to you.

18.

Hiram's Palace

David and his men moved from Hebron to an area occupied by the Jebusites. The Jebusites felt secure in their fortress, and they taunted David, saying that even their blind and lame could defend the walled city. David offered to make the man who led the charge against Jebus commander of Israel's army. Joab, David's nephew, led the charge and defeated the Jebusites.

David fortified the city that became known as Jerusalem—the City of David. He extended its borders, implemented building projects, and renovated buildings. During the citywide improvements, King Hiram sent construction materials along with commissioned carpenters and stonemasons to build a beautiful, luxurious palace for David as a congratulatory present.

Wanting a Permanent Home for God

After living in the palace, David thought it was odd for him to live in splendor while God, who is the King of kings, dwelled in a tent. "How can I live in extravagance like this when the God of all creation who created me, the Living God of Israel, the love of my life, dwells in a tent?" Therefore, David decided to build God a magnificent temple that would be famous throughout the world. No one had ever thought of building a permanent dwelling place in Israel, and God had never complained about it. God is vast, omnipresent, on the move, and therefore, not bound to one place. What could a man build that could contain the Almighty? The tent that housed the Ark of the Covenant suggested temporary arrangements. David was not satisfied with those arrangements, because he was serious about his relationship with God and wanted to give the love of his life a permanent home.

> "Heaven is my throne, and the earth is my footstool. Could you ever build me a temple as good as that?" asks the Lord. "Could you build

> a dwelling place for me? Didn't I make everything in heaven and earth?" *Acts 7:49–50*

With all the renovation and reconstruction, David did not lose sight of what was most important. In this way he was different from the Babylonian exiles who would return to Israel centuries later, who were so preoccupied with rebuilding their lives that they had to be reminded to tend to God's house. David was not so preoccupied with life's comforts and conveniences that he forgot about God. Without God there was no life; God was the most principal. God was first and foremost in his mind; therefore, David built his life centered around God. He was consumed by a desire to have more of God.

> You will show me the way of life, granting me the joy of your presence and the pleasures of living with you forever. *Psalm 16:11*

There are a number of reasons why David was so insistent on building the Lord God of all creation a permanent home in Israel. David knew that his success as Israel's leader depended upon maintaining God as his focal point. A good leader knows that it is hard to lead himself, let alone a host of people. David realized that he would have to rely on God's help to lead His people. One human cannot possibly meet the many and varied needs of a multitude of people. He wanted God near so that Israel would not suffer as a result of human mistakes, lack of judgment, and shortsightedness.

The second reason David was obsessed with establishing a place of permanence for God was that Israel needed Him; she could not survive without God. She had needed God to set her free when she was enslaved in Egypt; she had required His constant presence to guide and provide for her in the wilderness; she had needed God to defend her in battle as she entered into the Promised Land; and she needed God to deliver her from the entanglements of her sin. Israel could not survive without God. Although Israel kept pushing God away, she had God to thank for her very existence. Without God's assistance, Israel would have become extinct. How and where do you begin to live a life apart from God when He is responsible for your existence?

David took an interest in the desires of God's heart, which is one of the reasons God said David was a man after His heart. He loved God, and loving God meant loving what God loved. David wanted to please God, and he understood that God emphatically loved Israel and desired to have His relationship with her restored. David was obsessed with a desire to please God. God had permanently committed Himself to Israel, so David sought to satisfy God by giving Him permanent residence in Israel's heart.

Far greater than the other reasons for giving God a permanent house in Israel was David's love for God and desire to be with God always. David was not motivated by what he could get from God; he was more interested in what he could give God. David had a perfect love for God. His love for God was unlike what we commonly think of as love. Often we love people because of what they give us, how they benefit us, and how they make us feel. David did not love God because of the things he could get from Him. If David had been like most human beings, returning the Ark would have been enough to manipulate the Lord for a lifetime of favors. When a person is only committed to a relationship for what they can get out of it, the relationship soon sours. When a person gives and serves with an attitude that says, "I expect to be compensated for this," why even bother? Reciprocal relationships are so cheap, selfish, and tired. David was not in a manipulative relationship with God where he expected to be compensated for everything he did.

The Bible encourages reciprocity as a starting point in your relationship with God, but it should not remain that way. Those motivated by reciprocity are saying, "I trust you to give back what I gave." As you develop in your relationship with God, your relationship goes beyond simply trusting Him. As you develop intimacy with God, you grow to love, admire, and appreciate having God in your life. You realize that far greater than the things He gives is that He gives Himself, and there is no substitute for that. You realize that you cannot give anything to God that does not already belong to Him. He benefits you far more than you can ever benefit Him. It is no longer a matter of matching God's gifts and earning a return. Those in a committed relationship with God are motivated to give and serve from a desire to please Him.

"I do what I do simply because I love you and want to please you. I serve because it makes me feel good to be of benefit to you. My sustenance is to do your will. I am driven by a desire to please you, my Lord and my God."

David's relationship with God went far beyond reciprocity, which is why he proposed building a temple for God even though God did not request it. David had a loyalty to God that could not be broken, a loyalty stronger than his desire for life itself. "God, I need you more than I need my next breath."

> The one thing I ask of the LORD—the thing I seek most—is to live in the house of the LORD all the days of my life, delighting in the LORD's perfections and meditating in his Temple. *Psalm 27:4*

It's a Love Thing

David and God had an unbreakable relationship that was forged long before David emerged on the public scene, and nothing could come between them.

Every time God saved David He was giving David life, and David belonged to God. The value that God placed on David enabled David to love himself and to see his own worth. God valued David and showered His love upon him, and David responded to God's love by loving God in return. David expressed his love for God by taking an interest in what was important to God and championing God's causes.

"When I look back over my life, I can't help but have fond feelings for you, my God. I can see you on every page of my life story. I love you because you have affirmed your love for me time and time again. Your love for me caused me to love myself. You lightened the blows of my enemies, shielding me from the full force of their fury. You protected me from my enemies when they devised schemes to take my life.

"You understand and know me, and you are the only one I can trust with my sensitivities. You comforted me when I was down. You received a rejected, dejected person and loved the unloved. In your thoughtfulness you fulfilled the unspoken desires of my heart. You are my oldest, dearest, and best friend.

"I have felt the loneliest in a crowded room of supporters, yet I am not alone, because I know you are with me. You are my constant companion. You have shown yourself to be a true friend when everyone else forsook me and even threatened to take my life. You helped me breathe when those nearest to my heart struck the stinging blow of betrayal. When I cried tears deep from the well of my being and my body was wracked with pain and grief, I cried out and you restored me.

"You have been steadfast and unwavering in your love for me. You know all the dirt about me, even the stuff I have yet to uncover about myself, and still you love me. You lovingly correct me when I go astray. You don't turn your back on me during the time of storms. When all others abandoned my sinking ship, you stayed onboard and held my hand. You have been with me through thick and thin. You blow me away, because you stay by my side when you should have left a long time ago. Sometimes I wonder why you stay. If today you stopped doing all the things you have done in the past, I would tell you that you have done enough to last a lifetime."

David knew that he was not dealing with a God who set the world in motion, populated it, and then left it alone. He was dealing with a God who desired intimacy and loved all of His creation. He knew that God did not agree with the devil-inspired laissez-faire philosophy of man, because He knew they could not live without His love, care, and support. David loved God wholeheartedly and served Him not out of a sense of obligation but out of love and a willing heart. He accepted God's invitation to an intimate relationship.

If you want to understand David, you must understand that he was motivated solely by his intense love for God. David was a mere human trying to care for the God of all creation. He gave because it was all he could do to express his love for God. David had more than a cursory interest in the Lord, because you can spend a lifetime exploring God only to find that you have only scratched the surface. Once you have tasted the goodness of God and the indescribable peace He brings, your resounding response is a desire for MORE! David decided to build God a temple to keep Him permanently near. David was not scheming to get the things of God; he was trying to get God.

"God, you are my obsession. I am passionate about you. The closer I get to you, the more of you I want. I can't get enough of you, so to make sure I can always have you, I will build you a place so we can always be together. The things you give are nice, but all I really want is you. Nothing you could give me could top giving yourself to me. There's just no substitute for you."

When He created humanity, God's desire was for human beings to choose to love Him, not because He commanded or forced them. He hoped that human beings would experience His great love for them and that they would choose to love Him by their own accord. Unfortunately, sin severed humanity's connection to God and caused human beings to instinctively withdraw from God so that they could not experience a personal relationship with Him. As a result of the severed connection, instinctive withdrawal, and lack of personal relationship with God, humanity failed to experience God's love firsthand. Sin alienated humanity from God and caused humanity's love to grow cold.

Human beings can only love God the way God intended when God enables them to love. The only way people can love God (or love at all, for that matter) is by establishing a personal relationship with God and by experiencing the love God has for them. When a person experiences God's love and comes to appreciate the value He places on them, then God's love unlocks love in their heart, enabling them to love Him. With God's enabling love, a person can truly love God; then they grow to love themselves when they understand the value God places on them. That love spills over to the point that they love others without reservation, because they know the value God places on all humanity. God unlocks the power of love in a person when they pursue a love life with Him.

Because sin makes people instinctively withdraw from God, few people pursue a personal relationship with Him that will enable them to love without degree. Therefore, human beings operate with a conditional love. Human beings generally operate with the kind of love that has to be earned and that can be metered. Human beings choose where they will direct their love and who will be the recipient of their affections and loyalties. Human love is a decision, not a feeling—a decision to commit to another.

The nature of love is to give. If love is not freely given, it is not love. God cannot and will not *make* you love Him. Since human love has to be given freely, God commanded us to love Him and to love our neighbors as ourselves. Sin has caused human beings to operate with a low-grade type of love, one that is conditional, love that is controlled or measured. God settled for that low-grade human love and commands us to act in a loving manner. Once we practice observing His commands over time, acting in a loving manner will lead to an automatic way of behaving toward one another and God.

Of the millions of people who have walked this planet, only a small percentage have actually loved the way God desires. The Bible records only a handful of situations in which God experienced the type of love relationship He desires to have with a human being. God wants to be loved simply because of who He is, not for what He can do or what He gives. He wants to be loved without degree. To know God is to love Him.

The best love relationship is when a person loves the *intangible* you. They love you just because you are you. They love your spirit, your mind, and your heart. They are not hung up on your title, your status, the things you own, or the things you give. To them, the greatest present you can give them is to give yourself. They would go to the ends of the Earth to be with you. When a person loves you in that way, they start giving you their most treasured possessions, because you are more valuable than what they have treasured. When you are loved in this way, if you are healthy you return that love without degree.

The motto of a person in love with God in the way He wants to be loved is: "Whatever it takes to make you happy." A person in love with God wants to please Him. That person is not concerned with getting things from God, they are more concerned with giving things to God. To them nothing that God gives can be greater than God giving Himself to them. It is the combination of loving God and doing what He says that invites Him into a more committed relationship with them.

Enoch, Noah, Abraham, and Moses all experienced that type of love relationship with the Lord. God loved Enoch so much that He took him from the face of the Earth because He could no longer bear the distance between them.

> Enoch lived 365 years in all. He enjoyed a close relationship with God throughout his life. Then suddenly, he disappeared because God took him. *Genesis 5:23–24*

God also loved Noah so much that He preserved him and his family and used them to repopulate the Earth.

> Noah was a righteous man, the only blameless man living on earth at the time. He consistently followed God's will and enjoyed a close relationship with him. *Genesis 6:9*

God expressed His love for Abraham by giving his descendants the Promised Land and by using his descendants to bless all nations of the Earth. Abraham's faith touched God's heart, and God called him friend. Abraham did not withhold Isaac, the one thing he desired most in this world, from God. By doing that, he sent God a message that said, "You are more valuable than the things I treasure." God's love for Moses caused Him to preserve the nation of Israel when He wanted to wipe them out and start over with Moses. In Moses, God found a man who He could share His heart with and show His vulnerability to without fear of rejection. David belonged in the ranks of those men. They found favor with the Lord and enjoyed the most intimate relationship any human being could have with God. To love God like that and to be loved by Him in return should be every person's desire!

Since God loves us, His example shows what true love looks like. God loved human beings so much that He created an entire world for them. He put everything needed to sustain humanity on the Earth before he created them. God made human beings like Himself and breathed the spirit of life (a part of Himself) into them so that man became a living soul. When human beings died because of sin and severed their lifeline from God, God had a plan to reconnect with human beings. God loved human beings so much that He gave His only Son, the One most precious, His heart, in order to save human beings. When Jesus went back to heaven, God sent His Spirit. God started His relationship with human beings by giving, and He keeps giving and giving. God is emphatically in love with human beings. You do not have to do anything for God to love you. He loves you simply because you are His creation. God loves you.

David proposed building a temple for God because he wanted God to be with him forever. David's love for God caused him to give of himself wholeheartedly to please and serve God. In a real way, the relationship that David had with God was a marriage. God responded to David's love by giving David the most staggering gift of an eternal dynasty, and more important, God gave Himself to David, which was David's ultimate desire. The relationship that God experienced with David caused Him to go overboard in His response.

David, I've been with you all your life. I chose you when you were a shepherd boy. I have destroyed all your enemies. Now I will make you famous. I will build a house for you—a dynasty of kings! When you die, I will choose one of your descendants. I will make his kingdom strong. I will be his father—he will be my son. If he sins, I will not take my unfailing love from him as I did Saul, but I will use other nations to punish him. He will build my temple. Your throne will continue and be secure forever.

Monarchies are only as secure as they are militarily strong. Their durability relies on their ability to repress opposing factions. The gift God gave David can best be appreciated by looking at the Edomite kingdom. The kings of Edom did not have a dynasty. Once one king was gone, a new king from another "family" ruled, similar to the way the U.S. presidency operates. For instance, Bela of Dinhabah ruled for a time, but after his death, Jobab of Bozrah, who was not an immediate relative of Bela, became king.

When your family has a dynasty, your birthright gives you the highest position in the land. The gift God gave David guaranteed that one of David's descendants would be king forever. Understand the significance of the gift God gave David but do not get stuck on the gift, because those who are in a love relationship with God are not motivated by what God gives. Besides, if you are the type to snuggle up to God for what you can get, God is not fooled in the least.

After God had promised him a dynasty, David thanked Him, kneeling before the Lord, and prayed:

"Who am I that you have brought me so far? You know who I really am, a nobody, yet you have treated me like someone great. I don't deserve this great honor you are giving me, but I will receive it as an expression of your love. You've done so much for me already, and now you tell me that you will give me the gift of a lasting dynasty. Do you treat everyone this way? You blow me away; I am speechless. There is no other god like you. You have a history of doing things like this because you brought Israel from slavery to royalty. What miracles you performed, what awesome acts you performed! You chose them as your people and became their God. You protected them by removing the nations and gods that hindered them. Go ahead and bless me so your name will be established and honored forever. Do all that is in your heart to do for your glory and honor."

Heartchild

David had to wrestle with the hurt that comes from a reassigned project. It had never occurred to anyone to build God a temple; therefore, no one could build it in the way David conceived it. Considering the reasons he proposed the temple, no one could have had greater passion about the project than he did. Nathan told David that he would not be the one to build the temple. It became an issue that did not sit well with David. For God to refuse his gift was like God refusing his love. There is no record that Nathan gave David an explanation as to why God would not allow him to build the temple, so David went to God directly for an explanation.

David's side of the conversation might have gone like this: "Father, you know my heart. How can I hide anything from you? You know my thoughts before they are formed, and you know how I will respond to any situation. My heart aches, because I feel that you are refusing my love by denying me the right to build your temple. I will feel incomplete and unfulfilled if I can't do this for you, for us. Who could build your temple in the way I have envisioned it, since no one has ever considered building one?"

When David passed the torch to Solomon and charged the nation of Israel, he told them why he could not build the temple. "God would not allow me to build the temple because I have shed much blood before Him in battle. God has appointed my son Solomon as king of Israel. He will have rest from all his enemies so that he can give his undivided attention to building God's temple." Vessels are chosen and prepared for particular seasons. Israel was in a season of warfare, and God had appointed David to be her warrior. He could not build the temple because it was not a season of peace where he could focus his undivided attention on the temple's construction.

The fact that David continued with the plans for the temple shows his strength of character, his sense of duty and commitment to Israel, and his love for God. Many people facing the same situation would have quit. Their attitude would be: "If I can't design and build it, I want no part of it." However, David continued to plan for the temple, because it would benefit the nation of Israel. It was irrelevant who built the temple as long as it was built, because it was for the greater good of Israel. In order for Israel to prosper, she needed the Lord at her core, and God needed to have a permanent resting place in Israel. It was out of his love and passion for God that he proposed the temple in the first place, but his love did not die simply because he could not build the temple. David knew that God was not refusing his gift, the expression of his love. Therefore, he was committed to do whatever it took to make his vision a reality.

Building Fund

David accepted the explanation that God gave as to why he could not build the temple. He understood that God's denial was not a rejection of the gift, so he continued working, doing everything short of actually building the temple. Since he would not be the one to build the temple, he spelled out the plans in every minute detail to make certain the temple would be built exactly as he had envisioned it. He spent his entire administration making preparations for the temple. He began by gathering and dedicating to the Lord the plunder he had obtained from his enemies.

When David fought against Israel's enemies, the Lord assisted him. He gave David power and influence over the surrounding nations. Wherever David went, God gave him victory. God fulfilled His word to Israel by driving out nations and their gods (demonic strongholds) that withstood Israel. God wanted Israel to be blessed, victorious, and free. David understood that since the Israelites were God's chosen people, any nation fighting against Israel was an enemy to God. So David championed God's cause by subduing Israel's enemies for the glory of the Lord.

David fought and conquered many nations that were distant relatives of Israel. For instance, Israel's father Abraham was Aramaen. David defeated the Aramaens and placed garrisons in their capital, Damascus, and forced them to pay him tribute money. Moab and Ammon were children of Abraham's nephew Lot. David had close ties to Moab because his great grandmother Ruth was a Moabite. David received refuge from Moab for his parents while he was a fugitive. However, he conquered the land of Moab, executing nearly 70 percent of its population, because Moab had mistreated Israel when she fled from Egypt. David fought against and defeated the nation of Edom, descendants of Esau, Jacob's brother.

David fought and conquered many nations, and he amassed their wealth for God's temple. God did not have to struggle with David like He had with Saul. Saul felt that God was not good enough to receive the best gifts. He kept the best of the plunder for himself and his men, leaving the scraps for the Lord. David, on the other hand, defeated God's enemies and then took their wealth and gave it to God. It was within his right to keep the spoils of war, but he gave them freely to God, not to win his favor but because he loved Him and was committed to God's cause. The wealth from God's enemies would be a constant memorial to the Lord's victories. Every time sacrificial meat was handled with the gold meat hooks, it would represent the fact that God's enemies could not prevail over His people.

Take-home message: It's the combination of loving God and doing what He says that gets God's attention and invites Him into a deeper, more committed relationship with you.

19.

Legendary

Before David was king he was humble, yet he rose above his lowly circumstance, carrying countless others with him. He protected his countrymen and defended them at all costs. He consulted God in everything and even protected his enemies.

David was a good-hearted man. He was loyal and kind to people not because he felt he had to be but because he wanted to be. His attitude was, "I just want to be good to you." He went out of his way to honor his promises, show loyalty to those who were loyal to him, and redress wrongs. Fairness was one of the hallmarks of the early stages of his reign.

Honoring His Promises

David exhibited "private kindness" to Jonathan—the type of kindness you show when nobody is looking or keeping score. It is the Christian thing to do when you help your neighbor in times of need. How do you treat people in your life who have nothing to offer you? The answer to the question will define your private kindness.

David honored a vow he had made with Jonathan, even though Jonathan was not around to hold him accountable. Considering the kind of friendship David and Jonathan had shared and the fact that Jonathan had saved his life, David owed Jonathan a debt of gratitude. They had made a vow in confidence, between themselves and before God. If David had not honored his commitment, no one would have been the wiser from a human perspective. Of course, God knows all, He sits high and looks low, and nothing is hidden from Him. The only ones who would have known if the promise was honored would have been God, David, and Jonathan. David went out of his way to honor his commitment to find the survivors of Saul's family, which was a perfect example of David's character. He had promised Jonathan that he would show kindness to his offspring, and he did just that.

David did not just honor his commitments grudgingly. Some people honor their commitments with such a terrible attitude that it would have been better had they not honored their word at all. Once David found a surviving member of Jonathan's family, he lavished him with blessings and treated him as if he were his own son.

David contacted Ziba, one of Saul's servants, to find out if there were any survivors in Saul's family, and he told him there were at least eight. David was particularly interested in Jonathan's children. Ziba told him that Jonathan had a son, Mephibosheth, who lived with Makir bar Ammiel in Lo-debar. Jonathan had died when Mephibosheth was only five, and when news of Jonathan's death had reached Mephibosheth's nurse, she had grabbed him and fled, but she fell and dropped him, crippling him in both legs. However, even with his handicap and his fears, Mephibosheth managed to live a decent life in obscurity, eventually marrying and producing a son, Mica.

When David summoned Mephibosheth, he bowed low before the king, thinking he had finally met his doom. The day he most dreaded was upon him. But David immediately assuaged his fears. "Have no fear! I am glad I have found you so I can honor my word to your father. Everything that belonged to your grandfather, Saul, is yours. I want you to live with me in my palace. Ziba and Saul's men will be your servants." Mephibosheth moved to David's palace and ate at the king's table, like one of David's sons. God had given all of Saul's possessions to David to do with as he pleased. He gave them all to Mephibosheth with the same generous spirit that Jonathan had shown him.

Pride Is an Ugly Beast

David tried to show loyalty to those who viewed his kindness with suspicion. When King Nahash of Ammon died, his son, Hanun, ascended to the throne. Nahash was the one who had prompted Israel to ask for a king and threatened to take one eyeball from each of the inhabitants of Jabesh Gilead, but Saul had defeated him and saved the people of Jabesh. The Ammonites, like the Moabites, were descendants of Lot, relatives of Israel.

David wanted to honor the loyalty of King Nahash by being loyal to Hanun, so he sent ambassadors to offer his condolences for Nahash's death. However, unlike Mephibosheth, who received David's kindness without reservation, Hanun shunned it. Hanun allowed his advisors to convince him that David's show of loyalty was a guise to spy on him and to conquer the land, so he snubbed David by abusing his ambassadors.

To refuse David's kindness and to abuse his ambassadors was one thing that could have been excused. Hanun could have apologized, and there would have been no hard feelings. David would have allowed Hanun's blunder to roll off his back. But Hanun went from bad to worse in his interactions with David, and it ultimately cost him his kingdom and the lives of his allies. Once Hanun realized his blunder, instead of apologizing he hired thirty-three thousand ally troops to come to his aide. Many men lost their lives—and the freedom of their countries—because of Hanun's blunder. What kind of crazy madness would cause one to settle a dispute by summoning military forces when a simple apology and restitution would settle the matter? What is the world coming to when a person would rather jeopardize several nations than settle a dispute by discussion? Pride is destructive.

David sent Joab and the Israelite army to fight them, but doing this instead of accompanying them would be David's undoing. Joab fought on one front, and his brother, Abishai, fought on the other. The Ammonites and Arameans fled from the Israelites because they were no match, but Hadadezer summoned additional Aramean troops from the other side of the Euphrates. David summoned all the Israelite troops and led them to Helam, where they killed seven hundred charioteers and forty thousand horsemen, including Shobach, their commander. Hadadezer and his allies would not assist Hanun any longer, and they surrendered to David and became his subjects. Hanun had started a war that would last for at least twenty months, all because he lacked humility.

In the Wake of a Leader's Sins

The consequences of the sins, mistakes, and blunders made by leaders during their administration often surface long after their departure, leaving their constituents to pay the price. The administration that follows such a leader has the unsavory responsibility of making amends for the consequences. It behooves citizens, then, to avoid leaders who have a track record of mistakes. It is imperative for citizens to elect people who have operated with wisdom, knowledge, understanding, and integrity during their career.

David found himself thrust into a situation where he had to redress the wrongs of his predecessor, Saul. He could not ignore the problem, because Israel was suffering. By the time David consulted the Lord on Israel's behalf, Israel had suffered from a famine for three years. God told David that the famine was sent to alert Israel that restitution had to be made on behalf of the Gibeonites whom Saul had murdered in his efforts to wipe them out.

Saul was dead by the time the consequences of his actions surfaced, but the people of Israel suffered famine because he had reneged on a covenant. When the Israelites entered Canaan under Joshua's direction, God instructed them to wipe out the inhabitants of the land. The Gibeonites were descendants of the Amorites living in the land of Canaan. By pretending they were from a distant land, they tricked Joshua into making a peace treaty with them. After Joshua made the treaty, he discovered their deception, but he was still bound to his word because the Israelites had made that treaty before the Lord. As a result of the treaty, Israel could not destroy the Gibeonites, and Israel allowed them to remain in the land of Canaan.

David had to dispense justice to those who were wronged if he wanted to save his nation. That not only highlights the fact that David was a fair man but also shows that he interceded for the needs of his nation. He summoned the Gibeonites to determine how to resolve the conflict, eager to do whatever it took to restore Israel to a position of blessing.

> "What can I do for you to make amends? Tell me so that the LORD will bless his people again." "Well, money won't do it," the Gibeonites replied. "And we don't want to see the Israelites executed in revenge." "What can I do then?" David asked. "Just tell me and I will do it for you." Then they replied, "It was Saul who planned to destroy us, to keep us from having any place at all in Israel. So let seven of Saul's sons or grandsons be handed over to us, and we will execute them before the LORD at Gibeon, on the mountain of the LORD." "All right," the king said, "I will do it." *2 Samuel 21:3–6*

There are some things money cannot buy or repair. For instance, you cannot put a price on human life. There are some organ brokers who say human body parts are worth a million dollars, but human beings are worth more than the body parts that house their immortal soul. The totality of a human being is greater than the sum of its parts. God made human beings in His likeness and image, and put His Spirit in them so man became a living soul.

> What are mortals that you should think of us, mere humans that you should care for us? For you made us only a little lower than God, and you crowned us with glory and honor. *Psalm 8:4–5*

If human beings are made a little lower than God, we must measure God's worth to determine the worth of a human being. If we use the value system of this world, where people are valued by their possessions, it would not be a fair estimate of God's worth, since He owns everything. Since you cannot put a price on God, and God put His Spirit into human beings, you cannot put a price on humanity. Therefore, all the money in the world cannot compensate for the life of a single human being, because each person's life is invaluable.

Multiply invaluable by the number of Gibeonites Saul killed, and you come up with a price that cannot be fathomed, let alone paid. The Gibeonites thought it unfair to make innocent Israelites suffer for the sins of Saul, so they named a settlement price that would affect only Saul's family. If the price was paid, the curse of famine would be removed. To keep his covenant with Jonathan, David spared Mephibosheth's life. But he gave the men of Gibeon two sons of Saul's concubine Rizpah, and five sons of Saul's daughter Merab. The Gibeonites executed them before the Lord at the beginning of the barley harvest. The guilty party could not determine what a fair settlement would be; only the victims could determine what would settle the issue.

Heroes Do Not Deserve to Die Ignoble Deaths

Rizpah had lost her sons, the hope of her future. No parent ever expects to bury their children, and nothing can prepare a person for the depths of such grief. It is a pain a parent carries to the grave. No one can tell a mother how to grieve, and nothing can stop a mother's love. Each must grieve in her own way. Each must bring closure to a senseless tragedy. Rizpah's sons' only crime was being the offspring of their father, something they had no control over.

How does a mother come to terms with the fact that her children have been executed for something they did not do? What can she do when her children are forced to pay for a curse put in motion by their father? It is unfair for her children to pay for their father's sins, something they had nothing to do with. Rizpah felt helpless and hopeless, because she could do nothing to prevent the deaths of her children. Rizpah did the only thing she could do. She guarded the bodies of her sons after they had been executed. "It's bad enough that your lives were tragically cut short, but I will not let anyone profit from your death, adding insult to your injury."

There were many things that she could not control, but she would not allow her children to be violated any further. She bravely fought off vultures and wild animals, refusing to give up the fight for their dignity, because they were not criminals. They were not guilty of the crimes they had paid for, and she wanted people to recognize their innocence.

Rizpah guarded the bodies of her sons and Saul's grandsons throughout the barley harvest, attracting David's attention, and he validated her refusal to allow her sons to die ignoble deaths by championing her cause. He took the bones of Jonathan, Saul, and those executed by the Gibeonites and gave them a decent burial in the tomb of Kish.

Saul's sons and grandsons deserved to be honored as heroes, because their deaths had satisfied a curse; they had been executed for a crime they did not commit, saving the Israelites from dying of starvation.

Jesus, Thou Son of David, Have Mercy on Us

That situation also has a deeper spiritual significance. Since the Israelites were under spiritual reform, they should have been experiencing the blessings of God, but instead they were suffering under a curse. God withheld blessings to alert them to the fact that they had conflicts that needed to be resolved, and they could not experience the fullness of God's blessings until they made amends. They had repented and invited the Lord to return to live with them; they were living according to God's principles, shunning their evil idolatrous practices, and doing everything that would lead them to renewal and rebirth, yet they were suffering from a curse.

Such a situation is significant to the life of a believer, because it shows that even receiving Jesus as your Savior does not make you immune to the consequences of past sins. If you are doing all the right things by God's standards but are receiving curses instead of blessings, it is time for self-examination. I do not mean to imply that every time you encounter trials or tribulations it is an indication of your sin, but it is worth examination to find their source. If in your review process with the Lord you find that you are the cause of your current crisis, you need to ask God what you can do to restore His blessings. You may need to ask some people for forgiveness and find out what you can do to make things right. You may need to ask the Lord how to resolve some issues. Once you have made restitution and restoration, God will restore you to a place of blessings.

The entire nation of Israel suffered because of the sins of a few against an innocent group of people. God allowed the famine to alert Israel's leaders that restitution had to be made. If America is ever to be whole, restitution must be made. No one feels a need to address the issues, because we live in an inflated society that does a good job of covering up our poverty and the fact that we are bankrupt. We live in a society where we can lower interest rates or print more money to give people a false sense of security. If we allowed the economy to operate without interference, more people would be on their faces before the Lord. Crisis has a way of forcing people into an examination process with the Lord. If we are going to live in a blessed America, we must have national repentance where we shun sin and invite God back into the heart of the nation. Once we do that, we must tackle the social injustices from the past and the ongoing injustice.

Restitution must be made to the original occupants, the Native Americans, on their own terms. Restitution must also be made to those who were originally brought here as slaves, as well as the abused Italian and Asian immigrants who were cheated and treated like slaves. America was built on the backs of people it abused. Restitution for the millions of aborted babies must be made if we are going to live in a curse-free America; our land is filled with innocent blood. We must make restitution for the many times we have intervened in the affairs of other nations under the guise of protecting human rights when the real motive was economic gain, and for the times we have ignored human rights violations in other nations because it was unprofitable to confront them. How do you fight for human rights anywhere when you have unresolved human rights violations in your own country?

When the subject of restitution comes up, people who have benefited from the sins of their ancestors and the imbalances that have resulted grow uneasy. They argue that the past is the past and that we must move forward and do what is best for the greater good. That thinking invalidates the suffering of the disadvantaged and seeks to perpetuate imbalance. It was for the greater good and diplomacy that land was taken from Native Americans in the first place. Rules were made, adjusted, ignored, and broken to maintain the advantage of some at the expense of others. Then people argue that they were not around when their ancestors committed their sins against others, and they should not be held accountable for them. Although they did not commit the sins of their ancestors, they have benefited from the advantages that have resulted.

This biblical account demonstrates that something has to be done to make amends, and it is the offended who must determine what a fair settlement is. David did not suggest settlement terms, because only the offended could express the terms that would create justice. Justice under any terms other than those of the victim is not justice. The offender is indebted to the one offended and must pay whatever restitution the victim demands.

Take-home message: How you treat the person in your life who has nothing to offer defines your private kindness.

20.

Sucker Punched

When a person is riding a wave that reaches its zenith, it can be the most dangerous time of their lives, because they can come crashing down. When a person reaches a pinnacle in their career or ministry, it is time to be circumspect. It is at those times when a person has accomplished so much that they are in danger of pride, and pride comes before a fall.

It is not my intent to discourage you from scaling the upper limits or boldly going where few have gone. Pursue God with a passion! It is my intent to warn you to walk with the caution and skill of a person walking a tightrope. I want to admonish you to be on guard against snares, because the higher you ascend, the greater the potential for a long free fall. It is not inevitable that you will fall when scaling the upper regions, but as the angle of the slope increases, each step becomes critical. Carelessness on a steep slope will cause a fall that will not stop until you reach rock bottom.

Some have continued to ascend such a slope without faltering, even unto the time they left this Earth. I remember such a man who has now gone to be with the Lord. He was a man of great wisdom, discernment, and experiential knowledge with the Lord. Without being asked, one day in his sermon, he said, "I don't rest on past accomplishments. I continue to look forward to the task ahead of me."

That is the key. Never allow yourself to feel as if you have arrived, and never take stock of past accomplishments and rest on them. Leave that up to the scorekeepers and the historians. It sounds like advice that would come from the Apostle Paul, who pressed toward the mark of the high calling. When you are on a steep slope, you do not have time to look back and take stock.

Riding the Wave

David made unprecedented improvements in the nation of Israel. Although he acquired territory from enemies, thereby continuing the work of Joshua, turned enemies into subjects, built buildings, and fortified cities, those improvements were only cosmetic and therefore insignificant. Many church leaders would be satisfied with that type of superficial growth, but Satan yawns at those improvements. Satan only becomes disturbed when the size of the prayer group matches the membership roll. Satan becomes disturbed when the number of delivered people in the church matches the number on the membership roll.

David had such a positive impact on the nation that the heart of the nation was turned to the God of Israel. He was a man of God with a spiritual vision for his nation. He was determined to make Israel a godly nation. He lived a godly life and led by example. He revived the defunct class of Levites, and he returned the Ark of the Lord to have God near so Israel could be blessed. David was on a crest that kept rising and rising. His revival of the Levites caused them to fulfill their God-given purpose. He instituted 24/7 praise and worship before the Lord, because there is power in praise. The required daily sacrifices resumed. He sent Levites to teach God's word throughout the land, accompanied by praise and worship. Evil thrives where God's words are hidden. God's words challenge the hearers, causing them to wrestle with conflicting behaviors and attitudes. God's words know no boundaries. God's words can penetrate the heart of anyone who hears them, regardless of that person's station in life or creed. All it takes is a few appropriate words from God to make the stoutest heart crumble. That is why there is such resistance by today's powers that be to hearing God's words.

During David's reign, Israel learned that God was not her enemy and that He loved her. In the past, God had blessed her, but she kept refusing and rejecting His love. Because she had misunderstood God, she kept pushing Him away. Israel would not give God a chance to show that He loved her. When Moses led Israel through the wilderness, He had to confront her deep-seated idolatry issues that ignited His fury. Israel was uncommitted and was distracted by her voracious appetite for idols, and God was brokenhearted, hurt, and disgusted by Israel's unfaithfulness. God exploded because of Israel's behavior, and Israel resented God because of it. Israel harbored hostility and mistrust toward God; she felt God was stifling, irascible, and possessive. In a turbulent, tumultuous relationship, with flaring tempers and wounded feelings, it was hard for Israel to see that God loved her. It was hard for her to view anything God did without suspicion. As far as Israel was concerned, God was her enemy.

Israel's idolatry made it difficult for God to show His affectionate, soft side to Israel because she had a way of rubbing God the wrong way and bringing out the beast in Him. Israel and God had one of those "I can't live with you, but I can't live without you" relationships. From the time of Moses's leadership to David's, God and Israel were in a strained, antagonistic relationship, simply tolerating each other.

King David followed Moses's teachings to achieve a spiritual reformation in Israel. However, rules and regulations alone could not do what witnessing a man with a personal relationship with God could. Through King David, Israel had an opportunity to witness a man totally in love with God, and God totally in love with a man. King David's relationship with God allowed Israel to see God's softer side, and her perception of God began to change. Israel longed to have the kind of love life that David had with God.

During David's reign, things began to change for the better as Israel got a chance to see that the kind of relationship God desired was not bad; it was most desirable. David loved, worshiped, and served God with his whole heart, and God responded to David's love. God was able to reveal His true personality to Israel through His relationship with David. Israel saw that God was not the mean, angry, stifling tyrant she thought He was. God was beautiful, loving, tenderhearted, sensitive, thoughtful, kind, compassionate, and good. She had never seen that side of God, and His goodness melted her heart. How she longed to have the kind of relationship David had with God! It was not until David became king that she voluntarily dropped her other lovers in exchange for a sweet relationship with God.

David was blessed in all he did because God was with him, and the blessings of God spilled over onto the nation because of David's relationship with God. David had a reputation for being like "an angel of God," meaning he exercised wisdom and sound judgment. Justice characterized his leadership, and the Israelites did not suffer under his leadership as they had under Saul. David was known for his fairness, was a loyal man of integrity, and fought for justice for those wronged. He was a flawless man of impeccable character. Given David's reputation, he would never do anything to harm Israel. He loved God, and loving God meant loving what God loved.

Satan's Most-Wanted List

David presented a threat because he caused Satan to lose his stranglehold on Israel's soul. Israel wanted God and no one else, so she said goodbye to her other lovers and began a committed relationship with God. Because of this change in Israel, Satan lost his grip on Israel's heart and his control over her. King David's greater-than-Goliath spiritual reformation, combined with his uncensored public love life with God, caused Israel's heart to change in favor of God, which made King David the number one target on Satan's hit list. Therefore, Satan thought David must be removed. Once David was out of the picture, Satan felt certain that Israel would return to him.

Like an angry jilted lover who loses influence and power and wants to regain control and get their lover back, Satan designed the Bathsheba-Uriah incident to oust King David. David had crossed into a new line of warfare, spiritual warfare. David destroyed demonic strongholds in Israel by continuing Joshua's work of removing the prior occupants, and he also attacked engrained demonic strongholds within Israel's society. Turning the hearts of the Israelites back to the God of Israel meant that David had moved from fighting flesh and blood to waging spiritual warfare for the souls of the children of Israel. He had snatched the hearts of the Israelites from the grasp of the devil. That made David a prime target, and Satan set out to destroy David through sex, because sex was David's weak spot.

While David inherited a legacy of faith, he also inherited a generational curse of sexual perversion. Judah and Tamar, a Canaanite, had David's ancestor Perez. God forbade the Israelites from marrying the Canaanites because of their sexual immorality and spiritual idolatry. Rahab also introduced promiscuity into David's bloodline. Finally Ruth was a Moabite. Moabites were distant relatives of Israel whose ancestry resulted from incest.

To David it was not enough to live in the Promised Land; he also wanted Israel to experience absolute freedom from spiritual bondage to demons. David had accomplished great things in Israel, but that was his biggest feat ever. In fact, the greatest accomplishment any human being can achieve is to be instrumental in delivering captives from the hands of the demons and into the hands of God. There is a distinct difference between focusing on membership growth in a church and focusing on liberating its members from demonic strongholds and deep-seated ungodly habits. Any time you focus on the latter, the devil wants to take you out using any means necessary. Any time you challenge the devil's authority in your life or the lives of others, you are in for a fight. Spiritual warfare is different from fighting against human beings. Unlike human enemies, the devil knows your weak spots and attacks those areas.

When you are fighting in the spirit, physical weapons and human ability are ineffective. Those who can acknowledge that demons exist can also acknowledge that human beings are not equipped to fight demons. Movies like *Fallen* show how powerless human beings are when it comes to waging spiritual warfare with human ability. The message is to withdraw from challenging demonic oppression.

The Bible contains many examples of how God has given victory over demons. Satan is an archangel—he is not to be toyed with, but he is to be respected. When Satan was contending for the body of Moses, the archangel Michael said, "Satan, the Lord rebukes thee." When Satan was trying to tempt

Jesus in the wilderness, Jesus defeated Satan through the word of God. Jesus proved that understanding the intent behind God's words was more important than remembering God's words verbatim.

Those who resist evil and destroy demonic strongholds understand that although demons use human agents to do their bidding, agents are not the problem. The real problem is the demons that influence and control them. The battle against evil has never been physical. "For the weapons of our warfare are not carnal, but they are mighty through God to the pulling down of strongholds" (2 Corinthians 10:4, KJV). The point is not to avoid removing demonic strongholds but to do it by the power and authority of God. Draw near to God, resist the devil, and he will flee.

> Be strong with the Lord's mighty power. Put on all of God's armor so that you will be able to stand firm against all strategies and tricks of the Devil. For we are not fighting against people made of flesh and blood, but against the evil rulers and authorities of the unseen world, against those mighty powers of darkness who rule this world, and against wicked spirits in the heavenly realms. Use every piece of God's armor to resist the enemy in the time of evil, so that after the battle you will still be standing firm. Stand your ground, putting on the sturdy belt of truth and the body armor of God's righteousness. For shoes, put on the peace that comes from the Good News, so that you will be fully prepared. In every battle you will need faith as your shield to stop the fiery arrows aimed at you by Satan. Put on salvation as your helmet, and take the sword of the Spirit, which is the word of God. Pray at all times and on every occasion in the power of the Holy Spirit. Stay alert and be persistent in your prayers for all Christians everywhere. *Ephesians 6:10–18*

The inevitable truth is that some people are opportunists, because they take advantage of the bondage of others. It is an ugly truth that few would admit, but some secretly like the bondage of others because they can use it to their advantage. Therefore, when a bound person is set free, someone loses. Instead of rejoicing with you over your freedom, the opportunist seeks to find a way to put you back in your place to maintain their advantage.

People or industries gain their wealth from the bondage of others. The Apostle Paul preached in Ephesus and the provinces of Asia for more than two years. During that time he also used God's power to heal the sick and cast out evil spirits. People who were trapped in a life of sin, such as witchcraft, confessed, and after receiving Jesus as Savior, they burned their incantation books, valued in the millions, in a public bonfire. Business owners who derived their income from manufacturing shrines to the goddess Artemis (also known as Diana) became upset when Artemis lost prestige and influence, because the freedom of their countrymen interfered with their livelihood. So they incited a riot that would have led to the deaths of Paul's ministry companions if left unchecked. The illegal drug industry and its ancillary agencies is a modern example of an industry that benefits from the bondage of others in our society.

Modern ministers whose preaching sets people free from bondage join the ranks of David, Jesus, and the Apostle Paul. The attitude of spiritual-warfare ministers is, "It is not enough to be saved and heaven bound, but it is also important to experience absolute freedom in the kingdom of God." Anytime you are instrumental in the deliverance of one person or a mass of people, you attract the attention of the enemy of God. Those who benefited from a freed person's bondage lose out. Those who lose money, power, and other perceived benefits when a bound person gets their freedom will do anything to regain their advantages. That is why such ministers of the gospel come under assault today. Although it looks like the battle is between people, the real enemy is the enemy of God.

In the days of the apostles, it was not uncommon for their opposition to lie, incite riots, beat, imprison, and kill them. Those people were angry because of the influence the apostles had in the lives of those who were bound and because it affected their way of life. The opposition was religious leaders as well as nonbelievers during the apostles' time. Some in the media today have gone so far as to set traps for God's effective ministers just to have new material, but there is something sick, sinister, and diabolical about wanting so badly to see a spiritual-warfare minister fall that you set traps for them; woe unto you! The sad truth is that just as the media is hungry for the fall of God's ministers, many believers also relish those falls.

Some believers secretly hate those who belong to the upper spiritual echelon, because they are envious of the special relationship they have with the Lord and of the things they have accomplished. They do not realize that they could have the same type of relationship if they just spent time with God. You have paid the price that they are not willing to pay. They want what spiritual leaders have without putting forth the effort it takes to get it. Jealousy and envy cause people to hate and despise those who have reached great spiritual heights, scaled the limitless, and boldly gone where they never attempted to go. So when a spiritual giant falls, many people in Christian circles derive personal satisfaction from it. With glee, they shake their heads and say, "I just *knew* Minister So-and-So was really a sinner." Sad, but true.

After David became king over all Israel, his responsibilities increased, as did the number of people he governed. Before he was king, his role was mainly to protect the nation from human enemies. After he took the helm, he also took on the responsibility of reforming the church and looking after the spiritual well-being of Israel.

When David was a fugitive, he was the commander of his soldiers, but his influence waned after the men made it clear that they were opportunists. It did not help matters that Joab was aware of the sentiments of David's men and did not hesitate to use it to his advantage. When Joab killed Abner, it signaled that David was losing influence over the army.

David began to develop a habit of sending troops instead of leading them. During the battle against the Ammonite King Hanun, David sent Joab and Abishai to handle the situation. It was only when the Arameans sent for reinforcements that David led the entire Israelite army into battle against them. He defeated the Arameans so soundly that they became David's subjects and would no longer aid the Ammonites.

Israel requested a king because she wanted someone to defend her from her enemies in spite of her moral condition. Saul left Israel vulnerable many times while he was hounding David, but he still led the army in battle, even up to his death. Israel expected her king to fight against her enemies. Traditionally, kings went into battle in the spring; it was unusual for the king not to escort the troops. But David sent Joab and the Israelite army to destroy the Ammonites instead of leading them, and he stayed behind in Jerusalem, something the scriptures make a point of emphasizing. After the Ammonite nation had been destroyed, Joab sent for David so that he would get credit for the victory.

Since the Bible does not tell us why David did not lead the troops, we can only offer conjectures. Perhaps he was working on another project. Perhaps he was afraid that Joab would turn on him in battle and "accidentally" kill him. Regardless of the reason, David was out of position, and when you are not where you are supposed to be, you are not doing what you are supposed to be doing. It is also during those times that you will suffer your greatest defeats. There is protection in the will of God, but when you step out, you are free game for the devil's snares. David would have come through the situation unscathed had he prayed to the Lord for guidance.

What David needed at a time like that is what all accomplished spiritual leaders need, and that is a prayer covering. (Let me be clear about what I mean by "spiritual leader." There is a difference between a spiritual leader and a spiritualist. When I refer to a spiritual leader, I am talking about a man or woman of the true and living God. A spiritualist could be a person who invokes demon power or is even hostile toward God.) David needed to have people who prayed for him on a consistent basis to protect him against the snares of the evil one.

There are a few things that we can learn from David's situation that will help today's ministers avoid pitfalls. Do not rest on past accomplishments; keep moving toward the task ahead. Make sure you are always where God wants you to be, fulfilling your responsibilities. Proactively identify and attack your own weaknesses through prayer and fasting. Do not allow isolation; develop relationships with other men and women of God who you can go to when you need help. Draw close to God, resist the devil, and he will flee. Be vigilant and pray when you see your hour of temptation approaching.

Background Check

Considering what David had accomplished in Israel, it was logical for Satan to put a snare in David's path. The devil literally was on the warpath against David.

Humans are most vulnerable when they are sleepy or groggy. Late in the afternoon, after a nap, David arose from his bed. Half awake, he managed to stumble up to the roof of his palace for a "wake up" stroll where, in that sleepy state, he viewed a woman in her house bathing herself. Simple decency would usually cause a person to look away, but she was so beautiful that David could not take his eyes off her. Satan had thrown David a sucker punch, because men are sight-driven. The only way you can parade a beautiful naked woman by a man without eliciting a strong response is if he is dead or near death. Satan laid a snare that few men could resist. Sexual desire is a powerful force, and David took the bait—and from that point there was no turning back. Your Bible heralds one of the worst atrocities ever committed by one of God's chosen men.

In modern society, it is not uncommon for women to be scantily clad. We call it sexy when a woman leaves little to the imagination. A woman can walk around with so much cleavage exposed that there is not much left to hide, with hip-hugger jeans that barely cover the top of her private parts, and with thongs that rise above her jeans exposing the top of her buns, yet we act surprised and offended when a man has a natural sexual response. "He's a dog," we say. We act as if we do not know that men are sight-driven. It is cruel and diabolical to treat men this way. It is a control thing, and it is dangerous, because it is teasing a man, daring him to respond yet punishing him if he fails to suppress natural tendencies.

Immodestly dressed women cause unintended consequences for our society. When a man has been trained to suppress his natural arousal tendencies in a society of half-naked women, he has trouble responding to the sight of his own wife's nakedness. Perhaps some of the demand for erectile products comes from the need to physically override psychological suppression. If we train men to suppress their natural arousal at the sight of a naked woman, they stop responding and start dreading, fearing, and hating the thing that causes their natural response. Another consequence of a society of half-naked women is that after a man repeatedly fails to respond to his wife, he concludes he is gay. It behooves the women in our society to dress with propriety.

David investigated Bathsheba's background in a legitimate attempt to do the right thing. Had he found that she was a single, available woman, he would have asked for her hand in marriage. He learned that her name was Bathsheba, daughter of Eliam and wife of one of his soldiers, a Hittite named Uriah.

During his investigation, David had time to pause and consider his actions, but there was something diabolical about the situation, because David was not being rational and was acting totally out of character. How much time elapsed between the time David saw Bathsheba naked and when he had sex with her? (How much time have you spent pondering your sin?) David was normally a just and honorable man in private matters. A person's true character is what he or she does when no one is looking. David had proved himself to be a man of impeccable character when he honored his private promises to Jonathan, so what would have caused him to pursue an illegitimate relationship with a woman just because she was beautiful? All his wives were beautiful.

David had Abigail, who had beauty *and* brains, and Maacah, daughter of King Talmai, whose beauty can be inferred because she produced gorgeous children. He had a number of women at his disposal, but it was as if he was being pushed into a situation over which he had no control. Unseen forces were compelling him. He could not put on the brakes even if he tried. He had never been faced with such a situation before; the novelty threw him off guard. There was no legitimate, legal way that David could have had Bathsheba, because she was married and thus off limits, but it did not seem to matter to David. Seeing her had fueled his desire and ignited his passion—he had to have *her*. After he gathered all the information, he sent for Bathsheba and slept with her anyway.

Do you ever look back on a situation and ask with regret, "What would have happened if I had not been there? Where would I be if I hadn't met so-and-so?"

Take-home message: Those who destroy demonic strongholds become targets of the devil and need a prayer covering.

21.

Love Had Nothing to Do with It

Love had nothing to do with the situation; it was all about David satisfying his "need." How terrible it must feel to know that someone is using your body for their own pleasure and that you are simply the object of someone's desire! David's passion got the best of him, and he abused his authority with Bathsheba.

How do you refuse a king's sexual advances? She should have refused on the grounds of wanting to be faithful to her husband or that it was an immoral, illegal affair whose consequence would be death for both parties, especially if the sex was judged consensual. Everyone would have understood that she was not a willing participant if she had cried out for help. She could have fallen to the floor in tears and made an emotional appeal to David's honor. However, she did none of those things, because she was afraid to stand up to him.

David put Bathsheba in an awkward, powerless position. There was no dialogue between them, and Bathsheba felt she could not offer a voice of reason against powerful King David. She felt there was nothing she could do to save herself from the tragedy, so she succumbed. Who can fully understand the dynamics between the two? From David's standpoint, it was a "wham-bam-thank-you-ma'am" liaison. After his passion was spent, David sent her back home.

A similar thing happens when a woman parades around scantily clad. Men are sexually attracted, but when she draws unwanted attention from men, she's shocked. Certain men who have not yet learned to suppress their urges come on to a woman who dresses in a revealing manner. She mistakes that attention for personal interest in her, but nothing could be further from the truth. Men are responding to the sexual arousal she has ignited, and it has nothing to do with her personally, except that she was the object of their arousal. She mistakes sexual attraction for personal interest. When they end up in bed after a brief "introduction," she thinks the man loves her, but love had nothing to do with it. It was only physical. She is hurt to find out she was just a plaything, but he thinks that is what she wanted. She walks away hurt; he is confused.

The Cover-Up

The situation between David and Bathsheba got worse. The clandestine rendezvous would not be nice and tidy after all. Bathsheba got pregnant, but several months passed before she told him. The bombshell threw David into a state of panic. David wanted to cover it up, but sins are eventually found out. How many of you know that your sins will find you out? What is done in secret will one day be exposed by God.

God gives each person a gift, and we can choose to use it for good or evil. David was a master strategist in battle, and he used those same skills in an attempt to cover his sin. David had a perfect strategy, except for one flaw that he thought he could easily correct. David called Bathsheba's husband from the battlefield. He figured that if he could subtly persuade Uriah to sleep with Bathsheba, her pregnancy would be explained. It would be David and Bathsheba's little secret. The child would be well cared for and Bathsheba would receive "compensation" because she carried a child of the king in her womb, but that was not the way it turned out.

David masterminded a scheme to get Uriah to sleep with his wife, but he could not say anything about it without arousing suspicion. The plan would have worked had Uriah been the soldier of any army other than David's. David had trained his men not to sleep with women while they were on active duty. All Uriah had to do was go home, David thought, and the act would be consummated. After all, how could anyone refuse a woman of such alluring beauty that even disciplined King David could not resist? There would be no way for Uriah to resist the charms of his wife or to quell the hunger that grew from his long absence.

When Uriah arrived, David made small talk with him, asking how the battle was going. Then he sent Uriah home for some rest and relaxation. But Uriah was a man of integrity, a faithful and honorable man who refused any special treatment, so he stayed with the servants at the palace that night. The next day David asked him why he did not go home, and he replied:

> The Ark of the armies of Israel and Judah are living in tents, and Joab and his officers are camping in the open fields. How could I go home to wine and dine and sleep with my wife? I swear I will never be guilty of acting like that. *2 Samuel 11:11*

Uriah had unintentionally rebuked David, because David was guilty of that very behavior. He was guilty of indulging in pleasure when he should have, at the very least, been practicing abstinence in support of the army. He could have been called to battle at a moment's notice, and he should have been in a state of readiness. Uriah stayed at the palace for a couple more days, and during that time David got him drunk in an attempt to get him to go home to his wife, but Uriah slept at the palace entrance instead. Uriah had more integrity drunk than many do sober. Therefore, David had to resort to Plan B.

David's actions were motivated by self-preservation, but it is amazing how cruel people can be to those they consider insignificant. That is why God often reminded the children of Israel to be kind to foreigners. However, Uriah was not a foreigner. His ancestors had a long history in the land of Canaan. His family was there before Abraham ever set foot in Canaan. Abraham had bought a field that would become the permanent burial place for Israelite forefathers from the Hittite Ephron, son of Zohar.

The Hittites had a long history of friendship toward the Israelites, and the fact that Uriah was in the Israelite army bespeaks of their continued loyalty. The plight of the Hittites was that of a people remaining in conquered land, dependent upon the mercy of their conquerors. Even after you have shown hospitality toward the conquerors, you are downgraded to second-class citizen status. In the minds of conquerors, second-class citizens are insignificant. No one cares what happens to the powerless second-class citizens, and no one will hold you accountable for harming a nobody. Who would come to Uriah's defense or care if he died, and who would request an inquiry into the cause of his death? What's the matter, David? You won't touch God's anointed, but you'll lay your hand on this "no name," Uriah, a seemingly insignificant one?

David had a desperately urgent need to cover his tracks, because Bathsheba's belly was not getting any smaller. There was an ironclad penalty for adultery in Israel: they stoned the adulterers to death. Soon people would ask questions and seek explanations. David was trying to keep the thing under wraps. He was trying to preserve his own reputation and his life. If they questioned Bathsheba, David knew she would probably tell all. Why would she risk ruining her reputation and losing her husband and her life when there had been no love between David and her?

David would have made a good chess player, because he had planned far in advance. Nothing in his actions suggests that he was acting impetuously. He made cold, calculated moves and had many contingency plans. When he found Bathsheba was pregnant, he tried to get Uriah home to sleep with her. When the stubborn, principled Uriah refused, David got him drunk to weaken his defenses. That did not work. Plan B meant taking Uriah's life. With Uriah dead, he could marry Bathsheba without having to explain that her pregnancy was the result of adultery. When the baby was born early, he could say it was premature.

David further abused his authority by involving others in his sin. David used Uriah's strong sense of honor against him, sending him back to the battle with a letter of execution. Uriah never even thought about opening the king's letter, so he delivered the letter that sealed his fate. David instructed Joab to station Uriah on the frontlines where the battle was fiercest and then to back off so Uriah would be killed. Uriah was not the only one who lost his life as a result of David's sin—other soldiers fighting next to Uriah died as well.

There is an irrationality to sin that causes you to do things you would not ordinarily do—such as create unwanted partnerships. When Joab killed Abner, David made it clear that he did not agree with Joab's actions. If David had been able to exercise greater influence over the army, he would have cut all ties with his nephews Joab and Abishai. The reason David did not dismiss Joab was because he feared him and thought Joab was too powerful to control. David tolerated Joab and Abishai.

Knowing David's sentiment, what would cause him to involve Joab in his conspiracy? Why would David want to make himself more vulnerable to Joab by putting himself in a situation where he could be blackmailed? Was David getting sloppy in his sin? What would make David feel that his secret was safe with Joab? The last person to involve when you are in trouble and trying to cover up a scandal is an adversary, because they will expose you.

There is only one reason David could have felt comfortable involving Joab: he knew that Joab was a ruthless man. Involving Joab in the conspiracy forever cemented an unwanted relationship. David gave Joab the opportunity to prove his loyalty (by murdering Uriah) in order to secure his tenuous position as army commander. Who knows how far David was willing to go? Perhaps he planned to kill Joab.

When Bathsheba was informed that her husband had been killed in battle, she went into mourning, and after that mourning period, David brought her to the palace to become one of his wives. The question is: How much did Bathsheba know? There is no indication that Bathsheba was aware that David had Uriah at the palace, so she could not have been aware of his scheme to get Uriah to go home.

Although she may have suspected that Uriah's death was not coincidental, she could not confirm her suspicions. In the back of her mind, there would always be lingering doubt. Having Uriah out of the way was very convenient for David. David abused her by turning her life upside down for his own selfish pleasure. When everybody else looked at David, they saw a mighty man of God, an undefeated warrior, and an admirable man, but only Bathsheba knew about his ugliness and treachery.

David was successful in covering up his adultery. The only person who knew he had murdered Uriah was Joab (and whomever Joab told), but there had to have been whispers among staff members who were starting to put two and two together. The death of Uriah and the other soldiers had to raise some eyebrows.

If there wasn't a God who sits high and looks low, David could have breathed a sigh of relief. You may be able to fool every man living on this Earth, but you cannot fool God. God does not skip a beat. He even checks your thoughts out while you sleep. You may convince everybody that you are pristine, but God sees all and weighs your thoughts and the intent of your heart. You may be so slick that you can sin right in front of people and convince them that they did not see what they saw. You can easily deceive human beings, but not God—and David was no exception. God kept his eye on David all of his life, so what would make David think his sins would slip under God's radar undetected? Sin creates irrationality.

> But the LORD was very displeased with what David had done.
> *2 Samuel 11:27*

It's a Dirty Job, But the Prophet Has to Do It

It is important for a prophet not to placate leaders when they are sinning. The reason Christian leaders have such a credibility problem today is that some pastors and prophets flock to the defense of celebrity sinners. Sin is sin, no matter who commits it, whether it be a president, an athlete, or the CEO of a large corporation. Onlookers stop respecting Christian leaders and they blaspheme God when pastors defend a celebrity's sin. Why do we have higher standards for the average person than we do for a president? Unless a person, regardless of position, is remorseful, our only job is to warn them of their sins. If they have a contrite heart, it is our responsibility to restore them. Under no circumstances are we to tell them, "There, there, you did nothing wrong. You were just being human."

You do people a disservice when you do not show them their sins and the way out. The responsibility of a watchman is to warn people of the consequences of their sins. If a watchman fails to warn them, those people will die in their sins, and their blood will be on the watchman's hands. When a watchman warns people, he absolves himself.

God sent the prophet Nathan to confront David about his sins, but Nathan did not address the situation directly at first. To get David to see the error of his ways, he told a story to evoke David's indignation, because even though David had sinned and tried to cover it up, he was still a man who was naturally just. Sometimes you cannot directly address a person's sin, because it will put them on the defensive, and once that happens, you cannot get them to acknowledge their wrong. You have to present your case in a different light or from a different perspective to get a person to see their wrong.

Nathan presented a case concerning a wealthy man who owned a great deal of livestock and a poor man who owned only one lamb. The poor man's lamb was treated like a member of his family. When a visitor came to the wealthy man's house, he killed the poor man's lamb instead of one of his own to serve his guest. Everything the rich man possessed had been given to him, but the poor man had worked hard for the one thing he owned. David was incensed; the wheels of justice churned in his heart.

"That man deserves to die! He must repay four lambs for the one he stole," David exclaimed.

It is easy to be objective about the sins of others, but God had set David up, looking for that exact response. Nathan said, "You are that man! You murdered Uriah and stole his wife." A ton of bricks came crashing down on David. God knows . . .

God gave David everything that belonged to Saul because Saul had wrongfully oppressed him. God gave David all of Saul's wealth because of the years of oppression and torment he had put David through. He withheld nothing, and if David had said, "God, I want more," God would have given him what he requested. However, just as God had lavishly blessed David because of all he had suffered at the hands of Saul, He punished him just as lavishly for the evil deeds he had committed against Uriah, Bathsheba, and other innocents. God had to avenge the wrongful death of Uriah and the theft of his wife the same way He had avenged Saul's wrongful pursuit of David. Saul hounded David and besmirched his reputation but he did not lay one finger on him, yet God gave David everything that belonged to Saul. If God had blessed David abundantly in the past even though Saul was not successful at taking his life, what would David's punishment be since he actually did kill Uriah and other unnamed innocents?

If you could see the devastation and horror you unleash in your life and the lives of your family members as a result of five minutes of sin, you would reconsider your actions, because it is not worth it. Anytime you want to do something questionable, ask yourself, "What are the consequences, and can I live with them?"

That would cut down on a lot of heartache. Half the battle is thinking things through or praying when the temptation is strong. Sir, is that woman with the short, tight, low-cut dress really worth wrecking your marriage over? Ma'am, is that man who smells good, is attentive, and acts sensitive worth brokenhearted children? Is one act of selfishness worth having children who grow up conflicted, bitter, and angry? Is it all about you and your "happiness" to the exclusion of the happiness and well-being of your spouse and children?

Nathan told David what to expect as a result of his sins. David's sin opened the floodgates of murder, rebellion, and sexual dysfunction in his household. Everyone suffered because of David's sin, even those not directly involved.

> From this time on, the sword will be a constant threat to your family, because you have despised me by taking Uriah's wife to be your own. Because of what you have done, I, the Lord, will cause your own household to rebel against you. I will give your wives to another man, and he will go to bed with them in public view. You did it secretly, but I will do this to you openly in the sight of all Israel.
> *2 Samuel 12:10–12*

The private sins of a leader affect not only his family but also the people he or she leads. The aftershock of David's sins could not be confined to his family, since they also affected the mentality of the entire nation. David's sins spurned God's words, and all the progress David had made in leading Israel to spiritual reform was undone by his sins. People tend to discredit everything a fallen minister has accomplished. David's righteousness encouraged the Israelites to strive to live holy lives, but his sins discouraged them.

People give up trying to live right when their model fails. It is hard to demand holiness of others when you fail to exemplify it yourself. The sins of a minister have a way of lowering the standard and encouraging others to follow suit. So much rides on the righteousness of spiritual leaders that when they fail, everything crumbles. Moral failure in ministers proves that it is impossible to live according to God's words. The people figured that if David, God's anointed one, could sin, so could they.

"We are justified. If the man of God sins, why can't we? He proved that no one can live a godly life. We have sinned, but not as badly as David, so we are righteous. If we keep living as we're living, we will never be as bad as David. No one can live under the restrictions God sets forth anyway."

When men and women of God sin, it provides an opportunity for the enemies of God to mock Him. We are God's ambassadors, and anything we do reflects on Him. The enemies of God are given an opportunity to disrespect Him, to act irreverently toward Him, to mock Him, to belittle Him, and to make light of His holiness when a high-profile Christian falls. The media, actors, and comedians love it and have a field day when they have any opportunity to discredit God and run God's name through the mud because of the sins of one of His servants. They have fresh material that they can use with many spins for at least a year. It's like throwing raw meat to hungry dogs. It's entertaining to some to witness the fall of God's ministers.

> But they are glad now that I am in trouble; they gleefully join together against me. I am attacked by people I don't even know; they hurl slander at me continually. They mock me with the worst kind of profanity, and they snarl at me. *Psalm 35:15–16*

Take-home message: Don't kid yourself; God sees everything.

22.

A True Picture of Repentance

When Christians sin, God uses His Holy Spirit to convict, and when the convicting power of the Lord is upon you, you feel guilt and shame that does not easily fade away. Carrying the burden of sin weighs you down and causes weariness, because God's rebuke lingers for hours, days, or weeks. The replay of events is torturous. You kick yourself for your stupidity, even though there is no way to undo the past. God's heavy hand of discipline has a way of causing you to feel your errors physically—your stomach ties up in knots, your head hurts, and your body aches. He rakes you over the coals without laying a finger on you. Sleep eludes you and your appetite flees. It is a horrible spot to be in when the Lord is displeased with your actions. His heavy hand of discipline is not pleasant.

David's Anguish and Remorse

David was in this exact situation. When he was alone, he cried a river of tears, "soulish" cries, a deep wailing that came from within and could not be quelled. He was immobilized by the weight of his sins, but he could do nothing to comfort his soul. His sins had robbed him of his joy and peace. His desperate plea was for God to stop replaying the events of that fateful day in his mind.

> For I recognize my shameful deeds—they haunt me day and night. Against you, and you alone, have I sinned; I have done what is evil in your sight. You will be proved right in what you say, and your judgment against me is just. *Psalm 51:3–4*

"The punishment you have given me is perfectly just, because I deserve it. You are right, fair, and accurate in your assessment of me. I am a sinner. I am a broken wretch. I acknowledge the damage I have caused others. I have let you down and broken your heart."

When a prophet confronts you with your sin, the desired response is repentance, but simply being sorry you were caught is *not* repentance. That attitude suggests that if given the opportunity, you would do it again. Godly sorrow is what leads to true repentance; it is the kind of sorrow that causes you to ask God to forgive you for your sin and to beg God to cleanse you from future sins. That kind of sorrow will not rest until you set things straight. Once you sin in a particular way, you are destined to repeat it. Asking for forgiveness restores you to right standing before the Lord. Asking God to cleanse you of all ungodliness ensures that you will not repeat the sin.

David was not at peace about his actions. Before Nathan confronted him, he suffered anguish and remorse over what he had done, and his soul was in turmoil. It was the first time in his life he had royally botched things and the first time he had faced a major sin. Those who have lived a perfect life find their first major sin a crushing, devastating blow. It was the first time he had broken God's heart. Considering how much he loved God, David's guilt was compounded even more. Up to that time in his life, he had never harmed anyone. How does a man with his record handle the transition from being fair and generous to being a selfish destroyer? He was disgusted to discover the evil and treachery that resided within him. He absolutely abhorred himself. Facing the aftermath of his sin was worse than dying. He tried to hold his head up and go on with business as usual, but when he was alone, a tidal wave of tears gushed from his very soul. He needed relief from his anguish in a bad way. How do you spell relief? R·E·P·E·N·T·A·N·C·E.

> I am worn out from sobbing. Every night tears drench my bed; my pillow is wet from weeping. *Psalm 6:6*

Sin robs you of joy, silences you, blocks your ability to praise God by your voice and by offering sacrifices. The greatest sacrifice that can be given at a time like that is a broken heart and a contrite spirit. Unresolved sin hinders your prayer life. Sixty percent of the Ten Commandments deal with our relationship with one another, which means God is deeply concerned about how we treat one another. When we sin against one another, it is imperative that we seek forgiveness before we go to God. God is not interested in our offerings and sacrifices, because they cause a stench in His nostrils when we are unrepentant. God advises us to leave our offering beside the altar when we become aware that someone has something against us and go to that person and seek reconciliation. After we do that, we can offer our sacrifice to God.

By the time Nathan confronted David, he was ready to spill his guts; he was dying to confess his wrongdoing. Keeping his terrible secret was poisoning his soul. He needed to purge his soul, because his sins were burning and eating him alive. Confession was medicine to his soul, and it brought relief and cleansing that he could not have obtained otherwise. Confession is cathartic and cleanses the soul. Confess. Confess. Confess.

> When I refused to confess my sin, I was weak and miserable, and I groaned all day long. Day and night your hand of discipline was heavy on me. My strength evaporated like water in the summer heat. Finally, I confessed all my sins to you and stopped trying to hide them. I said to myself, "I confess my rebellion to the Lord." And you forgave me! All my guilt is gone. Therefore, let all the godly confess their rebellion to you while there is time, that they may not drown in the floodwaters of judgment. *Psalm 32:3–6*

General and Specific

David is a perfect example of how repentance is supposed to work. When confronted by Nathan, David did not play head games and try to redefine the meaning of sex. He was not in denial, and he did not lie to God, himself, or others. He did not try to justify his actions by saying, "A man has needs." He instantly confessed.

The first step in repentance is a general confession that you have inherited a sinful nature and that you have sinned. When Adam sinned, he unleashed a twofold curse. First of all, because every human being originated from Adam, we are contaminated by sin. The only thing that satisfies sin's demand is death. Therefore, everyone was condemned to die. The problem with a curse is that in order to stop it, four generations from the point of the initiating sin must not sin at all. Although they themselves will still suffer from the curse, their sinless lives can stop the curse starting at the fifth generation. How hard is that? The problem with this endeavor is that if you have been born with a proclivity toward sin, you will find it impossible to go against natural tendencies. Doing what is natural (committing sin) fuels the curse, because the punishment from the curse affects the next four generations and your sinful nature is passed on to your offspring. Inherited sin ensures that sin will continue, and sin reinforces the curse that condemns all to die. It is an unending, nauseating circle of sin that is impossible for humanity to break.

Second, Adam's sin severed his connection with God, causing him to die spiritually, and his offspring was born spiritually dead. Adam caused human beings to become walking dead, physically alive yet spiritually dead. The human body is a temporary shell that houses a person's spirit and soul, and it will perish. Immortality is wrapped in mortality. Since a person's soul is immortal, it will live forever, even after it sheds the body. An immortal soul has a spirit that is either dead or alive. A dead spirit is one that is permanently separated from God. To be permanently separated from God is the ultimate death. Spiritual life is dependent upon a connection to God. When a person gives themselves to God, He quickens their spirit by attaching His Spirit to theirs. God is to man's spirit what air is to man's body, and when Adam sinned, he severed humanity's connection to God.

If one human manages to live a sinless life, the curse can be broken, ensuring blessings for the generations to come. God lavishes His love and blessings on a person who loves and obeys Him for a thousand generations of their offspring. Jesus broke the twofold curse of sin by living a sinless life. Those born through Jesus are born with a righteous nature and are no longer condemned with the curse of a sinful nature. Jesus, in His death, satisfied the demands of the curse, broke the cycle of sin, and restored humanity's spiritual connection to God. Jesus through His sinless life and sacrificial death made forgiveness available to humanity and restored a right standing with God. Anybody who wants what Jesus offers has to make the general confession, and it is theirs.

David admitted that he had a sinful nature. To travel the road to repentance, you must follow David's path. In general, you must confess, like David, that humans are born with a sinful nature.

> For I was born a sinner—yes, from the moment my mother conceived me. *Psalm 51:5*

Until you admit that you have a sinful nature and that you have sinned, God cannot help you, because you first have to be able to humble yourself. Many people do not believe they are sinners, because they are good people. It is true that there are people who are morally good and possess better character than many Christians, but if being a good person is good enough to get you into heaven, why did Jesus need to sacrifice His life? If people can enter heaven on the basis of their own merits, Jesus died for nothing.

Comparisons between human beings are relative and faulty at best, because a compromised measuring tool is being used. When the proper standard is used as a comparison, people can truly see how they stack up. Jesus was the only human being who ever lived on this Earth who is worthy to be used as a comparative measure. When you stand before God, He will weigh you on a scale that has been calibrated by Jesus. Comparing your "righteousness" against others is a waste of time.

You cannot travel the road to repentance and recovery as long as you hold the belief that you are not a sinner. All human beings are contaminated with sin because of Adam's sin. Any human being who expects to be restored with a right standing before the God of the Universe must do so through the person of Jesus Christ, the Son of God. Therefore, on a general level, you must first admit that you have a sinful nature.

The next step on the road to repentance is specific confession of personal wrongdoing. Everybody, and I do mean everybody, faces an area of weakness where they consistently falter. The Bible calls them *besetting sins*. People are either born with a proclivity for a particular sin or develop it, like David did. You have to be honest with yourself and God over past and present unresolved sins. To obtain forgiveness for sinful actions, you have to be able to clearly identify your sins.

David instantly acknowledged his sins against Uriah and Bathsheba. More important, he admitted that his sins were against God. He also recognized that God could not help him unless he humbled himself.

> For I recognize my shameful deeds—they haunt me day and night. Against you, and you alone, have I sinned; I have done what is evil in your sight. . . But you desire honesty from the heart, so you can teach me to be wise in my inmost being. *Psalm 51:3–4, 6*

"I broke your heart by killing several of your children and taking what did not belong to me. I had no right to destroy what belongs to you. I coveted Uriah's wife by actively pursuing her and stole her. I took advantage of Bathsheba and abused my authority for my own selfish pleasure. I was selfish, self-centered, and self-indulgent. I took the beautiful gift of sexuality that you gave humanity and degraded it. My sins have caused a breakdown in the spiritual reform of Israel. My sins have given your enemies cause to despise and act irreverently toward you. People will use my sins as an excuse to sin against you."

There is such a cleansing in honest, sincere confession. Sometimes general and specific confessions happen at the same time, but for most people, it takes a maturing process in Christ before they realize that the actions and habits they once considered normal are sinful. For both general and specific confessions to happen concurrently, you must be tired of your inability to correct your actions, tired of suffering for your sins and tired of the suffering you cause others. It is wonderful to witness a person who comes to Jesus with both confessions at the same time because they are fed up with themselves and their sins. They had reached rock bottom and recognized their inability to fix things long before they heard of Jesus. When such a person meets Jesus

Christ, what a release and what a cleansing! It is a beautiful thing to see and an even more beautiful thing to experience. However, those types of confessions are rare and usually not public.

Some people give their hearts to Jesus in the middle of sin while they are at their lowest point. For instance, there was a man who regularly rented a hotel room so he could shoot drugs into his arm. His wife and children suffered because of his addiction, and he was failing as a husband, father, and employee. He was disgusted with himself and what he was doing, but he felt there was no way out. One day Jesus met him at the hotel room while he was shooting up, and the man fell on his knees and asked Jesus to deliver him from his destructive lifestyle. He poured out his many sins before Jesus and told Him how he had caused suffering in his family, depriving them financially and emotionally. His wife had done everything she could to help him and to hold things together, but he had refused her help. He admitted that he was not proud of himself and desperately wanted to be free but could not stop on his own. Jesus listened as the man poured out his heart and freed him on the spot, and that man is still free today. His wife is happy because she received a new man, a better man than the one she married, and his children are happy because they have their daddy back.

Ninety percent of altar calls invoke only general confessions; it is not the specific confessions that yield instant cleansing on the spot. Most Christians go through a progressive, gradual purification. That is why we observe unseemly behaviors in ourselves and fellow Christians. God graced us when we were saved, but He expects us to go on to perfection and work out our salvation with fear and trembling.

What does *graced us* mean? It depends on your level of maturity. For a seasoned Christian, it means He covers your sins, giving you the opportunity to repent. But for the new believer, He took your sins away because when you were saved, you were not able to handle much. Remember when Jesus rescued *you*? It was as though you were walking on the clouds; you were a new person. Many sinful behaviors vanished instantly, and even your family members could see the change. He did that because at the time you were not strong enough to get rid of your sinful habits, nor did you see a need. He got rid of them because He wanted to love you and to draw you close. He had been longing to wrap His arms around you. It is the goodness of God that leads to repentance. He wanted to assure you of His love so you would bravely face your internal ugliness. He wanted you to face your sins, knowing that He knows all about them—and loves you in spite of them.

When you become more mature in Christ, He uses His word to expose unresolved sins and character flaws. He brings them to your attention so you will confront them, seek deliverance, and allow Him to cleanse you of unrighteousness. When God confronts Christians with their sins, they tend to blame it on the devil, because he is the accuser of the brethren, after all. Many people mistakenly rebuke the devil for bringing up the past when it is God who brings deep-seated sins to the surface and initiates the purification process.

Go for Cleansing

Repentance is more than apologizing; it also involves changing your behavior. When you apologize, you are simply admitting your actions were wrong, but until you have changed your behavior, your repentance is incomplete. Nobody cares how sorry you are when you continue to do the same things that make them sorry. Show sorrow and repentance by terminating wrong behavior.

When John the Baptist was preaching in the wilderness, people came to him asking, "How do I repent?"

> Prove by the way you live that you have really turned from your sins and turned to God. *Matthew 3:8*

He told the tax collectors to stop taking more than was required. He told soldiers to stop being abusive. A positive behavioral shift is evidence that true repentance has taken place.

Some teach that repentance means changing your mind about God. Change your mind to recognize that what you considered normal is sin in God's eyes. It is true that *repentance* literally means "changing your mind," but it is not enough just to change your mind. Your soul is made up of mind, will, and emotions. Your mind is only a third, while your heart influences the other two thirds of your behavior. When the thoughts of your mind (the seat of logic and intellect) and heart are in disagreement, your heart wins because it carries more influence! Your heart dictates your behavior. Out of the abundance of the heart the mouth speaks. As a man thinks in his heart, so is he. If you understand with your heart, you will be converted. This is the reason David sought a clean heart.

> Create in me a clean heart, O God. Renew a right spirit within me. *Psalm 51:10*

David knew that trying to reform or rehabilitate himself would be faulty and temporary at best. It is easy to change your mind but much more difficult to change your heart. Only when change begins in your heart will your behavior change. Only the Master of the heart can deal with the complexities and contradictions of the heart; the job is too big for a human being.

> How can I know all the sins lurking in my heart? Cleanse me from these hidden faults. Keep me from deliberate sins! Don't let them control me. Then I will be free of guilt and innocent of great sin.
> *Psalm 19:12–13*

David wanted the assurance that he would never again commit the sinful acts he had committed, so he asked the Lord to cleanse him. David demonstrated the clearest "textbook" repentance in the Bible. The process of repentance in David's life is the process God wants everybody to walk through. David acknowledged his sins, confessed, received forgiveness, and asked for cleansing deliverance so that he would not repeat his sins.

> Purify me from my sins, and I will be clean; wash me, and I will be whiter than snow. Don't keep looking at my sins. Remove the stain of my guilt. *Psalm 51:7, 9*

"I am dissatisfied with my sinful ways and cannot endure living with the contradiction between my behavior and your Holy Word. I know that my actions were wrong, yet I continue do that which breaks your heart. I am discouraged and disgusted with myself. I cannot continue to live with duplicity. Wash the dirt off me. The ugliness within my soul is revolting. I cannot continue to live with an impure heart. I cannot bear the chasm that my sin causes between us. I do not like being separated from you like this. I feel lost and insecure without you. If there is going to be any improvement in my sinful condition, if there is going to be any cleansing deliverance, it will only take place through you, Lord God. If there is any hope for my recovery, it is in you. This is not the time to abandon me. It is the time to embrace me so you can heal me. If you leave me to myself, I will sin again."

> Do not banish me from your presence, and don't take your Holy Spirit from me. *Psalm 51:11*

This aspect of repentance involves making a personal effort to change your behavior and appealing to God for cleansing. All sins have the same penalty, but there are some sins that are more compelling than others, and some have greater power over one person than another. One man can get so drunk that he cannot remember his name and then resolve never to do it again. He may successfully live with that resolve because he does not have a problem with alcohol. Another person may find the intoxicating whispers of alcohol irresistible and be unable to maintain a resolve to avoid drunkenness on his own. That person will have to appeal to God for cleansing deliverance.

The ugliness of the sin within David was too great and the propensity for sinning in the same manner was too strong for him to try to correct on his own. Everything within him desired not to repeat his sins, and he resolved never to commit such acts again, but he understood that man's resolve is temporary at best and the power of his sin's addictiveness was too great for his resolve. Man's resolve will only be successful when he gets a commitment from God, who is omnipotent, to change him.

David understood that his actions had serious moral implications and signaled many character flaws. Innocent people had died because of his sin, so he sought cleansing deliverance, because even though his sin had been forgiven, the potential for repeating sin still remained. Only God can heal the depravity in a person's heart. Only God can heal your heart so that your behavior is permanently corrected. If you have sinned, that is not the time to run away from God. It is the time to run to God. Go for the cleansing! Trade sin, sickness, and shame for the glory of the Lord.

When a person becomes a believer by receiving salvation, the focus turns from salvation to purification. Purification is a process that happens whenever it is necessary. There are many things for which a person needs to be purified; once a person successfully resolves a particular sin, then God will present another sinful area that needs resolution. That cycle continues in a person's Christian walk until they leave this Earth; therefore, no one can ever reach a point where they feel they have arrived. Purification is a progressive work, because a person must be able to acknowledge their actions as sin. There are several ways a person can realize that their actions are sinful; one way is by reading and hearing God's words.

God initiates purification by His word. His word is so sharp that it exposes the deep-seated attitudes and beliefs behind our habits and behavior. Once God's words expose us, He uses them to cleanse us from all unrighteousness. He sends His word to correct, instruct, advise, and nurture us. His word is powerful and irresistible; it will accomplish His purpose in our lives.

Many people believe that Christians are weak-kneed, spineless, emotional cripples, but Christianity is not a wimpy way. God will confront you with your sins because He wants to purify you. He will make you face the ugliness within your soul. God shows you who you really are, and it will disgust you when you get a glimpse of the evil that lies within.

Most people cannot face themselves and do not allow themselves to feel the weight of sin until they reach rock bottom, and then it becomes unavoidable. Although you can try to ignore it, you know that something is terribly wrong. You just cannot stop crying or feeling a sense of dread. You cannot explain your mourning and grief. You use sleeping pills when sleep eludes you. You use other pills for your depression. You are in denial; somehow everyone else is to blame for your actions. Things will be a lot smoother if you just face the issues.

Christianity forces believers to bravely look at the evil within and to confess their need for cleansing deliverance. It takes strength to do objective introspection. It takes strength to admit you were wrong. The difference between a weak person and a strong person is being able to admit guilt and the need for restoration. Many people would rather take drugs, drink alcohol, overeat, watch TV, exercise, or do any number of other mind-numbing things rather than face themselves.

Forgiveness is not enough. The general and specific confession aspects of repentance lead to forgiveness, but forgiveness only restores you to right standing with God. David sought forgiveness and received it, but he did not stop there, because he realized that sin is highly addictive. Once you have committed a particular sin, it is highly probable that you will repeat it.

God commissioned churches to go out to the highways and byways and across this globe to preach the gospel and compel people to receive the eternal life that Jesus made available. As long as we believe that salvation and forgiveness of sins are enough, Christians will remain in bondage to sin. If we stop at the forgiveness stage, thinking our work is done, we only produce mental ascension. Mental ascension is dangerous; simply acknowledging sin is not enough, because it does nothing to correct future behavior. What mental ascension produces is a Christian who is stuck in a rut of the same sinful behavioral patterns, justifying the need to seek forgiveness for the same sin again. Nothing has been done to cleanse the person from the contamination of sin to prevent its future recurrence. Having Christians in the kingdom of God struggling with habitual sins is the same as the children of Israel in the Promised Land struggling with idolatry. You may be in the right position but still living an accursed life as a result of unresolved sins. No, we cannot stop at the salvation and forgiveness stage.

When God forgives you of sin, it is as if you have never sinned, because your sins are cast into the sea of forgetfulness, never to be remembered again. Does it not bother you, though, to keep going to the Father and requesting forgiveness for the same sin a thousand times a year? Something is desperately wrong. Although God has forgiven you, you need to be cleansed of the contamination of sin. Because the purification process is often neglected, it produces stunted Christians. Stunted Christians are jeopardizing their eternal life with Christ Jesus because the focus is not on purification where sinful attitudes, thoughts, and habits are addressed.

There is no condemnation for those who are in Christ Jesus. When Jesus died, He broke the power of sin and overcame death. Those who received Jesus as their Savior also died with Him; therefore, they share in the benefits of His death. They are dead to sin, and they live by the same power that raised Christ Jesus from the dead. Condemnation means there is no hope of transformation and a person is doomed to die; since Jesus broke sin's condemning power, a person can be set free.

Sin no longer has the power to lock you up forever—you do not have to be a slave to sin. Jesus set you free from sin's addictiveness so that when you sin, you are not bound to repeat it. Jesus broke the cycle of sin, giving you the power to choose to do right. Before you became a believer, you had no choice but to sin, because sin dominated you. But now Jesus has restored your choice. However, you become a slave to your choices. You can choose to continue in sin and allow it to master you, laying again a foundation of nonproductive behavior, or you can choose to become a slave to righteousness, laying a foundation of good works. This means that you can choose to go to Jesus with your sins and let Him break the power of sin in your life and do a perfect work in you. God's glorious power is enough to help you rise above your circumstances, because it is the same power He used to raise Jesus from the dead. He can give you the cleansing deliverance you need.

"If any man be in Christ, he is a new creature: old things are passed away; behold all things are become new" (2 Corinthians 5:17, KJV). You believe that verse is fulfilled passively and does not require any action on your part, but you can save yourself a lot of frustration if you consider how God works. When He says a thing, He considers it done. He talks about the end of a thing but does not tell you the process He will take you through to get you there. God considers the work done once He speaks it, but the process will be different for each person. Regardless of the process, every Christian should strive for cleansing deliverance and never be satisfied with "good enough."

> Search me, O God, and know my heart; test me and know my thoughts. Point out anything in me that offends you, and lead me along the path of everlasting life. *Psalm 139:23–24*

Let that be your heart's cry.

Not an "Oops, I Stepped on Your Foot" Type of Incident

God forgave David and told him that he would not die, but the immediate consequence from David's sin was the death of the son he and Bathsheba had conceived. After Nathan left, Bathsheba's baby became deathly ill, and David fasted and prayed for God to spare the child's life. Why should an innocent child die for his sins? Nothing can grieve a parent more than to know that their children are suffering as a direct result of their sins. In an attempt to save his son's life, David begged, groveled, wept, and mourned, but to no avail, because David's son died within seven days.

> David begged God to spare the child. He went without food and lay all night on the bare ground. The leaders of the nation pleaded with him to get up and eat with them, but he refused. *2 Samuel 12:16–17*

After the baby died, David got up from the ground, washed himself, put on lotions, and changed his clothes. Then he went to the Tabernacle and worshiped the Lord. Afterward, he returned to the palace and ate. Some people believe that David had it backward, feeling that he should have mourned the child's death more than he mourned when the child was sick. However, that was not the case. Intercede for your children while they are living and perhaps you can save their lives. Do not wait until they die to start crying, because by then it is too late.

> David replied, "I fasted and wept while the child was alive, for I said, 'Perhaps the LORD will be gracious to me and let the child live.' But why should I fast when he is dead? Can I bring him back again? I will go to him one day, but he cannot return to me." *2 Samuel 12:22–23*

Imagine the devastation Bathsheba felt. She went from being *the* apple of one man's eye to being only one of the apples in another man's eye. She went from being the special main dish to one man to being an appetizer to another. She lost the man she adored, the man to whom she had given her life. Gone was the opportunity to bear the children with the love of her life; there would be no little Uriahs running around. There would be no children who resembled Uriah or had his mannerisms. She lost her husband, her dignity, and her self-worth, and then, to top it all off, she lost her baby. David did not love her, and she knew it. He felt obligated to her, and obligatory relationships are often cold and sometimes hostile. It is one thing to be in a relationship because you want to be, but it is a different story when you are in a relationship because you have to be. What would your attitude be toward that kind of obligatory person in your life? He could have resented her because she was a reminder of his sin. Every time David saw Bathsheba she reminded him of the ugliness within his soul—he felt the guilt and shame. The natural tendency would be to hate her.

David could have resented her the same way a man resents a woman he has impregnated. He feels trapped, especially if he had no intention of marrying her. He was just out for pleasure, not the lifetime commitment a child requires. The baby binds them together, especially if he is the type of man determined to be a daddy and not just the man who fathered a child. A man views such a woman like she is a trap, and nobody likes traps. If David felt trapped, he did not show it. That was one of the things that made him great.

Complete repentance requires acknowledging sin, confessing, receiving forgiveness, asking for cleansing deliverance which reforms behavior, and making reparation. David received forgiveness, but he realized it was not just an "Oops, I stepped on your foot" type of incident that could be rectified by a simple apology. Sometimes you cannot wipe away a wrong with an apology; restitution must be made. David was responsible for restoring Bathsheba and went out of his way to give her preferential treatment. It is impossible to compensate a person for a loss like the one David caused in Bathsheba's life, but he did everything humanly possible for her and allowed God to do the rest. He comforted Bathsheba by making love to her, and she later conceived Solomon. David promised to make Solomon king, which meant that her descendants would sit on David's throne forever.

Bathsheba went from obscurity and disgrace to being the co-ancestor of David's dynasty, because he gave her his throne. It was a coveted position, so this caused friction among those who rightfully deserved that honor. David had seventeen sons by his wives and an undisclosed number of sons by his concubines. His oldest was Amnon, whose mother was Ahinoam of Jezreel. Wise Abigail had Kileab, and it would have been great had he inherited the throne. Absalom was the son of Maacah, daughter of Talmai, King of Geshur. Adonijah was the son of Haggith. Abital gave David Shephatiah, and Eglah gave David Ithream. Those children were born before David took the throne in Jerusalem. After he moved to Jerusalem, David and Bathsheba had Shimea, Shobab, Nathan, and Solomon. David also had Ibhar, Elishua, Elpelet, Nogah, Nepheg, Japhia, Elishama, Eliada, and Eliphelet.

According to Israelite custom, the eldest received a double portion of his father's possessions. In the case of ascendancy, Amnon should have inherited David's throne. Solomon's elder brothers and all their sons had to die in order for him to have a right to David's throne. Can you appreciate the gift David gave to Bathsheba? David was as generous in compensating Bathsheba as he had been in honoring his covenant to Jonathan. He did not adopt an attitude that said, "I will do the minimum—just enough to get by." He gave Bathsheba the best gift he had to offer. He was not trying to assuage his conscience. He was trying to do the best he could for her.

A powerful man of God spoke at our chapel one day. He mentioned that as an adult, he went back to the nickel-and-dime store he used to steal from in his childhood and paid the owner back with interest. I remember thinking that was petty, but what I now understand is that God causes us to revisit our wrongdoings and to make amends.

Love the Child—Hate the Conception Circumstances

The Lord loved Solomon and sent Nathan to change his name to Jedidiah, loved of God. That act was interesting, because some people have a tendency to despise children born under unfavorable circumstances. If a child is born out of wedlock to a teenage girl, some parents disown both her and the baby. Children of divorcees are sometimes resented by a new spouse. A cheated spouse may despise a child born as the result of an affair. The child born to the boy who said he loved his girlfriend but then rejected her after he found out she was pregnant may be hated by the boy. The child born to the woman executive who used her body as a ladder in the corporate world is so despised that she kills him. Millions of children aborted each year are so despised that they are not even given the dignity of a decent burial because that would add validity to their lives. Children have absolutely nothing to do with the circumstances under which they are conceived; yet to be born under unfavorable circumstances causes them to be treated with disdain. We would do well to follow God's example by loving all children even though we may hate the circumstances that produced them. Love life.

What can you give a dead man—a man who was murdered? If it were possible, you would give him back his life, but since that is not possible you give him the life of his assailant, though that does not mean the assailant has to die. God loved Solomon because David's union with Bathsheba produced Solomon in Uriah's stead. In Old Testament times, when a man took a wife and he died before they had children, his brother married his wife so that his seed would produce an heir for his dead brother. Perhaps God viewed Solomon as the child that would have belonged to Bathsheba and Uriah had David not killed him. Jedidiah would be raised as a memorial to Uriah. (This is not a remedy for murder in our day.)

Take-home message: Give your soul a break by completing the process of repentance.

23.

Consequences

Our actions always produce consequences, and Christians generally cringe when consequences are mentioned, because many feel that if God has forgiven us, there should be no repercussions for our actions. However, although God forgives us for our sins, the consequences remain. All people will be rewarded for their thoughts and deeds, regardless of whether they are good or evil in this life or in the life to come. God forgave David and preserved his life. God did a perfect work when He delivered David, because David never repeated those sins for the rest of his life. Nevertheless, David's sins unleashed horror in his family, and the aftershocks can still be felt by his descendants today.

A Generational Curse Unleashed

David's sins initiated a generational spirit that cursed his family. The curse of a spirit of rebellion, sexual dysfunction, premature death, and murder was unleashed in David's family because of his sins. The same sins David committed were the ones that engulfed his family. Most people view generational spirits as negative, but they can be good, bad, or both. A generational spirit can produce a family of pastors, physicians, or attorneys. It can produce a family of politicians who get trapped in sex scandals and die prematurely. Negative generational spirits grab attention because of the devastation that a constant pattern of dysfunction causes a particular family. Aunts and uncles, brothers and sisters, and even distant cousins display similar negative traits, even if they have not had much contact with one another, and they seem powerless to end the curse. However, to know why the negative traits are there, trace their family tree—the family's history will reveal the truth.

As we follow the life of David and his children, we will see how they suffered from David's sin. They suffered simply because of the family they were born into, not because they had opened the floodgates of sin. Sin destroys not only the perpetrator but also the lives of the perpetrator's family. No one can afford to pay the price of sin. Sin is an insatiable destroyer. It is never satisfied, even after countless lives have been ruined. The suffering caused by your sin is not worth the pleasure. When you sin, you give license for the destroyer to wreak havoc in your life and in the lives of your offspring. The Bible reveals at least four incidences of suffering under the curse initiated by David.

The consequences God spoke of through Nathan began to manifest. It began with the death of Bathsheba's first son and then engulfed the rest of his family. It is horrible to suffer for sins you committed, but it is an even greater agony to watch those you love suffer for them as well. David suffered each time he saw his children repeat the same sins he had committed. Every time he saw his children repeat his sins, it caused him to recall the events that caused their suffering, knowing he was helpless to end the curse. It would have been better for David to die for his sins than to have to watch his family suffer.

The second incident that resulted from David's sin started with Amnon and Tamar, took more than ten years to conclude, led to the deaths of three of his children, and affected his entire household and the nation of Israel. The subject of David's consequences starts here and concludes two chapters later.

Many of the elements present in the incident between David and Bathsheba were also present when Amnon raped Tamar. Tamar was the sister of Absalom, the granddaughter of King Talmai of Geshur, and the daughter of King David and Maacah. Tamar was royalty, child of a princess and daughter of a king. She had everything going for her and dreamed that one day her prince would come and sweep her off her feet. Hers was the life of a fairy tale. Tamar was a beautiful princess in the palace; nothing but blue skies ahead and dreams of happily ever after filled her head. Little did she know that her fairy tale would end and nightmares would begin, causing her to live a life far different from any she had ever imagined.

Tamar's beauty was so irresistible that her half brother Amnon fell deeply "in love" with her. Nothing could satisfy his obsession for her; he moped around day after day, lovesick and inconsolable. Amnon was the child of David and Ahinoam; the firstborn, and heir apparent to David's throne. The entire world was his, and he could want for nothing. However, the thing Amnon wanted most was the one thing he could not legally have. He wanted his virgin half sister to fulfill his "love" for her.

Even people born into privilege can desire things that are outside of their grasp. In the eyes of others, Amnon should have been on top of the world, but he was desperately unhappy, and his cousin Jonadab could not understand why. It was impossible to imagine that Amnon could lack anything. A person who has everything should never have a sad day. The very air was his servant. Yet he was not satisfied.

There was no legitimate way to address Amnon's dilemma, because Leviticus clearly denounced what he had in mind.

> Do not have sexual intercourse with your sister or half sister, whether she is your father's daughter or your mother's daughter, whether she was brought up in the same family or somewhere else.
> *Leviticus 18:9*

Amnon's problem sheds added light on the incident between David and Bathsheba. Amnon was the firstborn, a child with great promise. David was king of Israel; almost anything he wanted was his for the asking. Tamar was beautiful, and her beauty struck Amnon like a ton of bricks. It was Bathsheba's naked beauty that snagged David. The spirit of incest was brewing in Amnon's heart. It was sexual dysfunction that caused David to believe he could have another man's wife. Amnon had to have his half sister Tamar; no one else could satisfy him. David was obsessed with having Bathsheba, and although he had many wives no one else but Bathsheba could satisfy his need.

> Amnon became so obsessed with Tamar that he became ill. She was a virgin, and it seemed impossible that he could ever fulfill his love for her. *2 Samuel 13:2*

It seemed impossible to Amnon that he would ever be able to express his love, until his crafty cousin Jonadab intervened (some relatives are best kept at a distance). Together they planned an elaborate scheme to get her alone so that Amnon could satisfy his "lovesickness." Similarly, David was so obsessed with Bathsheba that he schemed to get her alone to satisfy his desire.

Although the participants and events were different, all the elements of David's original sin were present, and Amnon's future actions only added fuel to the curse. Amnon pretended to be sick, and he asked his father to send Tamar to cook him a special meal. Amnon's request seemed innocent enough that David, a discerning man, did not furrow his eyebrows.

Sex-Crazed

Tamar was not suspicious of Amnon's request, either. She went to the room where Amnon was lying down so he could watch her make some special bread for him. However, when she set the serving tray before him, he refused to eat, ordered all his servants to leave, and then told Tamar to take the food into his bedroom and serve it there. Tamar did as requested, but once Amnon and Tamar were alone, he made the most impossible request: he demanded that she have sex with him. Tamar vehemently refused and tried to talk some sense into him, but Amnon was not thinking with his head and could not be reasoned with. He was not relying on the rational part of him that would make logical decisions or he would have known that his actions would lead to shame and death in exchange for a few minutes of pleasure. No, in his heart he conceived the plan, and since the heart dictates a person's actions, no logic could overrule it.

"If you really have good intentions toward me, if it is love that you are feeling, you could ask the king to let you marry me," Tamar pleaded. "If I am that important to you, marry me, and then you can have me as much as you like. Honor my need for purity. I would rather walk down the aisle with you in honor and purity knowing that I have saved myself for you than to live with disgrace and shame. I want to be a victorious virgin. Wouldn't you rather have a lifetime of sustaining pleasure than a few minutes of reckless, abandoned pleasure? This crime is punishable by death. Does it make sense to throw away your future and all you have going for you just to have sex with me? What will happen to me once you have humiliated me?"

Tamar considered marrying the man who was out to destroy her. She wanted to give herself to just one man. As long as Amnon married her, she could fulfill the law and maintain her dignity. In today's world, people often mistake the kind of "love" Amnon felt for real love. You think he loves you when he can't get enough of your body, but that is only a physical addiction to sex, one of the most powerful, compelling forces in the world. The kind of "love" Amnon felt was only an imitation of love. Amnon's version of love was and is insatiable, immature, selfish, and destructive. That kind of love is indiscriminate, because anyone can be used to satisfy it and it is only concerned with selfish pleasure.

During sex outside of marriage, many confuse that "I love you" spoken in the heat of the moment with real love. You should not be fooled by that kind of love, because it has nothing to do with you personally; you just happen to be the channel of fulfillment. You are not loved as a person like you need and want to be loved; you are loved as an object that brings pleasure. If you want to test their level of commitment to you, stop having sex with them or ask them to marry you. Then you will find out where you really stand and how much you mean to them. A person can love a hotdog without emotional attachments; once the hotdog is gone so is the love. When the next hotdog comes along, the person once again says, "I love you," proving that it had nothing to do with the particular hotdog, just hotdogs in general.

Amnon would not listen to reason because he could not be rational; his passion had gotten the best of him. The kind of battle of wills that took place between Tamar and Amnon did not take place between Bathsheba and David. Bathsheba could not express her opposition because she was in a powerless position.

Amnon overpowered Tamar and raped her, and as soon as it was over, his "love" instantly turned into hate; he hated her more than he "loved" her. Since love had nothing to do with the situation, it can be called what it was from the very beginning—lust. Lust, in this case, was hate or imploded love. How does a person go from an amorous state to one of disdain in a matter of minutes? The answer: it was not love in the first place.

Although we treat sex as just another bodily function, one that does not engage the soul, the process involves every inch of our being—spirit, soul, and body. There is a convicting power in sex that either affirms or disaffirms your motives instantly on the spot. If your motives were good, it enhances you. If your motives were selfish, it convicts you. Sex outside of marriage is selfish, and under that condition motives are selfish rather than selfless; therefore, you will feel remorse. The contradictions of your actions convict you, and you feel guilt and anger.

If you enter a sexual encounter committed to give anything less than your own life, you cheat the process. Sex outside of marriage actually proves that you do not love the person, are not committed to that person's well-being, and are lazy, because you want something for nothing. If a sexual encounter is only about meeting physical needs, the nature of sex is violated. In sex, it is "my life for yours." If your attitude says, "I want to get as much as possible out of the encounter and give the least possible," you are not ready for sex. Sex outside of marriage is convicting because it immediately exposes your intentions. It exposes an attitude that says, "I am only in this for pleasure. I do not want all the other baggage. I do not want all of you; I just want your body. I am committed to physical pleasure, but I am not willing to give my life to you. I do not want to be bound or linked to your spirit and soul. I am only committed to you as long as you bring me physical pleasure. I want the rewards of the covenant without fulfilling its terms."

That is a selfish attitude, and sex under those circumstances causes resentment. You cannot walk away from sex without being irrevocably changed in the process. You know that you were linked in spirit and soul during sex, even though you did not want to be. Since sex creates a contract and demands accountability that you refuse to honor, you become angry. You feel as if you have been trapped into something you did not intend to commit to—sex ratifies a covenant. If you do not intend to honor that covenant you become angry, because it exposes your selfish motives. Sex binds you when you did not want to be bound.

After Amnon had raped Tamar, he could no longer stand the sight of her. He had turned sex, a thing of beauty under the right circumstances, into a grotesque and repulsive action. Having sex with Tamar had exposed the depravity of his soul and revealed his selfish motives. That, coupled with the look of brokenness and bewilderment on her face, was more than he could stand. Tamar became a constant reminder of his guilt and shame, and since he could not bear to look at her because the whole situation convicted him, he wanted her out of his sight.

Sex Is a Covenant Act

The most successful marriages are ones in which two people make a commitment to each other's spirit and soul before they seal the covenant through sex. Therefore, the process of dating should be used to get to know the intangible qualities of the person of interest. The emphasis should be on finding out how the other person thinks, how they feel about various issues, how they interact with others, their likes and dislikes, and their goals and dreams. During this process, enough information should be gathered about the person's history to construct a sketch of the person. The point is to know as much as you can about the other person so you can make an informed decision and know who you are committing to. During the process of exploration, you should ask yourself, "Can I commit to this person? Can I support their dreams and goals? Do I like this person's character?" Those same questions have to be answered in the reverse; it has to be a mutual relationship. If you take the time to know and love the intangible qualities of the other person (character, personality, dreams, and passions) before marriage, a long-lasting relationship can ensue.

At no time during general acquaintance, dating, or engagement should sex be an option. Many have concluded that sex is just sex because they have discovered that one body will respond to another's regardless. You do not have to be trained, and it does not take a special person or moment to get a response. As long as you mistakenly believe that sex is only a physical process that does not engage your spirit and soul, you will continue to abuse yourself and others. When sex is added to relationships outside of marriage, you lose objectivity and allow your body to dictate your feelings. Feelings are fleeting and, therefore, unreliable. But because your body loves sex, you interpret that to mean that you love that person when that may not be the case at all.

Because people embark on sex prematurely, many marriages today are based on physical pleasure. Once the physical thrill has worn off, people find themselves saying, "I'm not in love anymore, I'm not feeling it." Then they ask, "What have I gotten myself into? I cannot stand this person!" What they considered love was just the love of sex, and it loses its thrill when they get to know the person they married. They find themselves unhappy because once they get to know the person they married, they realize they cannot commit to them and vice versa. For this reason, many marriages fail today. People walk into marriage backward, by first making a commitment to sex and the feelings it evokes and then trying to commit to a person's soul and spirit. People allow their body's love of sex to cause them to enter into a covenant relationship with a person whom their spirit and soul cannot tolerate. Sex is wonderful, beautiful, amazing, powerful, incredible, and highly addictive. It is one of God's gifts to humanity and is meant to be enjoyed to the fullest in marriage, but it is a fringe benefit that comprises a small aspect of marriage. Sex is the easiest part of the marriage covenant and takes very little effort. Marriages based solely on sex are tenuous; when adversity comes, they crumble because they lack a substantial foundation.

We have the mechanics of sex down to an art, but we place little emphasis on the intangibles. Although we know about form and function, since there are scores of articles, books, and Web sites that will tell how to have "great sex," we have digressed in our understanding that the essence of humanity is wrapped in sexuality. Many articles give advice about how to spice up your marriage, but the emphasis is only on sex. Few talk about how to have a good marriage relationship apart from sex, because it requires work.

Our modern focus is totally and purely physical, but there is more to sex than just anatomical parts colliding—it involves the blending of souls, the exchange of life. Sex is a twofold process: through the giving of your body, you also give access to your soul. Sex is a package deal, blending two spirits together. Through sex his soul blends with hers, creating an amalgam—a soul blend that has not existed before, such that the participants will forever be changed in the process. Like it or not, a physical union through sex automatically interlaces the spirits and souls of those involved, and what happens in the spiritual realm is more significant and binding than what happens in the physical realm.

True marriage does not take place when you say, "I do." Marriage takes place when you have sex, because it is through the physical act of sex that spirits and souls are joined. Even if we could construct the greatest condom that would prevent the swapping of fluids, no condom ever made will prevent the blending of souls and spirits via sex; it is the nature of sex. Each time you have sex, a marriage takes place, because sex is a *covenant act*. Sex is the evidence that a covenant has been made.

In a court of law, a person can present a case for a broken contract without having the paperwork that spelled out the contract. Many people believe that if there is no written proof that a contract exists, it is not binding. Others believe that words and a handshake mean nothing. However, a court of law will accept the fact that a covenant was in place judging by the actions of the parties involved. The actions of two parties involved in a contract can be used to prove that a covenant was in force. Sex is a covenant act and having sex is more important than saying, "I do." Having sex not only says, "I do," it also says, "Not only do I but I have already ratified the covenant."

Sex is the evidence that a covenant is in place. Having sex involves giving one's self in order to express love to another. Love is not a feeling; it is a commitment. It is a covenant commitment that says, "My life for yours. I commit my soul and spirit to support *your* soul and spirit. I give my life in exchange for yours. I am committed to you as a person. I will support your dreams and plans. I am with you in good and bad times regardless of what comes our way. I am committed to sustaining you and helping you grow. Nothing but death will separate us."

Although it is impossible to prevent the exchange of spirit and soul during sex, it is possible to distance oneself and to refuse to commit to another during everyday life by actions outside of the bed. The joining and blending is automatic, but the fulfillment of the terms of the covenant is not. Sex ratifies a covenant, but it takes working effort apart from sex to fulfill that covenantal commitment.

Rape Is Murder

During the act of rape, the victim is robbed of something that cannot be replaced: dignity, self-worth, sense of security and control—but it goes deeper than that. The beauty and essence of life are stolen.

All people have three things that are exclusively theirs. You can be destitute with only the clothes on your back, yet you still have three valuable assets: your spirit, soul, and body. All three comprise the substance of life. Having sex involves the interchange of all three. You have the right to choose who will be the recipient of your treasures. You have the right to choose to whom you will give your life.

When people believe God, they receive eternal life not as a symbolic gesture but through the indwelling of the Holy Spirit and Jesus Christ. God, the Father, is in Jesus and they are in a person, making them all one, because they blend their Spirits with that person's spirit and soul, creating a spiritual amalgam. Since Jesus is eternal life, the person gains eternal life. While the human body does not present a barrier to God's Spirit, it does to other human beings. The human body houses the spirit and soul of a person, and it is what separates one person from another. The only way a normal person can access the spirit and soul of another, then, is through sex. Sexuality is the gateway to a person's soul and spirit.

God will not force Himself on anyone; He comes by invitation only. Rape is the taking of one's spirit and soul that was not given and forcing one's spirit and soul on another uninvited, producing an unwanted spiritual amalgam. Each person walks away from the experience irrevocably changed. If God, who is all powerful, will not force Himself on another, for a person to do so through the act of rape is a serious ungodly violation. It is demonic.

The act of rape involves forcefully taking what was not given; it involves robbing another of life. Rape is the theft of life; in other words, it is murder. A lost life is like spilled water: once spilled on the ground, it cannot be gathered up again. Because we take our sexuality so lightly by failing to realize that our lives (spirit and soul) are accessible through sex, we abuse others and ourselves. Our society today treats the sexual abuser as a victim and treats the victim as the abuser because we do not understand that sexuality is life.

> But if the man meets the engaged woman out in the country, and he rapes her, then only the man should die. Do nothing to the young woman; she has committed no crime worthy of death. This case is similar to that of someone who attacks and murders a neighbor. *Deuteronomy 22:25–26*

> After he had raped Tamar, Amnon snarled: "Get out!"
>
> "No, no!" Tamar cried. "To reject me now is a greater wrong than what you have already done to me . . ." *2 Samuel 13:16*

Amnon treated Tamar as if she were the villain, as if it were her fault that he had sinned against her. It was her fault that he had designs on her, that he schemed against her, and that he overpowered her. He treated her like a seductress who had lured him into a trap he could not avoid and had then exploited his weakness. In truth, she reminded him of his guilt. Sex had convicted him of hateful selfishness, and rape had condemned him as a murderer. Tamar did not necessarily want to be attached to Amnon, because something ugly and selfish had transpired between them; she was just trying to be validated as a human being.

Tamar was saying, "Not only have you taken my life, which I can never recover, but by rejecting me now, you are also saying that my life was not of value in the first place. You add insult to injury by doing this. Since the essence and the core of my being are wrapped up in my sexuality, by rejecting me after experiencing the intangible me, the best I have to give, you are denying my value as a human being."

Although it may seem like it was misguided for Tamar to want any further attachment to Amnon, she was on the right track, because according to the Torah, if a man raped a woman he had to marry her and could never divorce her. You can reject a person on the basis of social status, personal ability, or physical characteristics and it is of no significance, but to reject someone on the basis of sex is the ultimate rejection. It is cruel and murderous, because you are rejecting them at the core of who they are. Tamar lived the rest of her life in desolation because she had been robbed of her life and then told that her life was worthless.

Dashed into a Billion Pieces and Ground to Dust

In today's society, we place high value on things that are rare, such as platinum and gold. Purity is found in exclusivity. The scarcer a thing is, the greater its value. We apply those definitions to inanimate objects, yet we refuse to apply them to ourselves. God is holy because He is unique and there is no other like Him. Your value is also derived from your exclusivity. It does not make you a sexual stud if everybody and anybody who wants a piece of you can have you. That just means you do not recognize your value and neither does anyone else.

Tamar tore her beautiful robe (which symbolized purity), put ashes on her head, and walked away crying, her face in her hands. There are some wounds that take a lifetime to heal. Tamar's life had been dashed into a billion pieces and then ground to dust. She was a desolate woman, and God would spend time healing and rebuilding her life. Gone was her hope of marrying a wonderful man and being treated like she was his special gift. Gone was the hope of experiencing the beauty, joy, mystery, and inexplicable wonderfulness of the gift of sex. Gone was her chance for producing immortality. Gone were all the hopes and wishes that every princess dreams of.

In Israel, the penalty for a man sleeping with his sister or half sister was excommunication. The man was shunned and became an outcast. Being an Israelite had its advantages just as being a part of any society did, and a man who was cut off from the community forfeited those advantages. He could not conduct business with Israelites and did not enjoy the rights and protection of the law. He could not go to the temple to experience being in the presence of God and could not offer sacrifices to God. It was a miserable life, but it also could mean that God would directly punish the offender with a premature death. This law assumes consensual sex. For Tamar this was not the case.

> If a man has sexual intercourse with his sister, the daughter of either his father or his mother, it is a terrible disgrace. Both of them must be publicly cut off from the community. Since the man has had intercourse with his sister, he will suffer the consequences of his guilt. *Leviticus 20:17*

If we look at the case of Amnon's rape of Tamar without considering the fact that they were siblings, another law applied.

> If a man is caught in the act of raping a young woman who is not engaged, he must pay fifty pieces of silver to her father. Then he must marry the young woman because he violated her, and he will never be allowed to divorce her. *Deuteronomy 22:28–29*

Amnon could not marry Tamar (even if he had wanted to) because they were siblings, so being cut off from the community of Israel was the most appropriate action.

Theological teaching today regarding Tamar fails to consider the Israelite society when it came to issues such as incest and rape. Some preachers suggest that Tamar was not destroyed, just damaged, since she was still a person of value and had much to give. Those preachers advise women who find themselves in situations similar to the one Tamar faced to pick up the pieces and find someone who will value the princess within. However, such preaching addresses only the physical part of a human being; it does not address the spiritual issues. It also fails to consider the society in which Tamar lived. Virginity was highly prized and demanded—nobody wanted anything to do with a nonvirgin. Nonvirgins were considered taboo, and if they were allowed to live, they lived the life of a eunuch, so Tamar's prospects for marriage were destroyed. Nonvirgins lost the opportunity to have a healthy, loving marriage, which was why Tamar lived as a desolate woman in her brother's household for the rest of her life.

Take-home message: The sins of ancestors create a curse that repeats itself in generations to come.

24.

Shhh . . .

After Tamar was raped, no one said a word about it. As is often the case in such situations, it became an awkward issue that everyone wanted to brush under the rug. They buried the secret in their hearts, but everyone was left hurting and struggling with the incredible sense of loss. No one quite knew what to do.

Doing Nothing Doesn't Cut It

David was angry, but his anger may have stemmed from the knowledge that his sins had caused the calamity. Who can fully put words to what Tamar felt? Tamar's brother, Absalom, deeply resented Amnon for his actions, and Tamar's mother felt the loss of her daughter's hope, because every mother wishes the best for her princess. Amnon felt guilt and shame, realizing not only that he was capable of incomprehensible cruelty but also that he had destroyed an innocent person's life. Amnon's mother felt shame that her child could commit such a heinous crime, because his actions reflected upon her. Everybody was grieving with inner turmoil.

Some parents live in denial when their children tell them that family members have sexually abused them. That is the worst way to handle the situation, because nothing is done in the way of restoration. When a parent tries to sweep such issues under the rug, the injured child does not receive ministry, so no healing can take place. A child in such a situation is emotionally stunted, and even though they grow older mentally and physically, they are often stuck at the time when they were abused, because such damage does not heal on its own. Failure to deal with the issues also sends a message that you do not believe them and legitimizes the actions of the abuser. As long as the situation is unresolved, bitterness and resentment grow in the heart of the wounded person.

Many parents refuse to get help because they are embarrassed and ashamed to air their dirty laundry. A great deal of time is spent protecting the one who caused the offense, which prevents healing for all involved. Everyone involved needs restoration, including the abuser and the abused. Your silence and failure to address the issues leaves that person's understanding of their offense uncorrected and sets them up for sexual maladjustment in adulthood. Ignoring the issue does not heal the problem; it only magnifies it.

David took a passive stance toward Amnon's sins. David was angry about the incident, but he did nothing to resolve the situation. He took no disciplinary action. After all, how could David punish Amnon when he himself had received mercy from God for a similar indiscretion? After being thrown out of Amnon's house, Tamar tore her robe and began to mourn with bitter tears. She lived with Absalom for the rest of her life. The kind of healing she needed could only come from God, but David did not minister to her. David also did nothing in the way of counseling Absalom, or he would have been aware of Absalom's growing resentment toward Amnon.

God had not punished David with death as the law demanded, so perhaps David thought it was hypocritical to chastise Amnon. Many parents feel this way when they see their children committing the same sins they committed when they were younger. They do not address the sin because they feel that since they did it themselves, they cannot expect their children to live by a higher standard. Even worse, some parents find themselves still bound by the sin and are unable to offer any advice or help for sins they have not learned to master. Just because you have sinned does not mean you can sit idly by and watch your children fall into the same trap. You can hold out the lifeline. Your children can learn from your mistakes if you tell them where the road they are traveling on will lead. Do you want your children to have a better life than you did? If so, help them avoid the emotional pitfalls you encountered when you were their age

The only problem with dealing with pain privately and internally is that issues do not resolve themselves. They have a way of popping up as dysfunctions and maladjustments later in life. Unjust situations do not become just unless conflicts are resolved and justice is achieved. A "hands-off" approach does not make the conflict go away, and passivity in the face of emotional upheaval does not bring recovery. There are also some problems that can have no adequate resolution.

There are some things that only God can heal, and sexual abuse is one of them. Only God can deal with a broken human being, but that does not give you a license to do nothing. Keep in mind that you conceived and delivered your child into the world; your child is your gift from God and your gift to this world. You should seek professional counseling for the child and for the entire family, and medical care if necessary. Pray with and for the child on a daily basis, because it is essential to break further dysfunction and promote healing. Protect them from future abuse by separating them from their offender if possible. Affirm your love for them by spending time with them, keeping the lines of communication open, and addressing questions and concerns they have. Create an environment that is conducive to healing. Block unhealthy television shows, movies, music, and Web sites. Actively involve yourself in their life by knowing who their friends are and be brave enough to forbid unwholesome relationships. Examine your lifestyle and make sure you are not living in a way that invites mayhem in your house. Teach them about the beauty of sex within the boundary of marriage. The greatest gift you can give your children is you; spend time with them, value and esteem them, love them. The results will be astounding.

Absalom's Revenge

When people are left to deal with injustice in their own way, they may feel they have no recourse but to take drastic measures. Absalom was the kind of person who took matters into his own hands to create justice. He harbored animosity against Amnon for raping Tamar and against David for failing to correct the situation, and he was out for revenge. He viewed David's inaction as condoning what Amnon had done, and as making light of the devastation that Amnon had caused Tamar.

David should have seen the potential treachery brewing in his household since he operated with such discernment in national affairs, but he did not. The reason he was out of touch with the affairs of his own household is because of the curse of his sin. David was outside the wall of protection God once wrapped around him, and one of the devastating consequences of sin is that you lose God's protection against future onslaughts. Sometimes mayhem runs unhindered in households because the sins of the parents have opened the door and given license to the evil one. God was not obligated to protect him from it and did not warn him. It should have seemed strange that Amnon would specifically request Tamar to come and prepare food for him when there were plenty of capable servants. Perhaps Amnon's request seemed innocent enough not to arouse suspicion.

Absalom allowed two years to pass before he avenged his sister's rape, and he was very cunning and strategic. First, he never expressed his resentment to David or Amnon, so it appeared that he had allowed things to blow over. To remove suspicion further, Absalom planned a party and invited David and his servants. When David declined, as Absalom knew he would, Absalom requested Amnon's presence.

> "Well, then," Absalom said, "if you can't come, how about sending my brother Amnon instead?" "Why Amnon?" the king asked. But Absalom kept on pressing the king until he finally agreed to let all his sons attend, including Amnon. *2 Samuel 13:26–27*

Even a person without David's discernment would have had serious reservations about Absalom's request because of his specific insistence that Amnon attend his party, but David did not see a reason to deny the request. So all of David's sons attended Absalom's party. Absalom ordered his men to wait until Amnon was drunk and then kill him on his signal. The plan worked.

Absalom escaped to his grandfather King Talmai in Geshur, where he stayed for three years. But Absalom's resentment was not spent when he killed Amnon. He still had brewing resentment against his dad; he had an ax to grind. He was angry with his dad because David was king and possessed power yet he stood idly by and did nothing in a situation that was crying out for justice and healing. You may not be king, but you are the head of your household. It is your responsibility to make sure that justice is served. It is your responsibility to create an environment conducive to healing. If you do not exercise your authority to resolve conflict between your children, you never know what your children will do when they get older. You are setting your children up for future failure. They will rise up and lash out against you, because you represented authority and power in their lives when they were growing up. When they were vulnerable and in need of your protection, you failed them by doing nothing.

Take-home message: Sexual abuse does not resolve itself with time; the passage of time alone only produces maladjustment. Effort must be expended, in the way of prayer and counseling, to bring about healing and restoration.

25.

Absalom, O Absalom

David disowned and refused to receive Absalom after he killed Amnon, which did nothing to mend their broken relationship; it only widened the chasm of resentment. During the three years Absalom was with his grandfather, David did not visit or make contact in any way, making it easy for Absalom to conclude that his father favored Amnon. "My father disowned me because I killed Amnon, but he did not disown Amnon after he raped Tamar. He acted as if Amnon were above the law. Amnon received more favorable treatment than I did. He loved Amnon more than he loved my sister and me."

Mixed or blended families are challenged to make sure all the children receive the same amount of love; favoritism is prohibited. David eventually came to terms with Amnon's death and missed Absalom. Joab sensed David's shifting sentiments and mediated Absalom's return home.

David allowed Absalom to return to his own house but refused him audience for two years. It had been five long years since Absalom had seen his father.

"What's the point of bringing me home if you will have nothing to do with me? I might as well have stayed where I was," thought Absalom. At Absalom's request, Joab asked David to receive him. David finally received his estranged son, and although they made amends, their relationship was icy.

Rebellion

So Absalom lashed out against his father, because he wanted him to hurt as much as he felt his father had hurt him. Absalom was methodical in plotting his revenge toward his father, painstakingly fomenting a rebellion by exploiting a weakness in David's administration. His plan was to make the people think that they did not have adequate representation and that David was not concerned with their plight.

Each day, the people of Israel got up early and made their way to the city gate, because only a limited number of cases would be heard. That meant that many people had to wait a long time to receive justice and pointed to a judicial system that was either bogged down by inadequate staffing or did not consider the needs of the people a high priority. For four years, Absalom got up early every morning, stationed himself at the city gate, and listened to the problems of those seeking justice. Their worries and burdens concerned him.

Absalom planted a seed of doubt in the mind of the people that David was not concerned with their needs. He fostered discontent and frustration with David in the hearts of the people, convincing them that the king did not care enough to listen to their problems like he did. The problem with royalty at that time was that it was out of touch with the plight of the people. Absalom won the hearts of the people by befriending them and treating them as companions. When the people tried to bow to him, he would hug them instead. He convinced the people that he had his finger on their pulse and that his administration would overhaul the old system.

David knew nothing of Absalom's conspiracy or that he was stirring up a rebellion—until it was too late. However, once news of the coup reached him, David left the city to prevent war within Jerusalem's borders. A growing number of people thought Absalom had a valid point and joined with him, including David's advisor, Ahithophel, who eventually became an advisor to Absalom. Ahithophel told Absalom to sleep with David's concubines, because it would show Israel that he was not just a spoiled brat throwing a temper tantrum for David's attention who would later reconcile with his father. It was a symbolic gesture to signify that he had severed his relationship with the "old administration" and there would be no turning back.

Absalom did what Ahithophel advised, having sex with David's concubines in a tent on the roof of the palace in plain sight of the public, but in doing so, Absalom perpetuated the sexual dysfunction curse. It was a sin for a man to sleep with his father's wives or concubines, because it uncovered his father's nakedness. Ahithophel's advice came directly from God, because it fulfilled Nathan's prophecy. Although he had no knowledge of the prophecy Nathan had delivered to David, Absalom fulfilled it precisely.

Heartbroken and beaten down by the weight of his sins, David left Jerusalem, knowing that his past sins had created the present situation. It is easy to understand rebellion that rises from people you do not know or have a relationship with, but it is difficult to understand one that swell from your own ranks. It is downright overwhelming when the fruit of your loins ignites a coup. David was grief-stricken, because he knew that he had cultivated the rebellion in Absalom. Stubbornly imposing distance between Absalom and himself had fomented deep resentment and hostility that had been brewing for more than a decade. He had turned away from Absalom when Absalom needed a father to embrace and minister to him. Ultimately, David knew that although there was a cause-and-effect relationship to Absalom's behavior, his sin against Uriah was the root cause of the misfortune in his family, and he was powerless to stop it. Although he could see the events unfolding before his eyes, he could do nothing to ward off the attacks. Each time one of his children suffered, it was a grueling reminder of his sins.

Private Sins of Public Officials

The conversation between Nathan and King David had been private. No one knew that the disaster that struck David's family was a result of David's sin except God, the angels, the Holy Spirit, Jesus, Nathan, and David. David knew that Absalom's coup was a judgment from God. That is how God works: He tells you what will happen, but He does not give you details. David respected God's decision to dethrone him, so he left Jerusalem without putting up a fight. The tragedies at home and the political unrest were direct results of his sins.

David believed he was not worthy to be king of Israel any longer because of his sins, and he did not blame God for seeking out a man who would be a worthy replacement. He displayed genuine humility. He was always interested in the welfare of the nation. He wanted what was best and would bring peace to the nation rather than pursuing his personal ambition and need for security. Many leaders would do well to adopt David's attitude.

"I'm wrong, and I'm sorry for my sins. I will not resist God's judgment. If I am causing Israel to suffer, it is best that I be removed. When I am no longer a benefit and am standing in the way of progress, then I will step aside so that a man who is worthy can lead Israel into blessings."

A good leader will defer to another who can get the job done. When you bring shame upon your office and the nation suffers as a result of your personal sins, step aside and allow integrity and honor to be restored. If the Lord sees that you are still of value, He will bring you back. Only a selfish individual will continue to stay in office after his private immorality has adversely affected his public service. Only a selfish person will resist removal even though his or her sins are causing innocent people to suffer. Any political office requires integrity on the part of the one who holds it. Many people argue that their private life has no bearing on their public service, but that argument does not hold water.

David's decision to leave Jerusalem when the coup started was the only logical choice for a good shepherd. Good shepherds see to it that the people they lead remain unharmed and at peace. David wanted to spare the city from bloodshed and needless property loss. He would not allow a battle to take place in an area that was populated by civilians. After all, he knew that Absalom's number one objective was to kill him, so why stand his ground to protect his throne at the expense of others? To do anything other than leave would have been a mark of selfishness.

It is ludicrous to adopt an attitude that says, "If I go down, so will everyone else." If you deserve to go down, innocent people should not suffer for your sins. What kind of logic drives a person to force innocent people to suffer for their personal sins? Stand up and face the consequences of your actions like a man; show that you have some guts. Show some integrity; be accountable for your actions.

At the outset of the coup, David did not know what God's plans were; for all he knew, God was taking away his throne and giving it to Absalom. Nathan's prophecy could have been interpreted in many ways. Although Nathan did not specifically say that God would hand the kingdom to another man, it was not difficult to reach that conclusion given the information David had. When he fled Jerusalem, David did not know if he would ever see the city again. He especially mourned his inability to go to the Tabernacle to be in the presence of God. It was a period of uncertainty about God's love, and David did not know if God was for or against him. The fact that God did not warn him of Absalom's conspiracy shed doubt in David's mind about God's support.

> "If the LORD sees fit," David said, "he will bring me back to see the Ark and the Tabernacle again. But if he is through with me, then let him do what seems best to him." *2 Samuel 15:25–26*

Although David did not know God's intentions and was not on the best of terms with Him, he still prayed to God and asked for help to defeat Ahithophel's advice. When you have depended upon God all your life, where else do you turn?

In earlier times David could count on God's support because he was innocent, but in this case David did not have a defense, because his sin had created his current circumstances. David was unsure of God's plans, and in all the confusion it was difficult to determine God's intent, though he knew that whatever God did, He would be justified. If God wanted to use his enemies as instruments of correction, so be it. If God did not see fit to protect him, he did not deserve to be protected. He would not resist God's judgment.

"God, I don't know if you love me anymore. That breaks my heart more than what's going on around me. I don't know what your intentions are regarding me; everything is so uncertain. I don't blame you for your actions against me; I deserve every bit of it, and you have done what you said you would. I deserve this and more because of my sins, and I am deeply saddened because I have broken your heart. Although I understand why you are doing what you are doing, I cannot bear the thought of losing you; it makes my whole world fall apart. Life is not worth living if I don't have you. I can't bear the thought of never being around you. I don't know what I'll do if I can't see your smiling face, if I can't wrap my arms around you, if I can't feel your warmth. Losing the throne is not as terrible as losing you. Banish me from the throne, but don't banish me from your sweet presence. I can't live if I don't have you."

Get Out of Here, You Murdering Scoundrel!

When the Lord is correcting you, it is difficult to determine if attacks by others are from God or if they are using your calamity to kick you while you are down. If God had turned His back on David, what did it matter if others attacked him? David was distraught over Absalom's conspiracy and in no condition to fight. He left the city and God's presence in tears, his head covered and his feet bare because he was mourning. His soul was in anguish. Those who accompanied him were mourning as well; they were weary, discouraged, and faint with depression. Their heaviness was so thick that it was debilitating. It took every ounce of energy they could muster to climb mountains and travel through the wilderness. The last thing David needed at that moment was for his enemies to assault him. David was so down that he did not resist assaults, because he felt he deserved them. Maybe God was using them as instruments of righteousness, so who was he to resist God's chastening, no matter what form it took?

Many of Saul's relatives and loyalists used the rebellion as an opportunity to vent their animosity toward David. Shimei, son of Gera and a member of Saul's family, was emboldened by the situation. He assumed that the rebellion was a thing of permanence and that David no longer had authority as king of Israel, so Shimei pelted him with stones, insults, and lies.

> "Get out of here, you murderer, you scoundrel!" he shouted at David. "The LORD is paying you back for murdering Saul and his family. You stole his throne, and now the LORD has given it to your son Absalom. At last you will taste some of your own medicine, you murderer!"
> *2 Samuel 16:7–8*

It was a risky strategy, because even if David was no longer king, his men could have cut off Shimei's head. If David was as ruthless as Shimei said he was, what would have stopped David from having him killed? Shimei kept his distance in case he needed to flee, but he kept up with the procession, cursing and throwing rocks at David and his officers.

When Saul was king, David had defended Israel in spite of betrayals and the fact that he was regarded as an enemy of the state. During Saul's final battle with the Philistines on Mount Gilboa, many Israelite soldiers, including Saul and his sons, lost their lives. Some people believed that David was responsible for Saul's death because he did not take part in that battle, but since most (if not all) the battles Saul fought against the enemies of God were waged without David's assistance while David was a fugitive, why should Saul's last battle have been any different?

When Joab killed Abner, David had made it clear that he was not responsible for Abner's death, but Saul's loyalists still blamed David. Saul's remaining son, Ishbosheth, who was crowned king over Israel, was slain by men of his own raiding party acting on their own. Although David had nothing to do with Ishbosheth's death, some people still held him responsible.

When there was famine in Israel because of Saul's sins, David paid the price the Gibeonites demanded, which was seven of Saul's sons or grandsons. David never harmed Saul's family. The calamity that befell Saul's family was not David's doing—he was falsely accused, but Saul's relatives did not see it that way.

Although Shimei's accusations were mostly lies, his accusations did apply to the incident with David, Uriah, and Bathsheba. In that incident, David had been a scoundrel and a murderer, and God used Absalom's rebellion to pay David back for Uriah's murder and for stealing his wife, Bathsheba. The situation *was* designed to give David a taste of his own medicine, so when David's men asked for permission to kill Shimei, David refused.

David answered in a throaty tone that revealed his deep hurt, "No! If the Lord has told him to curse me, who am I to stop him?"

> My own son is trying to kill me. Shouldn't this relative of Saul have even more reason to do so? Leave him alone and let him curse, for the LORD has told him to do it. And perhaps the LORD will see that I am being wronged and will bless me because of these curses.
> *2 Samuel 16:11–12*

David was in a state of confusion and endured the attack, thinking God had directed it. David would not add the sin of defiance to his others. He was still feeling the shame of the Bathsheba incident and carrying the guilt from needless bloodshed. He relived the curse every time one of his children suffered.

"Go ahead and beat me over the head, I can use the distraction from my pain."

David knew that he deserved God's punishment. He would not resist God's chastisement or fight against God. He displayed a completely different attitude from Saul's. Saul had kept up the pretense that the Lord was with him even after God had rejected him, but David understood that he was an affront to God's holiness and did not blame God for withdrawing from him. David respected the Lord's decision; he would not resist God's chastening.

Seize the Moment

The best time to defeat a giant is when he is distracted with other problems, and Ahithophel knew that David and his men were weary, discouraged, and in no condition to put up a fight. A person is not operating at 100 percent when they are depressed. Emotional strain is more exhausting than physical exertion. When a person is depressed, normal tasks become taxing. Under normal circumstances, David could leap over a mountain in a single bound, but when he was weary he could barely step over a molehill. While David and his men were fleeing into the wilderness, Ahithophel was making plans to defeat them. He advised Absalom to let him go after David immediately to catch David and his people off guard and ensure victory.

> Let me choose twelve thousand men to start out after David tonight. I will catch up to him while he is weary and discouraged. He and his troops will panic, and everyone will run away. Then I will kill only the king. *2 Samuel 17:1–2*

Ahithophel was right; it was an excellent idea. If he took twelve thousand men to attack while David and his men were in a depressed state, it would have been easier to kill David. The beauty of his plan was that it did not put Absalom at risk. The people would give Absalom their full support, and no one would be harmed. It was a good plan and would have happened exactly as Ahithophel predicted had it been executed.

David sent another one of his advisors, Hushai, to Absalom to undermine Ahithophel's advice. Absalom decided to consult Hushai to see what he thought of Ahithophel's plan, and Hushai told him that Ahithophel's plan was flawed because it did not take into consideration the stature of men they would be pursuing. David and his men were experienced, courageous warriors, and they would be as enraged as a mother bear robbed of her cubs over Absalom's coup. Absalom's men would not stand a chance against them, so Hushai advised Absalom to mobilize the entire Israelite army and to lead them himself. Absalom and the leaders compared notes and decided Hushai's plan was best. Had it not been for Hushai's counteradvice, David would have died that day.

The Lord used Hushai to defeat Ahithophel's counsel and to destroy Absalom. The situation could have turned out either way: either David or Absalom could have died. God's promise of an eternal dynasty to David would still have been fulfilled. God had contingency plans. Everything hinged on David's response to God's chastening. If David had been incorrigible like Saul, God would have defeated him. If David had decided to resist the Lord's chastening and to fight to preserve his throne like Saul, God would have allowed Absalom to follow Ahithophel's advice. However, since David received his correction with humility and did not resist his punishment, God spared his life by arranging for Hushai to defeat Ahithophel's advice. Don't resist the chastening of the Lord, for God resists the proud and gives grace to the humble.

Hushai's advice bought David time to recuperate, because it would take time to mobilize the entire Israelite army. His advice also made Absalom vulnerable, because he would be the sole target of David's men, and a cause loses steam and followers flee when their leader is defeated. Hushai sent an urgent warning to David via the high priest's sons, Jonathan and Ahimaaz, to flee the wilderness to prevent his death. Hushai's message confirmed the fact that Ahithophel's advice was sound.

The high priest's sons were spotted leaving En-rogel, which was reported to Absalom, and although Absalom's men went after them, they could not find them. There were enough close calls to allow God to defeat either David or Absalom, but David's humility turned the tides in his favor. David and his men crossed the Jordan before dawn and went to Mahanaim.

Healing Oil

When a person is facing distress, if you cannot comfort them, remain neutral, because there are two types of people you do not forget when the Lord brings you through storms: those who stepped on you while you were down and those who comforted you. Thank God for people who show kindness to the bruised and broken. Thank God for people who pour oil instead of salt into the wounds of the hurting.

The weary, weak, and distressed travelers were greeted by the kindness of Shobi, an Ammonite, Makir of Lodebar, and Barzillai from Rogelim when they arrived at Mahanaim. These three provided comfort, encouragement, and sustenance. It is the kindness and thoughtfulness of others that soothes the heart of those who are troubled and battered by the weight of their sins.

> They brought sleeping mats, cooking pots, serving bowls, wheat and barley flour, roasted grain, beans, lentils, honey, butter, sheep, and cheese for David and those who were with him. For they said, "You all must be very tired and hungry and thirsty after your long march through the wilderness." *2 Samuel 17:28–29*

David and his men were soon refreshed and ready for battle. Six hundred of the men in his party that day were Gittites from Gath. Even at David's urging, they refused to leave him. The other people you do not forget when you are down and out are those who stand with you in your storm. David dismissed the Gittites but they refused to leave him.

> But Ittai said to the king, "I vow by the Lord and by your own life that I will go wherever you go, no matter what happens—whether it means life or death." *2 Samuel 15:21*

Some people have criticized David for having a foreign court, but when the Israelite army could be so easily persuaded to attack David, could he be blamed? The Israelite soldiers demonstrated disloyalty toward David again when Absalom used them to go against David. It would not have been possible if David had the loyalty of the army. How could a rebel who had only made unfulfilled promises persuade the Israelite army to go against the crowned king who had benefited them many times over? There was still resentment toward David. Those in the army remembered David as one who had not paid his dues. He was the quick upstart who became king. The disloyalty was still there, and anyone who could recognize that could use it to their advantage. Joab often taunted David about the army's disloyalty; why would a seed of David overlook such a fortuitous opportunity? To remain king, David needed a court composed of people who would remain loyal regardless of the circumstances, and if he could only find loyal subjects in foreigners, that was what he had to do.

David split his men into three groups, making Joab, Abishai, and Ittai commanders. When David announced that he was going along, everyone objected. They knew David was the object of Absalom's men. Absalom would not be satisfied with all their deaths if David managed to escape. As David's men left the city, he asked his commanders to spare Absalom.

"For my sake, have mercy on my child, for by harming him you are harming me. Have mercy on me because I cannot breathe, I cannot move if you harm the one I love."

During that battle, twenty thousand men died, the majority of them because of the forest and not by the sword. Absalom's head got caught in the thick branches of an oak tree, and he was dangling from the tree when Joab, ignoring David's request, killed him. When the Israelite army saw that Absalom was dead, they lost their courage and fled.

When the news of Absalom's death reached David, he was overcome with grief. As he went to his room, he burst into tears and said, "O my son Absalom! My son, my son Absalom! If only I could have died instead of you. O Absalom, my son, my son!" (2 Samuel 18:33)

It was not just that Absalom was his son. David also understood that the curse put into motion by his own rebellion against God had created the rebellion that grew in Absalom's heart. He had failed Absalom, and his son's death was his fault. More torturous than suffering personally for your own sin is to watch others of your household suffer as well. David had failed as a father and a husband because of his sin and had failed to protect his family from the devastation of rape, murder, and rebellion. Though innocent, they had paid the price of David's sin.

That was why he wailed, "O, Absalom." He was saying, "I failed you as a father; my failure has caused your death. Oh my dear darling prince, my beautiful son, my precious baby, I caused you to live an abridged life. If only I could have died in your stead."

David was a broken man. Absalom was the fourth of his children to die, and though all were innocent, their lives were cut short because of his sins. His sins had wreaked havoc in his family. He was helpless to stop the curse that was ravaging them. All he could do was helplessly watch the devastation. There is nothing worse than watching your children suffer and feeling powerless to put an end to that suffering.

"For my sake, have mercy on my children. It tears me up inside; I cannot bear the grief of watching them suffer. How many more of my children have to die before sin is satisfied? I am a mortal, mortals are weak, and there is only so much suffering a man can take before it kills him. Each time one of my children dies, I die a thousand deaths. I am a dead man; my life has been ground to dust. Take this cup of suffering from me, for it is too bitter to sip, and the fumes are caustic. I can't bear to mourn another second; this grief is too heavy for me. I can't catch my breath from crying, and my body is wracked with pain. Each time I cry, my whole body heaves under the greatest physical strain I have ever endured. My flesh burns internally. I'm all wrung out. Next time you want to take one of my children, take me instead. Please, God, I beg, I grovel for your mercy. Relieve my anguished soul."

David's crying could be heard in the courtyard, and everyone could feel his grief when the men returned from battle. Their heads hung in shame, as if they had suffered defeat. Every time David wailed, the men mourned. Every sob, every roar from David's soul shattered the men.

David's grieving would have continued had it not been for Joab, who reminded him, "You cannot cry over the death of your enemy when your men risked their lives to save you from him. We achieved a great victory today, but you seem to love your enemies more than those who are loyal to you. You would have liked nothing more than the death of all your men in exchange for Absalom. If you continue to act this way, you will send a message to your men that they are expendable, and they will leave you. Then see how far you get." Of the many tragedies of leadership, perhaps the greatest is the fact that you cannot show normal human emotions.

David cried privately for years over the destruction and misery he had caused his family. Bathsheba's firstborn had died shortly after his birth. Tamar had lost her life when Amnon raped her. Absalom had taken Amnon's life. Absalom had raped ten of David's concubines, who then suffered a great loss because they lost the ability to "commune" with David. Absalom had lost his life when he led a rebellion against David. Adonijah, David's fourth son, lead a rebellion to usurp David's throne as David neared his death. David was a witness to that rebellion, but he did not witness his son's death.

Solomon's life was a disaster. Although he was one of the wisest men who ever lived, all his wisdom could not save him from David's curse. He married many foreign women, who then turned his heart away from God by influencing him to practice idolatry. His sin caused a split in the kingdom of Israel. The only reason David's descendants remained in power was that God was honoring his covenant with David. These are the catastrophes in David's family that we know about, but there were and are many silent tragedies.

One man's sin has the power to ruin the lives of his offspring. The curse is never satisfied, even though it destroys life after life. You know you are involved in a curse when you watch generation after generation of family members fall into the same trap. No one can avoid the pitfalls. There is usually one person in a family who can recognize the pattern, but even they are unable to escape the trap. There is powerlessness in a generational curse. There is no hope for removing a curse without the power of God. Just as humanity's only hope for escaping the curse put in motion by Adam is Jesus, so is Jesus the only hope for the individual who wants to escape a generational curse.

"Lord, today my heart breaks for all those who are trapped in generational curses. Some don't even realize that the turmoil they are facing results from the sins of their fathers. They go through life facing one tragedy after another, oblivious to the cycle. It's even more torturous for those who are aware of the cycle but are powerless to stop it. When they look back over their lives and the lives of their family members, they see the aftermath of the curse running rampant through their family and their heart breaks. Their lives are filled with misery. They watch the curse destroy lives, and they brace themselves for the next blow. They are battered and bruised by the curse and are looking for a way out, but Lord, you are the only way out. Could you please help break the curse?"

Take-home message: Do not resist the chastening of the Lord, for God resists the proud and gives grace to the humble.

26.

Seeds of Division

After Joab killed Absalom, the coup lost its steam and David returned to his throne, though not without a hitch. After much debate, all of Israel except Judah decided to reinstate King David. They made an honest appraisal of David's reign and realized that his leadership had blessed them. They had chosen Absalom for their king, but he had not done anything for them except make promises.

> The king saved us from our enemies, the Philistines, but Absalom chased him out of the country. Now Absalom, whom we anointed to rule over us, is dead. Let's ask David to come back and be our king again. *2 Samuel 19:9–10*

A Case of Favoritism

David sent representatives to convince Judah, his own tribe, to reinstate him, but they were reluctant. They feared David would retaliate for their participation in the coup and the fact that Amasa, one of their own, had led the Israelite army against David. They wanted assurance that David bore no resentment toward them. David negotiated his reinstatement with Judah by appointing Amasa as army commander.

David was from the tribe of Judah, and Amasa was his nephew, and of all tribes they should have been the last to lift a finger against him. At the very least, they should have been the first tribe to reinstate him instead of forcing him to negotiate his reinstatement. Before he became king, he had given them gifts from the spoils of war. David was a blessing to everyone in general and especially to the tribe of Judah, but they had betrayed him and felt guilty for it. Consequently, they were overzealous in escorting David and his family across the Jordan, acting as if they were the only ones who had a right to escort the king. The other tribes felt slighted and voiced their concerns to David, but he did not settle the matter.

David should have created an inclusive environment, but his silence implied exclusivity. He let the tribe of Judah quarrel with the rest of the tribes. Judah's zeal and David's inaction caused a split, marking the beginning of the division that future kings of his lineage would experience. David's improper handling of the issue of favoritism thus fueled another rebellion.

> "The king is one of our own tribe. Why should this make you angry? We have charged him nothing. And he hasn't fed us or even given us gifts!" "But there are ten tribes in Israel," the others replied. "So we have ten times as much right to the king as you do. Why did you treat us with such contempt? Remember, we were the first to speak of bringing him back to be our king again." The argument continued back and forth, and the men of Judah were very harsh in their replies.
> *2 Samuel 19:42–43*

David could have laid all issues to rest if he had handled his reinstatement better. During any momentous occasion in Israel, all the tribes had representation. When David returned the Ark of the Covenant, all tribes were represented. The same was true when he reorganized the Levites. Involving every tribe in momentous events demonstrated unity, inclusion, and esteem, and David's reinstatement should have been no different. All of the tribes wanted to welcome him and expected him to honor their reception. David's response should have been one of gratitude, one that received and honored their acceptance. Although it seemed to be a trivial thing to allow all tribes representation, it was a huge symbolic issue in their minds. The message the rest of Israel received that day was that the tribe of Judah would always be favored above all other tribes as long as David's lineage ruled.

Sheba, son of Bicri of the tribe of Benjamin, essentially said, "Since David does not include us, we don't want anything to do with him. Let's go." The men of Israel followed Sheba, while the men of Judah stayed to escort David to Jerusalem. David sent Joab to crush the fomenting rebellion. Although Absalom was dead, the cause that had created the rebellion was still there—and the rebellion had a new leader.

Sheba mobilized the Bicri clan at the fortified city of Abel-beth-maacah. Abishai went to the city and built a ramp to batter the wall down. When a woman asked why he was attacking a loyal city, Abishai told her all he wanted was Sheba bar Bicri, who had revolted against King David. The people of the city beheaded Sheba and threw his head out to Abishai.

The coup gained momentum because the people felt they did not have adequate representation, justice was sluggish, and royalty was out of touch with their plight. That, coupled with the favoritism David displayed when he was reinstated, served to create a rift that would later divide Israel from Judah. David never addressed the cause of the coup, for several reasons. He believed the coup was built on false pretenses and exaggerations; therefore, it lacked substance and was unfounded. The coup was a consequence of David's sin, a one-time event without lasting repercussions. With the exception of the tribe of Judah, the people had invited him back without conditions. Nonetheless, any leader whose administration is suffering from a revolt should find out what needs are not being addressed in order to put an end to the unrest. The Israelites perceived a problem. Otherwise, why would they have selected a new king who did nothing but make promises over a man who had served and kept them in peace?

The kingdom of Israel would immediately have split from Judah if David had not forcibly prevented it. A revolt is not defused by killing its leader, because as long as it has a cause, another leader will emerge. It is killed by addressing the issues that fuel it. Although Sheba was dead and the rebellion was quashed, the resentment remained. Saul's family and loyalists had unfounded issues with David. Joab had killed Amasa, but his family held David accountable for not controlling his men. Sheba's family had grounds to resent David. The people of Israel believed that David favored the tribe of Judah above all others and that Sheba had just been trying to redress the situation.

Information Gap

David showed mercy toward Shimei when he stopped Joab and Abishai from killing him. David did not say that Shimei did not deserve to die—he only said it was a time to celebrate. David was uncertain of the Lord's intentions, but he was thrilled to find that God was allowing him to continue as king of Israel. He was in such a state of euphoria because of God's mercy that he spared Shimei.

When David was fleeing from Absalom, Mephibosheth's servant Ziba told him that Mephibosheth wanted to get Saul's throne back and would not come with David. If only David had been operating with spiritual discernment, he would have been able to see through Ziba's scheme. Mephibosheth later told David that Ziba had lied. Mephibosheth was handicapped and needed assistance to saddle and mount his horse; Ziba had refused to help him, making it impossible for him to come with David. After hearing this explanation David decided to give Ziba half of Mephibosheth's property, because he could not determine who was telling the truth.

> "All my relatives and I could expect only death from you, my lord, but instead you have honored me among those who eat at your own table! So how can I complain?" "All right," David replied. "My decision is that you and Ziba will divide your land equally between you." "Give him all of it," Mephibosheth said. "I am content just to have you back again, my lord!" *2 Samuel 19:28–30*

Mephibosheth's response makes a strong case that he was telling the truth, based on a similar case that Solomon judged. Unfortunately, David could not see that, because his sins had caused him to lose the gift of discernment.

There had been a spiritual breakdown in David's personal life and career as a result of his sin involving Uriah, Bathsheba, and other innocent people. That sin was a turning point in David's life and caused his life to descend. God took a few steps back in David's life. He did not completely abandon David as He had Saul, but He was distant. Back when David and God were closer, David had access to information and supernatural advice that enabled him to stay ahead of his enemies and ward off attacks. While he fought the enemies of the Lord, God always gave him information to help defeat his foes. However, after his sins, his armor began to crumble, making him susceptible to devastation in his personal life, increased threats to his survival, and poor decision making in his administration.

One of the many benefits of being in a relationship with God is that He provides advice that helps people avoid grief and devastation and protects them from the evil plans of the enemy. These plans are to kill, steal, and destroy God's people. David's sin exposed him to the onslaughts of the devil and caused him to lose God's hedge of protection. Sexual dysfunction and rebellion were two of the consequences of David's sin, so God withheld information about Amnon's plan to rape Tamar. God left David unaware of Absalom's conspiracy until it was in full bloom.

The other consequence of David's sin was that the sword would be poised against him and his family. David's sin gave Satan latitude to make attempts on his life. The close brush with death during a battle with the Philistines signaled that God had distanced Himself from David. It is a good thing that David inspired others to be giant killers. What kryptonite was to Superman, sin was to David (as it is to all of humanity). God did not spare David from the assaults against his life, but He did preserve him.

> Ishbi-benob was a descendent of the giants; his bronze spearhead weighed more than seven pounds, and he was armed with a new sword. He had cornered David and was about to kill him. But Abishai

> son of Zeruiah came to his rescue and killed the Philistine.
> *2 Samuel 21:16–17*

David had been regarded as an angel of God, displaying unusual wisdom in social affairs. However, he failed to see through Ziba's schemes and failed to exercise wisdom during his reinstatement. David was no longer operating by the spiritual discernment that comes from God but was relying on faulty, limited human knowledge. His administration began to suffer. What had made David powerful and great was his connection to God and having His favor.

Which Lord?

Satan was still on the warpath against David. God had preserved David through the many attempts Satan had made to take his life. Satan had designed the Bathsheba-Uriah incident to oust David. By rights David should have died, but what Satan did not take into account was David's humility and God's mercy. Satan had attempted to remove David through Absalom's rebellion but had failed for the same reason. Satan had tried to snuff out David's lights during his last battle with the Philistines, but God had thwarted his efforts. David's sins gave Satan license to attack him, but God kept preserving David, so Satan decided to take a different approach. The devil is cunning and crafty; he will leave you for a season, regroup, then attack again.

At the instruction of the Lord, David ordered Joab to take a census. Joab, as ruthless as he was, had reservations and tried to persuade David not to take the census. Nonetheless, Joab did as David had commanded, in spite of his reluctance, taking almost ten months to complete the task. Counting only men of military age, Joab reported that there were eight hundred thousand in Israel and five hundred thousand in Judah. After the census was complete, David's conscience began bothering him. He prayed to God, asking Him to forgive him for taking the census. If God had commanded him to take the census, why would David pray to God and ask for forgiveness for carrying out His command? There are two accounts in the Bible that try to explain why David took the census, but the accounts are conflicting and need further examination.

> Once again the anger of the LORD burned against Israel, and he caused David to harm them by taking a census. "Go and count the people of Israel and Judah," the LORD told him. *2 Samuel 24:1*

> SATAN rose up against Israel and caused David to take a census of the Israelites. *1 Chronicles 21:1*

Did God direct David to take the census, or did God allow Satan to provoke David to take it? Why would God command David to sin and then punish him for doing it? Did David get his wires crossed? Did David mistake Satan's voice for the voice of God? Through whom did David receive his instructions?

It does not make sense that God would be angry at Israel at that time. Israel was enjoying a spiritual reformation during David's leadership. If God was angry at Israel, He would explain the reason, but the Bible says nothing about that. It does not point out sinful behavior or wrongdoing that would justify His anger. The account given in 2 Samuel 24:1 presents a picture of an unjust and unreasonable God. It is as though He was trying to find a reason to punish Israel and when He could find none, He created a reason—but God does not get pleasure from causing pain. It is not in God's nature to tempt any man with sin. He cannot be tempted by sin and neither does He tempt any man to sin. Men are drawn away from God by their own desires.

God gave Moses instructions about how to conduct a census. If God expected David to take a census, He expected it to be conducted in the way He had already prescribed. David knew how to take the census properly because he had studied the Torah.

> And the LORD said to Moses, "Whenever you take a census of the people of Israel, each man who is counted must pay a ransom for himself to the LORD. Then there will be no plagues among the people as you count them. His payment to the LORD will be one-fifth of an ounce of silver. All who have reached their twentieth birthday must give this offering to the LORD. When this offering is given to the LORD to make atonement for yourselves, the rich must not give more, and the poor must not give less. Use this money for the care of the Tabernacle. It will bring you, the Israelites, to the LORD's attention, and it will make atonement for your lives." *Exodus 30:11–16*

The proper way of doing a census brought blessings, but the wrong way caused a plague. David counted the men of military age according to God's edict, but he did not collect the atonement offering. If God had called for the census, He intended to bless Israel by making amends through the atonement offering. Atonement means to harmonize, to compensate, and to balance. Blessed is the man who is not charged for his sins and whose iniquities have been forgiven. Since David took the census improperly, he brought a curse instead of a blessing upon Israel. The way David took the census brought the Israelites to the attention of God and highlighted their sins without making restitution.

If it was not God's intention to conduct a census, He allowed Satan to test David's heart. It puts a burden on distinguishing the difference between *testing* and *tempting*. If one is tested and sins, what is the difference between testing and tempting? God tests His children to expose their motives. God will test a person's motives to see if they are interesting in pleasing Him or in doing their own thing. It is entirely possible to anger God while fulfilling His commands, because it all comes down to motives. For example, in Balaam's case when God told him to go with Balak's men, the angel of the Lord withstood him and would have killed him were it not for his donkey. Why did God tell Balaam to go to Balak and then attempt to kill him for going? Because Balaam intended to please himself by aiding Balak instead of serving God.

God allowed Satan to provoke David to take the census, and it was meant as a test. Satan played upon the pride most leaders fall prey to, where they measure their accomplishments based on the number of people they govern, the size of their military, or the growth of financial assets. Pride is self-promoting and God-demoting. Taking a census was like taking inventory of human resources, relying on human effort, taking credit for God's handiwork, and ignoring God, who is the source of all blessings and victories. Satan used the census to remove David, to attack Israel, and to re-exert his dominion.

David's confession sheds light on what really happened. He did not confess that he had taken the census improperly; he confessed that he should not have taken it.

> But after he had taken the census, David's conscience began to bother him. And he said to the Lord, "I have sinned greatly and shouldn't have taken the census. Please forgive me, Lord, for doing this foolish thing." *2 Samuel 24:10*

Even those of us who have enjoyed an outstanding relationship with the Lord all of our lives can sometimes be fooled into believing that we are hearing from God. Although Joab instantly identified David's order as sin and tried to persuade him not to conduct the census, David was convinced that the God of Israel had issued the command and would not be persuaded otherwise. If a false spirit posing as God has never deceived you or led you astray, how would you know it is possible? David had always followed the voice of God and had never been disappointed by the outcome, so he issued orders to fulfill what he thought was God's command.

Often God's commands evoked a "No, that can't be right" response. People in David's inner circle had tried to discourage him from doing what God had told him to do in past situations, but he had obeyed God and reaped the benefits. He had never been disappointed by doing the will of God, in spite of the opposition and the fact that God's instructions went against the grain of human reasoning. David had grown accustomed to standing alone; that is what leaders do. People of vision and faith have accomplished the miraculous because they have trusted God. Visionaries do not get to where they are by succumbing to sight walking and human reasoning.

David had reached a point in his relationship with God where He was giving him the silent treatment. Unfortunately David did not realize this. Satan took advantage of the situation and used God's silence as an opportunity to deceive David. David mistook Satan's voice for God's and brought disaster upon Israel.

The real question is: How do you safeguard yourself against mistaking Satan's voice for God's voice? Satan can pose as an angel of light, deceiving the elect into believing that he is God. David had no apprehension about what he was doing, because he was convinced he was doing the will of God. It was not until after the census that David's conscience began to bother him, and only then did he realize that he had sinned. The majority of the time when David received commands from the Lord, they came through a prophet or he inquired of the Lord through a priest. The command to take the census does not appear to have been mediated by either. Therefore, the way for people of God to safeguard themselves against being confused is to consult counselors (prophets and other Christian leaders).

Under the best circumstances, a failure like that could cause David to question everything he heard, but under the worst circumstances, it had the power to destroy David's relationship with God. When your trusted line of communication has been contaminated, it is hard to take anything you hear in the spirit seriously. It created a crisis of faith. He could no longer operate in the supernatural. If David could not be sure that he was hearing from God in that situation, how could he be sure he had *ever* heard from God?

If the destroyer fails to take your life, he will settle for destroying your relationship with God, since being separated from God is a fate worse than death. When you go through a crisis of faith, you question whether God loves you, and you feel disqualified from being God's servant. Eventually you determine you are not a Christian. It can make you question whether you ever had a relationship with God. You wonder whom you were serving in the first place. Those who spring back from an assault by the devil know it only has to happen once to make you begin to second-guess everything you hear, rendering you ineffective and disabled from walking in the supernatural. Trust is easily granted, but once broken, it is difficult to regain. David did not have time to dwell on his damaged communication line and mistaken identity; he would have to sort that out later. He had more immediate issues to deal with in the wake of his sin.

Choose Your Punishment

David's mistaken identity cost Israel greatly. God spoke through David's personal prophet, Gad, and told him to choose one of three punishments: three years of famine, three months of flight from his enemies, or three days of severe plague. How could a shepherd sit by and watch his sheep suffer from famine for three years? More people would have died by that decision than by his ultimate choice. David chose three days of severe plague, choosing the hands of a merciful God over the unforgiving hands of man. David chose the punishment he thought would create the least suffering.

> "This is a desperate situation!" David replied to Gad. "But let me fall into the hands of the LORD, for his mercy is very great. Do not let me fall into human hands." *1 Chronicles 21:13*

It is far, far better to fall into the hands of a merciful God than into the cruel, unrelenting, unmerciful hands of humanity. God can be touched by our infirmities and is well acquainted with our frailties. He is sensitive and kind. The elements for a coup were present, so it would not have been difficult to inspire an uprising. There were people who would have jumped at the opportunity to attack David and would have been relentless in their pursuit. Being chased by his enemies was not palatable, because men are cruel. Human beings will grind each other to dust if restraints are not in place. The destroyer tendency in humanity was inherited from our ancestor's sin and has been cultivated by centuries of sin. Sin makes the love of many grow cold. David knew he would not stand a chance if he fell into the hands of his enemies. "Do whatever you feel is necessary but do not let me fall into the hands of evil beasts."

There was always the hope that God would relent and reduce the punishment when He considered that David had been deceived into believing that he was following His orders. David had been just as much of a victim as the rest of the Israelites.

David and the leaders of Israel were paralyzed with fear. They put on sackcloth and fell face down before the Lord to show their distress and appeal to His mercy. David interceded for the people because he had the heart of a true shepherd and was concerned about their welfare. He pleaded with the Lord on their behalf, "Why should they suffer for my sin? Let me and my family suffer." (As if they could use more suffering!) "It's my fault. I sinned, but these people are innocent. Do whatever you want to do with me, but please spare your people. I made a mistake. Please don't cause these people to suffer because of me. Hold me accountable for my sin."

A good shepherd will suffer personal loss if it will preserve the life of one sheep, and he would never want a sheep to die because of his error. David understood that his error had caused Israel to suffer, and it caused him great turmoil. However, one who is a hireling would not be concerned that people suffer as long as they personally do not have to feel the shock of their own sin. David did not take the attitude that as long as he was insulated and isolated from the devastation, he did not care what happened to the people. If you do not care about the plight of the people you are responsible for, if you just yawn when you hear that the people you are leading are suffering, if you do not have your finger on the pulse of the people, you are a mercenary. If the people are suffering because of your sins and you refuse to step aside to put an end to the suffering, you are selfish and unworthy of being a leader. It is terribly shocking to have others pay for your sin.

It is impossible to insulate people from the consequences of the sins of their leaders. People have a right to demand accountability if you are their leader. They have a right to question your morality and how it will influence your ability to lead. You cannot tell people "It's none of your business" when they question your sins. That response shows that either you do not care or you fail to understand that your constituents will pay for the consequences of your immorality. In either case, it shows unworthiness. The consequences of a leader's sins affect not only the leader personally but also the people exponentially. People pay a high price for the low living of their leaders. Therefore, they have a right to question your morality, and if they find that you lack remorse, they should reject you.

God resists the proud but gives grace to the humble. If David had possessed Saul's attitude, he would have died prematurely. David's redeeming quality was his humility. With God, humility can defuse a time bomb. When you are a sinner and do not have a righteous leg to stand on, it is imperative to appeal to a righteous, loving God for mercy. David took a chance that God's mercy would cause Him to lessen the impact of the punishment. The Lord heard the people's prayers and relented. God relented because of their intercession. He could also see the genuine anguish and remorse in David's heart.

Even though God was merciful, the death angel had killed more than seventy thousand people by the time he reached Jerusalem.

> And God sent an angel to destroy Jerusalem. But just as the angel was preparing to destroy it, the LORD relented and said to the death angel, "Stop! That is enough!" At that moment the angel of the LORD was standing by the threshing floor of Araunah the Jebusite.
> *1 Chronicles 21:15*

It is a good thing when God says, "Stop! That is enough!" to the consequences of sin. All God was looking for was remorse, a broken heart, and a contrite spirit. David, Gad, and Araunah could see the death angel, his sword poised and ready to strike Jerusalem, and it struck terror in their hearts. God's punishment broke David's pride; he was humiliated and lost his reputation as protector of Israel. For the second time in David's reign, Israel suffered for his mistakes, which was a big blow to a man who prided himself on being a blessing to Israel. It was terrible to watch the people suffer because of his sin, and his remorse was evident in his plea to God.

I Will Not Let You Pay My Debt

Praise and sacrifice are alike because both attract the attention of the Lord, and like praise, sacrifice cannot be offered for you—it is personal. Praise and sacrifice go straight from the heart of the sender to God. When Jesus visited the temple and watched the offering bucket, He was attracted to the widow's mite because it was a very personal sacrifice. Cornelius' prayer and alms caught God's attention in heaven. Personal sacrifices and personal praise attract God's attention.

> Then the angel of the LORD told Gad to instruct David to build an altar to the LORD at the threshing floor of Araunah the Jebusite.
> *1 Chronicles 21:18*

When David went to do what he was told, Araunah offered to give David everything he needed, but David refused to let someone else pay for his sin offering. A person is not being held accountable if the costs are passed along to someone else. Sacrifices are not sacrifices if they do not cost you anything.

David built an altar, made burnt offerings and peace offerings, and prayed, and the Lord accepted those prayers and sacrifices by sending fire from heaven to consume the sacrifice. Then the Lord commanded the death angel to put the sword away. There are only a few recorded cases in which the Lord supplied the fire to consume an offering, which makes David's case notable. Elijah built an altar, set the sacrifices on it, and then poured water on them. Then Elijah prayed for the Lord to send fire from heaven to consume the sacrifices to prove that he was serving the living God who could both see and hear.

$E=mc^2$

It is hard to imagine anyone believing that God limits Himself to only one place when He is omnipresent. Although you have a higher probability of finding God in church, you put limits on God when you fail to realize that you can find God anywhere. You may find Him while you are standing at the kitchen sink, walking down the street, sitting by a river, looking at a sunrise, picking apples, driving on the highway, staying in a hotel room, or receiving the smile of another person. God is everywhere and anywhere you need Him to be. When David proposed the temple, God explained that He had always lived in a tent and moved when the Israelites moved. In essence, God told David that He was a God on the move, yet David gave the distinct impression, especially during the plague, that he felt God could only be reached at Mount Gibeon, where the Tabernacle and the altar Moses had built were located.

Although taking the census was one of David's failures, some good things came from it. Since he discovered that Araunah's threshing floor was a place where God would answer prayers and receive offerings, David designated it as the site of the Lord's temple. He found a place to build the temple when he learned that God was not bound by time or space. He wanted to build the temple on the place where a sinner could reach God.

> When David saw that the Lord had answered his prayer, he offered sacrifices there at Araunah's threshing floor. Then David said, "This will be the location for the Temple of the LORD God and the place of the altar for Israel's burnt offerings!" *1 Chronicles 21:28, 22:1*

Triumph can often be found in tragedy, and out of David's tragedy came a blessing. All things work together for the good of them who love the Lord and are called according to his purpose. It is hard to be objective about that statement, because it usually takes a lifetime before the phenomenon can be observed. In the immediate sense, all you have is a mistake and the consequences it brings: regrets, guilt, shame, and suffering. While you are waiting to see God put the broken fragments of your life back together, God has provided an example through the life of David. When you have sinned so horribly that you just want to hide, be encouraged to know that God can mix the good and the bad to create something wonderful.

From this discussion of David's life you might conclude that you should sin for the sake of sinning because God will ultimately turn things around to your favor, but that is definitely not the case! If you live long enough, you will make some painful mistakes, but if you are contrite and continue to love God, He will take the sins in your life and turn them around to benefit yourself and others.

Take-home message: With God, humility is everything.

27.

Colossal Work in Progress

The Levites were a colossal work in progress that began when they returned the Ark of the Lord. The successful return of the Ark was solely attributed to David's study of the Torah. David led Torah seminars for the Levites to instruct them in their God-given responsibilities. David not only used the Levites for temple maintenance, construction supervision, government administration, and worship/preaching, but he also restored them to their responsibility of ministering before the Lord and His people.

The Levites operated on a limited basis during Saul's reign because they were a liability to God's cause. The high priest's sons, who were entrusted with the responsibility of ministering before the Lord and His people, were corrupt, and when the head is corrupt, it infects the whole body. God wanted a relationship with Israel and expected that relationship to be facilitated and cultivated by His ministers. When the Levites were discouraging the few people who were trying to connect to Him, God decided to relieve them of their duties, using Samuel to fill the gap. The Levites were a defunct class of has-beens until David restored them.

David placed a high priority on restoring the Levites because without them, he could not lead a reformation in Israel. He also understood that Israel would maintain her greatness not by military prowess but by strong spiritual leadership. He wanted the Levites fully operational by the time his son became king so they could help him lead. David envisioned a society with God at the helm, in which Israel was in love with God and had a healthy relationship with Him. David needed people who understood his vision and would implement it in order to transform society—and who better to do that than the Levites? God intended it to be that way, and their sheer numbers could make David's dream a reality. Thirty-eight thousand people carrying the same vision could change a nation the size of Israel. Using the Levites to carry out God's vision multiplied David's efforts.

No Favoritism

David held summit meetings that included the high priest, the family leaders of priests and Levites, some Levites, and the army commanders so everything would be done in fairness and in order. Leaders from each tribe in Israel also played an active role in the planning phase. David developed a flowchart outlining all of Levi's descendants so he could categorize each registered Levite according to his clan to make sure that all clans were represented and were qualified for particular responsibilities.

Levi had three sons: Gershon, Kohath, and Merari. Descendants of Gershon came from his sons, Libni and Shimei. Descendants of Merari came from his sons, Mahli and Mushi. Descendants of Kohath came from his sons, Izhar, Hebron, Uzziel, and Amram. David conducted two censuses of the Levites, the first included all Levites thirty years of age and older to serve in leadership positions.

David concentrated on the priests, descendants of Aaron, because they were responsible for everything involving the temple and the things of God. Aaron, Moses's older brother, was a son of Amram and a descendant of Kohath. Aaron had four sons: Nadab, Abihu, Eleazer, and Ithamar. All priests were descendants of either Eleazer or Ithamar, because Nadab and Abihu died in the wilderness. Only priests were qualified to dedicate the most holy things, offer sacrifices in the Lord's presence, make atonement for Israel, perform health and sanitation inspections, conduct purification ceremonies, and pronounce blessings in His name. Priests supervised the Levites. There were many qualified priests; therefore, all tasks were assigned by casting sacred lots in the presence of David, his priests Zadok and Ahimelech, and the family leaders of priests and Levites to avoid preferential treatment.

To maintain smooth operation in God's house, David ordered the second census of Levites and carefully registered all who were between the ages of twenty and twenty-nine. Then he qualified them to assist the priests in the Lord's house, freeing the priests to focus their attention on their primary responsibilities. These Levites were assigned to help perform purification ceremonies, to prepare sacred bread, to check weights and measures, and to guard the temple. David assigned Levites to protect the assets of the house of God. They were responsible for the treasury, which held all things dedicated to the Lord by Israel and its leaders. They were responsible for the utensils used in worship, checking them in and out to avoid loss. They were also responsible for the furnishings and supplies. Obed-edom and his family learned how to care for the Ark of the Lord when David left it at his home after his first attempt to return the Ark to Jerusalem failed. He used their experience to guard the Ark at Jerusalem and at the temple once it was constructed.

They were trustworthy men assigned to gates surrounding the property, the storehouse, and the courtyard.

It is difficult to produce lasting change in people without dealing with the society in which they live. David believed it was important to have the word of God publicly preached for the society to run efficiently. When God's words are hidden from a society, people cast off all restraint and do what is right in their own eyes. The sons of leading musicians also proclaimed God's messages by David's order to the accompaniment of the harp, cymbals, and lyre. So the musicians not only played skillfully, but they also preached with music as a backdrop (the origin of our modern church services). The reason those involved in praise and worship today cannot exempt themselves from Bible study is that they must also be well versed in God's words to proclaim His word at the most appropriate times.

David understood that having strong spiritual leadership was more important than military prowess, because God promised that His son would rule in peace. Consequently, David turned his attention from defense to running a well-ordered society. The Levites were assigned to fill official governmental positions within Israel.

Assigning certain Levite clans to particular positions supported every function that was needed to keep the Tabernacle operating and to support the necessary societal roles. David personally supervised the assignment of priests and Levites to all positions in order to prevent favoritism and ensure that every position was filled. Particular Levite families were permanently assigned to particular positions, so although specialization developed, each position was designed for the orderly fulfillment of Israel's needs. As long as each group fulfilled its task, the organization operated smoothly and no need went unmet.

Each denomination within the body of Christ is designed to perform a critical task to assist with the overall operation of the universal body of Christ. The diversity that results from denominations edifies the body and allows it to function smoothly. As long as each one is doing its task, no need goes unmet. Unfortunately, instead of appreciating and embracing our differences we often allow them to cause division. If the body of Christ is divided against itself, how shall it stand? One denomination refuses to accept the validity of other denominations because they do not perform its task. It refuses to respect the other denominations as Christian, believing it is the only one serving God correctly. It is chaos and a trick of the enemy of Christ when infighting occurs over the differences in our task. If the whole body of Christ conformed to perform the uniform task of one denomination, there would be a systemwide shutdown in the body of Christ, causing many needs to go unmet. If the whole body were an eye, how would it hear?

Restoring the Levites was a masterpiece—one of David's greatest accomplishments. He took the helm of the Levites the same way he would a military company. He organized them, outlined their responsibilities, and assigned tasks. He took a broken-down order and caused it to fulfill its potential according to God's will. No longer would the Levites be a class of dysfunctional, forgotten has-beens. They became an organization that fulfilled a crucial role in society. David was a charismatic leader who was an expert in motivating people to achieve goals higher than they thought possible. He was an expert in helping people to achieve their God-given purpose.

Praise Is What I Do

There are churches today that believe including musical instruments in praise and worship is against biblical standards. They also argue that since Jesus did not emphasize it, it is prohibited. Each church should govern itself according to its own conscience. However, there are scriptural references concerning the use of musical instruments to enhance praise. When Israel crossed the Red Sea, Miriam led praise and worship using the tambourine. Praise and worship using rams' horns preceded warfare. When Joshua led Israel against Jericho, they circled Jericho seven days. Armed guards sandwiched seven priests blowing horns and the priests that carried the Ark of the Lord. The priests blew the horns the entire time as they circled Jericho each day. On the seventh day, they blew their horns during the six times they circled the city, and on the seventh time around they sounded the long blast on their horn and the people shouted on Joshua's cue. Since carrying the Ark of the Lord into battle could be observed near the end of the Judges period, praise and worship preceding battle was still followed. David also followed that protocol when returning the Ark of the Lord to the tent in Jerusalem.

> Let the godly sing with joy to the LORD, for it is fitting to praise him. Praise the LORD with melodies on the lyre; make music for him on the ten-stringed harp. Sing new songs of praise to him; play skillfully on the harp and sing with joy. *Psalm 33:1–3*

David used Moses's teachings to learn how to return the Ark of God, to revive the Levites, to reorganize his society, and to teach Israel God's words. Moses gave God's commandments, principles, regulations, and laws; he instituted the many types of sacrifices; he designated the special commemorative days celebrating the history of God's involvement in Israel; and he outlined the priestly functions. Praise and worship were duties of the Levites during

Moses's time, but they were not as developed as David's design.

David put a greater emphasis on praise and worship than Moses did, taking them up a thousand notches to a whole new level. He created full-time positions for Levite musicians whose sole function was to praise God and teach God's word. David specifically created musical instruments to be used for praise and worship. Worship leaders used during the processional return of the Ark of the Lord were exempted from all other duties and appointed to give thanks to the Lord twenty-four hours a day for seven days a week. From the families of the lead musicians came 288 accomplished musicians to make music before the Lord. They were assigned to a specific term of duty by casting sacred lots without regard to age or experience.

David assigned a representative from each Levite clan to lead music. Heman of the Kohath clan was the lead musician, and his assistants were Asaph of the Gershon clan and Ethan of the Merari clan. They reported directly to David and followed the guidelines he gave them. They proclaimed God's messages across Israel to the accompaniment of harps, lyres, and cymbals. Modern-day church services arise from the design David and Asaph created. Two single-file choirs marched to the temple of God while singing praise to God to the accompaniment of trumpets under the direction of the choir director. The choir director conducted the choir in hymns of praise and worship to God. The choirs stood opposite each other during ceremonies, with one section responding to the other. All Israel stood during praise and worship.

Separation of Church and State?

When it came to using the Levites, there was no separation of church and state. To have a healthy society, the roles of king (or president), priest (or church), judges, administrators (or legislators), and prophets must be filled. When any of these elements are not operating, a society is crippled. David used the Levites as the base of his political support, employing them as administrators, judges, and government officials.

To qualify for a governmental position during David's administration, a person had to be a Levite with a proven track record of exercising wisdom and sound judgment. During the fortieth year of David's reign, he conducted a search to find capable men with unusual wisdom to help his son during his administration. When he located such people, he appointed them as governing leaders in charge of the tribes of Israel. For instance, Hashabiah and his relatives governed the Israelite tribes west of the Jordan River, while Jeriah and his relatives governed the Israelites east of the Jordan River.

When David sought leadership candidates, it was not enough to be a Levite; a person also had to operate in wisdom. The same holds true today for all Christians who aspire to politics. Those who work in politics must use discernment to understand the motives of others, have the wisdom and integrity to do the right thing, and also operate in the prophetic in order to be effective. It is sad to admit that notable Christian leaders of late have been misled by the political scams and maneuvers of others just to gain the Christian vote. Where are the prophets who can provide sound advice from the mind of God so Christians will not mistakenly align with dishonorable people? Now is the time for the prophets to come forth.

People question whether Christians should be involved in politics. The fact that the question exists proves that forces in our society have convinced many Christians that they do not have a right to serve as representatives. To question Christian involvement in politics is a sign of lack of knowledge concerning the things of God. In light of David's example and many scriptural references, the answer is a resounding yes; Christians should run for as many political offices as possible. Our involvement should not simply be the passive act of voting. Christians should run for offices, because oftentimes we are voting for the lesser of two evils when we are not presented with leaders who represent biblical values.

Many times we find ourselves using valuable time and energy trying to block immoral legislation—time that could be better spent to produce a healthy society. We are on the defensive when we should be on the offensive, being pacesetters and proposing government policy. The common belief in Christian circles is that politicians are corrupt, but the office takes on the character of the person holding the position and not vice versa. Out of the hearts of corrupt men come corrupt laws. If a righteous person holds a public office, there is a righteous tone to that person's administration.

When the subject of the church fulfilling its role as society's moral compass is discussed, some church leaders envision that involvement as a theocratic Israelite society or Islam, but nothing could be further from the truth. America's Bill of Rights, the first ten amendments to the Constitution, prohibits a government-controlled church; therefore, the church has to operate within those parameters. In today's society, the church must provide leadership the same way as any other group that attempts to influence the government. The church is responsible for defending the cause of righteousness—God's position on any issue that comes up for debate in the public arena.

Besides David's society, there are other examples in the Bible of using one's voice to influence society. Isaiah was a statesman who provided godly council to the king. Jeremiah warned kings and leaders of his time to do what God said or suffer the consequences. God told Ezekiel that he was a watchman, which made him responsible for warning society of the consequences of their actions, and if he failed his mission, they would die in their sins and their blood would be on his hands. Jesus is God, Lord, Master, and Savior, but while he was on Earth, He exposed the hypocrisy of the leadership of His day.

The list goes on, but a pattern emerges: Christian leaders who get involved in politics should operate in the prophetic realm, providing the prophetic voice that is needed in society. When the church involves itself in politics, it should use biblical principals as its basis. Christian leaders can warn people of the consequences of their actions, inform the society of God's will, and act as God's spokesmen to influence society to do the right thing. The influence they provide is just that—influence. While Christian leaders work to influence government policy, they do not impose their will on the majority and they do not force people to follow God any more than the prophets of the past did. Christian leaders can operate in American politics without imposing a government-controlled church and violating the Bill of Rights.

Twisted Interpretation

The actual phrase "separation of church and state" does not appear in the Declaration of Independence, the Constitution, or the Bill of Rights. However, the notion does appear in the First Amendment: "Congress shall make no law respecting an establishment of religion, or prohibiting the free exercise thereof; or abridging the freedom of speech, or of the press; or the right of the people peaceably to assemble, and to petition the government for a redress of grievances."

The First Amendment is interpreted and applied today in a manner opposite its original intent. The modern interpretation implies that the church has no right to influence the government, but the government can influence the church. The first settlers came to America fleeing the tyranny of a government-controlled church—because religion kills. If their conscience led them to believe that they should worship God differently, the government church used its power to persecute them, to rob them of their livelihood, to confiscate their property, to incarcerate them, to impose higher taxes on them, and if their differences were pronounced enough, to kill them. They were treated like criminals.

It defies logic that those who fled for their lives would want to continue that same type of government. Instead, they believed that the government should serve and be controlled by the people and not be allowed to favor or disfavor any particular religious belief.

The men who framed the Bill of Rights and those who signed it denied the establishment of a government-controlled church. The government has no right to pass laws to establish a church or impose a national religion, and it has no right to pass laws to regulate the activities or control the affairs of the church. The government cannot favor one religion to the exclusion of others and must protect the rights of its citizens to choose a religion that satisfies their personal convictions—without penalizing their choices.

What we have in America today is the exact situation the first settlers fled from—a government that is hostile to the expression of religious convictions. Since the meaning of the First Amendment has been twisted, today we have a stifling state-run church that is intolerant of and hostile toward Christianity. The one that prides itself for its tolerance is actually more intolerant than those it accuses of intolerance.

The First Amendment was meant to protect the rights of citizens from government-imposed religion, but that does not prohibit Christians from influencing government policy. Governments are instituted among men, and the power to govern is derived from the governed. If government is made up of people and established to represent the interests of people, then people (regardless of religious creed) have a right to propose laws, influence policy, and petition the government. Any citizen of the United States has as much say in how they are governed as the next person, because everyone is equal. Any citizen of the United States can propose legislation, but a majority has to agree to ratify that legislation.

Violation, Violation

If any group has a right to complain that there has been a violation of the First Amendment, it is the Christian church. In the recent past, Christians have been treated as second-class citizens with rights and privileges inferior to other citizens. Christian values and traditions have been tossed aside as "conservative and narrow-minded." The dominant thought in political arenas is that Christians should not be involved in politics, implying that Christians are not ordinary citizens and thus should not be able to form a political bloc. Many politicians were annoyed by the fact that the Christian vote became a dominant force to be reckoned with in recent elections. However, the First Amendment protects the rights of U.S. citizens, regardless of creed, to choose their religion, to speak freely, to assemble peaceably, and to petition the government. The First Amendment was meant to protect the rights of citizens. It is unconstitutional to disavow petitions by a person or a group because of their religious convictions.

Christian churches that are "funded" by the government cannot be involved in the political process. Some leaders in the church argue that the government is not funding them even though they have 501(c)(3) status. The government taxes every individual earning income above a certain level and every for-profit business. When the government does not take taxes but allows an organization to keep what it normally takes, it is the same as giving money. The single largest contributor to churches today is the U.S. government, because it exempts churches from the taxes it charges citizens and corporations. Those who offer substantial financial support to a Christian church feel they have a right to dictate how things are done.

Representation without taxation is unconstitutional; therefore, churches with the 501(c)(3) designation are barred from the political process and rightly so. When a tax-exempt church involves itself in political affairs, it violates the political process. The funding the government gives to support charitable organizations should not be used to lobby or endorse political candidates. If the government provides financial support to an organization, that financial support cannot be used to work against the government. That is why political candidates run for office by obtaining funds from private sources, not governmental sources.

Since many churches in the United States have the 501(c)(3) designation, pastors do not have a right to free speech where government is concerned. Organizations that have the 501(c)(3) designation may not attempt to influence legislation or participate in campaign activity for or against political candidates. They can, however, be involved in peripheral activities such as conducting voter-registration drives and political educational initiatives. They cannot publicly support or oppose a particular candidate nor can they lobby to influence legislation. A Christian church is guilty of violating this policy if more than 10 or 20 percent of its activities are devoted to lobbying or campaigning. The government has shut down churches in violation of this policy by revoking their tax-exempt status and imposing excise taxes, financially crippling the church to the point that it can no longer operate. If the government has the right to shut down a church and seize its assets, it implies that the government has ownership of the church, which is a violation of the First Amendment.

Many Christian churches across America are in jeopardy because they have allowed government infiltration, and the government has a stranglehold on churches because of the tax-exempt status it gives them. The government maintains this control to prevent the church from being a moral guide and spiritual compass for society and to prevent churches from participating in the political process. The government "funds" the Christian church to prevent it from becoming the dominant political force God intended it to be. It pays hush money to silence and control the church, but the government should not fund any church, because that is the same as establishing a state religion.

That is the clearest textbook example of a violation of the First Amendment ever presented.

The First Amendment really means the government does not have a right to pass laws to regulate churches. It does not mean churches do not have a right to influence government policy. Christian churches should be screaming, "violation of the First Amendment," because the government has infiltrated the church. But they will not scream out, because it would cause them to lose substantial funds or even the church itself.

The American Civil Liberties Union (ACLU) actively fights to enforce the "separation of church and state" in the way it is commonly interpreted today. They fight to protect the government from the influences of the church. They also fight against public prayer that specifically mentions Jesus at the opening of legislative sessions, prayer at high school graduations, displaying the Ten Commandments on courtroom walls, and placing nativity scenes on government property. The ACLU fights to protect government from the influence of the church and to ensure that the government is not imposing religion.

Do we uphold the rights of citizens to free speech, or do we infringe upon their rights in the name of the separation of church and state? No one loses their First Amendment rights just because they partake of government-provided provisions. Are valedictorians at high school commencements, who cannot even vote, government representatives or ordinary U.S. citizens with a right to free speech? Do politicians have a right to free speech because they are U.S. citizens or do they lose their rights to free speech because they are politicians? When politicians exercise their right to free speech where God is concerned, does it mean that the government is imposing a state-run religion or does it mean that the individual is exercising their right to free speech by expressing their opinion? Do we violate the First Amendment in order to uphold it?

The First Amendment prohibits governmental involvement in the church, prohibits the government from interfering with the exercise of an individual's religion, and prohibits the government from abridging the freedom of speech or press. The First Amendment gives power to individual U.S. citizens and bans the government from usurping their rights. This means that the activity of banning prayer at schools and at legislative sessions is a violation of the First Amendment.

The ACLU does not fight against the financial support the government gives to churches because it has twisted the First Amendment to mean that the government can regulate the affairs of the church but not vice versa. Some people argue that the church is a charitable organization, and all charitable organizations are tax-exempt, but government money is used to fund churches, which is the same as establishing a religion. We strain at a gnat and swallow a camel! The ACLU understands the delicate balance of control the government is trying to maintain by funding churches. They understand that to reverse the financial support the government gives churches would give the church license to influence the government. It is in everybody's best interest to keep silent about the fact that the government is in gross violation of the First Amendment.

The role of the church is charitable, but it also functions as a moral compass for society. If the church is going to fulfill its God-given moral function, it is impossible to retain tax-exempt status without violating the provisions that come with it. If Christian churches are ever going to rebound to their rightful position in American society, they are going to have to shed their nonprofit 501(c)(3) status. They will have to shake off the shackles of government control. Instead of putting up more buildings, they need to make it a priority to incorporate. Incorporation will cost the church nearly 40 percent of its "revenue," but it will allow it to reclaim 100 percent of its God-given function. There are no barriers to becoming the church God envisions.

One chief operating officer of a church was able to identify the encumbrances that the 501(c)(3) status imposes upon the church, but at the same time he could not envision his church without it. He acknowledged the fear he felt when witnessing church leaders violate the terms of the 501(c)(3) provisions. The officer also acknowledged that pastors, church leaders, and church outreach programs are constrained by the rules set forth in the 501(c)(3) status, but he felt that the church has adapted. According to him, only a small percentage of Christians tithe and those who do only do so because they can write it off as a tax deduction. If a church incorporated and changed its tax status, the percentage of people who tithed would drop and the church could not function. According to him, the church does not operate in faith, because it is not practical when people do not operate in faith.

But what happened to trusting in God? God said, "Bring all the tithes in the storehouse so there may be meat in my house. Test me to see if I don't open up the windows of heaven and pour out a blessing that you are not able to contain." He did not say that the government was responsible for blessing those who tithe or that it was responsible for producing the miraculous. The church is supposed to be self-contained.

God issued a challenge; He said, "try me," and it is up to churches to rise to the occasion. When they do, people will follow suit. Church leaders must start operating in faith, and the people will follow. The reformation that is needed in the area of church finance will be more effective if it begins with the leadership. Reformation in this area can lead to reformation in other aspects of the church. Successful alignment with God's words and living by the book realizes the benefits and provisions thereof, and when incremental successes are gained, they will encourage further alignment. Cumulative alignment with God's words and operating by His principles will lead to reformation.

Take-home message: In order to produce a healthy society, the church must fulfill its God-given role.

28.

Plans for the Heart Child

David discovered the site for the temple by accident. When he learned that Araunah's threshing floor was a place where God would answer prayers and receive offerings, he designated it as the site of the Lord's temple. It was a surprise to many that David chose Araunah's threshing floor instead of Mount Gibeon, where the Tabernacle and the altar were located. It was a revelation to David that God was not bound by space, and Araunah's threshing floor would forever symbolize a place where a sinner could get in touch with God our Savior for deliverance and mercy. It was the perfect place for the temple, considering its purpose.

David proposed building a temple where God's footstool could rest permanently, but he was denied the privilege of actually building it. Nonetheless, David continued with the preparations and did everything but build it. David wanted to honor God because he loved God. He spent his life making room for the Lord in his life and in the lives of the Israelites. He made the Lord the centerpiece in the hearts of the Israelites. David gathered the resources needed to build a magnificent place for the Lord, including paying top dollar for Araunah's threshing floor.

David restructured the Levites to restore them to their rightful function and to employ them in the temple construction. More than half of the Levites who were qualified for leadership positions were assigned as construction supervisors. David recruited skilled carpenters, craftsmen, stonemasons, goldsmiths, silversmiths, and workers of bronze and iron. He assigned general labor to foreigners living in Israel for preparing blocks and stones, and many people volunteered their help. David groomed Solomon and put leadership in place to provide support for him.

God Chose Solomon

Can anyone else be as passionate about your baby, your heart child, as you? How can they provide the same energy and enthusiasm for something you conceived? How can they envision the details and intricacies? David's dilemma caused him to question God about why he could not build the temple. The prophet Nathan simply told David that he would not be the one to build the temple, but he did not tell him why, so David went to God for an explanation.

> "I wanted to build a Temple to honor the name of the LORD my God," David told him. "But the LORD said to me, 'You have killed many men in the great battles you have fought. And since you have shed so much blood before me, you will not be the one to build a Temple to honor my name. But you will have a son who will experience peace and rest. I will give him peace with his enemies in all the surrounding lands. His name will be Solomon, and I will give peace and quiet to Israel during his reign. He is the one who will build a Temple to honor my name. He will be my son, and I will be his father. And I will establish the throne of his kingdom over Israel forever.'"
> *1 Chronicles 22:7–10*

God is amazing because He loves us in spite of what He knows about us. There are certain attitudes and behaviors we possess that have not yet surfaced. If we knew the depths of evil lurking within, it would sicken us. The heart is desperately wicked—but who can know it? Only God knows. He loves us in spite of what He knows about our future, in spite of the ugly things we will do that will break His heart. A sinner who does not know God as Savior will naturally sin, but it is hard to swallow the realization that people in a committed relationship with God will also sin and break God's heart. God loves us in spite of the unknown propensity for evil within us.

Before David and Bathsheba met and before Solomon's existence was possible, God named Solomon as David's successor. In order for Solomon to exist, David had to sin against Uriah, Bathsheba, and other unnamed men. God knew that David would sin the way he did before David did so. David did not have a history of behaving the way he did during the scandal with Bathsheba, so there was no way for him to suspect that he would ever sin like that. By naming Solomon as David's successor before the circumstances arose to make it possible for Solomon's birth, God demonstrated that He already knew about the disaster David would create, yet He did not allow future circumstances to cloud their relationship. Even though He already knew about

David's future sins, God still loved him. God knows about the events waiting to happen in our lives that will reveal our sinful attitudes and behaviors, yet still He loves us—and there is no greater love.

A pastor introduced a taped sermon he had preached about David and Bathsheba. He said that David and Bathsheba were supposed to marry and produce Solomon. Bathsheba was supposed to be David's wife, even though she was married to Uriah, according to that pastor. The theory he proposed was revolting because it implied that God condones seduction, adultery, murder, deceit, and robbery. The pastor suggested that since God named Solomon as David's successor before the circumstances were possible for Solomon to exist, it meant that He intended for David and Bathsheba to marry and conceive Solomon. Bathsheba was married to the wrong man, so all the circumstances had to take place to bring her to David, the right man.

Nothing could be further from the truth! God, in His omniscience, knew what would happen and decided to turn a bad situation into something good. All things work together for the good of those that love the Lord and are called according to His purpose. David had many sons who did not have the scandal surrounding them like Solomon. If Kileab was anything like his mother Abigail, he would have made a great king. But God chose Solomon, proving that he can take the mistakes in life and turn them around for good. God knows everything about your life, from start to finish. He weaves everything together, the good, the bad, and the ugly, to produce a wonderful outcome—but it does *not* mean He condones sin.

Blueprints and Building Materials

God creates each individual for a task only that person can fulfill. Therefore, everyone on this planet has a purpose. If everyone fulfilled their God-given purpose, no need would go unmet. David left the task of building the temple to Solomon because the Lord had chosen him.

Because David's life was inextricably linked to the temple, he left nothing to chance. David spent the rest of his life making the preparations for the temple, so all Solomon had to do was follow the instructions God gave his father. The task would overwhelm the most ambitious person, let alone a novice. David realized that the task of building God's temple might be overwhelming for Solomon, so he spent a great deal of time instructing his son. It took faith on David's part to leave the building of the temple to Solomon—or to anybody else, for that matter. "How can I entrust the responsibility of building God's throne room on Earth to someone so young and inexperienced?"

David even gave Solomon instructions regarding the items in the Lord's temple to be used for worship and sacrifice, including the amount of gold or silver needed for each item. For example, he designated the amount of gold or silver needed for the lamps and lamp stands, for the table that would hold the Bread of the Presence, and for the altar of incense and gold cherubim. David left no room for confusion, spelling out everything.

David gave Solomon the blueprints of the temple, planned in minute detail—the rooms that surrounded the temple, the treasuries, the inner sanctuary where the Ark would be kept, were all clearly specified. It was not the first time a man had received blueprints from God. God gave specific instructions to Noah for the ark, and gave instructions to Moses for building the Ark of the Lord and the Tabernacle. Given what we know about those men, it speaks volumes about David. In order to receive the instructions, David had to have a special relationship with God. David did not assume anything; he had ideas about how to design the temple, but he laid them aside and asked God how he could best accommodate Him. When David passed the blueprints on to Solomon, he told him that he had obtained the blueprints from the Lord.

David collected vast quantities of building materials throughout his reign, because he knew that Solomon was "young and inexperienced." He did not want to take a chance that Solomon would become discouraged by shortages and abort the project. David gathered tons of precious metals for the construction of the temple. Based on the small glimpses God gives us of heaven—streets paved with gold, pearly gates, costly stones, and precious jewels representing each tribe of Israel—the temple might have been meant as a miniature replica of God's throne in heaven.

David initially provided four thousand tons of gold and forty thousand tons of silver for the project, but as he approached the end of his life, he donated more gold and silver, as well as great quantities of onyx, precious stones, fine stone, and marble.

As David neared his final days, he was concerned about how the nation and his son would fare after his departure. He was also concerned about the temple, since it was more than a task—it was a vision. In case there were not enough resources, David asked the people to follow his example, summoning all his officials to Jerusalem and addressing them.

> My brothers and my people! It was my desire to build a temple where the Ark of the LORD's covenant, God's footstool, could rest permanently. I made the necessary preparations for building it. . . . And now because of my devotion to the Temple of my God, I am giving all of my own private treasures of gold and silver to help in the construction. This is in addition to the building materials I have already collected for his holy Temple. . . . Now then, who will follow my example? Who

is willing to give offerings to the LORD today?
1 Chronicles 28:2, 29:3, 5

A Heart Condition

When David began to rule in Israel, the people were hostile to God. Israel had a history of rejecting God and treating Him like an intrusion. The Israelites chose a king because they did not want to be governed by the stifling God of the universe who doted on them so much. There was no place in Israel's life for God because He required exclusivity while Israel lustfully sought to give her love and affection to the gods of the people of Canaan.

The Israelites wanted nothing to do with God. They did not love or trust Him. They viewed God as an unwelcome guest who interfered in their lives. They did not recognize His worth or appreciate how His involvement blessed them. They were not interested in the least in pleasing Him or being in a relationship with Him. The Israelites feared God, misunderstood His intentions, and pushed Him away. They felt God wanted to restrict them, limit their happiness, and punish them over the slightest offenses. The Israelites adopted a favorable attitude toward God only when they needed Him to get them out of a bind. Then they manipulated God to deliver them by temporarily ridding themselves of their idols. Once He had delivered them and all was well, they pushed Him aside. This attitude prevailed in Israel's leaders as well as the society.

Through David the people had seen firsthand that God wanted to be their God and that He would defend, protect, and provide for them. He wanted them to see His love, care, compassion, protection, and provision without the anger and frustration He had demonstrated in the past. He was committed to them, and He wanted them to see what a loving relationship with Him looked like. Through David, Israel witnessed a side of God she could not see in the past.

David's lifestyle, his consistent teaching of God's words across Israel, and his relationship with God provided a model for Israel and produced the potential for lasting change. David loved God and lived for Him. Through His relationship with David, God was able to demonstrate His intentions and to show the people what He would do for those who loved and obeyed him. God wanted Israel to realize that He would not withhold good gifts from people who walked in righteousness. The nation was blessed because of David's relationship with God. She enjoyed success, prosperity, and protection because of David's devotion to the Lord. The people saw God give David victory against Israel's enemies. As a result, they learned that God considered it a personal assault when other nations attacked His children and that He would address the situation accordingly. They watched God restore David during the coup and witnessed God's response when David sinned against Him. They saw God's mercy and learned that He would not despise a broken heart and a contrite spirit. God is not waiting for an opportunity to destroy a sinner. While actions have consequences, God is in the business of restoration. God is gracious.

> The God of Israel spoke. The Rock of Israel said to me: "The person who rules righteously, who rules in the fear of God, he is like the light of the morning, like the sunrise bursting forth in a cloudless sky, like the refreshing rains that bring tender grass from the earth."
> *2 Samuel 23:3–4*

As a good shepherd, David was concerned about how Israel would fare in his absence. He understood that having leaders in place who had a heart for God would insure that they would rule in righteousness and Israel would be blessed. When the righteous are in authority, the people rejoice, but when the ungodly rule, the people mourn. The people not only mourn but also do not rise above the level of righteousness displayed by their leaders. Having god-fearing leaders guarantees godly influence. That is why David invited family leaders, commanders of the twelve army divisions, the general and captains of the army, his administrative officers, and all the warriors of the kingdom to make donations. If those people had healthy hearts, they would lead through righteousness.

Giving to God is motivated by reciprocity, trust, and love. There are principles in the Bible that encourage reciprocal giving. A person who gives to the poor, lends to God. Cast your bread on the water and it will be returned. A person who sows sparingly will reap sparingly, but a person who sows generously will reap generously. Give and it shall be given to you in good measure. Anyone, believer or nonbeliever, can implement this type of giving, and the biblical principles will work for them. People who give God what He asks for trust God to honor His word. Therefore, giving is an act of faith. *Bring all the tithes into the storehouse, and I will open the windows of heaven and pour out blessings that you will be unable to contain.* A person who gives to God on this level trusts God to meet their needs. Those who give to God out of love express appreciation for Him and a desire to be in a relationship with Him. They give up their treasures in exchange for a relationship with Him, because He is more valuable than the things they treasure. They derive joy from being able to please God.

People who have a hostile attitude toward God will not give to Him without being manipulated. Those who do not trust God will not give, because they do not believe He will honor His word. If David had invited the people to give at the beginning of his reign, his request would have received a lukewarm reception at best. The people would have given with reluctance because they believed it was the correct thing to do; however, the sincerity would not have been there. David's invitation to the people to donate to the building of the temple was a litmus test. How Israel responded to David's invitation would reveal David's impact on the nation, the condition of Israel's heart, and how she would fare in his absence. If both Israel and her leaders demonstrated a healthy heart, she would face a positive future.

The people responded positively and gave enthusiastically, without hesitation, and willingly for the construction of the temple of God. How they gave was more important than what they gave. The moment was significant because the people's giving pointed to a change in the condition of their hearts. The people knew they were on the road to recovery and were glad. It sent an unmistakable message that the nation had a new heart: gone was the stony, unfaithful heart, and in its place was a heart of flesh, a faithful heart that desired to do all within her power to express her undying love toward her Creator. The heart is deceitful and desperately wicked. The only one who can give a heart transplant is the maker of the heart, and that is God. God transformed Israel's heart, and she rejoiced at the changes He created in her heart.

Everybody at the assembly rejoiced over the gifts, not because of the gifts themselves but because of their significance. The people rejoiced because they gave willingly and wholeheartedly to God. They were thankful for God's presence, and God had finally become Israel's acknowledged King.

"Lord, we love you and we acknowledge you as our King. We love you enough to give you our best, because you are worth it! We are thankful for you and appreciate all you do for us! We rejoice because it is an indication of an attitude shift. Our hearts are healthy. We went from being suspicious and hostile toward you to trusting and welcoming you. We are glad to see the progress we have made; we have come a long way. We love you, God of our ancestors. We are excited over the opportunity to give to you as an expression of our love. Even more important, we are excited about you. You are our most treasured possession; nothing is too good for you. There is nothing to give that expresses your worth; but such as we have, we give to you."

There was a chain reaction of praise and festivity when the people gave. They brought a thousand bulls, a thousand rams, and a thousand male lambs for burnt offerings to the Lord. They also brought drink offerings and other sacrifices. They feasted and drank in the Lord's presence with great joy that day. Their praise and gifts signified a heart change. A heart change is more significant than a temporary behavior change because a heart change permanently changes behavior.

The greatest accomplishment any person can achieve is the testimony that people turned to God because of their lifestyle and leadership. That was the most gratifying day in David's life, because he could go to his grave knowing that his life had influenced others to develop a relationship with the Lord. The generous outpouring the people demonstrated that day would not have occurred at the beginning of David's reign. King David's joy did not stem from relief that the building fund had been filled. His joy stemmed from what the gifts signified. David had witnessed a heart transplant. Israel had exchanged a sin-diseased heart for a healthy one. Therefore, Israel would continue to enjoy God's blessings in his absence.

> The people rejoiced over the offerings, for they had given freely and wholeheartedly to the LORD, and King David was filled with joy.
> *1 Chronicles 29:9*

All Praise to You, My King

David praised God for the people's giving, because he understood it was not what they gave that was important; it was the fact that they gave—and how they gave. People who do not trust and love God will not give, but people who love God will give without hesitation.

David praised the Lord in the presence of the whole assembly, "You are great and powerful, majestic, victorious, and full of glory. Everything belongs to you, even this kingdom. Riches and honor come from you, power and might are in your hands, and you give to whomever you choose. How could we give you anything, for everything we have comes from you! The materials we have gathered to build a temple to honor your holy name belong to you. You have examined our hearts, and you know there are integrity and good motives there. We want you to know that in our hearts we put you above all riches. We're giving you the best we've got because in our hearts we sincerely love you. My heart swells with love for you, my passion overflows for you, and my heart is hungry for you. We don't consider these gifts as important as the recipient of the gifts. The greatest gift of all is you."

David had so impressed God that Israel and Solomon benefited from the promises God had made him, even after his death. There was an abundance of wealth in the nation. The influx of wealth could be attributed to their giving, which was done cheerfully and not manipulatively. They gave with gratitude, appreciated God, and wanted to show that they would not withhold anything from Him, even their most treasured possessions.

They did not give with the expectation of reciprocity—for that is not giving, it is exchanging. As far as they were concerned, what God had already given was priceless. He did not have to do anything more to prove His love. Israel also enjoyed peace with her enemies during Solomon's reign, just as God had promised David.

Take-home message: Giving is an expression of love. Giving to God is an indication of a healthy heart and a healthy relationship with God.

29.

A Dying Shepherd's Wishes

Even as a dying shepherd, David was still concerned with the plight of the sheep. He wanted Israel to continue to enjoy God's blessings and charged them to obey Him.

> So now, with God as our witness, I give you this charge for all Israel, the LORD's assembly: Be careful to obey all the commands of the LORD your God, so that you may possess this good land and leave it to your children as a permanent inheritance. *1 Chronicles 28:8*

If Israel continued to follow God, she would possess the good land, and possessing the good land meant enjoying the benefits and provisions the land produced. The good land that the Lord gave the Israelites was producing before they arrived in Canaan. They did not have to build houses or work to produce fertile ground that would yield bumper crops; they were already there for their enjoyment. The Israelites' continued obedience had both present and future benefits. In the present, they would continue to reap the bounty the land produced, and in the future, their children would receive the land as a permanent inheritance, passed on from generation to generation.

If you want to enjoy a good life and ensure that your offspring will too, obey God. Obedience sees miracles and receives the blessings of God. Obedience gives God's will precedence. Life would be dramatically different if every Christian made it a personal endeavor to obey God. If you are at all interested in seeing that your children live the good life, live a life in subjection to God.

David's Prayer

Adults do not like to believe that their lifestyle decisions have any bearing on the quality of life their children experience or the kind of adults they become.

Some would rather believe that their children live in a cocoon unaffected by their mistakes and bad choices, but this is not so. Children learn by observation and tend to become adults similar to their parents. If you never model godly living, how can you expect your child to choose that way naturally? It is a bitter pill to swallow to see our children following the erroneous paths we took. While it is true that children do not have to choose the lifestyles of their parents, it takes tremendous effort to overcome that predisposition. Prayer provides the overcoming force against the inertia of predisposition.

Prayer can accomplish what years of advice, training, teaching, and preaching cannot. To ensure that the nation would live right, David prayed that Israel would stay with God. Israel had come a long way since David became king. Before his leadership she had rejected God and refused to be governed by Him, but during David's leadership she invited the Lord back. David prayed that God would give the Israelites the desire to obey Him. He wanted them to continue to trust and love God in his absence.

David faced the same dilemma all good parents face. They spend a couple of decades teaching their children to live right, and then they face a time of letting go, during which they find out if their children "got it." Prayer is the best assurance of continued right living when children are no longer under your tutelage.

David understood that Israel would only continue in God's favor if her king and leaders continued to follow the Lord. Leadership is critical, because the righteousness of a nation will not exceed that of its leaders. David understood that if Israel were to continue to follow righteousness, its leaders would have to do so first. That was why he placed a great emphasis on reviving the Levites and on Solomon's training. Israel's prosperity was riding on Solomon's obedience to God.

> But if you abandon me and disobey the laws and commands I have given you, and if you go and worship other gods, then I will uproot the people of Israel from this land of mine that I have given them. *2 Chronicles 7:19–20*

Jedidiah—Loved of God

David issued four directives to Solomon: continue to obey the Lord, seek the Lord and get to know Him, serve and worship Him, and build the temple.

God highly favored Solomon and chose him as Israel's next king. Because David lived a life in subjection to the Lord, Solomon's leadership showed great potential. All Solomon had to do was continue to obey the Lord to enjoy success during his reign.

> Observe the requirements of the Lord your God and follow all his ways. Keep each of the laws, commands, regulations, and stipulations written in the law of Moses so that you will be successful in all you do and wherever you go. If you do this, then the Lord will keep the promise he made to me: "If your descendants live as they should and follow me faithfully with all their heart and soul, one of them will always sit on the throne of Israel." *1 Kings 2:3–4*

David said, "I am going to rest with my ancestors and be with the Lord, the love of my life. I will not be with you much longer, but I will not leave you fatherless. God has promised me that He will be your Father; He has chosen you as His son. If you continue to obey God, He will give you a lasting kingdom. It is not enough to be obedient while I am still alive; continue to do so after my death. God has promised you peace, but if you turn away from Him, He will use your enemies to chastise you."

Near the end of his life, David passed the secret of his success, his devotion to and his dependence on God, to his son. "Solomon, if you want to enjoy the success, prosperity, and victory that I have enjoyed all my life, get to know God."

Get close to God and explore Him. I promise you will not be disappointed. You can spend a lifetime studying God and never get bored. You can explore Him, and He will satisfy your curiosity. He is an absolute pleasure and total delight to be with. If you earnestly hunger and thirst after Him, you will be filled. It pleases Him when you show an interest in Him. The more time you spend with God, the more you want to be with Him. God knows the heart of every person, however. He knows if you are genuinely interested in Him or are just pretending; you cannot fool God. Do not kid yourself into thinking that you can fool Him. God weighs the hearts and intents of each person. He knows if you are interested in Him or not; He knows if you are hot or cold toward Him. If you want nothing to do with Him, He will back off. Once you come to know the Lord by developing a relationship with Him, serving and worshipping come automatically. It is not about religion; it is about relationship, having a personal, one-on-one relationship with God, the Creator of the universe.

> And Solomon, my son, get to know the God of your ancestors. Worship and serve him with your whole heart and with a willing mind. For the Lord sees every heart and understands and knows every plan and thought. If you seek him, you will find him. But if you forsake him, he will reject you forever. *1 Chronicles 28:9*

Worship involves a person's spirit, soul, and body. It is more than just an emotional response resulting from God's blessings; it is a logical response that comes from knowing the Lord. Praising God is about acknowledging Him for who He is. It is because of who He is in all of His glory that praise and honor are due Him. Praising God is also about gratitude; once you realize how greatly He blesses you, worship is automatic. When you realize how much He loves you, you will begin to love Him in return. There comes a time in the Christian journey when pleasure is derived from worshiping and serving God out of love for Him.

David's last mandate to Solomon was to build the temple. "I am leaving you a project, the building of the temple, that will exercise your faith and prove your reliance upon God. At the end of the project, you will either have failed miserably because you failed to follow God, or you will come to know, appreciate, and love God as I do. If you trust and acknowledge the Lord and lean not to your own understanding, He will direct your path.

"What you are inheriting is the opportunity to know God. I know the task before you is challenging and overwhelming, because it is not just another building, it is the Lord's temple. You have evaluated yourself and correctly found yourself inadequate. You feel that you do not have what it takes and you are in over your head, but do not lose heart or be afraid. It is a monumental task, but God is with you, and as long as He is with you, there is nothing you cannot accomplish. Knowing that the Lord is with you will empower you to accomplish the impossible!"

David's farewell address to Solomon and the nation of Israel showed that he was heavily influenced by Moses's teachings. The charge he gave Solomon sounds exactly like the one Moses gave Joshua:

> Be strong, and courageous, and do the work. Don't be afraid or discouraged by the size of the task, for the LORD God, my God, is with you. He will see to it that all the work related to the Temple of the LORD is finished correctly. *1 Chronicles 28:20*

The similarities between the lives of David and Moses are astounding. Just as Moses received plans to build the Tabernacle, the Ark, and the priestly garments, David received the plans for the temple. The blueprints David gave to Solomon came directly from the hand of the Lord. Moses outlined the duties and functions of the Levites, and David followed those instructions to realign the Levites according to God's will. David would not have returned the Ark and would not have reorganized the Levites had it not been for Moses's teachings. Moses delivered the people from slavery in Egypt, while David delivered them from slavery to idols and turned their hearts back to their God. Like Moses, David was an intercessor for the nation of Israel. Moses taught Israel from the Torah, and David commissioned the Levites to teach it to all Israel. David prayed for his successor because he wanted Israel to continue being blessed just as Moses did.

Moses's teachings and leadership produced conformity in Israel, but conformity does not mean wholehearted agreement and acceptance. The people either obeyed out of fear or failed to obey and died. Their fear of reprisals was greater than their desire to follow an independent path. The people Moses led through the wilderness did not internalize his teachings. They played by the rules as a means of coping. David followed Moses's teachings to achieve spiritual reformation in Israel, but he knew that rules and regulations alone could not do what witnessing a man with a personal relationship with God could. Through David, Israel had an opportunity to witness a man totally in love with God—and God in love with a man. David's love for God allowed Israel to see God's softer side, which changed her perception of Him. She saw God as passionate, kind, thoughtful, sensitive, and generous, and Israel longed to have the kind of relationship David had with God. So she said goodbye to her idols and entered a committed relationship with God.

If we leave our children nothing else, it is imperative that we leave them a spiritual heritage, for it is a person's spirit that will overcome all infirmities. Many of the troubles we face in this life cannot be solved by money or material possessions. As children embark upon the journey of life, they will find themselves in situations where they need to consult someone at a moment's notice. Since parents cannot be everywhere at all times for their children, it is important to introduce them to an omnipresent God—a God who is within earshot and has all-power. We cripple our children when we fail to teach them to rely on God. We fail them when we do not help them dedicate their lives to the God who entrusted us with them in the first place.

If you journey back into your own past, you will find that God favored you and brought you through many difficulties. If you wrote your life story, God would be the central theme, for He was always there to give you a helping hand. Children should be taught that God is their Father and intimately concerned about them. Although they may lack human companions at times, they are never alone, because God is with them.

David ensured a smooth transition from his leadership to Solomon's. He gathered the human resources and raw materials to build the temple. He assigned people to assist Solomon. David reorganized the Levites because he knew they would be an important part of Solomon's support system. He knew that if the country's leaders had healthy hearts, they would lead by righteousness and Israel would fare well. He charged his son and all Israel to obey God's commandments so they could continue to possess the good land and pass the goodness on to their children.

> O Lord, the God of our ancestors Abraham, Isaac, and Israel, make your people always want to obey you. See to it that their love for you never changes. Give my son Solomon the wholehearted desire to obey all your commands, decrees, and principles, and to build this Temple, for which I have made all these preparations.
> *1 Chronicles 29:18–19*

Considering how David carefully mentored and groomed Solomon, how could another man conspire to take his throne and convince the people that he should be the next king?

The Hired Men Sang "Long Live King Adonijah"

As David neared death, he could not get warm, no matter how many blankets were placed on him. They scoured the kingdom to find the beautiful virgin Abishag to tend to David, but he did not even touch her, which signified that death was not far off. He had not officially appointed his successor, so barring any prior arrangements, the eldest son was entitled to the throne, and with Amnon and Absalom dead, Kileab, Abigail's son, was next in line. It is not clear whether Kileab was also dead or he knew and respected his father's desire for Solomon to succeed him, but whatever the reason, he did not come forward to claim the throne. If Kileab was deceased, the next in line was Adonijah. As David's death drew nearer, Adonijah decided to appoint himself king of Israel.

Adonijah, son of Haggith, was David's fourth child. He was gorgeous and very spoiled. David never put the brakes on Adonijah, and he never opposed him, thereby creating a monster. Adonijah took advantage of his father's condition and his lack of an appointed heir to promote himself and make himself king. Self-promotion is the highest form of arrogance and the quickest path to ruin. David was not exactly in touch with current affairs. Maybe he was too far gone to address mundane issues. In the absence of a preemptive official appointment, and if Kileab was deceased, Adonijah was the rightful heir. People not aware of David's wishes would have supported Adonijah without knowing they were betraying David.

Since it was commonly known, at least among David's immediate family and officials, that David had promised Bathsheba that Solomon would be heir to his throne, Adonijah decided to seize power by stealth. He gained the support of Joab, son of Zeruiah, the army commander, and Abiathar, the priest, both high-ranking officials in David's cabinet. Adonijah had military and religious support (and by default he had political support); he had everything he needed to enforce his ascension.

It was a wise move for Adonijah to gain Joab's support, because Joab had the power to enforce a coup. Adonijah knew there was contention between Joab and David. Joab only maintained his position because he killed everyone David appointed, and David tolerated Joab because he felt powerless against him. Adonijah used that tension to his advantage. He hoped that David would not challenge him because of his fear of Joab, and he hoped Joab would join the coup to maintain his tenure as army commander.

During Absalom's rebellion, both Joab and Abiathar supported David, at that time because David was still a force to be reckoned with. Because David was dying during Adonijah's coup, both Abiathar, who owed his loyalty to David because David had protected him when Saul sought his life, and Joab felt no fear of reprisal for betraying him. Having the support of a high priest also gave Adonijah influence with the people. Adonijah used persuasion to win the support of the people, and force to silence the opposition. His tactics were ugly and manipulative, but shrewd. He was a son of David, after all.

Adonijah threw a party to celebrate his self-appointment, inviting all but dissenters. He supplied chariots and horses, recruited fifty men to run before him, and invited all of David's sons—with the exception of Solomon. Since he also did not invite high-ranking officials who remained loyal to David and would not support his endeavor, David's bodyguard Benaiah, priest Zadok, and prophet Nathan did not attend. Self-promoters will only surround themselves with "yes people," not challengers. Adonijah's action proved that he knew Solomon was heir and that he was surreptitiously trying to take the throne. He was hoping that his dying father would be out of touch, self-absorbed, and too focused on his next journey to respond to a rebellion. Confusion and lack of communication would be his allies.

His party was as riotous as any coronation celebration. The guests at the party shouted, "Long live King Adonijah," even though it was commonly known that David had chosen Solomon as his successor. David was not making public appearances. Adonijah's self-promotion and David's silence caused the people to think that David had changed his mind. Death can bring out ugliness in the survivors. In the absence of an official will, relatives can fight over the belongings of the decedent. Lifetime feuds and broken relationships result when relatives are left to surmise the decedent's intent about inheritance issues.

Fortunately for Bathsheba, David was still alive and could make his wishes known. She had to perform the unsavory task of interrupting David's pre-death reverie. She had to overcome the dread of troubling a dying man with the affairs of the living. It was a matter of life and death for Bathsheba to receive the fulfillment of David's promise. Receiving a promise and having the promise fulfilled are two different things. Sometimes you have to fight for the realization of the promise, because there are always those who will try to block you from receiving the fulfillment of it by claiming your promise for themselves. Taking a passive approach to the fulfillment of a promise may cause you to lose it. If you sit there hoping wrongs will be corrected in time and everything will straighten itself out, you may miss out on what was designated and earmarked for you.

If Adonijah was the natural heir to David's throne and if David passed away during Adonijah's self-appointed coronation, all Israel would assume he was David's intended heir and would support his right to the throne. Under those circumstances, anybody who challenged his right to the throne would be killed. Those who claimed a right to the throne and those who refused to support his ascension would face execution. It was imperative, then, to get David to make an official public appointment before his death.

While Adonijah threw his own coronation party, Bathsheba and Nathan held an audience with David. As Adonijah rode in a chariot behind the men he had hired and as he sacrificed sheep, oxen, and fattened calves for his party guests, Bathsheba reported his activities to David. She then asked why Adonijah had been made king when he had promised the throne to Solomon. Nathan confirmed her report, which propelled David into action. He vowed to appoint Solomon to his throne that very day.

David summoned his priest Zadok, his prophet Nathan, and his bodyguard Benaiah to take Solomon on his personal mule to Gihon Spring, where Zadok and Nathan anointed Solomon king over Israel, just as David commanded. They blew trumpets and shouted, "Long live King Solomon!" The celebration could be heard and felt for miles, and when they returned, Solomon was the new king. Although David did not make a public appearance, he dispelled all doubts about who would be king of Israel. If the promoted does not rise to prominence with the tokens and blessings of his predecessor, one has to question the legitimacy of the promotion.

Jonathan, son of Abiathar, went to Adonijah's celebration to announce that David had appointed Solomon as king of Israel and that Solomon was seated on the throne at that very moment. Forks dropped, handkerchiefs fell, chairs scooted back from the table, and people kicked up dust. With that news, everybody at the celebration left quickly, because they knew Adonijah would soon be dead. They did not want to be discovered supporting a dead cause. Adonijah went to the sacred tent and caught hold of the horns of the altar, where Solomon promised not to harm him as long as he showed loyalty. Adonijah agreed, and Solomon sent him home.

Tying Up Loose Ends

David gave Solomon instructions for tying up loose ends. He instructed Solomon to arrange for the death of Joab and Shimei. Joab had killed two of David's army commanders as well as Absalom. Joab should have been charged for war crimes and executed at the beginning of David's reign over Israel. It did not help matters that he had betrayed David by supporting Adonijah's coup attempt. David asked Solomon to do something that he himself had not managed to do. He advised Solomon to make life difficult for Joab, a man he had not been able to manage while he was king.

David should have addressed Shimei's insolence when he was confronted with the situation, not years later. Shimei deserved to die because he had cursed David and thrown stones at him when he was fleeing from Absalom. David had vowed not to kill Shimei, but that did not mean he was innocent—and David's vow did not apply to Solomon. David pardoned Shimei but used a technicality to make sure his deeds did not go unpunished.

As his last request, David asked Solomon to show kindness to the sons of Barzillai by making them his permanent guests, in return for the kindness Barzillai had showed him when he was on the run from Absalom.

Adonijah had a hard time coming to terms with the fact that Solomon was king instead of him, but he made a deadly mistake when he asked Bathsheba to ask Solomon to give him Abishag for his wife. Solomon had many older brothers, but Adonijah was the only one exerting his "rights." Adonijah thought he should have a consolation prize since the kingdom had been taken from him, but Solomon saw things differently. If Adonijah thought he was entitled to Abishag, Solomon believed he must also think he was entitled to the throne, and it would not be long before he took steps to get it. Adonijah had the support of key people and could launch a coup.

> As you know, the kingdom was mine; everyone expected me to be the next king. But the tables were turned, and everything went to my brother instead; for that is the way the LORD wanted it. So now I have just one favor to ask of you. Please don't turn me down.
> *1 Kings 2:15–16*

History is full of examples of wars that have been fought and kingdoms destroyed over women, because one way a man can show dominance over another is by having his wife. Therefore, Solomon decided to ward off trouble before it began by sentencing Adonijah to death for his request.

> "How could you possibly ask me to give Abishag to Adonijah?" Solomon demanded. "You might as well be asking me to give him the kingdom! You know that he is my older brother, and that he has Abiathar the priest and Joab son of Zeruiah on his side." Then King Solomon swore solemnly by the LORD: "May God strike me dead if Adonijah has not sealed his fate with this request. . . . So as surely as the LORD lives, Adonijah will die this very day!" *1 Kings 2:22–24*

Solomon secured his throne by tying up other loose ends as well, including dealing with anyone who could potentially depose him. David had identified people he wanted Solomon to deal with, but there were also those who had supported Adonijah's rebellion.

> So Solomon deposed Abiathar from his position as priest of the LORD, thereby fulfilling the decree the LORD had made at Shiloh concerning the descendants of Eli. *1 Kings 2:27*

God does not make empty promises or threats, and delay is not a denial; it is just a delay. God made a threat He intended to carry out against Eli's family. During Eli's tenure as high priest, God promised to cut his family line off from being priests. He also told Eli that his two sons would both die on the same day, which they did.

> I will put an end to your family, so it will no longer serve as my priests. All the members of your family will die before their time. None will live to a ripe old age. *1 Samuel 2:31*

During Saul's reign, God had nearly fulfilled his promise against Eli when Saul ordered Doeg to kill Ahimelech, along with his entire family. The executions were ghastly, but they were a fulfillment of God's promise. Although Saul's administration took on a distinct anti-God tone, he was fulfilling God's promise when he ordered the priests' execution. Abiathar, one of Ahimelech's sons, was the only one to escape execution. David took Abiathar under his wing, protected him, and gave him a position of authority by making him a priest. When Abiathar fled from Nob, all he had was his life, but he went on to get married, have children, and lead a normal life.

Abiathar was honored as a priest, along with Zadok, during the Levite census and job appointments. Abiathar and his immediate family had blossomed under David, which made his betrayal even harder to bear. At the beginning of Solomon's reign, he disqualified Abiathar and his descendants from serving as priests, which was the final fulfillment of God's word. Priests from Ithamar's clan were banned from serving as priests. When God makes a promise or threat, He may not fulfill it instantaneously, but He will fulfill it. God does things according to His own timing.

Solomon was firmly established as king shortly before David died. Solomon had Joab executed while he was holding on to the horns of the altar for joining Adonijah's revolt and for the murder of two innocent men. The last person executed in the early years of Solomon's reign was Shimei, the man who had cursed David. Solomon first put Shimei under arrest in the city of Jerusalem. He was free to roam the city, but he could not leave—leaving the city would be punished by death. Three years later, Shimei left Jerusalem for Gath, so Solomon had him executed. With all known dissenters dead, Solomon gained a firm grip on Israel.

Take-home message: God keeps his word.

30.

Liberator

Israel had an idolatry problem, but the difference between Israel and other nations is that the God of all creation took a personal interest in her, and His jealousy would not allow Him to tolerate Israel's unfaithfulness. Idolatry was an issue God had to address immediately, because He was personally present with Israel.

Moses had fought against idolatry in the wilderness but had only achieved compliance. Compliance does not mean there is a heartfelt agreement; it means only that people consider the consequences of following their own path too costly. If you knew that you would die on the spot for engaging in idolatry, or worse, that your whole family would die and that the entire nation would suffer, it would have a strong influence on your choice to abstain from idolatry. But that is not really a choice, is it? God gave Israel an offer she could not refuse: obey or die. Zero tolerance was the policy during Moses's administration. It did not cause Israel to internalize change that would lead to a permanent transformation.

Moses had an up-close, face-to-face relationship with the Lord, and although he spent a great deal of time with God, his resounding request was, "More, God, I want more of you. I feel as though I barely know you. I have barely scratched the surface in my relationship with you."

Although Israel witnessed their relationship, it did not cause her to desire the same type of relationship with God. When God visited, precautions had to be taken so that Israel would not die during the encounter. If Israel touched Mount Sinai, where God was, it was a mistake corrected by death. Israel feared God and did not want to get close to Him. Israel's response to God was, "Moses, tell God to keep Himself at a distance from us or else we will die."

When God tried to lead Israel into the Promised Land, Israel resisted. Having a promise that you have to fight for is as good as having no promise at all. He did not tell Israel that He planned to use her to make the miracle happen in her life. Israel thought God had set her up for failure. When God was ready to take her in, she wanted to turn back to bondage because she knew what to expect and had been comfortable there. She knew she was not up for a fight, and she did not trust God, so she refused to cooperate. Consequently, God left her in the wilderness until her stubborn resistance and refusal-to-fight mentality died.

Joshua, a By-the-Book Type

Joshua was God's replacement for Moses, although he did not enjoy the same type of relationship with God as Moses had. Israel needed a man who would obey God, a by-the-book type, to lead her into the Promised Land, and she needed a warrior for the next phase of her life. She found that man in Joshua. Joshua taught Israel that the sins of one person had the power to wreak havoc on the entire nation. Either all were going to get right by choosing to obey God or those who chose to live a life contrary to God's will would get left behind. Israel could not afford to carry the dead weight of besetting sin. Israel could not afford to fight her enemies on one front and have God as an enemy on another front as a result of unresolved sins. Under Joshua's leadership, Israel could choose to live a life contrary to God, which would result in separation from the commonwealth of Israel.

Joshua led Israel victoriously in battle, but when his time of departure was at hand, there was no central leader waiting to replace him. Joshua had to do what every parent has to do: he had to push his fledglings out of the nest and let them fly on their own. He had to stand back and let Israel do what he had trained her to do.

Joshua hoped that the tribes of Israel would do what Caleb had done. He had asked for land that was promised to him, and Joshua had granted it. The land was inhabited, though, which meant that Caleb had to use his faith to fight and had to rely on God to gain victory. Unfortunately, the tribes of Israel responded as most Christians do today. They failed to exercise faith, expecting someone else to do it for them. They failed to look at their obstacles from God's point of view; there is nothing that can resist the will of God. They were defeated and began to lose what they had already gained because they did not internalize Joshua's teachings. They failed to realize that while victory was assured, there could be no victory without a fight.

When Joshua and all of the other leaders of his era died, a new generation arose, but it did not know God. It did not know how to fight and did not understand the importance of obedience to God. No one had taught the new generation about Israel's history with God. The noble race of people who had once been feared began to suffer defeat and starvation at the hands of her merciless enemies. The new generation did not know that victory on the battlefront requires purity. Israel's sins and idolatry finally brought her to a point of suffering that caused her to cry out to God for deliverance. God, who can be touched by our infirmities, sent judges (deliverers) who defeated Israel's enemies and led Israel into a short-lived reformation—the kind of reformation most people have when they are in trouble.

"Just get me out of this, Lord, and I promise never to do this again."

The Levites, who represented the church, were in as much of a quagmire as the rest of Israel. The church suffered from internal corruption at the highest levels and was in no condition to be the moral compass it was intended to be. God tried to correct the situation, but high priest Eli repeatedly refused correction.

God does not find pleasure in your soul's death—a permanent, irrevocable separation from Him. He wants you to receive His conviction, repent, correct the situation, and live. What is the point of dying? Where is the glory in that? Eli's situation proved that God is long-suffering and will give you time to repent. God does not condemn you—He only convicts you. You condemn yourself by refusing to correct unresolved sin. God is in the business of restoration. Since the Levites were a liability to God's cause, discouraging the few Israelites who were trying to live right, God decided to relieve them of their duties and find a new leader.

Samuel, Leading Israel in a National Repentance

Any time communication ceases in a relationship, there is no hope of recovery. You can silence many things in this life, but when God becomes silent, it is cause for concern, because all life is dependent upon every word that proceeds from the mouth of God. Israel reached that point with God where there was a dearth of His word in the land, and it was a time of great fear and uncertainty. However, God found Samuel and used His relationship with Samuel to speak to Israel. Israel was depressed because she needed God and He was so distant. Samuel led Israel in a national repentance.

"Do you want God to return? Are you willing to do anything to get Him back?"

"Yes, anything."

"Good. Get rid of your idols, repent in sackcloth and ashes, draw close to God, confess your unresolved sins to Him, and He will draw close to you."

All was well under Samuel's leadership until it was time for him to pass the baton to his sons. His sons could be bribed to twist justice and Israel would not have it, so Israel decided she needed a king. Her request for a king was an attempt to oust God. Israel knew that when she did not have a spiritual leader she would revert to idolatry, and history would repeat itself. Her enemies would cruelly oppress her, she would cry out to God for deliverance, there would be a short reprieve from sin until the leader died, and then she would find herself in the same rut. She wanted a king to protect her from her enemies without regard to her moral condition.

God granted Israel's request and was not entirely opposed to the idea of Israel having a king. In Deuteronomy, He had made provisions for such an occasion. What He was opposed to, however, was the motive behind Israel's request. She wanted to sever all ties with Him. Israel was mistaken in her belief that when an old administration leaves, so do its ways of governing. God let Israel know that theirs was a permanent relationship, and even with a king, she would still be accountable to Him. If Israel and her king obeyed, respected, and worshiped Him, all would go well; if not, God would discipline her.

Saul, the King Who Disobeyed God's Instructions

God chose Saul, from the tribe of Benjamin, to be Israel's king. Initially, Saul received a lukewarm reception from the people, because he displayed fear during his public introduction. Israel needed a warrior, not a wimp, but Saul eventually won acceptance when he defeated the Ammonite king Nahash. Saul was a manager, not a visionary like his son, Jonathan. After the battle with Nahash, Saul sent all but three thousand troops home because he did not expect to have to fight again. His plan was to use the troops he retained to put out fires; he did not intend to launch offensive assaults. The problem with his plan was that he did not take Jonathan into account.

Jonathan refused to live under Philistine oppression and challenged their right to oppress Israel. He was not content to live with the status quo, which forced Saul into a battle he did not intend to fight. Saul lost his dynasty and his authority during that battle. He lost his dynasty because he offered a sacrifice, which was akin to claiming God had authorized something when He had not. At some point in every new leader's reign, his or her authority is challenged, and the outcome of the challenge determines whether that person is a leader in name only or in deed. The troops challenged and prevailed against Saul, causing Saul to lose his authority, which would haunt him later in his reign.

Although Saul won many battles and the respect of Israel, he suffered severe personal losses. God had a personal score to settle with the Amalekites, and considering the importance of the battle to God, it is easy to see why Saul lost his destiny when he failed to follow God's instructions. The root cause of Saul's failure was that he feared men. Even though he had God's support, he never relied on it. Instead, he allowed his men to prevail over him, making it impossible to obey God. In Saul's thinking, it was better to snub a God he could not see than to disappoint an entire army he could see. A man proves his love to God by his obedience. A man who disobeys God's instructions despises Him.

Saul lost his dynasty, his destiny, and the presence of the Holy Spirit. His administration took on a distinctive anti-God tone. Losing his dynasty was not so bad, because that did not affect his future. When he lost his destiny and God's Spirit, however, he became a raving madman, bent on preserving his throne at any cost. Saul forced Samuel to worship with him in order to keep up appearances. He had an entire family of priests killed (only one survivor escaped), and he hounded David, a man with God's Spirit.

It would have been possible for Saul to keep his throne legitimately, but he chose to subvert the will of God. If Saul had demonstrated any humility, God would have accepted it. If Saul had rounded up the treasure from the Amalekite battle and given it to God, it would have been a step in the right direction. If Saul had fallen on his face before God in sackcloth and ashes, repented, and begged God to cleanse him of rebellion, God would have honored that. If Saul had confessed his flaws and asked God to help him overcome his fear of men, his inability to obey and to wait on God in a crisis, God would have helped him. However, Saul did none of those things. He did not demonstrate the kind of remorse that leads to repentance and cleansing. He was just sorry he had gotten caught. He always made excuses when confronted about wrongdoings; he was incorrigible. Saul subverted God's will at every opportunity, and it ultimately cost him his life.

Grooming David

God could not afford to have another Saul on his hands, so he searched for a man after His own heart. In his search, He found David. David had three notable ancestors, and from them, he inherited three types of faith: breakthrough, negotiating, and sacrificial. He grew up in a family that recognized that he was gifted but was not healthy enough to handle his giftedness. They mistreated, discouraged, and isolated him, unknowingly shaping him into a fine leader, because God used that time of separation for demonstration.

God personally introduced Himself to David. He put David into situations where he was helpless from a human perspective so He could break David's self-reliance. He taught him to judge situations from His perspective so David could see that no one could resist God's power. He taught David that He would magnify his efforts because He wanted a warrior who understood that victory was assured when He was involved. He also esteemed David so that David would not have to derive his self-esteem from men. Through David's training, God developed a man who knew how to trust Him in a crisis. He also earned David's loyalty by saving David's life.

Saul recognized David's potential and tried to include him in his entourage. Once you have tasted of the Spirit of God, you can recognize Him in the lives of others. Saul saw God's Spirit on David and lashed out at him like a jealous, jilted lover. He lashed out at David because Israel swooned to him. He wanted to remove David, either by death or public disgrace, but when his stealthy efforts failed, he dropped all pretenses and hounded him openly.

Saul's actions forced David to become a fugitive and thrust him into phase two of his training, during which David learned the painful lesson that all great leaders learn. People who are blessed by your efforts will betray you in a heartbeat. The people you bless might not pat you on the back, but to be consistent, you must remember that it is God you are ultimately serving. David also learned to respect leadership, even if that person is out to destroy you.

David's move from phase two to three of his training was subtle. During phase three, God wanted to see if David would trust Him to address Saul's injustice or if he would take revenge against Saul himself. God handed Saul to David by putting Saul and his men into a deep sleep. If there was vengeance in David's heart, that would have been the time for it to surface. Instead of taking his revenge, David respected God's leader and rebuked Saul's men for not protecting their king. In that final phase, David also discovered that the men he took under his wing and ministered to were disloyal and could not be trusted. Loyalty cannot be taught—you either have it or you don't.

After Saul's death, the transition from fugitive to king was not as smooth as it should have been for David. Abner, commander of Saul's army, carried the spirit of Saul, and although he knew that David was God's choice to replace Saul, he decided to subvert God's will and initiated a civil war. When he realized he could not win, Abner tried to hand the kingdom to David peaceably, but Joab, David's nephew, prevented it.

What do you do when people and circumstances prevent you from fulfilling your destiny? When you are trying to reach your destiny, it is critical that you surround yourself with people who will assist in the process. You will discover that you need to let some people go, even if they are precious to you, because they are blocking your progress. The sooner you do this, the sooner you will reach your destiny. David failed to do this, and it delayed his destiny as king for seven years and would later haunt him in his administration.

What a Difference a King Makes

An immediate difference could be seen when David became king. As a man in love with God, David was preoccupied with bringing the Ark of the Lord back to the center of Israel. He did not issue executive orders or force his will on Israel. He obtained the people's permission to invite the Holy One of Israel back to His rightful place. It was imperative that David did it that way, because God will not force Himself on any person—He only comes by invitation. When Israel gave God a personal invitation to return, she was also committing to restoring her relationship with Him. What David did was get buy-in from Israel; they invited God back by choice. Inherent in that personal choice was an agreement to honor God.

David loved God and did not hide his relationship. He had a strong love life with God that was on public display, giving Israel an opportunity to witness a man totally in love with God and God in love with a man. One of the things God loved so much about David was his obedience; He could trust David to do whatever He said. David had a rare relationship with God; he was married to God. Most people are in relationships with one another and with God for what they can get, not for what they can give, but David did not have a reciprocal relationship with God. He was not the type to use and manipulate God.

David gave to God without keeping score. All he wanted was God, not the things God could give. He wanted the nearness of God more than his next breath. Everything he did was to please God. He returned the Ark of the Lord, he waged war against Israel's enemies, he dedicated the spoils of war to fund the temple project, he made detailed plans for the temple so Israel and God could be together, and he restored the Levites so they could teach God's words, resume sacrifices to God, worship God, and provide political leadership. Restoring the Levites to their God-given function was especially significant, because it helped to fulfill David's spiritual vision and produced a transformation in Israel.

As in any relationship, getting to know God personally takes time and effort. Unfortunately, many people are content with a surface relationship with God where they know of Him, but they do not know Him personally. The only way most people ever take their relationship with God to the next level is by seeing it modeled in another person's life, and David gave Israel that opportunity. Witnessing David's and God's relationship caused Israel to see a side of God she had never seen. Israel saw God's soft, sweet side through His relationship with David. When Israel observed David and God, she wanted to experience the same relationship with Him. Israel shunned her idols not because she was forced or afraid of retribution, but because she loved God and wanted to be in a relationship with Him, thus internalizing change. Israel willfully sought God, to the exclusion of all her other gods.

When you make such strides in the kingdom of God, you become a target for the enemy of God. Bigger buildings and increasing membership rolls are great, but they are cosmetic. Satan did not mind the return of the Ark, the building projects, or the renewal of daily sacrifices, because they were cosmetic. When the Ark was present and daily sacrifices were performed in the past, that did not stop him from having a stronghold in Israel; in fact, he used it to his advantage.

You can increase the membership rolls, but as long as your members remain in bondage, true transformation has not taken place, and the enemy of God is allowed to continue his domination. When you successfully break strongholds and wage warfare in the spirit realm, it attracts the attention of the devil. When you challenge and prevail over the powers of darkness in your life and the lives of others, you have crossed into dangerous territory. When your preaching challenges listeners to release deep-seated sinful habits and to get delivered from demonic oppression, you have caused the enemy of God to lose his domination and oppression. For instance, if you preach in an area where witchcraft prevails, causing the spirit of witchcraft to break in the lives of listeners, you are in for a fight, just as Paul was when he ministered in Ephesus. If you preach to a nation bound by drugs and they get delivered, the devil will fight you and so will the people who benefit from drug trafficking.

David's lifestyle and leadership influenced the hearts of the children of Israel to turn to God, sparking a transformation had not existed in Israel before—one that caused Satan to lose his stronghold in Israel. That marked a crossing of the spiritual line of warfare for David. He accomplished by himself more than Moses, Joshua, and Samuel had accomplished altogether. He was a reformer, restorer, warrior, minister, and prophet, but his greatest accomplishment was to become Israel's liberator. David followed Moses's teachings to achieve spiritual reformation in Israel, but he knew that rules and regulations alone could not do what witnessing a man with a personal relationship with God could. When Israel renounced idolatry, it put things on another level entirely. When Israel embraced God, Satan lost his power base—and no one gives up power without putting up a fight.

Number One on Satan's Hit List

David became number one on Satan's hit list. Satan had to remove him at all costs so he could regain his authority in Israel. Strength for strength, human beings are no match for demons. Fighting demons is not a physical battle, and it is not about matching wits. Fighting demonic oppression is difficult because it is not a physical battle against an enemy you can see; it is a spiritual battle against an enemy you cannot see but who sees you and knows your weak spots. The devil knows your weaknesses better than anybody else, since he constantly stands before God accusing you of your faults, and he knows exactly how and when to attack to make you crumble. He knows which blows will have the greatest impact. Although Satan is not to be toyed with by human beings, he is no match for God. With God's help, the devil can be conquered.

Satan sucker-punched David by throwing a blow few men could handle or even resist. Men are sight-driven, so seeing Bathsheba naked was no accident; it was by the design of the devil. Satan intended to destroy David through sex because sex is a powerful, irresistible force, and David had a weakness in the area of sex. It was as though David was forced into a situation he had no control over. Unseen forces compelled him; he could not put on the brakes. He had never been faced with such a situation, and the novelty threw him off guard. After that, David behaved in a way that was totally uncharacteristic. The attack was designed by Satan to snuff out David's life.

What David needed most at that time is what all accomplished ministers of God need, a prayer covering. David faced the fight of his life totally unequipped. Israel had an ironclad way of dealing with adulterers, and Satan figured that when David was caught in adultery, he would be stoned to death, thereby solving Satan's problems.

Any unresolved sins and ungodly tendencies you fail to deal with are prime tools the enemy of God can use to attack and destroy you when you step into his territory. If you attack and eradicate sinful habits and demonic strongholds in your life at the beginning of your ministry, the enemy of God will have little to deal with when you cross into his territory. However, the devil will find something that will necessitate a strong prayer covering. Even Jesus needed a prayer covering during his hour of need, and it especially becomes evident when an attack by the devil leaves you dumbfounded and unable to utter one word in prayer. A prayer covering is composed of a group of people, prayer warriors, who can pray you through. One will put a thousand to flight, two puts ten thousand, and three puts one hundred thousand to flight, so you only need two or three spiritually attuned nongossiping prayer warriors fighting on your behalf.

The devil was confounded when the Bathsheba incident failed to oust David. No one was exempt from the consequences of adultery, not even the king. The devil did not count on the effect that David's humility would have on God. David had made a horrible mistake but took a far different approach to his sins from the one Saul took. One of the distinct difference between David and Saul was humility. Humility is number one in God's book. David did not make excuses and blame others when confronted with his sins. In David, we find a textbook repentance, because he was not just sorry he had been caught. He was truly remorseful, which produced cleansing change.

> How can I know all the sins lurking in my heart? Cleanse me from these hidden faults. Keep me from deliberate sins! Don't let them control me. Then I will be free of guilt and innocent of great sin.
> *Psalm 19:12–13*

He begged God to purge and purify him so every trace of his sin would be eradicated. God forgave him and cleansed him from all unrighteousness. That is the approach we all need to take toward our sins if we want to be free. Through David's repentance we see that the nature of the sin and who is affected by it determines what needs to be done in the way of restoration—it is not enough to say you are sorry. You do everything in your power to restore the person, and for whatever you cannot do, you ask for God's help. Although God forgave David, it did not release him from the consequences of his sins. David's precious loved ones paid the price and are still paying for his sins today. All people are responsible for their own sins, and although God will hold each person accountable for the things they do and say, we cannot deny that the sins of parents affect their offspring. The sins of parents have a way of producing proclivities in their children, making it harder for their children to resist repeating the parent's sins.

When the devil's carefully crafted attempt failed, he made another attempt against David's life through a census. He inspired David to not only conduct the census but to do it improperly by appealing to his pride. Whenever human beings pull out the scorecards to measure their accomplishments, it is an indication that they are content with what they have accomplished and points to a pride problem. Reflection on your accomplishments, especially without the acknowledgment of God as the source of your success, leads to the danger of falling from pride. Pride comes before destruction. Leave it to the historians to count your track record while you continue to move forward by the power of God.

Although David allowed his pride to blindside him during the census, his consistent characteristic of humility saved him once again. When God saw David's humility, he told the death angel, "Stop it, that is enough." Your humility has the same power to end your misery. God loves humility; He resists the proud and gives grace to the humble. He makes allowances for your sins and shortcomings, giving you the space to repent. Despite commonly held beliefs, especially among the young in Christ and those who do not have a personal relationship with God, God does not sit around waiting for you to fail so He can pounce on you.

God is gracious when it comes to our sins and failures. He will surprise you when you go to Him and say, "I don't have a leg to stand on. I'm just flat wrong, and whatever actions you take against me are justifiable." He will not throw the book at you. Instead, He will look beyond your sins and see your need for love and affirmation. Only human beings, the devil, and your own self are merciless. When it comes to your sins and failures, no one can beat you down better than you can. Stop beating yourself up over your sins and go to your Heavenly Father, who will welcome you with open arms and forgive you.

"You trusted me, and allowed me to get close to you, so close that I breathed you, but I betrayed you. I've let you down, broken your heart, and created a deep wound in you. My sins have torn us apart. I don't deserve you, Lord; I am not worthy to be in your presence, and I am not worthy to worship you, but I will worship you because you deserve it—just because you are you. Not even death can stop me from loving you. I hurt because I have lost you, the most important person in my life, and I can never again have what we once had. I may not be able to have the closeness we once shared, but I beg you not to banish me from your presence or I will suffocate. I don't want anyone else. There is no one like you."

Israel saw David's sins, his repentance in sackcloth and ashes, and she observed God's gracious response. God has a soft heart and can be moved by our distress over our sins. Israel concluded that it was better to fall into the hands of a merciful God.

Continuing to Serve God

Although David had damaged his relationship with God, he continued to serve, worship, and please God. His attitude was, "Though you slay me, yet will I trust, yet will I serve you."

David discovered the site of the temple by accident, the place where he learned that God was not bound by time and space, and it would forever be a place where sinners could reach their Savior. David spent his administration preparing for the temple, although he knew he would not be the one to build it. He acquired building materials, funding, skilled and general laborers, and construction supervisors. He reorganized and revived the Levites so they could assist in the project. He was included in a small elite group of great men, such as Moses and Noah, because God gave him the blueprints for the temple. God gave Noah instruction for building the ark, and He gave Moses instructions for building the Ark of the Covenant and the Tabernacle. David planned everything in minute detail, including the exact amount of gold and silver that was to be used in lamps, furniture, and utensils.

God named Solomon as David's successor and the one who would build the temple long before the circumstances existed to create Solomon. That was remarkable, because it demonstrated God's omniscience. In spite of what He knows about our future, God still loves us and weaves the good with the bad of our lives to create something wonderful. I am not saying that you should sin for the sake of sinning so God's grace may abound, God forbid. I am saying that if you live long enough, you will make mistakes. Evil resides in the heart of every human being, and it only takes the right circumstances to reveal it. Those who are in die-hard relationships with God will make painful mistakes, breaking God's heart, but God loves us in spite of our human frailties. All things work together for the good of those who love the Lord and are called according to His purpose.

David amassed the wealth taken from the enemies of God to build the temple. He also gave from his personal treasures and then invited Israel's leaders to give. That invitation turned out to be a litmus test whose outcome would indicate the condition of Israel's heart. Giving is significant because it points to the condition of your heart. If your heart is not healthy, giving to God is difficult. If you have a healthy heart, you give because giving is an expression of trust and love. There are many levels of giving; the lowest is reciprocity and the highest is giving without keeping score. God started His relationship with humanity by giving, and He keeps giving and giving, proving that He loves us more than we can fathom.

Since giving is an indicator of the heart's condition, much was riding on Israel's response to David's invitation. Israel's response would be evidence that she wanted to please God. It would give David an indication of how well he had influenced change in Israel and how Israel would fare after his departure. Much was riding on her response.

Israel had a hearty, healthy response toward giving to God, which proved that a transformation had taken place under David's leadership. What they gave was not as significant as how they gave, because giving to and praising God is an indication of the healthiness of one's heart. The people responded positively and gave enthusiastically without hesitation for the construction of the temple of God. Israel's contribution to the temple of God sent a message that she wanted God to be a permanent part of her life. God, David, and all the people were delighted at their response.

What a complete reversal for a people who had once asked for a king to oust God! Before David, Israel and God were in an antagonistic relationship. Israel viewed God with hostility and did not want anything to do with Him, even though she could not live without Him. Asking for a king was an attempt to remove the shackles of her relationship with God. God loved Israel, but she kept hurting Him with her unfaithfulness. Israel could not see that God had her best interests at heart. God used His relationship with David to model what He expected, and Israel saw that God was loving, kind, generous, and, in spite of mistakes, God, was merciful. David's consistent leadership, persistent teaching, and devotion to God made a permanent change in Israel. Thus, her giving signified healthiness and recovery. She loved God and wanted Him to be part of her life.

Take Your Concerns to God

When you are making significant strides in the kingdom of God, you should expect attacks from the enemy of God. Should a blow from the devil cause you to fall, humble yourself in the sight of the Lord, and He will lift you up. You may think that you cannot recover from your embarrassing and painful situation, the devil may continually replay the tape of your sins, and people may never let you live it down, but the important thing is to repent, seek God's forgiveness, and beg Him to cleanse you of all unrighteousness. Forgiveness is not enough; do not settle until you have been cleansed. Once you have been cleansed, restore those who were hurt and damaged by your sins as much as you can, and ask for God's help with what you cannot do. Then get up, dust yourself off, and continue to work in the kingdom of God. God is offering you redemption. Get up, you mighty warrior, and accomplish God's will for you.

It would be easy to conclude that with your personal characteristics, God cannot use you because you are a hindrance to His cause. However, do an honest self-assessment and then take your concerns to God. Humble yourself and ask for forgiveness. Tell God that you love Him but you cannot seem to do His will, and seek cleansing deliverance from God.

The apostle Paul was a man who started his career in ministry in opposition to God, but God turned his life around and used him, with all his flaws, to turn the world upside down by spreading the gospel. You may wrestle with habitual sins that leave you desperate for deliverance and cause you to cry out, "O wretched man that I am, who shall deliver me from the body of this death?"

You may find it hard to deal with the dichotomy of wanting to do right but doing evil instead. You know the will of God but disappoint Him by doing the opposite of what He intended. Paul had personal struggles, as evidenced by the desperate cry over his thorn in the flesh. He sought out the Lord three times about getting delivered.

God's response to Paul is the same as His response to you: "My grace is sufficient for thee." In other words, "I've got you covered. My strength is made perfect in your weakness."

With that knowledge in mind, go—with all your flaws, humility, and God's grace—and spread the good news, and turn this world upside down!

Index